PETRONII ARBITRI

CENA
TRIMALCHIONIS

PETRONII ARBITRI
CENA
TRIMALCHIONIS

EDITED BY

MARTIN S. SMITH

OXFORD

AT THE CLARENDON PRESS

1975

Oxford University Press, Ely House, London W. 1

GLASGOW NEW YORK TORONTO MELBOURNE WELLINGTON
CAPE TOWN IBADAN NAIROBI DAR ES SALAAM LUSAKA ADDIS ABABA
DELHI BOMBAY CALCUTTA MADRAS KARACHI LAHORE DACCA
KUALA LUMPUR SINGAPORE HONG KONG TOKYO

ISBN 0 19 814444 X

© *Oxford University Press 1975*

*Printed in Great Britain
at the University Press, Oxford
by Vivian Ridler
Printer to the University*

E5605/3

PREFACE

DESPITE the recent growth of interest in Petronius there has been no up-to-date English edition of the *Cena Trimalchionis* meant primarily for undergraduates. The present work sets out to provide a commentary more advanced than that of Sedgwick and comparable in scope with those of Friedlaender, Marmorale, and Perrochat.

I am grateful to Professors G. W. Williams and R. G. M. Nisbet for the encouragement they have given me, and to Dr. Elaine Fantham, Dr. A. S. Gratwick, Mr. J. S. Rainbird, and Dr. G. E. Rickman for their advice over details. Two of my colleagues deserve particular mention for their generous help: Mr. P. A. George discussed the text and commentary at every stage, and readily made available the results of his own work on Petronius; and Mr. J. H. Simon scrutinized the later drafts and the proofs with his usual precision and judgement, and enabled me to remove errors and to repair omissions. I must also acknowledge the courtesy of Professor Konrad Müller in permitting me to base the text and apparatus substantially on that of his two editions. Occasionally I have adopted conjectures from elsewhere, but my debt to him is considerable. In addition, I wish to express my appreciation of the helpfulness at all times of the staffs of the Academic Division of the O.U.P. and the Printer to the University. Finally my thanks are due to my wife for her help and encouragement, not to mention her fortitude, throughout the preparation of this commentary.

M. S. S.

St. Andrews
September 1974

CONTENTS

ABBREVIATIONS

AJP	*American Journal of Philology*
ALL	*Archiv für lateinische Lexicographie und Grammatik*
BSR	*Papers of the British School at Rome*
CGL	*Corpus Glossariorum Latinorum*
CIL	*Corpus Inscriptionum Latinarum*
Cod.	Justinian, *Codex*
CP	*Classical Philology*
CQ	*Classical Quarterly*
CR	*Classical Review*
CRF	Ribbeck, *Comicorum Romanorum Fragmenta*
D.–S.	Daremberg and Saglio, *Dictionnaire des antiquités grecques et romaines*
Ernout–Meillet	Ernout and Meillet, *Dictionnaire étymologique de la langue latine*
Hof. *LU*	Hofmann, *Lateinische Umgangssprache*
K.–S.	Kühner and Stegmann, *Ausführliche Grammatik der lateinischen Sprache*
L.–H.–S.	Leumann and Hofmann, *Lateinische Syntax und Stylistik*, 3rd ed. rev. by Szantyr
L.–S.–J.	Liddell and Scott, *Greek–English Lexicon*, 9th ed., revised by H. Stuart Jones
Marq. *Prl.*	Marquardt, *Privatleben der Römer*
OCD	*Oxford Classical Dictionary*
OLD	*Oxford Latin Dictionary*
Paroem. Gr.	Leutsch and Schneidewin, *Corpus Paroemiographorum Graecorum*
Philol.	*Philologus*
PSI	*Papiri greci e latini*
RE	Pauly–Wissowa, *Real-Encyclopädie der Classischen Altertumswissenschaft*
RÉL	*Revue des études latines*
Rev. Phil.	*Revue de philologie*
Rh. Mus.	*Rheinisches Museum für Philologie*

SG^8	Friedlaender, *Darstellung aus der Sittenge-schichte Roms*, 8th ed.
SHA	Scriptores Historiae Augustae
TAPA	*Transactions of the American Philological Association*
TLL	*Thesaurus Linguae Latinae*
Wien. St.	*Wiener Studien*

INTRODUCTION

THERE is no evidence on the reception given to the *Satyricon*, the novel of which the *Cena Trimalchionis* forms part, by those who first read or heard it. In later antiquity it won praise even when the mutilation, whether accidental or deliberate, which has left the novel in its present fragmentary state may already have begun to take place. By the time classical learning revived, the greater part of the work, including most of the *Cena*, had been lost; yet scholars still responded to Petronius' elegant style, even if they could not bring themselves to approve altogether of his choice of subject-matter (one sixteenth-century writer[1] even wondered whether it might be advisable to change Giton, the boy-friend of the 'hero' Encolpius, into a girl, Gitona). In an enthusiastic letter[2] to a friend Lipsius (1547–1606) expresses his admiration of Petronius' attractive, incisive style; he regrets the scandalous nature of some passages but is ready to forgive such blemishes: 'ioci me delectant, urbanitas capit.'

The rediscovery in 1650 of a nearly complete text of the *Cena* (see III below) brought a great increase in Petronius' popularity. His skill in handling an episode of some length was more obvious than before; the dinner-party, a theme long familiar in literature, was seen to be treated with a liveliness and breadth not seen in his predecessors, and his masterly portrait of a section of society not usually thought worthy of a serious writer's attention attracted readers towards not merely the *Cena* but the fragments already known. The *Cena* made it possible to guess more plausibly at the scope of the novel as a whole. The inclusion of this

---

[1] Burmann[1], ii. 253.   [2] Ibid. 260.

substantial, carefully elaborated interlude suggested that the plot was a vehicle for a series of similar brilliant episodes. While it is no doubt a pity that the other extant portions of the *Satyricon* have been somewhat neglected, the *Cena* fully deserves its pre-eminence. As well as presenting on its own a fascinating microcosm of Roman life and manners, it amply illustrates Petronius' versatility, his wide range of humour, his subtle characterization, his skilful interweaving of traditional literary motifs and techniques, and his unerring appreciation of the mentality of common people and the nuances of their speech. All these qualities combine to offer us something unique and refreshing in ancient literature.

I. THE *SATYRICON*

A. *Date and Authorship*

The earliest citations from the *Satyricon* or references to *an author* named Petronius occur about A.D. 200. It is generally agreed, however, that the economic background and the language of the novel point to the first century A.D. rather than later (Marmorale's arguments in favour of a late-second-century date are rightly rejected). Difficulties arise when a more precise date is sought. At any rate in the extant parts of the *Satyricon* Petronius has chosen to give few, if any, indications of the date he had in mind for his setting, which presumably is contemporary with himself. The reference to *Caesar* in 51. 2 clearly places the action in the Imperial period, but it does not specify any particular emperor. Again, several gladiators and other entertainers named in the *Cena* may belong to the middle of the first century. The gladiator Petraites of 52. 3 and 71. 6 may be Neronian;[1] the Menecrates whose songs Trimalchio sings at 73. 3 could be the *citharoedus* of the Neronian period mentioned in Suet.

[1] H. T. Rowell, 'The Gladiator Petraites and the Date of the *Satyricon*', *TAPA* lxxxix (1958), 12 ff.

Nero 30. 2; when at 64. 4 Plocamus boasts that in his youth the only singer to equal him was Apelles, this could be the singer of that name[1] who was popular in the time of Caligula. In each case the identification consistent with a Neronian date may be correct, but the same objection is possible each time: performers on the stage and in the arena, as in other professions, quite often used traditional names.[2] Thus the Neronian date for the gladiator Petraites itself depends on this recurrence of names: a known Caligulan gladiator named Columbus has to be discarded in favour of a hypothetical Neronian namesake in order to maintain the Neronian date for Hermeros and Petraites.[3]

It is doubtful whether details like these would have seemed sufficient in themselves to prove that Petronius wrote during the reign of Nero. Three further questions, all crucial, must be considered: (i) was the author of the *Satyricon* the same as the C.(?)[4] Petronius mentioned in Tac. *Ann.* xvi. 17 ff. (see Appendix IA and Testimonia)? If he was, then the *Satyricon* must have been written not later than early in A.D. 66; (ii) did Petronius base his poem on the Civil War (chs. 119–24) on Lucan's *De Bello Civili*, whether he wrote it as a parody or as a demonstration how the subject ought to have been treated or in some other direct relationship (see Appendix IB)? If he did, at least that part of the *Satyricon* cannot have been written before, say, A.D. 64, when some knowledge of Lucan's poem may have begun to be available (he left it incomplete when he died in his 26th year in 65). If the identification with the Tacitean Petronius and the direct relationship with Lucan are both accepted, the composition of Petronius' *Civil War* must be placed

[1] Suet. *Calig.* 33. 1.

[2] Sen. *NQ* vii. 32. 3 'at quanta cura laboratur ne cuius pantomimi nomen intercidat', *SG*[8] ii. 634 ff.

[3] See note on 52. 3.

[4] It should not be forgotten that the reading depends essentially on one manuscript.

between 64 and 66; (iii) did Petronius draw on the *Epistulae Morales* of Seneca (see Appendix IC)? If he did, he cannot have composed the *Satyricon* earlier than *c.* 60–5. In the three sections of Appendix I, as in the relevant parts of the Commentary, it is suggested, not that a late Neronian date is impossible, but rather that the evidence for it has been pressed too far. In any case the significance of this whole controversy should not be exaggerated. The common ground needs emphasis as much as the area of disagreement. Thus, for example, in chapter 71, where Petronius clearly satirizes those who parade their kindness towards their slaves, the satire is equally effective whether or not we think that it is aimed at Seneca in particular.

B. *Title*

The novel is by convention referred to as the *Satyricon*, but it is agreed that this title is not a neuter singular but a genitive plural (= Greek σατυρικῶν), lit. 'satyr-like adventures'. The word σατυρικός is not connected with the Latin *satura* or with its adjective *satiricus*[1] but it is difficult to believe that Petronius did not intend a play on words,[2] especially since the subject-matter of the *Satyricon* overlaps that of *satura*.

C. *Length*

The length of the original work is impossible to determine. The extant portions, of which the *Cena* amounts to rather more than a third, do not provide us with either the beginning or the ending of the story, and they contain numerous breaks. There are indications in the *codex Traguriensis* and elsewhere that what we have comes from books xiv–xvi, but these do not enable us even to calculate the length of any one book (Sullivan divides as follows: bk. xiv—12 to

[1] Cf. Schol. Juv. 1. 20 'Lucilium satiricum dicit.'

[2] So, for example, Walsh, p. 72; against this view see B. E. Perry, *The Ancient Romances*, 192.

26. 6; bk. xv—1 to 11, 26. 7 to 99; bk. xvi—100 to the end. Müller prefers to divide: bk. xiv—1 to 26. 6; bk. xv—26. 7 to 78; bks. xvi f.—79 to 141). Even if we assume that we can guess the average length of a book, we cannot tell how many books there were originally, but merely that there were at least sixteen. The most likely supposition is that the original novel was of considerable length (the tale of travel and adventure written by Antonius Diogenes in the second century A.D. had 24 books).

D. *Genre*

No other work in Greek or Latin literature closely resembles the *Satyricon*, so it is hardly surprising that modern writers have disagreed greatly on how to classify it, or even whether it can be classified at all.

(*a*) The *Satyricon* may be in part a parody of the conventional Greek romance, which sought to edify the reader by telling how two lovers are separated, undergo appalling hardships and dangers, and are finally reunited. The nature of these romances is illustrated by Chariton's *Chaereas and Callirhoe*, now dated not later than the second century A.D. (The more familiar sophistic romances of writers like Achilles Tatius, Longus, and Heliodorus represent a development from the simpler type.[1]) In the *Satyricon*, instead of a young man and woman, eternally faithful to one another, Petronius presents a pair of homosexuals, Encolpius and the faithless Giton, who behave unheroically when faced with the standard misadventures of romance—seductions, pirates, storms, and shipwrecks.

Several objections have been made to this interpretation. Firstly, there is no firm evidence that the Greek romance, at any rate if the term is confined to works of considerable length, can be traced back as early as Petronius,[2] although

[1] See Perry, *The Ancient Romances*, 96 ff. on the nineteenth-century mistake of regarding the sophistic romances as the basic type.

[2] See on this question Sullivan, p. 95, Walsh, p. 8.

recent papyrus discoveries remove some of the force in this objection. Secondly, many of the parallels adduced between the *Satyricon* and Greek romance are inconclusive, since epic and romance have some features in common (see (*c*) below). Furthermore, the length of the *Cena* episode, which may not have been the only substantial self-contained episode in the novel, suggests that parody, whether of romance or of epic, was far from being Petronius' main concern, even if it helped to provide a narrative framework.

(*b*) In chs. 111 f. a cynical tale is told of a widow of Ephesus whose respect for her dead husband very soon gave place to her passion for a new lover. This story, like that of the Pergamene boy (chs. 85 ff.) must be in the tradition of the scandalous Milesian tales of Aristeides (second century B.C.), which were translated into Latin by Sisenna (early first century B.C.). It remains uncertain whether Petronius could have found more than isolated incidents in Aristeides and his followers, since we have no knowledge that they joined stories together to form a continuous narrative.[1]

(*c*) The *Satyricon* has also been seen as a parody of epic, in particular the *Odyssey* and the *Aeneid*. Instead of the hero Odysseus, pursued by the angry god Poseidon during various adventures, the cowardly Encolpius is pursued by Priapus and afflicted with embarrassing attacks of impotence. Sometimes the link with epic is made explicit, as, for instance, when Encolpius meets a lady called Circe (127 ff.), and is himself referred to as Polyaenus, an epithet of Odysseus. Mock-epic passages are used to add to the absurdity of the story; e.g. in ch. 108 the dispute on board ship, which has already been treated in an exaggerated, theatrical manner, is brought to an end by Tryphaena's lines:

> 'quis furor' exclamat 'pacem convertit in arma?
> quid nostrae meruere manus? non Troius heros
> hac in classe vehit decepti pignus Atridae . . .'

---

[1] See Walsh, pp. 10 ff., 15 ff.

This interpretation of the plot could account for various adventures which have been taken to suggest a parody of romance. Even the picture-gallery incident of ch. 83, which might indicate a motif from romance,[1] may be based on epic passages such as the description of the shield of Achilles at *Iliad* xviii. 478 ff. or the pictures in Dido's temple at *Aen.* i. 456 ff. But although parody of epic is undoubtedly present in the plot it is unwise to use this as an argument for excluding parody of romance as a partial and complementary explanation of the plot.

(*d*) Another genre which has influenced Petronius in some details is the mime, low farce with a very simple plot.[2] Several times he makes an explicit comparison; cf. 19. 1 'omnia mimico risu exsonuerunt', 31. 7 'pantomimi chorum, non patris familiae triclinium crederes.' Even where it is not explicit, a close resemblance can often be seen; note, for instance, the various imitations offered by guests and slaves at the *Cena* (41. 6, 64. 5, 68. 3, 69. 4, 70. 13), the mock-funeral scene (77 f.), the quick changes of scene, and the abrupt ending of the episode.[3]

(*e*) Some material may come from Menippean and Lucilian satire. The form of the novel has led some to lay emphasis on the influence of the Menippean satires of Varro (116–27 B.C.) and his model, Menippus of Gadara (early third century B.C.), who both used a mixture of prose and verse in order to handle miscellaneous subjects. This explanation of the form of the *Satyricon* would be more helpful if we had more evidence on the relative proportions of prose and verse in the work as a whole, or for that matter in Varro and Menippus. In Petronius the prose element far predominates; the verse element is mainly contained in the longest verse passages, the *Troiae Halosis* (89) and the *Bellum*

---

[1] Cf. Ach. Tat. i. 1.   [2] Cf. Beare, *The Roman Stage*, 149 ff.

[3] Cf. Cic. *Cael.* 65 'mimi ergo iam exitus, non fabulae; in quo cum clausula non invenitur, fugit aliquis e manibus, dein scabilla concrepant, aulaeum tollitur.'

Civile (119–24), which are both spoken by the poet Eumolpus and are not part of the main narrative. The subject-matter of the *Satyricon* could point equally well to the Lucilian form of satire. For example, the theme of legacy-hunting (116 ff.) occurs in Hor. *Sat.* ii. 5, and that of the vulgar host in *Sat.* ii. 8; we should, however, beware of deriving such passages solely from Horace.[1]

All these genres seem to have helped to shape Petronius' novel, but his skill in combining them has not always been properly recognized. Any attempt to find one single unifying link is misplaced. If we had the entire novel we might find that the plot was less important than a series of diverse scenes such as the rhetorical-school episode of the opening chapters of the extant text, or the *Cena*, or the legacy-hunters of Croton. The links needed to get the heroes from one scene to another were not necessarily alike—parody of the *Odyssey* in one place, of the *Aeneid* in another, of romance and tragedy elsewhere; perhaps in the lost passages parody of the *Iliad* and other works found a place. If this hypothesis is sound, the *Satyricon* could in fact be seen as satire in the Roman sense, a mixture of diverse elements, but satire more involved and ambitious than any of which we have knowledge.

II. THE *CENA TRIMALCHIONIS*

A. *Location*

The episode known as the *Cena Trimalchionis* (26. 7–78. 8) is set in a Campanian town, several times referred to as a *colonia* (cf. 44. 12, 44. 16, 57. 9, 76. 10) and as *Graeca urbs* at 81. 3. Mommsen identified the town as Cumae,[2] but in recent years a stronger case has been put for Puteoli.[3] Possibly the original text of the narrative before the *Cena*

---

[1] See N. Rudd, *The Satires of Horace*, 224 ff., 302 ff.; and IIB in this Introduction.

[2] *Hermes* xiii (1878), 106 ff.   [3] See Sullivan, pp. 46 f.

gave the name of the town. In addition one or two of the personal names which occur, such as the magistrate Norbanus in 45. 10, 46. 8, may have been significant to Petronius' contemporaries, although the average Roman reader, even the average Neronian courtier, was surely not expected to recognize the names of dignitaries of another town, even a large sea-port like Puteoli. Topographical and institutional details are vague (cf. 44. 18 *clivus*, 57. 9 *basilica*, 44. 3, 44. 13 *aediles*). It is quite possible, then, that Petronius did not attach much importance to the precise location of the *Cena*. Walsh (p. 76) goes rather further: 'This *Graeca urbs* which is a Roman colony with a decaying harbour is a composite creation'; but in chs. 116 ff. Petronius names an actual town, Croton, even though his account of it is a satirical fantasy.

B. *Literary Background*

The description of a dinner-party was a familiar topic in Latin and Greek literature since it could accommodate anything from serious discussion to amusing comments on social behaviour.[1] As it happens, the two best-known exploitations of this setting, the *Symposium* of Plato[2] and the *Cena Nasidieni* of Horace[3] (*Sat.* ii. 8), have both been confidently seen as direct sources for Petronius' *Cena*. The connection with Plato is remote: the late arrival of the drunken Habinnas at 65 gains only a little if we regard it as a take-off or an echo of the late arrival of Alcibiades in the *Symposium* (212 c ff.). If Petronius had been thinking of the *Symposium*, it would have been more appropriate to show Habinnas making comical advances to some male guest. Again, the sketch of his own life and character given

[1] Cf. N. Rudd, *The Satires of Horace*, 213 ff., *OCD*[2] s.v. 'Symposium Literature', *RE* s.v. 'Symposion-Literatur'.

[2] Averil Cameron, 'Petronius and Plato', *CQ* xix (1969), 367–70, Sullivan, p. 125.

[3] J. Révay, 'Horaz und Petron', *CP* xvii (1922), 202 ff., Sullivan, pp. 82, 92, 126 ff.

by Trimalchio at 75. 5 ff. owes nothing to Alcibiades' description of Socrates at *Symp.* 215 a ff. (contrast the explicit reference to Plato at 128. 7). The resemblances between the *Cena Nasidieni* and the *Cena Trimalchionis* are rather greater: e.g. the acrobat's fall in *Sat.* 54 is somewhat similar to the fall of the awning in Hor. *Sat.* ii. 8. 54; and the mishap is in each case greeted with some banal reflections on Fortune (*Sat.* 55. 3; *Sat.* ii. 8. 61 ff.), by Trimalchio himself at his dinner, by a guest Nomentanus at Nasidienus' dinner. But if he had Horace's satire in mind, Petronius has obviously reworked the material completely. Like Horace, he draws attention to the host's vulgarity and bad taste, yet as the meal proceeds Petronius' attitude to the scene becomes more complex than Horace's. The difference lies partly in the narrative technique employed. By using Encolpius, himself so disreputable, as the narrator who exposes the failings of Trimalchio and his friends, Petronius ensures that the reader's contempt is not directed exclusively towards them.[1] Furthermore, he has allowed himself an altogether ampler scale than Horace on which to portray his *nouveau riche* host, so that any debt to him becomes relatively insignificant.

c. *Language and Characterization*

Throughout the *Satyricon* Petronius uses variations in style to indicate distinctions in character. In the *Cena*, as elsewhere, he faces a major problem over Encolpius: he wants to show him as naïve, but he also wants to use him as the narrator. He could not afford to be too much circumscribed by the limitations of Encolpius, so at times he appears to hesitate over how far he should credit him with his own reactions to situations or make him a completely consistent character.[2]

[1] See notes on 29. 1, 60. 7, 70. 8.
[2] See P. A. George, 'Style and Character in the *Satyricon*', *Arion* v (1966), 354, P. Veyne, 'Le "je" dans le *Satiricon*', *RÉL* xlii (1964), 301 ff.

In the *Cena* a clear distinction is made between the elegant Latin of the narrative and the speech of Trimalchio and his freedman guests. Petronius sets out not merely to reproduce colloquial speech in general but to give at least the flavour of lower-class speech. The differentiation is obvious enough for the most part, but the corrupt state of the text in *H*, our only evidence for most of the *Cena*, leaves various details doubtful. When *H* credits Encolpius with an occasional Vulgarism, we are entitled to suspect it *a priori* as a scribal error; when the Vulgarism occurs in the speech of the freedmen we cannot be sure whether it has been deliberately introduced by Petronius or is simply another scribal error. As well as distinguishing the language of the freedmen from that of the narration, Petronius attempts to make a distinction between the speech of one freedman and another. For instance, Echion's speech (45–6) has numerous solecisms throughout but most noticeably when he addresses the rhetorician Agamemnon at 46. 1 and when he praises the value of education at 46. 7–8. But even where the Vulgarisms most abound Petronius is still careful not to come too close to the actual speech of lower-class Italians, especially in phonology; too close an approximation would have meant boring or mystifying the sophisticated reader.

In Appendix II some illustrations are given of the abnormalities in the speech of the freedmen, but we should not attempt to make too sharp a distinction between the speech of less cultivated Romans and that of the better educated.

III. THE TEXT OF THE *CENA TRIMALCHIONIS*

For an extended discussion of the textual tradition of the *Satyricon* as a whole see Müller's first edition pp. vii ff. or his second edition pp. 381 ff. ;[1] for the difficulties involved in

---

[1] See also E. H. Warmington in the second edition of the Loeb translation, pp. xix ff.

his account see pp. xxiii f. below. Here it will suffice to give
a summary of the facts, confined mainly to what concerns
the *Cena*.

Manuscripts of Petronius fall into four groups:

(*a*) The *excerpta vulgaria* (*O*) contain short passages from
chapters 1–26. 5 and 80. 9–137. 9, but nothing from the
Cena except ch. 55. In this group the oldest manuscript is
the *codex Bernensis* (*B*), written at Auxerre in the second
half of the ninth century; it was used by Pierre Pithou in
his editions of 1577 (*p*[1]) and 1587 (*p*[2]) (which chiefly reflect
the *L* group). There are two somewhat inferior twelfth-
century French manuscripts, not direct copies of *B*, Paris.
lat. 6842 D (*R*) and Paris. lat. 8049 (*P*). A number of
fifteenth-century Italian manuscripts of less value belong
to this class, all of them derived from one (δ) which was discovered by the Florentine scholar Poggio in 1420. In the
apparatus of ch. 55 one or two readings are cited from *s*, the
edition published in Antwerp in 1565 by Ioannes Sambucus,
who consulted one of these later manuscripts.

(*b*) The so-called longer excerpts (*L*) contain much more
of the extant part of the *Satyricon* than *O*. They have much
of the *Cena* as far as 37. 5, but very little after that. No surviving manuscript of this class is earlier than the latter part
of the sixteenth century. Several sixteenth-century editions,
including those of Jean de Tournes and Pierre Pithou, are
based mainly on manuscripts of this family.

(*c*) A number of *Florilegia* (φ) of the twelfth to the four-
teenth centuries contain fragments of the *Satyricon*. Of the
Cena they have only 34. 10, 43. 6, 44. 17, 45. 2, 55. 3, 56. 6,
59. 2, 75. 1.

(*d*) For the text of most of the *Cena* we depend entirely on
a single manuscript, the *Traguriensis* (*H* =Paris. lat. 7989),
which was discovered in 1650 at Trau in Dalmatia. It contains firstly the works of Tibullus, Propertius, and Catullus,
along with one of the *Heroides* of Ovid, then the *excerpta*
vulgaria from the *Satyricon* (= the MS. *A* of the *O* class),

and finally, from some different source but written in the same hand, the *Cena*. It was written in 1423, and it can be assumed to be closely connected with a manuscript which the Florentine scholar Poggio Bracciolini is known to have had in his possession in that year along with a manuscript of the *O* class. The ancestry of *H* is obscure, but John of Salisbury (twelfth century) was able to give a free version of ch. 51, a passage not in *L* or *O* (see Testimonia).

It must be emphasized that *H* has many errors, far more than are noted in the apparatus of this edition or in either of Müller's. In many cases these can be easily corrected, but in the speech of the freedmen it is sometimes extremely difficult to distinguish between scribal errors and solecisms introduced by Petronius. Many of the *hapax legomena* in *H* should also be regarded with suspicion: e.g. 41. 2 *bacalusias*, 41. 10 *pataracina*, 41. 12 *staminatas*.

The precise relationship between *O, L*, and *H* is uncertain, but it is clear that the *O* group has been excerpted from an incomplete text containing no more than the ancestor of *L*. The excerptor has worked on several different principles, choosing verse passages and aphorisms, but not attempting to preserve a narrative framework and therefore not marking gaps. *H*, on the other hand, was derived from an almost complete text. It is more difficult, however, to detect any rational principle according to which the material in *λ*, the hypothetical ancestor of *L* and *O*, could have been selected. *λ* seems to have contained what could be salvaged once that part of the work had suffered serious destruction and dislocation, i.e. after the text was in a worse state than when some ancestor of *H* was made. No dates can be assigned with confidence for these developments.

The history of the text suggested above differs to some extent from Müller's view. Convinced that interpolations common to *L* and *H* are Carolingian in date, he argues that the divergence of *L* and *H* cannot be earlier than the ninth century, and moreover that the same scribe who selected and patched together what we know through the *L* group also copied out the whole of the *Cena* in an ancestor of *H*. This would mean that when he more or less abandoned the *Cena* after 37. 5 in the course of excerpting for an ancestor of *L* he did so from choice and not from necessity. Müller's dating of the interpolations is open to question, as also is his account of the derivation of *L*, which has been more widely accepted.

TESTIMONIA

Tacitus, *Ann*. xvi. 17 (A.D. 66): eodem agmine Annaeus Mela, Cerialis Anicius, Rufrius Crispinus, C.[1] Petronius cecidere. *tum in capite 18*: de C. Petronio pauca supra repetenda sunt. nam illi dies per somnum, nox officiis et oblectamentis vitae transigebatur; utque alios industria, ita hunc ignavia ad famam protulerat, habebaturque non ganeo et profligator ut plerique sua haurientium, sed erudito luxu. ac dicta factaque eius quanto solutiora et quandam sui neglegentiam praeferentia, tanto gratius in speciem simplicitatis accipiebantur. pro consule tamen Bithyniae et mox consul vigentem se ac parem negotiis ostendit. dein revolutus ad vitia seu vitiorum imitatione inter paucos familiarium Neroni adsumptus est, elegantiae arbiter, dum nihil amoenum et molle adfluentia putat, nisi quod ei Petronius adprobavisset. unde invidia Tigellini quasi adversus aemulum et scientia voluptatum potiorem. ergo crudelitatem principis, cui ceterae libidines cedebant, aggreditur, amicitiam Scaevini Petronio obiectans, corrupto ad indicium servo ademptaque defensione et maiore parte familiae in vincla rapta. *19*. forte illis diebus Campaniam petiverat Caesar, et Cumas usque progressus Petronius illic attinebatur. nec tulit ultra timoris aut spei moras. neque tamen praeceps vitam expulit, sed incisas venas, ut libitum, obligatas aperire rursum et adloqui amicos, non per seria aut quibus gloriam constantiae peteret. audiebatque referentes nihil de immortalitate animae et sapientium placitis, sed levia carmina et faciles versus. servorum alios largitione, quosdam verberibus affecit. iniit epulas, somno indulsit, ut quamquam coacta mors fortuitae similis esset. ne codicillis quidem, quod plerique pereuntium, Neronem aut Tigellinum aut quem alium potentium

[1] C. *Wesenberg*: ac *M*: ac T. *Nipperdey*.

adulatus est, sed flagitia principis sub nominibus exoletorum feminarumque et novitatem cuiusque stupri perscripsit atque obsignata misit Neroni; fregitque anulum, ne mox usui esset ad facienda pericula. *20*. ambigenti Neroni, quonam modo noctium suarum ingenia notescerent, offertur Silia, matrimonio senatoris haud ignota et ipsi ad omnem libidinem adscita ac Petronio perquam familiaris. agitur in exilium, tamquam non siluisset quae viderat per-tuleratque, proprio odio.

Pliny, *NH* xxxvii. 20: T. Petronius consularis moriturus invidia Neronis, ut mensam eius exheredaret, trullam myrrhinam HS $\overline{\text{CCC}}$ emptam fregit.

Plutarch, *Mor.* 60 e: ὅταν (οἱ κόλακες) . . . τοὺς ἀσώτους καὶ πολυτελεῖς εἰς μικρολογίαν καὶ ῥυπαρίαν ὀνειδίζωσιν, ὥσπερ Νέρωνα Τίτος Πετρώνιος: 'when flatterers reproach profligate and lavish spenders with meanness and sordidness (as Titus Petronius did with Nero)'.

John of Salisbury, *Policraticus* iv. 5 (vol. i, p. 248. 22 ff. Webb): Apud Petronium Trimalchio refert fabrum fuisse, qui vitrea vasa faceret tenacitatis tantae ut non magis quam aurea vel argentea frangerentur. cum ergo fialam huiusmodi de vitro purissimo et solo (ut putabat) dignam Cesare fabri-casset, cum munere suo Cesarem adiens, admissus est. laudata est species muneris, commendata manus artificis, acceptata est devotio donantis. faber vero, ut admirationem intuentium verteret in stuporem, et sibi plenius gratiam conciliaret imperatoris, petitam de manu Cesaris fialam recepit, eamque validius proiecit in pavimentum tanto impetu ut nec solidissima et constantissima eris materia maneret illesa. Cesar autem ad haec non magis stupuit quam expavit. at ille de terra sustulit fialam, quae quidem non fracta erat sed collisa, ac si eris substantia vitri speciem induisset. deinde martiolum de sinu proferens vitium correxit aptissime, et tamquam collisum vas eneum crebris ictibus reparavit. quo facto se celum Iovis tenere arbitratus est, eo quod familiaritatem Cesaris et admirationem omnium se promeruisse credebat. sed secus accidit. quaesivit enim Cesar an alius sciret hanc condituram vitreorum. quod cum negaret, eum decollari praecepit imperator dicens quia, si hoc artificium innotesceret, aurum et argentum vilescerent quasi lutum. an vera sit relatio et fidelis incertum est, et de facto Cesaris diversi diversa sentiunt.

Isidore, *Etym.* xvi. 16. 6: ferunt autem sub Tiberio Caesare quendam artificem excogitasse vitri temperamentum, ut flexibile esset et ductile. qui dum admissus fuisset ad Caesarem, porrexit phialam Caesari, quam ille indignatus in pavimentum proiecit. artifex autem sustulit phialam de pavimento, quae conplicaverat se tamquam vas aeneum; deinde marculum de sinu protulit et phialam correxit. hoc facto Caesar dixit artifici: 'numquid alius scit hanc condituram vitrorum?' postquam ille iurans negavit alterum hoc scire, iussit illum Caesar decollari, ne dum hoc cognitum fieret, aurum pro luto haberetur et omnium metallorum pretia abstraherentur; et revera, quia si vasa vitrea non frangerentur, melius essent quam aurum et argentum.

BIBLIOGRAPHY

For works on Petronius up to 1909 see Stephen Gaselee, 'The Bibliography of Petronius', *Transactions of the Bibliographical Society*, vol. x, pp. 141–233; for 1908–40 see Müller[1], p. li.

MUTH, R. *Anzeiger für die Altertumswissenschaft* ix (1956), 1–22. [1941–55.]

SCHMELING, G. 'Petronian Scholarship since 1957', *Classical World* lxii (1969), 157–64.

SCHNUR, H. C. 'Recent Petronian Scholarship', *Classical Weekly* l (1957), 133–46, 141–3. [1940–1956.]

Editions and Commentaries

(i) Complete

BUECHELER, F. (*editio maior*), Berlin, 1862; 6th ed., rev. by W. Heraeus, 1922.

BURMANN, P. Utrecht, 1709; 2nd ed., Amsterdam, 1743.

ERNOUT, A. 4th ed., Paris, 1958 (with French trans.).

MÜLLER, K. Munich, 1961; 2nd ed. (with German trans. by W. Ehlers, and some notes), 1965.

(A commentary by J. P. Sullivan is in course of completion.)

(ii) *Cena Trimalchionis* only

FRIEDLAENDER, L. 2nd ed., Leipzig, 1906 (with German trans. and commentary).

MAIURI, A. Naples, 1945 (with Italian commentary).

MARMORALE, E. V. 2nd ed., Florence, 1961 (with Italian commentary).

PERROCHAT, P. 3rd ed., Paris, 1962 (French commentary without text).

SEDGWICK, W. B. 2nd ed., Oxford, 1950.

English Translations

ARROWSMITH, W. Ann Arbor, 1959.

HESELTINE, M. 2nd ed. (rev. by E. H. Warmington), 1969 (Loeb Classical Library).

SULLIVAN, J. P. Penguin Classics, 1965, rev. 1969.

General works on Petronius and the novel

BAGNANI, G. *Arbiter of Elegance*, Toronto, 1954 (*Phoenix* Suppl. ii).

COLLIGNON, A. *Étude sur Pétrone*, Paris, 1892.

PERRY, B. E. *The Ancient Romances*, Berkeley, 1967 (*Sather Classical Lectures*, vol. xxxvii).

RAITH, O. *Petronius, ein Epikureer*, Nuremberg, 1963.

SULLIVAN, J. P. *The* Satyricon *of Petronius: A Literary Study*, London, 1968.

TRENKNER, S. *The Greek Novella in the Classical Period*, Cambridge, 1958.

WALSH, P. G. *The Roman Novel*, Cambridge, 1970.

Language

COOPER, F. T. *Word Formation in the Roman* Sermo Plebeius, N.Y., 1895.

ELCOCK, W. D. *The Romance Languages*, London, 1960.

GOETZ, G. *Corpus Glossariorum Latinorum*, Leipzig, 1888–1923.

GRANDGENT, C. H. *An Introduction to Vulgar Latin*, Boston, 1907.

HERAEUS, W. 'Die Sprache des Petronius und die Glossen', reprinted in his *Kleine Schriften*, Heidelberg, 1937.

HOFMANN, J. B. *Lateinische Umgangssprache*, 3rd ed., Heidelberg, 1951.

KÜHNER, R., and STEGMANN, C. *Ausführliche Grammatik der lateinischen Sprache*, Pt. ii, 3rd ed., rev. by A. Thierfelder, Hanover, 1955.

xxx   BIBLIOGRAPHY

LEUMANN, M. and HOFMANN, J. B. *Lateinische Syntax und Stilistik*, 3rd ed., rev. by A. Szantyr, Munich, 1965.

LEUTSCH, E. L. v., and SCHNEIDEWIN, F. W. *Corpus Paroemiographorum Graecorum*, Göttingen, 1839–51.

LÖFSTEDT, E. *Philologischer Kommentar zur Peregrinatio Aetheriae*, Uppsala, 1911.

—— *Syntactica, Studien und Beiträge zur historischen Syntax des Lateins*, Lund, i, 1928 (2nd ed. 1942); ii, 1933.

—— *Vermischte Studien zur lateinischen Sprachkunde und Syntax*, Lund, 1936 (*Skrifter utgivna av Vetenskaps-Societeten i Lund*, xxiii).

MEYER-LÜBKE, W. *Romanisches Etymologisches Wörterbuch*, Heidelberg, 1938.

NELSON, H. L. W. *Petronius en zijn 'vulgair' Latijn*, Utrecht, 1947.

NEUE, F. *Formenlehre der lateinischen Sprache*, 3rd ed. by C. Wagener, Berlin, 1902–5.

OTTO, A. *Die Sprichwörter und sprichwörterlichen Redensarten der Römer*, Leipzig, 1890.

PALMER, L. R. *The Latin Language*, London, 1954.

SALONIUS, A. H. *Die Griechen und das Griechische in Petrons Cena Trimalchionis*, Helsingfors, 1927 (*Soc. Scient. Fennica, Commentationes Human. Litt.* ii. 1).

SEGEBADE, J., and LOMMATZSCH, E. *Lexicon Petronianum*, Leipzig, 1898.

STEFENELLI, A. *Die Volkssprache im Werk des Petron*, Vienna, 1962.

SÜSS, G. *De eo quem dicunt inesse Trimalchionis Cenae sermone vulgari*, Dorpat, 1926 (*Univ. Tartuensis: Acta et Commentationes B.* ix. 4).

SWANSON, D. C. *A Formal Analysis of Petronius' Vocabulary*, Minneapolis, 1963.

VÄÄNÄNEN, V. *Introduction au latin vulgaire*, Paris, 1963.

—— *Le Latin vulgaire des inscriptions pompéiennes*, 3rd ed., Berlin, 1966.

Antiquities, etc.

ANDRÉ, J. *L'Alimentation et la cuisine à Rome*, Paris, 1961.

BALSDON, J. P. V. D. *Life and Leisure in Ancient Rome*, London, 1969.

CARCOPINO, J. *Daily Life in Ancient Rome* (trans. Lorimer), London, 1962.

DAREMBERG, C., and SAGLIO, E. *Dictionnaire des antiquités grecques et romaines*, Paris, 1877–1919.

DE VREESE, J. G. W. M. *Petron 39 und die Astrologie*, Amsterdam, 1927.

FRIEDLAENDER, L. *Darstellungen aus der Sittengeschichte Roms*, Leipzig, 8th ed. 1910; 10th ed. (rev. Wissowa), 1921–3.

—— *Roman Life and Manners under the Early Empire* (English trans. of 7th ed.), London, 1908–13.

MARQUARDT, J. *Privatleben der Römer*, 2nd ed., Leipzig, 1886.

MARROU, H.-I. *A History of Education in Antiquity* (trans. Lamb), London, 1956.

RICCOBONO, S. *Fontes Iuris Romani Antejustiniani*, Florence, 1940–3.

RUGGIERO, E. DE. *Dizionario epigrafico di antichità romana*, Rome, 1886– .

Articles

ABBOTT, F. F. 'The Use of Language as a Means of Characterisation in Petronius', *CP* ii (1907), 43 ff.

—— 'The origin of the Realistic Romance among the Romans', *CP* vi (1911), 257 ff.

BENDZ, G. 'Sprachliche Bemerkungen zu Petron', *Eranos* xxxix (1941), 27 f.

BLÜMNER, H. 'Kritisch-exegetische Bemerkungen zu Petrons *Cena Trimalchionis*', *Philol.* lxxvi (1920), 331 ff.

BROWNING, R. 'The Date of Petronius', *CR* lxiii (1949), 12 ff., 28 f.

CAMERON, AVERIL. 'Petronius and Plato', *CQ* N.S. xix (1969), 367 ff.

COURTNEY, E. 'Parody and Literary Allusion in Menippean Satire', *Philol.* cvi (1962), 86 ff.

DELZ, J. Review of Müller's 1st ed., *Gnomon* xxxiv (1962), 676 ff.

DUNCAN-JONES, R. 'An Epigraphic Survey of Costs in Roman Italy', *BSR* N.S. xx (1965), 189 ff.

FUCHS, H. 'Verderbnisse im Petrontext', *Studien zur Textgeschichte und Textkritik*, ed. H. Dahlmann and R. Merkelbach, Cologne, 1959.

GASELEE, S. 'Petroniana', *CQ* xxxviii (1944), 76 f.

GEORGE, P. A. 'Style and Character in the *Satyricon*', *Arion* v (1966), 336 ff.

—— 'Petroniana', *CQ* N.S. xvii (1967), 130 ff.

—— 'Petronius and Lucan, *de Bello Civili*', *CQ* xxiv (1974), 119 ff.

HALEY, H. W. 'Quaestiones Petronianae', *HSCP* ii (1891), 1 ff.

HIGHET, G. 'Petronius the Moralist', *TAPA* lxxii (1941), 176 ff.

HUG, A. *RE* s.v. 'Symposion-Literatur'.

LILJA, S. 'Terms of Abuse in Roman Comedy', *Annales Acad. Scient. Fennicae* cxli. 3 (1965).

MENDELL, C. W. 'Petronius and the Greek Romance', *CP* xii (1917), 158 ff.

MOMIGLIANO, A. 'Literary Chronology of the Neronian Age', *CQ* xxxviii (1944), 96 ff.

MOMMSEN, T. 'Trimalchios Heimath und Grabschrift', *Hermes* xiii (1878), 107 ff.

NISBET, R. G. M. Review of Müller's 1st ed., *JRS* lii (1962), 227 ff.

ORELLI, J. K. 'Lectiones Petronianae', Ind. Lect. Zürich, 1836.

ORIOLI, F. 'In Petronii Arbitri frag. Trag. Notulae', *Nuova collezione d'opusc. lett.* (1824), 53, 111.

PRESTON, K. 'Some sources of the Comic Effect in Petronius', *CP* x (1915), 260 ff.

RÉVAY, J. 'Horaz und Petron', *CP* xvii (1922), 202 ff.

ROSE, K. F. C. 'The Date and Author of the *Satyricon*', Leiden, 1971 (*Mnemosyne* Suppl. xvi).

ROWELL, H. T. 'The Gladiator Petraites and the Date of the *Satyricon*', *TAPA* lxxxix (1958), 12 ff.

SANDY, G. 'Satire in the *Satyricon*', *AJP* xc (1969), 293 ff.

SCHISSEL VON FLESCHENBERG, O. 'Die künstlerische Absicht in Petrons *Cena Trimalchionis*', *Wiener Studien* xxxiii (1911), 264 ff.

SCHNUR, H. C. 'The Economic Background of the *Satyricon*', *Latomus* xviii (1959), 790 ff.

SCHUSTER, M. 'Der Werwolf und die Hexen', *Wiener Studien* xlviii (1930), 149 ff., xlix (1931), 83 ff.

SHERO, L. R. 'The *Cena* in Roman Satire', *CP* xviii (1923), 126 ff.

STÖCKER, C. 'Humor bei Petron', Diss., Erlangen, 1969.

STRELITZ, A. 'Emendationes Petr. *Sat.*', *Neue Jahrb. f. class. Philologie* cxix (1879), 629 ff., 833 ff.

STUBBE, H. 'Die Verseinlagen im Petron', *Philol.* Suppl. xxv (1933).

STUDER, G. 'Observationes in Petronii Cenam Trimalchionis', *Lect. Gymn.* Bern, 1839.

—— 'Über das Zeitalter des Petronius Arbiter', *Rh. Mus.* ii (1843), 50 ff., 202 ff.

SULLIVAN, J. P. 'Satire and Realism in Petronius' (in *Critical Essays on Roman Literature: Satire*, ed. Sullivan, London, 1963, 73 ff.).

—— 'Petronius, Seneca and Lucan: A Neronian Literary Feud?', *TAPA* xcix (1968), 453 ff.

SVENNUNG, J. 'Anredeformen', *Skrifter utgivna av Vetenskaps-Societeten i Lund*, xlii (1958).

VEYNE, P. 'Le "je" dans le *Satiricon*', *RÉL* xlii (1964), 301 ff.

WEHLE, W. 'Observationes Criticae in Petronium', Diss., Bonn, 1861.

Gaselee's bibliography is particularly useful for tracing the works of early editors and critics. Burmann's *Variorum* editions are the most accessible source for the suggestions of Dousa, Goesius, I. F. Gronovius, Hadrianides, Heinsius, Mentel (= Tilebomenus), Muncker, Reinesius, and Reiske. Buecheler's edition includes much of this earlier work and has in addition emendations by Iac. Gronovius, Jacobs, Jahn, and Orelli. Müller's editions contain a more rigorous selection of earlier emendations, and are the source for the suggestions of Leo, Kaibel, and Fraenkel.

SIGLA

L = consensus librorum *l m r t p* vel eorum qui quoque loco exstant

  l = codex Leidensis Scaligeranus 61, scriptus anno 1571

  m = codex Vaticanus lat. 11428, scriptus post annum 1565

  r = codex Lambethanus 693, a Daniele Rogers ante annum 1572 scriptus

  t = editio Tornaesiana, Lugduni 1575

  p = consensus utriusque editionis Pithoeanae

    *p*¹ = editio Pithoeana prior, Parisiis 1577

    *p*² = editio Pithoeana altera, Parisiis 1587

Memm. = lectiones codicis Memmiani a Turnebo aliisque exscriptae

Tol. = lectiones codicis Tolosani a Pithoeo in *p*² relatae

vetus Pithoei = lectiones a Pithoeo e codice Benedictino nunc deperdito excerptae

c = Scaligeri Catalecta, Lugduni 1573

O = consensus codicum *B R P*

  B = codex Bernensis 357 et codex Leidensis Vossianus 4° 30 (saec. IX)

  R = codex Parisiensis lat. 6842 D (saec. XII)

  P = codex Parisiensis lat. 8049 (saec. XII)

    Bit. = lectiones a Pithoeo e codice, qui fuerat Ioannis Biturigum ducis, excerptae

δ = codex a Poggio Florentino anno 1420 repertus, nunc deperditus, ex quo pendent libri novicii saeculo XV scripti omnes

  M = codex deperditus ex quo editio princeps expressa est

  s = editio Sambuci, Antverpiae 1565

O* = consensus librorum *O* et δ

SIGLA

H = codicis Parisiensis lat. 7989 olim Traguriensis ea pars
   quae cenam Trimalchionis continet, scriptus anno 1423

patav. = Cenae editio princeps, Patavii 1664

ϕ = archetypus Florilegiorum

Ioan. Sar. = Ioannes Saresberiensis (saec. xv)

λ = consensus LO

ω = consensus HL (in c. 55 ω = consensus HLO)

CENA TRIMALCHIONIS

Venerat iam tertius dies, id est expectatio liberae cenae, 7
sed tot vulneribus confossis fuga magis placebat quam
quies. itaque cum maesti deliberaremus quonam genere 8
praesentem evitaremus procellam, unus servus Agamemnonis interpellavit trepidantes et 'quid? vos' inquit 'nesci- 9
tis, hodie apud quem fiat? Trimalchio, lautissimus homo ⟨∗⟩
horologium in triclinio et bucinatorem habet subornatum,
ut subinde sciat quantum de vita perdiderit.' amicimur ergo 10
diligenter obliti omnium malorum, et Gitona libentissime
servile officium tuentem [usque hoc] iubemus in balneum
sequi. ⟨∗⟩ nos interim vestiti errare coepimus, immo iocari 27
magis et circulis ludentium accedere, cum subito videmus
senem calvum, tunica vestitum russea, inter pueros capillatos
ludentem pila. nec tam pueri nos, quamquam erat operae 2
pretium, ad spectaculum duxerant, quam ipse pater familiae,
qui soleatus pila prasina exercebatur. nec amplius eam re-
petebat quae terram contigerat, sed follem plenum habebat
servus sufficiebatque ludentibus. notavimus etiam res novas. 3
nam duo spadones in diversa parte circuli stabant, quorum
alter matellam tenebat argenteam, alter numerabat pilas,
non quidem eas quae inter manus lusu expellente vibrabant,
sed eas quae in terram decidebant. cum has ergo miraremur 4
lautitias, accurrit Menelaus et 'hic est' inquit 'apud quem

---

26 7 *non sanum;* id . . . cenae *secl. Müller, auctore Buecheler*
9 *lac. ind. Strelitz*   10 usque hoc *del. Heraeus*   balneum *Bue-*
cheler in adn.: balneo *H*   *lac. post* sequi *ind. Friedlaender*
   27 1 iocari *H*: morari *Nisbet*: otiari *Heinsius*: *lac. ante* immo *ind.*
Buecheler   ludentum (*sic*) *Heinsius*: ludentem *H*: *del. Buecheler*: circulis ludentes *Delz*   2 qui *L*: quia *H*   3 *verbum post* etiam
excidisse videtur   lusu *H*: luxu *LMemm.*: *fortasse* [lusu] expellentes

pres. for fut.

cubitum ponitis, et quidem iam principium cenae videtis.'
5 etiamnum loquebatur Menelaus, cum Trimalchio digitos
concrepuit, ad quod signum matellam spado ludenti subiecit.
6 exonerata ille vesica aquam poposcit ad manus, digitosque
paululum adspersos in capite pueri tersit.

very little

⟨*⟩

28 longum erat singula excipere. itaque intravimus balneum,
et sudore calfacti momento temporis ad frigidam eximus.
2 iam Trimalchio unguento perfusus tergebatur, non linteis,
3 sed palliis ex lana mollissima factis. tres interim iatraliptae
in conspectu eius Falernum potabant, et cum plurimum
rixantes effunderent, Trimalchio hoc suum propin esse dice-
4 bat. hinc involutus coccina gausapa lecticae impositus est
praecedentibus phaleratis cursoribus quattuor et chiramaxio, in quo deliciae eius vehebantur, puer vetulus, lippus,
5 domino Trimalchione deformior. cum ergo auferretur, ad
caput eius cum minimis symphoniacus tibiis accessit et tamquam in aurem aliquid secreto diceret, toto itinere cantavit.
6 sequimur nos admiratione iam saturi et cum Agamemnone
ad ianuam pervenimus, in cuius poste libellus erat cum
7 hac inscriptione fixus: 'quisquis servus sine dominico iussu
8 foras exierit, accipiet plagas centum.' in aditu autem ipso
stabat ostiarius prasinatus, cerasino succinctus cingulo,
9 atque in lance argentea pisum purgabat. super limen autem
cavea pendebat aurea, in qua pica varia intrantes salutabat.
29 ceterum ego dum omnia stupeo, paene resupinatus crura
mea fregi. ad sinistram enim intrantibus non longe ab
ostiarii cella canis ingens, catena vinctus, in pariete erat
2 pictus superque quadrata littera scriptum 'cave canem.' et

---

4 ponitis *H*: ponetis *Scheffer*   quidem *Buecheler*: quid *H*
5 etiamnum *Scheffer*: et iam non *H*   Trimalcio lautissimus homo *L*
6 *lac. ind. Buecheler*

28 3 propin esse *Heraeus*: propinasse *H*   5 cum minimis symphoniacus *H* (symphoniacis *L*): symphoniacus cum minimis *Wehle*
8 autem *om. L*   lance *om. H*

collegae quidem mei riserunt, ego autem collecto spiritu non ~~*diil not cay*~~
destiti totum parietem persequi. erat autem venalicium 3
⟨cum⟩ titulis pictum, et ipse Trimalchio capillatus caduceum
tenebat Minervaque ducente Romam intrabat. hinc quem- 4
admodum ratiocinari didicisset deinque dispensator factus
esset, omnia diligenter curiosus pictor cum inscriptione red-
diderat. in deficiente vero iam porticu levatum mento in 5
tribunal excelsum Mercurius rapiebat. praesto erat Fortuna 6
⟨cum⟩ cornu abundanti [copiosa] et tres Parcae aurea pensa
torquentes. notavi etiam in porticu gregem cursorum cum 7
magistro se exercentem. praeterea grande armarium in 8
angulo vidi, in cuius aedicula erant Lares argentei positi
Venerisque signum marmoreum et pyxis aurea non pusilla,
in qua barbam ipsius conditam esse dicebant.

of the master

⟨∗⟩

interrogare ergo atriensem coepi, quas in medio picturas 9
haberent. 'Iliada et Odyssian' inquit 'ac Laenatis gladia-
torium munus.' non licebat †multaciam† considerare   **30**

⟨∗⟩

nos iam ad triclinium perveneramus, in cuius parte prima
procurator rationes accipiebat. et quod praecipue miratus
sum, in postibus triclinii fasces erant cum securibus fixi,
quorum imam partem quasi embolum navis aeneum finie-
bat, in quo erat scriptum: 'C. Pompeio Trimalchioni, seviro 2
Augustali, Cinnamus dispensator.' sub eodem titulo et 3

---

29 3 cum *add. Burmann*   Romam *H*: tema *l vetus Pithoei*: tema
mr: tenia *tp*: moenia *Heinsius*   4 deinque *H*: dein *lmrp*: deinde *t*
5 mento *Hlp*: merito *mrt*: de pavimento *Fraenkel dubitanter*: porticu
de pavimento in tribunal excelsum eum *item Fraenkel*   6 cum
add. Wehle   copiosa *del. Goesius*   8 *lac. ind. Buecheler*
9 ergo *H*: ego *L*   medio *H*: medica *L*
   30 1 multaciam *H*: multa iam *Anton*: multa etiam *Scheffer*   *post*
considerare *lac. ind. Buecheler*   triclinii *del. Müller*[1]   imam *m*[m]:
unam *Hlmrtp*[1]

lucerna bilychnis de camera pendebat, ⟨erant⟩ et duae tabu-
lae in utroque poste defixae, quarum altera, si bene memini,
hoc habebat inscriptum: 'III. et pridie kalendas Ianuarias
4 C. noster foras cenat', altera lunae cursum stellarumque
septem imagines pictas; et qui dies boni quique incommodi
essent, distinguente bulla notabantur.

5 his repleti voluptatibus cum conaremur [in triclinium]
intrare, exclamavit unus ex pueris qui supra hoc officium
6 erat positus: 'dextro pede.' sine dubio paulisper trepidavi-
mus, ne contra praeceptum aliquis nostrum limen transiret.
7 ceterum ut pariter movimus dextros gressus, servus nobis
despoliatus procubuit ad pedes ac rogare coepit, ut se
poenae eriperemus: nec magnum esse peccatum suum,
8 propter quod periclitaretur; subducta enim sibi vestimenta
dispensatoris in balneo, quae vix fuissent X̄ sestertiorum.
9 rettulimus ergo dextros pedes dispensatoremque in oecario
aureos numerantem deprecati sumus, ut servo remitteret
10 poenam. superbus ille sustulit vultum et 'non tam iactura
11 me movet' inquit 'quam neglegentia nequissimi servi. vestimenta mea cubitoria perdidit, quae mihi natali meo cliens
quidam donaverat, Tyria sine dubio, sed iam semel lota.
quid ergo est? dono vobis eum.'

31 obligati tam grandi beneficio cum intrassemus triclinium,
occurrit nobis ille idem servus, pro quo rogaveramus, et
stupentibus spississima basia impegit gratias agens humani-
2 tati nostrae. 'ad summam, statim scietis' ait 'cui dederitis
beneficium. vinum dominicum ministratoris gratia est.'

3 tandem ergo discubuimus pueris Alexandrinis aquam in
manus nivatam infundentibus aliisque insequentibus ad
4 pedes ac paronychia cum ingenti subtilitate tollentibus. ac
ne in hoc quidem tam molesto tacebant officio, sed obiter

3 ⟨erant⟩ et *Buecheler in adn.*   5 in triclinium *del. Müller*
qui ... positus *del. Fraenkel (cf. 56. 8)*   7, 9 dextros *del. Fraenkel*
8 X̄ sestertiorum *L*: decem sexterciorum *H*: X HS *vetus Pithoei*
9 oecario *Heraeus*: precario *H*: atrio *Heinsius*: procoetone denarios
Müller²

cantabant. ego experiri volui an tota familia cantaret, 5
itaque potionem poposci. paratissimus puer non minus me 6
acido cantico excepit, et quisquis aliquid rogatus erat ut 7
daret: pantomimi chorum, non patris familiae triclinium
crederes. allata est tamen gustatio valde lauta; nam iam 8
omnes discubuerant praeter unum Trimalchionem, cui locus
novo more primus servabatur. ceterum in promulsidari 9
asellus erat Corinthius cum bisaccio positus, qui habebat
olivas in altera parte albas, in altera nigras. tegebant asellum 10
duae lances, in quarum marginibus nomen Trimalchionis
inscriptum erat et argenti pondus. ponticuli etiam ferruminati sustinebant glires melle ac papavere sparsos. fuerunt et 11
tomacula ferventia supra craticulam argenteam posita, et
infra [craticulam] Syriaca pruna cum granis Punici mali.

in his eramus lautitiis, cum ipse Trimalchio ad sympho- 32
niam allatus est positusque inter cervicalia minutissima expressit imprudentibus risum. pallio enim coccineo adrasum 2
excluserat caput circaque oneratas veste cervices laticlaviam immiserat mappam fimbriis hinc atque illinc pen-
dentibus. habebat etiam in minimo digito sinistrae manus 3
anulum grandem subauratum, extremo vero articulo digiti
sequentis minorem, ut mihi videbatur, totum aureum, sed
plane ferreis veluti stellis ferruminatum. et ne has tantum 4
ostenderet divitias, dextrum nudavit lacertum armilla aurea
cultum et eboreo circulo lamina splendente conexo. ut 33
deinde pinna argentea dentes perfodit, 'amici,' inquit 'nondum mihi suave erat in triclinium venire, sed ne diutius
absentivus morae vobis essem, omnem voluptatem mihi

31 7 et quisquis . . . daret *vix sanum*   8 tamen *H*: tum *L*
unum *H*: ipsum *LMemm.*   11 ferventia *ante* supra *collocavit t*ᵐ,
ante argenteam *habet* ω   craticulam *del. Müller*

32 1 minutissima *L*: munitissima *H*   2 coccineo *H*: coccino *L*
4 conexo *Buecheler*: conexum ω

33 1 in triclinium venire sed ne diutius absentius essem omnem
voluptatem *lrtMemm.* (diutius *in margine adscripto t*), (absentivus *p*):
in triclinium absens more vobis venire, sed ne diutius absenti vos
essem voluptatem *H corr. Heinsius*

2 negavi. permittitis tamen finiri lusum.' sequebatur puer
cum tabula terebinthina et crystallinis tesseris, notavique
rem omnium delicatissimam. pro calculis enim albis ac
3 nigris aureos argenteosque habebat denarios. interim dum
ille omnium †textorum dicta inter lusum consumit, gustanti-
bus adhuc nobis repositorium allatum est cum corbe, in quo
gallina erat lignea patentibus in orbem alis, quales esse
4 solent quae incubant ova. accessere continuo duo servi et
symphonia strepente scrutari paleam coeperunt erutaque
5 subinde pavonina ova divisere convivis. convertit ad
hanc scaenam Trimalchio vultum, et 'amici' ait 'pavonis
ova gallinae iussi supponi, et mehercules timeo ne iam
concepti sint; temptemus tamen, si adhuc sorbilia sunt.'
6 accipimus nos cochlearia non minus selibras pendentia
7 ovaque ex farina pingui figurata pertundimus. ego quidem
paene proieci partem meam, nam videbatur mihi iam in
8 pullum coisse. deinde ut audivi veterem convivam: 'hic
nescio quid boni debet esse', persecutus putamen manu
pinguissimam ficedulam inveni piperato vitello circumdatam.

34 iam Trimalchio eadem omnia lusu intermisso poposcerat
feceratque potestatem clara voce, si quis nostrum iterum
vellet mulsum sumere, cum subito signum symphonia datur
2 et gustatoria pariter a choro cantante rapiuntur. ceterum
inter tumultum cum forte paropsis excidisset et puer iacen-
tem sustulisset, animadvertit Trimalchio colaphisque obiur-
3 gari puerum ac proicere rursus paropsidem iussit. insecutus
est ⟨supel⟩lecticarius argentumque inter reliqua purgamenta
4 scopis coepit verrere. subinde intraverunt duo Aethiopes
capillati cum pusillis utribus, quales solent esse qui hare-

---

2 permittitis *Hlp*: permittetis *mrt* ac *H*: aut *LMemm*.
3 textorum *H*: testorum *LMemm*.: tonsorum *vel* lusorum *Burmann*
dicta *om. LMemm.* 5 sorberi possunt *post* sorbilia sunt *add.* H
8 circumdatam *H*: piperatam *L*

34 3 supellecticarius *Dousa*: lecticarius *ω* verrere *ω*: everrere
Goesius

nam in amphitheatro spargunt, vinumque dedere in manus;
aquam enim nemo porrexit.

laudatus propter elegantias dominus 'aequum' inquit 5
'Mars amat. itaque iussi suam cuique mensam assignari.
obiter et putidissimi servi minorem nobis aestum frequentia
sua facient.'

statim allatae sunt amphorae vitreae diligenter gypsatae, 6
quarum in cervicibus pittacia erant affixa cum hoc titulo:
'Falernum Opimianum annorum centum.' dum titulos per- 7
legimus, complosit Trimalchio manus et 'eheu' inquit 'ergo
diutius vivit vinum quam homuncio. quare tangomenas
faciamus. vinum vita est. verum Opimianum praesto. heri
non tam bonum posui, et multo honestiores cenabant.'
potantibus ergo et accuratissime nobis lautitias mirantibus 8
larvam argenteam attulit servus sic aptatam, ut articuli eius
vertebraeque luxatae in omnem partem flecterentur. hanc 9
cum super mensam semel iterumque abiecisset, et catenatio
mobilis aliquot figuras exprimeret, Trimalchio adiecit:

'eheu nos miseros, quam totus homuncio nil est!   10
sic erimus cuncti, postquam nos auferet Orcus.
    ergo vivamus, dum licet esse bene.'

laudationem ferculum est insecutum plane non pro expe- 35
ctatione magnum; novitas tamen omnium convertit oculos.
rotundum enim repositorium duodecim habebat signa in 2
orbe disposita, super quae proprium convenientemque
materiae structor imposuerat cibum: super arietem cicer ari- 3
etinum, super taurum bubulae frustum, super geminos testiculos ac rienes, super cancrum coronam, super leonem ficum
Africanam, super virginem steriliculam, super libram stateram 4

5 iussi *Burmann*: iussit *H*: iussit senex *L*   putidissimi *Heinsius*: pudissimi *H*: p̄dissimi *lp vetus Pithoei*: praedissum *t*: p̄disum *mr*
7 tangomenas *H*: τέγγε πνεύμονας *Muncker, probante Buecheler*
8 accuratissime *L*: curatissime *H*   aptatam *H*: aptam *L*   luxatae
Heinsius: laxatae *H*: locatae *L*   9 et *ω*: ut *Jahn*
    35 1 *vel ante vel post* laudationem *aliquid deesse susp. Müller*   3 fru-
stum *L*: frustrum *H*

in cuius altera parte scriblita erat, in altera placenta, super
scorpionem ⟨*⟩[pisciculum marinum], super sagittarium
oclopetam, super capricornum locustam marinam, super
5 aquarium anserem, super pisces duos mullos. in medio
6 autem caespes cum herbis excisus favum sustinebat. circumferebat Aegyptius puer clibano argenteo panem

⟨*⟩

atque ipse etiam taeterrima voce de Laserpiciario mimo
7 canticum extorsit. nos ut tristiores ad tam viles accessimus
cibos, 'suadeo' inquit Trimalchio 'cenemus; hoc est ius
36 cenae.' haec ut dixit, ad symphoniam quattuor tripudiantes
procurrerunt superioremque partem repositorii abstulerunt.
2 quo facto videmus infra [scilicet in altero ferculo] altilia et
sumina leporemque in medio pinnis subornatum, ut Pegasus
3 videretur. notavimus etiam circa angulos repositorii Marsyas quattuor, ex quorum utriculis garum piperatum curre-
4 bat super pisces, qui quasi in euripo natabant. damus
omnes plausum a familia inceptum et res electissimas ridentes
5 aggredimur. non minus et Trimalchio eiusmodi methodio
6 laetus 'Carpe' inquit. processit statim scissor et ad symphoniam gesticulatus ita laceravit obsonium, ut putares
7 essedarium hydraule cantante pugnare. ingerebat nihilo
minus Trimalchio lentissima voce: 'Carpe, Carpe.' ego suspicatus ad aliquam urbanitatem totiens iteratam vocem
pertinere, non erubui eum qui supra me accumbebat hoc
8 ipsum interrogare. at ille, qui saepius eiusmodi ludos spe-
ctaverat, 'vides illum' inquit 'qui obsonium carpit: Carpus
vocatur. itaque quotienscumque dicit "Carpe", eodem verbo
et vocat et imperat.'

4 pisciculum marinum *susp. Gaselee*   oclopetam *H*: odopetam *ltp*:
odepotam *Memm.mr*: oclopectam *Buecheler*   capricornum *H*: capri-
cornua *lp*   in quo cornua erant *post* capricornum *add. H*   6 *lac.*
ind. Buecheler   7 ius *ltp*: in ius *Memm.mr*: in *H*

36 2 scilicet in altero ferculo *om. p²*   3 utriculis *Hp*: int'culis
(*i.e.* intriculis *quod Tolosanum habere testatur p²) lmr*: int culis *t*
8 itaque *L*: ita *H*

non potui amplius quicquam gustare, sed conversus ad 37
eum, ut quam plurima exciperem, longe accersere fabulas
coepi sciscitarique, quae esset mulier illa, quae huc atque
illuc discurreret. 'uxor' inquit 'Trimalchionis, Fortunata 2
appellatur, quae nummos modio metitur. et modo modo 3
quid fuit? ignoscet mihi genius tuus, noluisses de manu
illius panem accipere. nunc, nec quid nec quare, in cae- 4
lum abiit et Trimalchionis topanta est. ad summam, mero 5
meridie si dixerit illi tenebras esse, credet. ipse nescit quid 6
habeat, adeo saplutus est; sed haec lupatria providet omnia,
est ubi non putes. est sicca, sobria, bonorum consiliorum— 7
tantum auri vides—est tamen malae linguae, pica pulvinaris.
quem amat, amat; quem non amat, non amat. ipse [Trimal- 8
chio] fundos habet, quantum milvi volant, nummorum nummos. argentum in ostiarii illius cella plus iacet quam quisquam
in fortunis habet. familia vero babae babae, non mehercules 9
puto decumam partem esse quae dominum suum noverit.
ad summam, quemvis ex istis babaecalis in rutae folium 10
coniciet. nec est quod putes illum quicquam emere. omnia 38
domi nascuntur: laina, cedria, piper; lacte gallinaceum si
quaesieris, invenies. ad summam, parum illi bona lana 2
nascebatur: arietes a Tarento emit et eos culavit in gregem.
mel Atticum ut domi nasceretur, apes ab Athenis iussit 3
afferri; obiter et vernaculae quae sunt, meliusculae a Graeculis fient. ecce intra hos dies scripsit, ut illi ex India semen 4
boletorum mitteretur. nam mulam quidem nullam habet
quae non ex onagro nata sit. vides tot culcit[r]as: nulla non 5
aut conchyliatum aut coccineum tomentum habet. tanta
est animi beatitudo. reliquos autem collibertos eius cave 6

37 1 accersere *Hl*: arcessere *mrtpMemm*.   6 est ubi *Müller²*:
et ubi *H*   7 *verba* tantum auri vides *eiecit Nodot, probante
Buecheler; tuentur cum alii tum Süss* 60   8 Trimalchio *secl.
Müller*   quantum *Scheffer*: qua *H*   10 'ut coniiciatur in rute-
folium, cuius Petronius in poenam delinquentium meminit' (cf. 58. 5)
Ioan. Sar. epist. 205 (scripta anno 1167)*
38 1 laina *George*: lana *H*   credrae *H*: citrea *Jacobs*   5 animi
susp. Scheffer

7 contemnas. valde sucos[s]i sunt. vides illum qui in imo
imus recumbit: hodie sua octingenta possidet. de nihilo
8 crevit. modo solebat collo suo ligna portare. sed quomodo
dicunt—ego nihil scio, sed audivi—cum Incuboni pilleum
9 rapuisset, [et] thesaurum invenit. ego nemini invideo, si
quid deus dedit. est tamen subalapa et non vult sibi male.
10 itaque proxime cenaculum hoc titulo proscripsit: "C. Pompeius Diogenes ex kalendis Iuliis cenaculum locat; ipse enim
11 domum emit." quid ille qui libertino loco iacet, quam bene
12 se habuit. non impropero illi. sestertium suum vidit decies,
sed male vacillavit. non puto illum capillos liberos habere,
nec mehercules sua culpa; ipso enim homo melior non est;
13 sed liberti scelerati, qui omnia ad se fecerunt. scito autem:
sociorum olla male fervet, et ubi semel res inclinata est,
14 amici de medio. et quam honestam negotiationem exercuit,
15 quod illum sic vides. libitinarius fuit. solebat sic cenare
quomodo rex: apros gausapatos, opera pistoria, †vis† ⟨*⟩
cocos, pistores. plus vini sub mensa effundebatur, quam
16 aliquis in cella habet. phantasia, non homo. inclinatis
quoque rebus suis, cum timeret ne creditores illum conturbare existimarent, hoc titulo auctionem proscripsit:
"⟨C.⟩ Iulius Proculus auctionem faciet rerum supervacu-
arum." '

39   interpellavit tam dulces fabulas Trimalchio; nam iam
sublatum erat ferculum, hilaresque convivae vino sermoni-
2 busque publicatis operam coeperant dare. is ergo reclinatus
in cubitum 'hoc vinum' inquit 'vos oportet suave faciatis.
3 pisces natare oportet. rogo, me putatis illa cena esse con-

---

8 et *del. Scheffer*   9 quid *Buecheler*: quo *H*: quoi *Goesius*: quod
Scheffer   subalapa *coniunxit Buecheler*: sub alapa *H*: subalapo *vel*
subalapator *Heraeus Kl. Schr. 110*   10 cenaculum *Buecheler*: oecum
Iac. Gronovius: cum *H*: *post* cum *aliquid perisse suspicatur Fraenkel*
(*item Fuchs*)   11 libertino *Heinsius*: libertini *H*   15 opera
pistoria *delebat Jacobs*   vis *H*: avis *Scheffer*: avis bis coctos pistorenses *Immisch*: *lacunam suspicatus est Buecheler*   16 T. *vel* C. *prae-*
nomen intercidisse censet Buecheler   auctionem *Scheffer*: caucionem *H*
    39 1 interpellabit *H*

tentum, quam in theca repositorii videratis? "sic notus
Ulixes?" quid ergo est? oportet etiam inter cenandum
philologiam nosse. patrono meo ossa bene quiescant, qui 4
me hominem inter homines voluit esse. nam mihi nihil novi
potest afferri, sicut ille fer[i]culus †ta mel habuit praxim†.
caelus hic, in quo duodecim dii habitant, in totidem se 5
figuras convertit, et modo fit aries. itaque quisquis nascitur illo signo, multa pecora habet, multum lanae, caput
praeterea durum, frontem expudoratam, cornum acutum.
plurimi hoc signo scholastici nascuntur et arietilli.' laudamus 6
urbanitatem mathematici; itaque adiecit: 'deinde totus
caelus taurulus fit. itaque tunc calcitrosi nascuntur et
bubulci et qui se ipsi pascunt. in geminis autem nascuntur 7
bigae et boves et colei et qui utrosque parietes linunt. in 8
cancro ego natus sum. ideo multis pedibus sto, et in mari
et in terra multa possideo; nam cancer et hoc et illoc qua-
drat. et ideo iam dudum nihil supra illum posui, ne genesim
meam premerem. in leone cataphagae nascuntur et im- 9
periosi; in virgine mulierosi et fugitivi et compediti; in libra 10
laniones et unguentarii et quicumque aliquid expendunt; in 11
scorpione venenarii et percussores; in sagittario strabones,
qui holera spectant, lardum tollunt; in capricorno aeru- 12
mnosi, quibus prae mala sua cornua nascuntur; in aquario
copones et cucurbitae; in piscibus obsonatores et rhetores. 13
sic orbis vertitur tamquam mola, et semper aliquid mali
facit, ut homines aut nascantur aut pereant. quod autem 14
in medio caespitem videtis et super caespitem favum, nihil
sine ratione facio. terra mater est in medio quasi ovum 15
corrotundata, et omnia bona in se habet tamquam
favus.'

'sophos' universi clamamus et sublatis manibus ad came- **40**
ram iuramus Hipparchum Aratumque comparandos illi

---

3 videbatis *Heinsius*   4 fericulusta mel *H, unde* ferculus *primus
seiunxit I. F. Gronovius*: iam semel *Heraeus*: talem *Studer*   praxim
H: apodixin *Jacobs*   10 mulierosi *Iac. Gronovius*: mulieres *H*
expendunt *Burmann*: expediunt *H*

homines non fuisse, donec advenerunt ministri ac toralia
proposuerunt [toris], in quibus retia erant picta subsesso-
2 resque cum venabulis et totus venationis apparatus. necdum
sciebamus, ⟨quo⟩ mitteremus suspiciones nostras, cum extra
triclinium clamor sublatus est ingens, et ecce canes Laconici
3 etiam circa mensam discurrere coeperunt. secutum est hos
repositorium, in quo positus erat primae magnitudinis aper,
et quidem pilleatus, e cuius dentibus sportellae dependebant
duae palmulis textae, altera caryotis altera thebaicis repleta.
4 circa autem minores porcelli ex coptoplacentis facti, quasi
uberibus imminerent, scrofam esse positam significabant.
5 et hi quidem apophoreti fuerunt. ceterum ad scindendum
aprum non ille Carpus accessit, qui altilia laceraverat, sed
barbatus ingens, fasciis cruralibus alligatus et alicula subornatus polymita, strictoque venatorio cultro latus apri vehe-
6 menter percussit, ex cuius plaga turdi evolaverunt. parati
aucupes cum harundinibus fuerunt et eos circa triclinium
7 volitantes momento exceperunt. inde cum suum cuique
iussisset referri Trimalchio, adiecit: 'et iam videte, quam
8 porcus ille silvaticus lotam comederit glandem.' statim
pueri ad sportellas accesserunt quae pendebant e dentibus
thebaicasque et caryotas ad numerum divisere cenantibus.
41 interim ego, qui privatum habebam secessum, in multas
cogitationes diductus sum, quare aper pilleatus intrasset.
2 postquam itaque omnis bacalusias consumpsi, duravi inter-
3 rogare illum interpretem meum quod me torqueret. at ille:
'plane etiam hoc servus tuus indicare potest; non enim
4 aenigma est, sed res aperta. hic aper, cum heri summa cena
eum vindicasset, a convivis dimissus ⟨est⟩; itaque hodie

40 1 homines *fortasse corruptum. delendum putat Müller*: homini
Heinsius   toralia *Mentel*: tolaria *H*   proposuerunt *H*: praeposuerunt *Mentel*   toris *secl. Fraenkel*   2 quo *add. Mentel*   5 qui
altilia laceraverat *secl. Sullivan*   7 lotam *Muncker*: totam *H*
8 quae . . . dentibus *secl. Müller*[1]

41 2 bacalusias *fort. corruptum*: baucalesis *Buecheler in adn.*   quod
Buecheler: quid *H*   4 est *add. Heinsius*: a convivis dimissus *interpolatum censet George*

tamquam libertus in convivium revertitur.' damnavi ego 5
stuporem meum et nihil amplius interrogavi, ne viderer
numquam inter honestos cenasse.

dum haec loquimur, puer speciosus, vitibus hederisque 6
redimitus, modo Bromium, interdum Lyaeum Euhiumque
confessus, calathisco uvas circumtulit et poemata domini
sui acutissima voce traduxit. ad quem sonum conversus 7
Trimalchio 'Dionyse' inquit 'Liber esto.' puer detraxit pilleum apro capitique suo imposuit. tum Trimalchio rursus 8
adiecit 'non negabitis me' inquit 'habere liberum patrem.'
laudavimus dictum [Trimalchionis] et circumeuntem puerum
sane perbasiamus.

ab hoc ferculo Trimalchio ad lasanum surrexit. nos 9
libertatem sine tyranno nacti coepimus invitare convivarum sermones. Dama itaque primus cum pataracina 10
poposcisset, 'dies' inquit 'nihil est. dum versas te, nox fit.
itaque nihil est melius quam de cubiculo recta in triclinium
ire. et mundum frigus habuimus. vix me balneus calfecit. 11
tamen calda potio vestiarius est. staminatas duxi, et plane 12
matus sum. vinus mihi in cerebrum abiit.'

excepit Seleucus fabulae partem et 'ego' inquit 'non cotidie 42
lavor; baliscus enim fullo est, aqua dentes habet, et cor 2
nostrum cotidie liquescit. sed cum mulsi pultarium obduxi,
frigori laecasin dico. nec sane lavare potui; fui enim hodie
in funus. homo bellus, tam bonus Chrysanthus animam 3
ebulliit. modo modo me appellavit. videor mihi cum illo 4
loqui. heu, eheu. utres inflati ambulamus. minoris quam
muscae sumus, ⟨muscae⟩ tamen aliquam virtutem habent,
nos non pluris sumus quam bullae. et quid si non abstinax 5

7 conversus *del. Fraenkel*   8 rursus adiecit *del. Fraenkel*
Trimalchionis *del. Fraenkel*   circumeuntem *Scheffer*: circumeuntes *H*
9 invitare *fortasse non sanum*   10 Dama *Heinsius*: clamat *H*
pataracina *obscurum*: acrata (*i.e.* ἄκρατα) vina *Müller*²   12 staminatas *dubium*: staminarias *Muncker*: heminarias *I. F. Gronovius*

42 2 baliscus *H*: balniscus *Scheffer*   cotidie *secl. Rose* (*cf.* C. et M. *xxvi*
(*1965*), *224 s.*)   laecasin *Burmann*: laecasim *H*   4 minoris *Scheffer*:
minores *H*   sumus *H*ᵐ: suus *H*   muscae *add. Heinsius*: illae *Ernout*

fuisset! quinque dies aquam in os suum non coniecit, non
micam panis. tamen abiit ad plures. medici illum perdiderunt, immo magis malus fatus; medicus enim nihil aliud est
6 quam animi consolatio. tamen bene elatus est, vitali lecto,
stragulis bonis. planctus est optime—manu misit aliquot—
7 etiam si maligne illum ploravit uxor. quid si non illam
optime accepisset! sed mulier quae mulier milvinum genus.
neminem nihil boni facere oportet; aeque est enim ac si in
puteum conicias. sed antiquus amor cancer est.'

43   molestus fuit, Philerosque proclamavit: 'vivorum meminerimus. ille habet, quod sibi debebatur: honeste vixit,
honeste obiit. quid habet quod queratur? ab asse crevit
et paratus fuit quadrantem de stercore mordicus tollere.
2 itaque crevit quicquid tetigit tamquam favus. puto mehercules illum reliquisse solida centum, et omnia in nummis
3 habuit. de re tamen ego verum dicam, qui linguam caninam
comedi: durae buccae fuit, linguosus, discordia, non homo
4 —frater eius fortis fuit, amicus amico, manu plena, uncta
mensa—et inter initia malam parram pilavit, sed recorrexit
costas illius prima vindemia: vendidit enim vinum, quantum ipse voluit. et quod illius mentum sustulit, hereditatem accepit, ex qua plus involavit quam illi relictum est.
5 et ille stips, dum fratri suo irascitur, nescio cui terrae filio
patrimonium elegavit. longe fugit, quisquis suos fugit.
6 habuit autem oracularios servos, qui illum pessum dederunt.
numquam autem recte faciet, qui cito credit, utique homo
negotians. tamen verum quod frunitus est, quam diu vixit.
7 †cui datum est, non cui destinatum. plane Fortunae filius,
in manu illius plumbum aurum fiebat. facile est autem, ubi

5 ad *Scheffer*: at *H*   6 stragulis *patav.*: stagulis *H*   planctus
patav.: plautus *H*   manu misit *patav.*: manum misit *H*
    43 1 Philerosque *Buecheler*: Phileros qui *H*   abbas secrevit *H*:
corr. Scheffer   tetigit *Delz*: crevit *H*   3 quia linguam caninam
comedit *Delz*   4 plena uncta *post Reinesium Heinsius*: uncta
plena *H*   5 longe fugit *patav.*: longe fuit *H*   6 oracularios
H: oricularios *Reinesius*   verum . . . vixit *vix sanum*   7 *quaedam excidisse videntur*. cui ⟨datum est⟩, datum est *Muncker*

omnia quadrata currunt. et quot putas illum annos secum
tulisse? septuaginta et supra. sed corneolus fuit, aetatem
bene ferebat, niger tamquam corvus. noveram hominem 8
olim oliorum, et adhuc salax erat. non mehercules illum puto
in domo canem reliquisse. immo etiam pullarius erat, omnis
minervae homo. nec improbo, hoc solum enim secum tulit.'

haec Phileros dixit, illa Ganymedes: 'narratis quod nec 44
ad caelum nec ad terram pertinet, cum interim nemo curat,
quid annona mordet. non mehercules hodie buccam panis 2
invenire potui. et quomodo siccitas perseverat. iam annum 3
esur⟨it⟩io fuit. aediles male eveniat, qui cum pistoribus
colludunt. "serva me, servabo te." itaque populus minutus
laborat; nam isti maiores maxillae semper Saturnalia agunt.
o si haberemus illos leones, quos ego hic inveni, cum primum 4
ex Asia veni. illud erat vivere. ⟨si⟩ simila Siciliae inferior 5
erat, larvas sic istos percolopabant, ut illis Iuppiter iratus
esset. [sed] memini Safinium: tunc habitabat ad arcum 6
veterem, me puero, piper, non homo. is quacumque ibat, 7
terram adurebat. sed rectus, sed certus, amicus amico, cum
quo audacter posses in tenebris micare. in curia autem 8
quomodo singulos [vel pilabat] tractabat, nec schemas
loquebatur sed derectum. cum ageret porro in foro, sic illius 9
vox crescebat tamquam tuba. nec sudavit umquam nec
expuit, puto eum nescio quid assi a dis habuisse. et quam 10
benignus resalutare, nomina omnium reddere, tamquam
unus de nobis. itaque illo tempore annona pro luto erat.
asse panem quem emisses, non potuisses cum altero 11
devorare. nunc oculum bublum vidi maiorem. heu heu,

8 oliorum *dubium*   pullarius *Burmann*: puellarius *H*
  44 3 esuritio *Buecheler*: esurio *H*   5 si simila Siciliae inferior
erat *Simon*: similia sicilia interiores et *H*: cum simila silicia interesset
(*sc. fraude pistorum*) *Heraeus, praeeunte Buecheler*: si milia si cilia
(= χίλια) interiores et *Whittick*, CR *N.S. ii* (*1952*), *11*: (si milia si
cilia *Heraeus*)   6 sed *del. Scheffer*   8 vel pilabat *secl.
George*: [vel] pilabat [tractabat] *Jacobs et Wehle, praeeunte Scheffer*
derectum *Reiske*: dilectum *H*   9 eum *Mentel*: enim *H*   assi a
dis *Burmann*: asia dis *H*: assi lapidis *Süss*

12 quotidie peius. haec colonia retroversus crescit tamquam
13 coda vituli. sed quare? [non] habemus aedilem ⟨non⟩ trium
cauniarum, qui sibi mavult assem quam vitam nostram.
itaque domi gaudet, plus in die nummorum accipit, quam
14 alter patrimonium habet. iam scio unde acceperit denarios
mille aureos. sed si nos coleos haberemus, non tantum
sibi placeret. nunc populus est domi leones, foras vulpes.
15 quod ad me attinet, iam pannos meos comedi, et si per-
16 severat haec annona, casulas meas vendam. quid enim
futurum est, si nec dii nec homines huius coloniae miseren-
tur? ita meos fruniscar, ut ego puto omnia illa a diibus fieri.
17 nemo enim caelum caelum putat, nemo ieiunium servat,
nemo Iovem pili facit, sed omnes opertis oculis bona sua
18 computant. antea stolatae ibant nudis pedibus in clivum,
passis capillis, mentibus puris, et Iovem aquam exorabant.
itaque statim urceatim plovebat: aut tunc aut numquam: et
omnes redibant udi tamquam mures. itaque dii pedes lanatos habent, quia nos religiosi non sumus. agri iacent—'
45 2 'oro te' inquit Echion centonarius 'melius loquere. "modo
sic, modo sic" inquit rusticus; varium porcum perdiderat.
3 quod hodie non est, cras erit: sic vita truditur. non mehercules patria melior dici potest, si homines haberet. sed
laborat hoc tempore, nec haec sola. non debemus delicati
4 esse, ubique medius caelus est. tu si aliubi fueris, dices hic
porcos coctos ambulare. et ecce habituri sumus munus
excellente in triduo die festa; familia non lanisticia, sed
5 plurimi liberti. et Titus noster magnum animum habet et
est caldicerebrius: aut hoc aut illud, erit quid utique. nam
6 illi domesticus sum, non est mixcix. ferrum optimum daturus

---

13 :a interpunxit *Delz*: non *del. Müller*[1], *ante* trium *posuit Buecheler*:
nos *Mentel* 16 huius *Scheffer*: eius *H* a diibus *Buecheler*:
aedilibus *H* fieri *Mentel*: fleri *H* 18 mentibus *H*: vestibus *Leo*
redibant *Jacobs et Wehle*: ridebant *H* udi *Triller*: uvidi *Reiske*:
ut dii *H*

45 2 truditur *Lφ*: tiditur *H* 3 sola *Reiske*: sua *H* 4 aliubi
Scheffer: alicubi *H* in triduo *Heinsius*: inter duo *H* 5 quid
Muncker et Heinsius: quod *H*

est, sine fuga, carnarium in medio, ut amphitheater videat.
et habet unde: relictum est illi sestertium trecenties, decessit
illius pater †male† ut quadringenta impendat, non sentiet
patrimonium illius, et sempiterno nominabitur. iam nannos 7
aliquot habet et mulierem essedariam et dispensatorem
Glyconis, qui deprehensus est, cum dominam suam delectaretur. videbis populi rixam inter zelotypos et amasiunculos. Glyco autem, sestertiarius homo, dispensatorem ad 8
bestias dedit. hoc est se ipsum traducere. quid servus pecca-
vit, qui coactus est facere? magis illa matella digna fuit
quam taurus iactaret. sed qui asinum non potest, stratum
caedit. quid autem Glyco putabat Hermogenis filicem um- 9
quam bonum exitum facturam? ille milvo volanti poterat
ungues resecare; colubra restem non parit. Glyco, Glyco
dedit suas; itaque quamdiu vixerit, habebit stigmam, nec
illam nisi Orcus delebit. sed sibi quisque peccat. sed subol- 10
facio quia nobis epulum daturus est Mammea, binos denarios
mihi et meis. quod si hoc fecerit, eripiet Norbano totum
favorem. scias oportet plenis velis hunc vinciturum. et 11
revera, quid ille nobis boni fecit? dedit gladiatores sester-
tiarios iam decrepitos, quos si sufflasses cecidissent; iam
meliores bestiarios vidi. occidit de lucerna equites, putares
eos gallos gallinaceos; alter burdubasta, alter loripes, tertiarius mortuus pro mortuo, qui habe⟨ba⟩t nervia praecisa.
unus alicuius flaturae fuit Thraex, qui et ipse ad dictata 12
pugnavit. ad summam, omnes postea secti sunt; adeo de
magna turba "adhibete" acceperant, plane fugae merae.
"munus tamen" inquit "tibi dedi": et ego tibi plodo. com- 13
puta, et tibi plus do quam accepi. manus manum lavat.
videris mihi, Agamemnon, dicere: "quid iste argutat mole- **46**
stus?" quia tu, qui potes loquere, non loquis. non es nostrae

6 fuga *Scheffer*: fuca *H*   amphitheater *Buecheler*: ampli-
teatur *H*   male! *interpunxit Müller*[2]: ⟨factum⟩ male *Ehlers*
7 nannos *Buecheler, praeeuntibus Scheff. et Heinsio*: Manios *H*
10 eripiet *Scheffer*: erripiat *H*   11 habebat *Buecheler*: habet *H*
  46 1 loquis *Burmann*: loqui *H*

fasciae, et ideo pauperorum verba derides. scimus te prae
2 litteras fatuum esse. quid ergo est? aliqua die te persuadeam, ut ad villam venias et videas casulas nostras? inveniemus quod manducemus, pullum, ova: belle erit, etiam si
omnia hoc anno tempestas disparpallavit: inveniemus ergo
3 unde saturi fiamus. et iam tibi discipulus crescit cicaro
meus. iam quattuor partes dicit; si vixerit, habebis ad latus
servulum. nam quicquid illi vacat, caput de tabula non
tollit. ingeniosus est et bono filo, etiam si in aves morbosus
4 est. ego illi iam tres cardeles occidi, et dixi quia mustella
comedit. invenit tamen alias nenias, et libentissime pingit.
5 ceterum iam Graeculis calcem impingit et Latinas coepit
non male appetere, etiam si magister eius sibi placens fit nec
uno loco consistit, sed venit ⟨*⟩ scit quidem litteras, sed non
6 vult laborare. est et alter non quidem doctus, sed curiosus,
qui plus docet quam scit. itaque feriatis diebus solet domum
7 venire, et quicquid dederis, contentus est. emi ergo nunc
puero aliquot libra rubricata, quia volo illum ad domusionem
aliquid de iure gustare. habet haec res panem. nam litteris
satis inquinatus est. quod si resilierit, destinavi illum artificium docere, aut tonstrinum aut praeconem aut certe causi-
8 dicum, quod illi auferre non possit nisi Orcus. ideo illi cotidie
clamo: "Primigeni, crede mihi, quicquid discis, tibi discis.
vides Phileronem causidicum: si non didicisset, hodie famem
a labris non abigeret. modo modo collo suo circumferebat
onera venalia, nunc etiam adversus Norbanum se extendit.
litterae thesaurum est, et artificium numquam moritur."'
47 eiusmodi fabulae vibrabant, cum Trimalchio intravit et
detersa fronte unguento manus lavit spatioque minimo
2 interposito 'ignoscite mihi' inquit 'amici, multis iam diebus

2 disparpallavit *Cholodniak*: dissipavit *Heinsius*: depravavit
Müller[2]: dispare pallavit *H*   3 partes *Scheffer*: parti *H*   aves
Triller et Reiske: naves *H*   5 fit *Buecheler*: sit *H*   *lac. indicavi*:
sed it redit. scit quidem litteras sed *Jacobs*: sed venit abit. scit quidem
litteras sed *Wehle*: sed venit dem litteras sed *H*   7 artificium
Scheffer: artificii *H*   tonstrinum *Scheffer*: constreinum *H*

venter mihi non respondit. nec medici se inveniunt. profuit
mihi tamen malicorium et taeda ex aceto. spero tamen, iam 3
veterem pudorem sibi imponit. alioquin circa stomachum
mihi sonat, putes taurum. itaque si quis vestrum voluerit 4
sua re causa facere, non est quod illum pudeatur. nemo
nostrum solide natus est. ego nullum puto tam magnum
tormentum esse quam continere. hoc solum vetare ne Iovis
potest. rides, Fortunata, quae soles me nocte desomnem 5
facere? nec tamen in triclinio ullum vetui facere quod se
iuvet, et medici vetant continere. vel si quid plus venit,
omnia foras parata sunt: aqua, lasani et cetera minutalia.
credite mihi, anathymiasis in cerebrum it et in toto corpore 6
fluctum facit. multos scio sic periisse, dum nolunt sibi
verum dicere.' gratias agimus liberalitati indulgentiaeque 7
eius, et subinde castigamus crebris potiunculis risum. nec 8
adhuc sciebamus nos in medio [lautitiarum], quod aiunt,
clivo laborare. nam commundatis ad symphoniam mensis
tres albi sues in triclinium adducti sunt capistris et tintinna-
bulis culti, quorum unum bimum nomenculator esse dicebat,
alterum trimum, tertium vero iam se⟨xen⟩nem. ego puta- 9
bam petauristarios intrasse et porcos, sicut in circulis mos
est, portenta aliqua facturos; sed Trimalchio expectatione 10
discussa 'quem' inquit 'ex eis vultis in cenam statim fieri?
gallum enim gallinaceum, penthiacum et eiusmodi nenias
rustici faciunt: mei coci etiam vitulos oenococtos solent
facere.' continuoque cocum vocari iussit, et non expectata 11
electione nostra, maximum natu iussit occidi, et clara voce:
'ex quota decuria es?' cum ille se ex quadragesima respon- 12
disset, 'empticius an' inquit 'domi natus?' 'neutrum' inquit
cocus 'sed testamento Pansae tibi relictus sum.' 'vide ergo' 13

47 2 malicorium *Scheffer*: maleicorum *H*   3 veterem *Heinsius*:
ventrem *H*: *del. Müller*   imponit *H*: imponet *Buecheler*   4 vetare
del. Kaibel   5 vetui *H*: vetuo *Buecheler*   lasani *Buecheler*:
lasanum *Scheffer*: lassant *H*   8 lautitiarum *del. Fraenkel*
quod *Heinsius*: quo *H*   commundatis *Heinsius*: cum mundatis *H*
sexennem *Wehle*: senem *H*   10 penthiacum *H*: phasiacum
Reinesius   oenococtos *Orioli*: aeno coctos *Mentel*: eno cocto *H*

ait 'ut diligenter ponas; si non, te iubebo in decuriam viatorum conici.' et cocum quidem potentiae admonitum in
48 culinam obsonium duxit, Trimalchio autem miti ad nos
vultu respexit et 'vinum' inquit 'si non placet, mutabo; vos
2 illud oportet bonum faciatis. deorum beneficio non emo,
sed nunc quicquid ad salivam facit, in suburbano nascitur
eo, quod ego adhuc non novi. dicitur confine esse Tarraci-
3 niensibus et Tarentinis. nunc coniungere agellis Siciliam
volo, ut cum Africam libuerit ire, per meos fines navigem.
4 sed narra tu mihi, Agamemnon, quam controversiam hodie
declamasti? ego etiam si causas non ago, in domusionem
tamen litteras didici. et ne me putes studia fastiditum,
II bybliothecas habeo, unam Graecam, alteram Latinam.
5 dic ergo, si me amas, peristasim declamationis tuae.' cum
dixisset Agamemnon: 'pauper et dives inimici erant', ait
Trimalchio 'quid est pauper?' 'urbane' inquit Agamemnon
6 et nescio quam controversiam exposuit. statim Trimalchio
'hoc' inquit 'si factum est, controversia non est; si factum
7 non est, nihil est.' haec aliaque cum effusissimis prosequeremur laudationibus, 'rogo' inquit 'Agamemnon mihi carissime, numquid duodecim aerumnas Herculis tenes, aut de
Ulixe fabulam, quemadmodum illi Cyclops pollicem †pori-
cino† extorsit? solebam haec ego puer apud Homerum
8 legere. nam Sibyllam quidem Cumis ego ipse oculis meis
vidi in ampulla pendere, et cum illi pueri dicerent: Σίβυλλα,
τί θέλεις; respondebat illa: ἀποθανεῖν θέλω.'
49 nondum efflaverat omnia, cum repositorium cum sue in-
2 genti mensam occupavit. mirari nos celeritatem coepimus
et iurare, ne gallum quidem gallinaceum tam cito percoqui
3 potuisse, tanto quidem magis, quod longe maior nobis porcus videbatur esse quam paulo ante apparuerat. deinde

13 potentiae *Scheffer*: potentia *H*
    48 4 etiam si *Wehle*: autem si *H*   domusionem *Wehle*: divisione
H   II *Buecheler* (duas *Mentel*): tres *H*   7 poricino *corruptum*:
del. Fuchs: porcino *Buecheler*
    49 2 coepimus *del. Fraenkel*   3 apparuerat *Heinsius*: aper
fuerat *H*: quam . . . fuerat *del. Müller*[1]

magis magisque Trimalchio intuens eum 'quid? quid?' 4
inquit 'porcus hic non est exinteratus? non mehercules est.
voca, voca cocum in medio.' cum constitisset ad mensam 5
cocus tristis et diceret se oblitum esse exinterare, 'quid?
oblitus?' Trimalchio exclamat 'putes illum piper et cuminum non coniecisse. despolia.' non fit mora, despoliatur 6
cocus atque inter duos tortores maestus consistit. deprecari
tamen omnes coeperunt et dicere: 'solet fieri; rogamus,
mittas; postea si fecerit, nemo nostrum pro illo rogabit.'
ego, crudelissimae severitatis, non potui me tenere, sed 7
inclinatus ad aurem Agamemnonis 'plane' inquam 'hic debet
servus esse nequissimus; aliquis oblivisceretur porcum exinterare? non mehercules illi ignoscerem, si piscem praeterisset.' at non Trimalchio, qui relaxato in hilaritatem vultu 8
'ergo' inquit 'quia tam malae memoriae es, palam nobis
illum exintera.' recepta cocus tunica cultrum arripuit por- 9
cique ventrem hinc atque illinc timida manu secuit. nec 10
mora, ex plagis ponderis inclinatione crescentibus tomacula
cum botulis effusa sunt.

plausum post hoc automatum familia dedit et 'Gaio feli- 50
citer' conclamavit. nec non cocus potione honoratus est
et[iam] argentea corona, poculumque in lance accepit Corinthia. quam cum Agamemnon propius consideraret, ait 2
Trimalchio: 'solus sum qui vera Corinthea habeam.' expe- 3
ctabam, ut pro reliqua insolentia diceret sibi vasa Corintho
afferri. sed ille melius: 'et forsitan' inquit 'quaeris, quare 4
solus Corinthea vera possideam: quia scilicet aerarius, a quo
emo, Corinthus vocatur. quid est autem Corintheum, nisi
quis Corinthum habet? et ne me putetis nesapium esse, valde 5
bene scio, unde primum Corinthea nata sint. cum Ilium
captum est, Hannibal, homo vafer et magnus stelio, omnes

6 coeperunt *del. Fraenkel*   mittas *Heinsius*: mittes *H*
50 1 honoratus *Scheffer*: oneratus *H*   etiam *H*: *corr. Buecheler*
4 nisi quis Corinthum *vix sanum*: nisi quis a Corintho *dubitanter*
Müller   habet *Buecheler*: habeat *H*   5 *cf. Isid. Etym. xvi. 20. 4*
stelio *Heinsius*: scelio *H*

statuas aeneas et aureas et argenteas in unum rogum con-
gessit et eas incendit; factae sunt in unum aera miscellanea.
6 ita ex hac massa fabri sustulerunt et fecerunt catilla et
paropsides ⟨et⟩ statuncula. sic Corinthea nata sunt, ex
7 omnibus in unum, nec hoc nec illud. ignoscetis mihi quod
dixero: ego malo mihi vitrea, certe non olunt. quod si non
frangerentur, mallem mihi quam aurum; nunc autem vilia
51 sunt. fuit tamen faber qui fecit phialam vitream, quae non
2 frangebatur. admissus ergo Caesarem est cum suo munere
⟨*⟩ deinde fecit reporrigere Caesarem et illam in pavimen-
3 tum proiecit. Caesar non pote valdius quam expavit. at
ille sustulit phialam de terra; collisa erat tamquam vasum
4 aeneum; deinde martiolum de sinu protulit et phialam otio
5 belle correxit. hoc facto putabat se solium Iovis tenere,
utique postquam ille dixit: "numquid alius scit hanc con-
6 dituram vitreorum?" vide modo. postquam negavit, iussit
illum Caesar decollari: quia enim, si scitum esset, aurum
52 pro luto haberemus. in argento plane studiosus sum. habeo
scyphos urnales plus minus ⟨*⟩ quemadmodum Cassandra
occidit filios suos, et pueri mortui iacent sic ut vivere putes.
2 habeo capidem quam reliquit †patronorum meus†, ubi
3 Daedalus Niobam in equum Troianum includit. nam Hermerotis pugnas et Petraitis in poculis habeo, omnia pon-
derosa; meum enim intellegere nulla pecunia vendo.'
4   haec dum refert, puer calicem proiecit. ad quem respiciens
Trimalchio 'cito' inquit 'te ipsum caede, quia nugax es.'

miscellanea *patav.*: muscillania *H*   6 et *add. Scheffer*   7 quod[1]
Muncker: quid *H*   non olunt *Buecheler*: nolunt *H*
   51 1 *cf. Isid. Etym. xvi. 16. 6, Ioan. Sar. Policr. iv. 5*   2 *lac.
post* munere *ind. Fuchs*   Caesarem *Scheffer*: Caesari *H*: *del. Fraenkel*   3 validius *H*   5 solium *Heinsius*: coleum *H*: coelum
Ioan. Sar.   ille *Heinsius*: illi *H*: Caesar illi *Buecheler*
   52 1 *lac. ind. Heinsius et Goesius*: C *add. Wehle, addendum praeterea*
quibus effictum *Goesius putavit*   sic ut vivere *Heinsius*: sicuti vere
H   2 capidem quam *patav.*: capidem quas *H*: capides ⟨M⟩ quas
Buecheler   patrono meo Mummius *Buecheler*   3 Hermerotis
Reinesius: hemerotis *H*   pugnas et *Burmann*: pugnasset *H*

statim puer demisso labro ⟨ora⟩re ⟨coepit⟩. at ille 'quid me' 5
inquit 'rogas? tamquam ego tibi molestus sim. suadeo, a te
impetres, ne sis nugax.' tandem ergo exoratus a nobis mis- 6
sionem dedit puero. ille dimissus circa mensam percucurrit

⟨*⟩

et 'aquam foras, vinum intro' clamavit. excipimus urbani- 7
tatem iocantis, et ante omnes Agamemnon qui sciebat
quibus meritis revocaretur ad cenam. ceterum laudatus 8
Trimalchio hilarius bibit et iam ebrio proximus 'nemo'
inquit 'vestrum rogat Fortunatam meam ut saltet? credite
mihi: cordacem nemo melius ducit.' atque ipse erectis supra 9
frontem manibus Syrum histrionem exhibebat concinente
tota familia: madeia perimadeia. et prodisset in medium, 10
nisi Fortunata ad aurem accessisset; [et] credo, dixerit non
decere gravitatem eius tam humiles ineptias. nihil autem 11
tam inaequale erat; nam modo Fortunatam suam †reverte-
batur modo ad naturam.

et plane interpellavit saltationis libidinem actuarius, qui 53
tamquam urbis acta recitavit: 'VII. kalendas Sextiles: in 2
praedio Cumano quod est Trimalchionis nati sunt pueri
XXX, puellae XL; sublata in horreum ex area tritici millia
modium quingenta; boves domiti quingenti. eodem die: 3
Mithridates servus in crucem actus est, quia Gai nostri genio
male dixerat. eodem die: in arcam relatum est quod collo- 4
cari non potuit, sestertium centies. eodem die: incendium 5
factum est in hortis Pompeianis, ortum ex aedibus Nastae
vilici.' 'quid?' inquit Trimalchio 'quando mihi Pompeiani 6
horti empti sunt?' 'anno priore' inquit actuarius 'et ideo 7

5 labro orare *Scheffer*: labrore *H*: ⟨coepit⟩ *add. Strelitz*   6 *lac.
ind. Buecheler*   10 et *del. Buecheler*   11 *non sanum*: revertebatur *Heinsius*: Fortunatam suam ⟨verebatur⟩ modo revertebatur ad
naturam *Buecheler*: Fortunatam suam ⟨verebatur⟩ revertebat modo
ad naturam *Gaselee*: Fortunatam ⟨verebatur⟩, modo ad naturam
suam revertebatur *Müller*
53 2 quod est Trimalchionis *secl. Müller*

8 in rationem nondum venerunt.' excanduit Trimalchio et
'quicumque' inquit 'mihi fundi empti fuerint, nisi intra sex-
9 tum mensem sciero, in rationes meas inferri vetuo.' iam
etiam edicta aedilium recitabantur et saltuariorum testa-
10 menta, quibus Trimalchio cum elogio exheredabatur; iam
nomina vilicorum et repudiata a circ[um]itore liberta in
balneatoris contubernio deprehensa et atriensis Baias relegatus; iam reus factus dispensator et iudicium inter cubicularios actum.

11   petauristarii autem tandem venerunt. baro insulsissimus
cum scalis constitit puerumque iussit per gradus et in summa
parte odaria saltare, circulos deinde ardentes trans⟨il⟩ire et
12 dentibus amphoram sustinere. mirabatur haec solus Trimalchio dicebatque ingratum artificium esse. ceterum duo esse
in rebus humanis quae libentissime spectaret, petauristarios
et cornic⟨in⟩es; reliqua [animalia] acroamata tricas meras
13 esse. 'nam et comoedos' inquit 'emeram, sed malui illos
Atell⟨an⟩am facere, et choraulen meum iussi Latine cantare.'
54   cum maxime haec dicente eo puer ⟨∗⟩ Trimalchionis de-
lapsus est. conclamavit familia, nec minus convivae, non
propter hominem tam putidum, cuius etiam cervices fractas
libenter vidissent, sed propter malum exitum cenae, ne
2 necesse haberent alienum mortuum plorare. ipse Trimalchio
cum graviter ingemuisset superque bracchium tamquam
laesum incubuisset, concurrere medici, et inter primos Fortunata crinibus passis cum scypho, miseramque se atque
3 infelicem proclamavit. nam puer quidem qui ceciderat
circumibat iam dudum pedes nostros et missionem rogabat.
pessime mihi erat, ne his precibus per ⟨rid⟩iculum aliquid

9 elogio *patav.*: elegio *H*   10 circitore *Buecheler*: circumitore
H   11 transilire *Heinsius*: transire *H*   12 cornicines
Heinsius: cornices *H*   animalia *del. Buecheler*   acroamata tricas
Scheffer: cromataricas *H*   13 sed *Heinsius*: et *H*   Atellanam
Scheffer: Atellaniam *Buecheler*: atellam *H*
     54 1 eo *Müller*: Gaio *H*   *lac. ind. Scheffer*   3 per ridiculum
Keller, Rh. Mus. *xvi (1861) 539*: periculo *H*: periculo nostro . . .
catastrophae *Buecheler* (catastrophae *Scheffer*)

catastropha quaereretur. nec enim adhuc exciderat cocus
ille qui oblitus fuerat porcum exinterare. itaque totum 4
circumspicere triclinium coepi, ne per parietem automatum
aliquod exiret, utique postquam servus verberari coepit, qui
bracchium domini contusum alba potius quam conchyliata
involverat lana. nec longe aberravit suspicio mea; in vicem 5
enim poenae venit decretum Trimalchionis quo puerum
iussit liberum esse, ne quis posset dicere tantum virum esse
a servo livoratum.

comprobamus nos factum et quam in praecipiti res hu- 55
manae essent vario sermone garrimus. 'ita' inquit Trimal- 2
chio 'non oportet hunc casum sine inscriptione transire'
statimque codicillos poposcit et non diu cogitatione distortus
haec recitavit:

> 'quod non expectes, ex transverso fit ∪ – ∪̆   3
> – et supra nos Fortuna negotia curat.
> quare da nobis vina Falerna, puer.'

ab hoc epigrammate coepit poetarum esse mentio diuque 4
summa carminis penes Mopsum Thracem memorata est,
donec Trimalchio 'rogo,' inquit 'magister, quid putas inter 5
Ciceronem et Pub⟨li⟩lium interesse? ego alterum puto diser-
tiorem fuisse, alterum honestiorem. quid enim his melius
dici potest?

> "luxuriae rictu Martis marcent moenia.   6
> tuo palato clausus pavo pascitur
> plumato amictus aureo Babylonico,
> gallina tibi Numidica, tibi gallus spado;
> ciconia etiam, grata peregrina hospita   5

5 poenae *Hadrianides*: cene *H*   livoratum *Delz*: vulneratum
Scheffer: liberatum *H*

55 2 distortus *Fuchs*: distorta *H*   3 expectes *Hφ*: expectas
L   fit ubique, nostra et *Heinsius*   4 memorata *HmrtpO**:
commorata *sl*   5 putas *H*: putes *λ*   Publilium *Buecheler*:
Publium *ω*   6 pascitur *Scaliger*: nascitur *ω*   aureo *LMsc*:
auro *HO**   Babylonico *ω*: Babylonicus *Fraenkel*

pietaticultrix gracilipes crotalistria,
avis exul hiemis, titulus tepidi temporis,
nequitiae nidum in caccabo fecit tuae.
quo margaritam caram tibi, bacam Indicam?
an ut matrona ornata phaleris pelagiis   10
tollat pedes indomita in strato extraneo?
zmaragdum ad quam rem viridem, pretiosum vitrum?
quo Carchedonios optas ignes lapideos?
nisi ut scintillet probitas e carbunculis.
aequum est induere nuptam ventum textilem,   15
palam prostare nudam in nebula linea?"

56   quod autem' inquit 'putamus secundum litteras difficilli-
2 mum esse artificium? ego puto medicum et nummularium:
medicus, qui scit quid homunciones intra praecordia sua
3 habeant et quando febris veniat, etiam si illos odi pessime,
quod mihi iubent saepe anatinam parari; nummularius, qui
4 per argentum aes videt. nam mutae bestiae laboriosissimae
boves et oves: boves, quorum beneficio panem manduca-
5 mus; oves, quod lana illae nos gloriosos faciunt. et facinus
6 indignum, aliquis ovillam est et tunicam habet. apes enim
ego divinas bestias puto, quae mel vomunt, etiam si dicuntur illud a Iove afferre; ideo autem pungunt, quia ubicum-
que dulce est, ibi et acidum invenies.'
7 iam etiam philosophos de negotio deiciebat, cum pittacia
8 in scypho circumferri coeperunt, puerque super hoc positus
officium apophoreta recitavit. 'argentum sceleratum': allata
est perna, supra quam acetabula erant posita. 'cervical': offla
collaris allata est. 'serisapia et contumelia': xerophagiae

pietaticultrix *lcmtp*: pietatis cultrix *HO*sr*   tuae *Fraenkel*: meo
ω: tuo *Heinsius*: modo *Jacobs, Buecheler*   margaritam caram *Ribbeck*: margarita cara ω   tibi, bacam Indicam *Heinsius*: tibi bac(c)a
indica *OBit.lct*^m: tribac(c)a indica *Hmrtp*δ: tribacca ac Indica *s*
an *lpOH*: aut *mrt*   ornata *lOH*: onerata *mrtp*   carbunculis *Buecheler*: carbunculos *rpO*: carbunculus *HMslcmt*
  56 3 anethinam *Jahn*   8 xerophagiae *Reiske*: aecrophagie *H*

e sale datae sunt et contus cum malo. 'porri et persica': 9
flagellum et cultrum accepit; 'passeres et muscarium':
uvam passam et mel Atticum. 'cenatoria et forensia': offlam
et tabulas accepit. 'canale et pedale': lepus et solea est
allata. 'muraena et littera': murem cum rana alligata
fascemque betae ⟨accepit⟩. diu risimus: sexcenta huiusmodi 10
fuerunt, quae iam exciderunt memoriae meae.

ceterum Ascyltos, intemperantis licentiae, cum omnia 57
sublatis manibus eluderet et usque ad lacrimas rideret, unus
ex conlibertis Trimalchionis excanduit—is ipse qui supra me
discumbebat—et 'quid rides' inquit 'vervex? an tibi non 2
placent lautitiae domini mei? tu enim beatior es et convivare melius soles. ita tutelam huius loci habeam propitiam,
ut ego si secundum illum discumberem, iam illi balatum
clusissem. bellum pomum, qui rideatur alios; larifuga nescio 3
quis, nocturnus, qui non valet lotium suum. ad summam,
si circumminxero illum, nesciet qua fugiat. non mehercules
soleo cito fervere, sed in molli carne vermes nascuntur.
ridet. quid habet quod rideat? numquid pater fetum emit 4
lamna? eques Romanus es: et ego regis filius. "quare ergo
servivisti?" quia ipse me dedi in servitutem et malui civis
Romanus esse quam tributarius. et nunc spero me sic
vivere, ut nemini iocus sim. homo inter homines sum, capite 5
aperto ambulo; assem aerarium nemini debeo; constitutum
habui numquam; nemo mihi in foro dixit "redde quod
debes." glebulas emi, lamellulas paravi; viginti ventres 6
pasco et canem; contubernalem meam redemi, ne quis in

e sale *Burmann*: saele *H*   contus *Burmann*: centus *H*   9 *verba*
canale . . . allata *post* Atticum *posuit Fraenkel*   canale *Buecheler*:
canalem *H*   pedale *Hadrianides*: pedalem *H*   murenam et litteram
H: *corr. Buecheler*   alligata *Buecheler*: alligatam *H*   accepit *add.*
Buecheler   10 exciderunt *Hadrianides*: ceciderunt *H*

57 1 is ipse . . . discumbebat *secl. Fraenkel (cf. 36. 7)*   2 vervex
*H*m: berbex *H*   balatum *sine causa suspectum*: alapam *Scheffer*:
colaphum *Reiske*: talatrum *Heraeus*   clusissem *Friedlaender*: duxissem *H*   3 rideatur *H*: rideat *patav.*   mehercules *Buecheler*:
me herculem *H*   5 sum *Burmann*: suos *H*

⟨capillis⟩ illius manus tergeret; mille denarios pro capite
solvi; sevir gratis factus sum; spero, sic moriar, ut mortuus
7 non erubescam. tu autem tam laboriosus es, ut post te non
respicias? in alio peduclum vides, in te ricinum non vides.
8 tibi soli ridicl[e]i videmur; ecce magister tuus, homo maior
natus: placemus illi. tu lacticulosus, nec mu nec ma argutas,
9 vasus fictilis, immo lorus in aqua, lentior, non melior. tu
beatior es: bis prande, bis cena. ego fidem meam malo quam
thesauros. ad summam, quisquam me bis poposcit? annis
quadraginta servivi; nemo tamen sciit utrum servus essem
an liber. et puer capillatus in hanc coloniam veni; adhuc
10 basilica non erat facta. dedi tamen operam ut domino satis
facerem, homini malista [et] dignitos[s]o, cuius pluris erat
unguis quam tu totus es. et habebam in domo qui mihi
pedem opponerent hac illac; tamen—genio illius gratias—
11 enatavi. haec sunt vera athla; nam [in] ingenuum nasci
tam facile est quam "accede istoc." quid nunc stupes tamquam hircus in ervilia?'

58   post hoc dictum Giton, qui ad pedes stabat, risum iam
diu compressum etiam indecenter effudit. quod cum animad-
2 vertisset adversarius Ascylti, flexit convicium in puerum et
'tu autem' inquit 'etiam tu rides, cepa cirrata? io Saturnalia, rogo, mensis december est? quando vicesimam numerasti? ⟨*⟩ quid faciat, crucis offla, corvorum cibaria.
curabo, iam tibi Iovis iratus sit, et isti qui tibi non imperat.
3 ita satur pane fiam, ut ego istud conliberto meo dono; alioquin iam tibi depraesentiarum reddidissem. bene nos habemus, at isti eug' euge—[qui tibi non imperant]—plane qualis

6 capillis *add. Burmann*: sinu *Heinsius*: capite *Reinesius*   7 ricinum *Mentel*: ricium *H*   8 lacticulosus *Scheffer*: laeticulosus *H*
9 sciit *Scheffer*: scit *H*   10 malista [et] *George* (malisto *Scheffer*):
maiesto *Muncker*: maiestoso *Immisch*: mali isto *H*   11 in *del.*
Buecheler: *servat Süss* (*cf. 62. 10 in larvam intravi*)
    58 2 cirrata *Reinesius*: pirrata *H*   *lac. ind. Buecheler* (nescit
suppl. in adn.)   faciat *H*: facias *Scheffer*   3 conliberto *Scheffer*:
cum liberto *H*   eug' euge *Salonius*: —euge! *Süss*: nugae *Buecheler*:
geuge *H*   qui . . . imperant *del. Fraenkel*

dominus, talis et servus. vix me teneo, nec sum natura 4
caldicerebrius, ⟨sed⟩ cum coepi, matrem meam dupundii non
facio. recte, videbo te in publicum, mus, immo terrae tuber:
nec sursum nec deorsum non cresco, nisi dominum tuum in 5
rutae folium non conieci, nec tibi parsero, licet mehercules
Iovem Olympium clames. curabo, longe tibi sit comula ista
besalis et dominus dupunduarius. recte, venies sub dentem: 6
aut ego non me novi, aut non deridebis, licet barbam auream
habeas. Athana tibi irata sit, curabo, et ⟨ei⟩ qui te primus 7
'deuro de' fecit. non didici geometrias, critica †et alogias
menias†, sed lapidarias litteras scio, partes centum dico ad
aes, ad pondus, ad nummum. ad summam, si quid vis, ego 8
et tu sponsiunculam: exi, defero lamnam. iam scies patrem
tuum mercedes perdidisse, quamvis et rhetoricam scis. ecce

"qui de nobis longe venio, late venio? solve me."

dicam tibi, qui de nobis currit et de loco non movetur; qui 9
de nobis crescit et minor fit. curris, stupes, satagis, tamquam mus in matella. ergo aut tace aut meliorem noli 10
molestare, qui te natum non putat; nisi si me iudicas anulos
buxeos curare, quos amicae tuae involasti. Occuponem pro- 11
pitium. eamus in forum et pecunias mutuemur: iam scies
hoc ferrum fidem habere. vah, bella res est volpis uda. ita 12
lucrum faciam et ita bene moriar aut populus per exitum
meum iuret, nisi te ubique toga perversa fuero persecutus.
bella res et iste qui te haec docet, mufrius, non magister. 13
⟨nos aliter⟩ didicimus, dicebat enim magister: "sunt vestra
salva? recta domum; cave, circumspicias; cave, maiorem

---

4 caldicerebrius *Jahn* (*cf. 45. 5*): caldus cicer eius *H*   sed *suppl.*
Buecheler   5 conieci *Scheffer*: coniecit *H*   parsero *Reinesius*:
par ero *H*   7 Athana *Heinsius*: sathana *H*   ei *add. Reinesius*
deuro de ('δεῦρο δή *i.e. accedere ad se vel sequi ut delicium' Buecheler*) *H*
critica *Reiske*: cretica *H*   alogias *H*: alogas *Scheffer*   menias
H: nenias *Scheffer*: meras *Mentel*   8 lamnam *Heinsius*: lamna *H*
scis *Reiske*: scio *H*   qui de *Buecheler*: quidem *H*   9 curris *H*:
muttis *vel* minurris *Buecheler*   12 aut *H*: ut *post Heinsium Jahn*
13 nos aliter *suppl. Heraeus*: nos magis *Jacobs*

14 maledicas." at nunc mera mapalia: nemo dupondii evadit.
ego, quod me sic vides, propter artificium meum diis gratias
ago.'

59 coeperat Ascyltos respondere convicio, sed Trimalchio
delectatus colliberti eloquentia 'agite' inquit 'scordalias de
medio. suaviter sit potius, et tu, Hermeros, parce adulescen-
2 tulo. sanguen illi fervet, tu melior esto. semper in hac re
qui vincitur vincit. et tu cum esses capo, cocococo, aeque
cor non habebas. simus ergo, quod melius est, a primitiis
3 hilares et Homeristas spectemus.' intravit factio statim
hastisque scuta concrepuit. ipse Trimalchio in pulvino consedit, et cum Homeristae Graecis versibus colloquerentur,
ut insolenter solent, ille canora voce Latine legebat librum.
mox silentio facto 'scitis' inquit 'quam fabulam agant?
4 Diomedes et Ganymedes duo fratres fuerunt. horum soror
erat Helena. Agamemnon illam rapuit et Dianae cervam
subiecit. ita nunc Homeros dicit quemadmodum inter se
5 pugnent Troiani et Tarentini. vicit scilicet et Iphigeniam,
filiam suam, Achilli dedit uxorem. ob eam rem Aiax insanit
6 et statim argumentum explicabit.' haec ut dixit Trimalchio, clamorem Homeristae sustulerunt, interque familiam
discurrentem vitulus in lance du⟨ce⟩naria elixus allatus est,
7 et quidem galeatus. secutus est Aiax strictoque gladio,
tamquam insaniret, concidit, ac modo versa modo supina
gesticulatus mucrone frust[r]a collegit mirantibusque vitulum partitus est.

60 nec diu mirari licuit tam elegantes strophas; nam repente
lacunaria sonare coeperunt totumque triclinium intremuit.
2 consternatus ego exsurrexi et timui, ne per tectum petau-
ristarius aliquis descenderet. nec minus reliqui convivae

14 at nunc mera *Heraeus*: aut tu mera *Iac. Gronovius*: aut
numera *H*

59 2 aeque *Heinsius*: atque *H*   habebas *Mentel*: habeas *H*   a
primitiis *Buecheler*: a primitis *H*   4 Tarentini *Scheffer*: Parentini *H*
5 scilicet Agamemnon *Scheffer*: scilicet *et* Iphigeniam *fort. delenda esse
censet George*   6 ducenaria *Burmann*: dunaria *H*   7 frustra
H: *corr. patav.*   vitulum *ante* concidit *transposuit Müller*

mirantes erexere vultus, expectantes quid novi de caelo
nuntiaretur. ecce autem diductis lacunaribus subito circulus 3
ingens [de cupa videlicet grandi excussus] demittitur, cuius
per totum orbem coronae aureae cum alabastris unguenti
pendebant. dum haec apophoreta iubemur sumere, respi- 4
ciens ad mensam

⟨*⟩

iam illic repositorium cum placentis aliquot erat positum,
quod medium Priapus a pistore factus tenebat, gremioque
satis amplo omnis generis poma et uvas sustinebat more
vulgato. avidius ad pompam manus porreximus, et repente 5
nova ludorum commissio hilaritatem hinc effecit. omnes 6
enim placentae omniaque poma etiam minima vexatione
contacta coeperunt effundere crocum, et usque ad [n]os
⟨nobis⟩ molestus umor accidere. rati ergo sacrum esse 7
fer[i]culum tam religioso apparatu perfusum, consurreximus
altius et 'Augusto, patri patriae, feliciter' diximus. quibusdam tamen etiam post hanc venerationem poma rapientibus
et ipsi mappas implevimus, ego praecipue, qui nullo satis
amplo munere putabam me onerare Gitonis sinum.

inter haec tres pueri candidas succincti tunicas intrave- 8
runt, quorum duo Lares bullatos super mensam posuerunt,
unus pateram vini circumferens 'dii propitii' clamabat.

⟨*⟩

aiebat autem unum Cerdonem, alterum Felicionem, tertium Lucrionem vocari. nos etiam veram imaginem 9

---

60 2 mirantes *del. Fraenkel* 3 diductis *Scheffer*: deductus *H*
de cupa . . . excussus *del. Fraenkel (cf. Müller pp. xli s.)* 4 *lac.*
ind. Buecheler 5 commissio *Delz*: missio *Buecheler*: remissio *H*
hinc effecit *Delz*: hic refecit *H* (hic *del. Friedlaender*) 6 os *Bue-*
cheler: nos *H* nobis *add. Delz* accidere *Buecheler*: accedere *H*
7 ferculum: fericulum *Reinesius*: periculum *H* ipsi *Buecheler*: ipsi
iis *Heinsius*: ipsas *H* sinum *patav.*: unum *H* 8 *post* clamabat
lac. ind. Buecheler 9 veram *H*: auream *Jahn*: ceream *Reinesius*

ipsius Trimalchionis, cum iam omnes basiarent, erubuimus
praeterire.

61 postquam ergo omnes bonam mentem bonamque valetudinem sibi optarunt, Trimalchio ad Nicerotem respexit et
2 'solebas' inquit 'suavius esse in convictu; nescio quid nunc
taces nec muttis. oro te, sic felicem me videas, narra illud
3 quod tibi usu venit.' Niceros delectatus affabilitate amici
'omne me' inquit 'lucrum transeat, nisi iam dudum gaudi-
4 monio dissilio, quod te talem video. itaque hilaria mera sint,
etsi timeo istos scholasticos, ne me [de]rideant. viderint:
narrabo tamen; quid enim mihi aufert qui ridet? satius est
5 rideri quam derideri.' 'haec ubi dicta dedit', talem fabulam
exorsus est:

6 'cum adhuc servirem, habitabamus in vico angusto; nunc
Gavillae domus est. ibi, quomodo dii volunt, amare coepi
uxorem Terentii coponis: noveratis Melissam Tarentinam,
7 pulcherrimum bacciballum. sed ego non mehercules cor-
poraliter ⟨illam⟩ [autem] aut propter res vene[ra]rias curavi,
8 sed magis quod benemoria fuit. si quid ab illa petii, numquam mihi negatum; fecit assem, semissem habui; ⟨*⟩ in
9 illius sinum demandavi, nec umquam fefellitus sum. huius
contubernalis ad villam supremum diem obiit. itaque per
scutum per ocream egi aginavi, quemadmodum ad illam
pervenirem: ⟨scitis⟩ autem, in angustiis amici apparent.
62 forte dominus Capuae exierat ad scruta [scita] expedienda.
2 nactus ego occasionem persuadeo hospitem nostrum ut

61 2 nunc *Scheffer*: nec *H*   muttis *Scheffer*: mutes *H*   3 dissilio *patav.*: dissileo *H*   4 rideant *Scheffer*: derideant *H*   viderint *patav.*: riserint *Scheffer*: viderit *H*   7 illam *add. Buecheler*:
autem *om. patav.*: autem [aut] *Bendz* (*cf. 73. 4*): auten (= αὐτήν)
George   venerarias *H*   benemoria *Orelli*: bene morata *Hadrianides*: bene moriar *H*   8 *in lac.* quicquid habui *add. Buecheler*:
omnia *add. Jacobs*: fecit *post* petii *transp. Fuchs, qui* quicquid *post*
semissem *add.*   *locum sic interpunxit Delz*: . . . negatum. ⟨*⟩ fecit:
assem semissem habui, in illius . . .   9 scitis *suppl. Buecheler*:
in angustiis autem *transp. Hadrianides*
62 1 Capue *H*: Capuam *Scheffer*   scita *del. George*

mecum ad quintum miliarium veniat. erat autem miles, fortis tamquam Orcus. apoculamus nos circa gallicinia, luna 3 lucebat tamquam meridie. venimus inter monimenta: homo 4 meus coepit ad stelas facere, secedo ego cantabundus et stelas numero. deinde ut respexi ad comitem, ille exuit se et 5 omnia vestimenta secundum viam posuit. mihi [in] anima in naso esse, stabam tamquam mortuus. at ille circumminxit 6 vestimenta sua, et subito lupus factus est. nolite me iocari putare; ut mentiar, nullius patrimonium tanti facio. sed, 7 quod coeperam dicere, postquam lupus factus est, ululare coepit et in silvas fugit. ego primitus nesciebam ubi essem, 8 deinde accessi, ut vestimenta eius tollerem: illa autem lapidea facta sunt. qui mori timore nisi ego? gladium 9 tamen strinxi et †matauitatau† umbras cecidi, donec ad villam amicae meae pervenirem. in larvam intravi, paene 10 animam ebullivi, sudor mihi per bifurcum undabat, oculi mortui, vix umquam refectus sum. Melissa mea mirari 11 coepit, quod tam sero ambularem, et "si ante" inquit "venisses, saltem nobis adiutasses; lupus enim villam intravit et omnia pecora ⟨*⟩: tamquam lanius sanguinem illis misit. nec tamen derisit, etiam si fugit; servus enim noster lancea collum eius traiecit." haec ut audivi, operire oculos 12 amplius non potui, sed luce clara †hac nostri† domum fugi tamquam copo compilatus, et postquam veni in illum locum in quo lapidea vestimenta erant facta, nihil inveni nisi sanguinem. ut vero domum veni, iacebat miles meus 13 in lecto tamquam bovis, et collum illius medicus curabat. intellexi illum versipellem esse, nec postea cum illo panem

3 apoculamus *Scheffer*: apoculanius *H*   4 ad stelas *Reiske*: ad stellas *H*   secedo ego *Delz*: sed ego pergo *Heraeus*: sedeo ego *Scheffer*: sed ego *H*   cantabundus *H*: cunctabundus *Delz*   5 [in] anima *Muncker*: in animo *H*   9 in tota via *Scheffer*: matutinas *Heinsius*: matavi tetavi *Watson*   10 in larvam *H*: [in] larva[m] *Fraenkel*: ut larva *Buecheler*   undabat *Nisbet*: manabat *Fuchs*: volabat *H*   11 coepit *del. Fraenkel*   villam *H*: ovilia *dubitanter George*   perculit *post* pecora *add. Buecheler*: praemordit *add. Müller*[2]   12 hac n̄ri *H*: maturius *Ehlers*: Gai nostri *Buecheler*: raptim *Müller*[1]

14 gustare potui, non si me occidisses. viderint alii quid de hoc
exopinissent; ego si mentior, genios vestros iratos habeam.'
63 attonitis admiratione universis 'salvo' inquit 'tuo sermone' Trimalchio 'si qua fides est, ut mihi pili inhorruerunt,
quia scio Niceronem nihil nugarum narrare: immo certus
2 est et minime linguosus. nam et ipse vobis rem horribilem
3 narrabo: asinus in tegulis. cum adhuc capillatus essem,
nam a puero vitam Chiam gessi, ipsimi nostri delicatus
decessit, mehercules margaritum, †caccitus† et omnium
4 numerum. cum ergo illum mater misella plangeret et nostrum plures in tristimonio essemus, subito strigae coeperunt:
5 putares canem leporem persequi. habebamus tunc hominem
Cappadocem, longum, valde audaculum et qui valebat:
6 poterat bovem iratum tollere. hic audacter stricto gladio
extra ostium procucurrit, involuta sinistra manu curiose, et
mulierem tamquam hoc loco—salvum sit quod tango—
mediam traiecit. audimus gemitum, et—plane non mentiar
7 —ipsas non vidimus. baro autem noster introversus se
proiecit in lectum, et corpus totum lividum habebat quasi
flagellis caesus [quia scilicet illum tetigerat mala manus].
8 nos cluso ostio redimus iterum ad officium, sed dum mater
amplexaret corpus filii sui, tangit et videt manuciolum de
stramentis factum. non cor habebat, non intestina, non
quicquam: scilicet iam puerum strigae involaverant et sup-
9 posuerant stramenticium vavatonem. rogo vos, oportet
credatis, sunt mulieres plussciae, sunt Nocturnae, et quod
10 sursum est, deorsum faciunt. ceterum baro ille longus post
hoc factum numquam coloris sui fuit, immo post paucos
dies phreneticus periit.'

14 alii quid de hoc *Buecheler* (quid de hoc alii *Heinsius*): qui hoc de
alibi *H*
   63 3 ipsimi nostri *Scheffer, Buecheler*: ipim mostri *H*   caccitus *H*:
catamitus *Jacobs*: zacritus *Rönsch*   4 nostrum plures *Heinsius*:
plorantes *Müller*[2]: comploratores *Delz*: nos tum plures *H*   strigae
⟨stridere⟩ *Jacobs*   5 poterat *om. patav.*   bovem *Reiske*: iovem *H*
7 quia ... manus *del. Fraenkel*   9 *verba* sunt Nocturnae *ex 64. 1
interpolata esse suspicatur Fraenkel*

miramur nos et pariter credimus, osculatique mensam **64**
rogamus Nocturnas ut suis se teneant, dum redimus a cena.⟨*⟩

et sane iam lucernae mihi plures videbantur ardere totum- 2
que triclinium esse mutatum, cum Trimalchio 'tibi dico'
inquit 'Plocame, nihil narras? nihil nos delectaris? et solebas suavius esse, canturire belle deverbia, adicere melicam.
heu heu, abistis dulces caricae.' 'iam' inquit ille 'quadrigae 3
meae decucurrerunt, ex quo podagricus factus sum. alioquin cum essem adulescentulus, cantando paene tisicus
factus sum. quid saltare? quid deverbia? quid tonstri- 4
num? quando parem habui nisi unum Apelletem?' opposi- 5
taque ad os manu nescio quid taetrum exsibilavit, quod
postea Graecum esse affirmabat.

nec non Trimalchio ipse cum tubicines esset imitatus, ad
delicias suas respexit, quem Croesum appellabat. puer 6
autem lippus, sordidissimis dentibus, catellam nigram atque
indecenter pinguem prasina involvebat fascia panemque
semesum ponebat supra torum [atque] ac nausea recusan-
tem saginabat. quo admonitus officio Trimalchio Scylacem 7
iussit adduci 'praesidium domus familiaeque'. nec mora,
ingentis formae adductus est canis catena vinctus, admonitusque ostiarii calce ut cubaret, ante mensam se posuit. tum 8
Trimalchio iactans candidum panem 'nemo' inquit 'in domo
mea me plus amat.' indignatus puer, quod Scylacem tam 9
effuse laudaret, catellam in terram deposuit hortatusque
⟨est⟩ ut ad rixam properaret. Scylax, canino scilicet usus
ingenio, taeterrimo latratu triclinium implevit Margaritam-
que Croesi paene laceravit. nec intra rixam tumultus con- 10
stitit, sed candelabrum etiam supra mensam eversum et

64 1 *lac. ind. Buecheler* ('*relatum erat de augescente convivarum
suaque ebrietate*')   2 suavius *Buecheler*: suavis *H*   melicam *H*:
melica *Scheffer*   belle diverbia dicere, melica canturire *Buecheler*
3 dulces caricae *Scheffer*: dulcis carica *H*   5 oppositaque *H*: appo-
sitaque *Heinsius*   6 semesum *Burmann*: semissem *H*   [atque
ac *Buecheler in adn.*: atque hac *H*   7 admonitus officio *H*: admonitus officii *Buecheler*: ⟨adspectu⟩ admonitus officii *Müller*   9 est
add. Buecheler

vasa omnia crystallina comminuit et oleo ferventi aliquot
11 convivas respersit. Trimalchio ne videretur iactura motus,
basiavit puerum ac iussit supra dorsum ascendere suum.
12 non moratus ille usus ⟨est⟩ equo manuque plana scapulas
eius subinde verberavit, interque risum proclamavit: 'bucca,
13 bucca, quot sunt hic?' repressus ergo aliquamdiu Trimalchio camellam grandem iussit misceri ⟨et⟩ potiones dividi
omnibus servis, qui ad pedes sedebant, adiecta exceptione:
'si quis' inquit 'noluerit accipere, caput illi perfunde. inter-
diu severa, nunc hilaria.'

65 hanc humanitatem insecutae sunt matteae, quarum etiam
2 recordatio me, si qua est dicenti fides, offendit. singulae
enim gallinae altiles pro turdis circumlatae sunt et ova
anserina pilleata, quae ut comessemus, ambitiosissime ⟨a⟩
3 nobis Trimalchio petiit dicens exossatas esse gallinas. inter
haec triclinii valvas lictor percussit, amictusque veste alba
4 cum ingenti frequentia comissator intravit. ego maiestate
conterritus praetorem putabam venisse. itaque temptavi
5 assurgere et nudos pedes in terram deferre. risit hanc trepi-
dationem Agamemnon et 'contine te' inquit 'homo stultis-
sime. Habinnas sevir est idemque lapidarius [qui videretur
monumenta optime facere].'

6 recreatus hoc sermone reposui cubitum, Habinnamque
7 intrantem cum admiratione ingenti spectabam. ille autem
iam ebrius uxoris suae umeris imposuerat manus, oneratus-
que aliquot coronis et unguento per frontem in oculos fluente
praetorio loco se posuit continuoque vinum et caldam popo-
8 scit. delectatus hac Trimalchio hilaritate et ipse capaciorem
poposcit scyphum quaesivitque quomodo acceptus esset.
9 'omnia' inquit 'habuimus praeter te; oculi enim mei hic
10 erant. et mehercules bene fuit. Scissa lautum novendiale

---

12 est *add. Buecheler*   plana *Scheffer*: plena *H*   13 repressus *H*:
compressus *Delz*   et *add. Anton*
  65 2 a *add. Scheffer*   5 qui . . . facere *secl. Müller* (*cf. 71. 5 ss.*)
videretur *H*: videtur *Scheffer*   10 lautum novendiale *Buecheler*:
laucum novendialem *H*: lautam novendialem (*sc. cenam*) *Heinsius*

servo suo misello faciebat, quem mortuum manu miserat. et
puto, cum vicensimariis magnam †mantissam habet; quinquaginta enim millibus aestimant mortuum. sed tamen 11
suaviter fuit, etiam si coacti sumus dimidias potiones supra
ossucula eius effundere.' 'tamen' inquit Trimalchio 'quid 66
habuistis in cena?' 'dicam' inquit 'si potuero; nam tam
bonae memoriae sum, ut frequenter nomen meum obliviscar.
habuimus tamen in primo porcum botulo coronatum et circa 2
sangunculum et gizeria optime facta et certe betam et
panem autopyrum de suo sibi, quem ego malo quam candidum; et vires facit, et cum mea re causa facio, non ploro.
sequens ferculum fuit sc[i]rib[i]lita frigida et supra mel 3
caldum infusum excellente Hispanum. itaque de sc[i]rib[i]-
lita quidem non minimum edi, de melle me usque tetigi.
circa cicer et lupinum, calvae arbitratu et mala singula. ego 4
tamen duo sustuli et ecce in mappa alligata habeo; nam si
aliquid muneris meo vernulae non tulero, habebo convicium.
bene me admonet domina mea. in prospectu habuimus 5
ursinae frust[r]um, de quo cum imprudens Scintilla gustas-
set, paene intestina sua vomuit; ego contra plus libram 6
comedi, nam ipsum aprum sapiebat. et si, inquam, ursus
homuncionem comest, quanto magis homuncio debet ursum
comesse? in summo habuimus caseum mollem ex sapa et 7
cocleas singulas et cordae frusta et hepatia in catillis et ova
pilleata et rapam et senape et catillum †concagatum, pax
Palamedes. etiam in alveo circumlata sunt oxycomina, unde
quidam etiam improbe ternos pugnos sustulerunt. nam
pernae missionem dedimus. sed narra mihi, Gai, rogo, For- 67
tunata quare non recumbit?' 'quomodo nosti' inquit 'illam' 2

mantissam *dubium*

66 2 botulo *Iac. Gronovius*: poculo *H*   sangunculum *Heraeus*:
saucunculum *H*   causa *del. Buecheler*   3 scribilita *H*: *corr.
patav.*   5 in prospectu *non probat Delz*   frustum *patav.*: frustrum *H*   7 ex sapa *Buecheler*: et sapa *H*   concagatum *H*:
concacatum *Burmann*   anguillam conchas garum, mox pelamidas
post senape et *Warmington*   improbe ternos pugnos *praeeunte Iac.
Gronovio Buecheler*: improbiter nos pugno *H*

Trimalchio 'nisi argentum composuerit, nisi reliquias pueris
3 diviserit, aquam in os suum non coniciet.' 'atqui' respondit
Habinnas 'nisi illa discumbit, ego me apoculo' et coeperat
surgere, nisi signo dato Fortunata quater amplius a tota
4 familia esset vocata. venit ergo galbino succincta cingillo,
ita ut infra cerasina appareret tunica et periscelides tortae
5 phaecasiaeque inauratae. tunc sudario manus tergens, quod
in collo habebat, applicat se illi toro, in quo [Scintilla]
Habinnae discumbebat uxor, osculataque plaudentem 'est
te' inquit 'videre?'
6   eo deinde perventum est, ut Fortunata armillas suas cras-
sissimis detraheret lacertis Scintillaeque miranti ostenderet.
ultimo etiam periscelides resolvit et reticulum aureum,
7 quem ex obrussa esse dicebat. notavit haec Trimalchio
iussitque afferri omnia et 'videtis' inquit 'mulieris compedes:
sic nos barcalae despoliamur. sex pondo et selibram debet
habere. et ipse nihilo minus habeo decem pondo armillam
8 ex millesimis Mercurii factam.' ultimo etiam, ne mentiri
videretur, stateram iussit afferri et circumlatum approbari
9 pondus. nec melior Scintilla, quae de cervice sua capsellam
detraxit aureolam, quam Felicionem appellabat. inde duo
crotalia protulit et Fortunatae in vicem consideranda dedit
10 et 'domini' inquit 'mei beneficio nemo habet meliora.' 'quid?'
inquit Habinnas 'excatarissasti me, ut tibi emerem fabam
vitream. plane si filiam haberem, auriculas illi praeciderem.
mulieres si non essent, omnia pro luto haberemus; nunc hoc
est caldum meiere et frigidum potare.'
11   interim mulieres sauciae inter se riserunt ebriaque iunxe-
runt oscula, dum altera diligentiam matris familiae iactat,
12 altera delicias et indulgentiam viri. dumque sic cohae-
rent, Habinnas furtim consurrexit pedesque Fortunatae

67 3 apoculo *patav.*: apocalo *H*   5 Scintilla *del. Fraenkel*
6 ex obrussa: ex sobriissa *H*   7 mulieris *Mentel*: mulieres *H*
8 circumlatum *Heinsius*: circulatum *H*   11 ebriaque *Müller*
(*cl. 79. 9 remisissem ebrias manus*): ebrieque *H*: ebriaeque *vulgo*   indulgentiam *patav.*: indiligentiam *H*

correptos super lectum immisit. 'au au' illa proclamavit 13
aberrante tunica super genua. composita ergo in gremio
Scintillae incensissimam rubore faciem sudario abscondit.

interposito deinde spatio cum secundas mensas Trimalchio 68
iussisset afferri, sustulerunt servi omnes mensas et alias
attulerunt, scobemque croco et minio tinctam sparserunt et,
quod numquam ante videram, ex lapide speculari pulverem
tritum. statim Trimalchio 'poteram quidem' inquit 'hoc 2
fer[i]culo esse contentus; secundas enim mensas habetis.
⟨sed⟩ si quid belli habes, affer.'

interim puer Alexandrinus, qui caldam ministrabat, lusci- 3
nias coepit imitari clamante Trimalchione subinde: 'muta.'
ecce alius ludus. servus qui ad pedes Habinnae sedebat, 4
iussus, credo, a domino suo proclamavit subito canora voce:

'interea medium Aeneas iam classe tenebat.'

nullus sonus umquam acidior percussit aures meas; nam 5
praeter errantis barbariae aut adiectum aut deminutum
clamorem miscebat Atellanicos versus, ut tunc primum me
etiam Vergilius offenderit. lassus tamen cum aliquando 6
desisset, adiecit Habinnas 'et num⟨quam' in⟩quit 'didicit,
sed ego ad circulatores eum mittendo erudibam. itaque 7
parem non habet, sive muliones volet sive circulatores imitari. desperatum valde ingeniosus est: idem sutor est, idem
cocus, idem pistor, omnis musae mancipium. duo tamen 8
vitia habet, quae si non haberet, esset omnium numerum:
recutitus est et stertit. nam quod strabonus est, non curo:
sicut Venus spectat. ideo nihil latet, vix oculo mortuo

12 correptos *Scheffer*: correctos *H*   13 incensissimam *vel*
indecentissimam *Reinesius*: indecens imam *H*
  68 2 ferculo *patav.*: fericulo *H*   sed *add. Buecheler*   5 adiectum *Scheffer*: abiectum *H*   deminutum *Scheffer*: diminutum *H*
6 desisset *Scheffer*: dedisset *H*   adiecit *del. Fraenkel*   numquam
inquit *Buecheler*: numquid *H*   erudibam *Buecheler, praeeunte Jahn*:
audibant *H*   7 desperatum *Buecheler*: desperatus *H*   8 vitia
patav.: vina *H*   numerum *Haase*: numerorum *Scheffer*: nummorum
H   latet *Delz*: tacet *H*

69 umquam. illum emi trecentis denariis.' interpellavit loquentem Scintilla et 'plane' inquit 'non omnia artificia servi nequam narras. agaga est; at curabo, stigmam habeat.'
2 risit Trimalchio et 'adcognosco' inquit 'Cappadocem: nihil sibi defraudat, et mehercules laudo illum; hoc enim nemo parentat. tu autem, Scintilla, noli zelotypa esse. crede
3 mihi, et vos novimus. sic me salvum habeatis, ut ego sic solebam ipsumam meam debattuere, ut etiam dominus suspicaretur; et ideo me in vilicationem relegavit. sed tace,
4 lingua, dabo panem.' tamquam laudatus esset nequissimus servus, lucernam de sinu fictilem protulit et amplius semihora tubicines imitatus est succinente Habinna et inferius
5 labrum manu deprimente. ultimo etiam in medium processit et modo harundinibus quassis choraulas imitatus est modo lacernatus cum flagello mulionum fata egit, donec vocatum ad se Habinnas basiavit, potionemque illi porrexit et 'tanto melior,' inquit 'Massa, dono tibi caligas.'
6 nec ullus tot malorum finis fuisset, nisi epidipnis esset
7 allata, turdi siliginei uvis passis nucibusque farsi. insecuta sunt Cydonia etiam mala spinis confixa, ut echinos efficerent. et haec quidem tolerabilia erant, si non fer[i]culum longe
8 monstrosius effecisset ut vel fame perire mallemus. nam cum positus esset, ut nos putabamus, anser altilis circaque pisces et omnium genera avium, '⟨amici,⟩' inquit Trimalchio 'quicquid videtis hic positum, de uno corpore est factum.'
9 ego, scilicet homo prudentissimus, statim intellexi quid esset, et respiciens Agamemnonem 'mirabor' inquam 'nisi omnia ista de ⟨*⟩ facta sunt aut certe de luto. vidi Romae
70 Saturnalibus eiusmodi cenarum imaginem fieri.' necdum finieram sermonem, cum Trimalchio ait: 'ita crescam patri-

---

69 2 defraudat *Hadrianides*: defraudit *H*   3 lingua *Scheffer*: linguam *H*   5 imitatus est *secl. Fraenkel*   molionum fata *H*: morionum fatua *dubitanter George*   6 turdi siliginei *Heinsius*: turdis iligine *H*   farsi *Heinsius*: farsis *H*   7 ferculum *patav.*: fericulum *H*   8 omnium *H*: omnia *Buecheler*   amici *add. Buecheler* 9 cera *suppl. Buecheler*   aut certe de luto *fort. interpolatum putat George*

monio, non corpore, ut ista cocus meus de porco fecit. non 2
potest esse pretiosior homo. volueris, de vulva faciet piscem,
de lardo palumbum, de perna turturem, de colepio gallinam.
et ideo ingenio meo impositum est illi nomen bellissimum;
nam Daedalus vocatur. et quia bonam mentem habet, 3
attuli illi Roma munus cultros Norico ferro.' quos statim
iussit afferri inspectosque miratus est. etiam nobis potestatem fecit, ut mucronem ad buccam probaremus.

subito intraverunt duo servi, tamquam qui rixam ad 4
lacum fecissent; certe in collo adhuc amphoras habebant.
cum ergo Trimalchio ius inter litigantes diceret, neuter 5
sententiam tulit decernentis, sed alterius amphoram fuste
percussit. consternati nos insolentia ebriorum intentavimus 6
oculos in proeliantes notavimusque ostrea pectinesque e
gastris labentia, quae collecta puer lance circumtulit. has 7
lautitias aequavit ingeniosus cocus; in craticula enim argentea cochleas attulit et tremula taeterrimaque voce cantavit.

pudet referre quae secuntur: inaudito enim more pueri 8
capillati attulerunt unguentum in argentea pelve pedesque
recumbentium unxerunt, cum ante crura talosque corollis
vinxissent. hinc ex eodem unguento in vinarium atque 9
lucernam liquatum est [infusum].

iam coeperat Fortunata velle saltare, iam Scintilla fre- 10
quentius plaudebat quam loquebatur, cum Trimalchio 'permitto' inquit 'Philargyre [et Cario], etsi prasinianus es
famosus, dic et Menophilae, contubernali tuae, discumbat.'
quid multa? paene de lectis deiecti sumus, adeo totum 11
triclinium familia occupaverat. certe ego notavi super me 12
positum cocum, qui de porco anserem fecerat, muria condi-
mentisque fetentem. nec contentus fuit recumbere, sed 13
continuo Ephesum tragoedum coepit imitari et subinde

---

70 2 vulva *Hadrianides*: bulba *Scheffer*: bulla *H*   3 attuli *Hein-*
sius: attulit *H*   Roma munus *Heinsius*: romā unus *H*   4 collo
Heinsius: loco *H*   6 gastris *Muncker*: castris *H*   9 liquatum
H: aliquantum *Heinsius*   infusum *secl. Salonius*   10 et Cario
secl. Kaibel (*cf. 71. 2*)   12 qui ... fecerat *del. Fraenkel* (*cf. 70. 1*)

dominum suum sponsione provocare 'si prasinus proximis circensibus primam palmam'.

71 diffusus hac contentione Trimalchio 'amici,' inquit 'et servi homines sunt et aeque unum lactem biberunt, etiam si illos malus fatus oppresserit. tamen me salvo cito aquam liberam gustabunt. ad summam, omnes illos in testamento 2 meo manu mitto. Philargyro etiam fundum lego et contubernalem suam, Carioni quoque insulam et vicesimam et 3 lectum stratum. nam Fortunatam meam heredem facio, et commendo illam omnibus amicis meis. et haec ideo omnia publico, ut familia mea iam nunc sic me amet tamquam 4 mortuum.' gratias agere omnes indulgentiae coeperant domini, cum ille oblitus nugarum exemplar testamenti iussit afferri et totum a primo ad ultimum ingemescente familia 5 recitavit. respiciens deinde Habinnam 'quid dicis' inquit 'amice carissime? aedificas monumentum meum, quemad- 6 modum te iussi? valde te rogo ut secundum pedes statuae meae catellam fingas et coronas et unguenta et Petraitis omnes pugnas, ut mihi contingat tuo beneficio post mortem vivere; praeterea ut sint in fronte pedes centum, in agrum 7 pedes ducenti. omne genus enim poma volo sint circa cineres meos, et vinearum largiter. valde enim falsum est vivo quidem domos cultas esse, non curari eas, ubi diutius nobis habitandum est. et ideo ante omnia adici volo: "hoc 8 monumentum heredem non sequatur." ceterum erit mihi curae ut testamento caveam ne mortuus iniuriam accipiam. praeponam enim unum ex libertis sepulcro meo custodiae causa, ne in monumentum meum populus cacatum currat. 9 te rogo ut naves etiam [monumenti mei] facias plenis velis euntes, et me in tribunali sedentem praetextatum cum anulis aureis quinque et nummos in publico de sacculo effundentem; scis enim quod epulum dedi binos denarios.

71 1 oppresserit *H*: oppressit *Buecheler*   6 fingas *Scheffer*: ponas *Buecheler*: pingas *H*   7 sequatur *H*: sequitur *Buecheler* 9 monumenti mei *del. Müller²*: ⟨in fronte⟩ monumenti mei *Keller* (*cf.* Rh. Mus. *xvi* (*1861*), *548*): ⟨in lateribus⟩ monumenti mei *Buecheler in adn.*

faciantur, si tibi videtur, et triclinia. facias et totum popu- 10
lum sibi suaviter facientem. ad dexteram meam ponas 11
statuam Fortunatae meae columbam tenentem: et catellam
cingulo alligatam ducat: et cicaronem meum, et amphoras
copiose gypsatas, ne effluant vinum. et unam licet fractam
sculpas, et super eam puerum plorantem. horologium in
medio, ut quisquis horas inspiciet, velit nolit, nomen meum
legat. inscriptio quoque vide diligenter si haec satis idonea 12
tibi videtur: "C. Pompeius Trimalchio Maecenatianus hic
requiescit. huic seviratus absenti decretus est. cum posset
in omnibus decuriis Romae esse, tamen noluit. pius, fortis,
fidelis, ex parvo crevit; sestertium reliquit trecenties, nec
umquam philosophum audivit. vale: et tu."'

haec ut dixit Trimalchio, flere coepit ubertim. flebat et **72**
Fortunata, flebat et Habinnas, tota denique familia, tamquam in funus rogata, lamentatione triclinium implevit.
immo iam coeperam etiam ego plorare, cum Trimalchio 2
'ergo' inquit 'cum sciamus nos morituros esse, quare non
vivamus? sic vos felices videam, coniciamus nos in bal- 3
neum, meo periculo, non paenitebit. sic calet tamquam fur-
nus.' 'vero, vero' inquit Habinnas 'de una die duas facere, 4
nihil malo' nudisque consurrexit pedibus et Trimalchionem
gaudentem subsequi ⟨coepit⟩.

ego respiciens ad Ascylton 'quid cogitas?' inquam 'ego 5
enim si videro balneum, statim expirabo.' 'assentemur' ait 6
ille 'et dum illi balneum petunt, nos in turba exeamus.' cum 7
haec placuissent, ducente per porticum Gitone ad ianuam
venimus, ubi canis catenarius tanto nos tumultu excepit, ut
Ascyltos etiam in piscinam ceciderit. nec non ego quoque
ebrius [qui etiam pictum timueram canem], dum natanti
opem fero, in eundem gurgitem tractus sum. servavit nos 8

10 faciantur *Goesius*: faciatur *H*   facias *Buecheler*: facies *H*
11 ponas *vulgo*: pones *H*   copiose *George*: copiosas *H*   unam *H*:
urnam *Iac. Gronovius*
    72 4 gaudentem *H*: plaudentem *Jacobs, Wehle*   coepit *add. Bur-*
mann   7 qui . . . canem *secl. Müller*

tamen atriensis, qui interventu suo et canem placavit et nos
9 trementes extraxit in siccum. et Giton quidem iam dudum
se ratione acutissima redemerat a cane; quicquid enim a
nobis acceperat de cena, latranti sparserat, at ille avocatus
10 cibo furorem suppresserat. ceterum cum algentes udique
petissemus ab atriense ut nos extra ianuam emitteret,
'erras' inquit 'si putas te exire hac posse qua venisti. nemo
umquam convivarum per eandem ianuam emissus est; alia
73 intrant, alia exeunt.' quid faciamus homines miserrimi et
novi generis labyrintho inclusi, quibus lavari iam coeperat
2 votum esse? ultro ergo rogavimus ut nos ad balneum
duceret, proiectisque vestimentis, quae Giton in aditu sic-
care coepit, balneum intravimus, [angustum scilicet et] cisternae frigidariae simile, in quo Trimalchio rectus stabat. ac
ne sic quidem putidissimam eius iactationem licuit effugere;
nam nihil melius esse dicebat quam sine turba lavari, et eo
3 ipso loco aliquando pistrinum fuisse. deinde ut lassatus
consedit, invitatus balnei sono diduxit [usque ad cameram]
os ebrium et coepit Menecratis cantica lacerare, sicut illi
4 dicebant qui linguam eius intellegebant. ceteri convivae
circa labrum manibus nexis currebant et gingilipho ingenti
clamore exsonabant. alii autem [aut] restrictis manibus
anulos de pavimento conabantur tollere aut posito genu
cervices post terga flectere et pedum extremos pollices tan-
5 gere. nos, dum illi sibi ludos faciunt, in solium, quod Trimalchioni servabatur, descendimus.

9 se ratione *Scheffer*: servatione *H*   10 udique *Buecheler*: utique *H*
73 2 angustum scilicet et *secl. George*: angustum . . . simile *secl.*
Sullivan   in quo *Buecheler*: in qua *H*   eius iactationem *Heinsius*:
ei actionem *H*   3 usque ad cameram *del. Nisbet*   4 ingenti
clamore *fort. interpolatum*   *post* exsonabant *aliqua deesse videntur*
autem [aut] *Buecheler*: aut aut (*i.e.* autem autem) *H ante corr., sed
lineolam super alterum* aut *del. H*[c] *ut fieret* autem aut 〈dentibus〉
conabantur *vel* conabantur 〈ore〉 *coni. Burmann*   5 dum illi
Buecheler in adn.: dum alii alios *Kaibel*: dum alii *H*   solium
Buecheler: solio *Scheffer*: solo *H*   servabatur *George*: temperabatur
Heinsius: pervapatur *H*: ał parabatur *H*[m]

ergo ebrietate discussa in aliud triclinium deducti sumus,
ubi Fortunata disposuerat lautitias suas [ita ut supra] ⟨*⟩
lucernas aeneolosque piscatores notavimus et mensas totas
argenteas calicesque circa fictiles inauratos et vinum in conspectu sacco defluens. tum Trimalchio 'amici,' inquit 'hodie 6
servus meus barbatoriam fecit, homo praefiscini frugi et
micarius. itaque tangomenas faciamus et usque in lucem
cenemus.' haec dicente eo gallus gallinaceus cantavit. qua 74
voce confusus Trimalchio vinum sub mensa iussit effundi
lucernamque etiam mero spargi. immo anulum traiecit in 2
dexteram manum et 'non sine causa' inquit 'hic bucinus
signum dedit; nam aut incendium oportet fiat, aut aliquis in
vicinia animam abiciet. longe a nobis. itaque quisquis hunc 3
indicem attulerit, corollarium accipiet.' dicto citius [de 4
vicinia] gallus allatus est, quem Trimalchio iussit ut oenococtus fieret. laceratus igitur ab illo doctissimo coco qui 5
paulo ante de porco aves piscesque fecerat in caccabum
est coniectus. dumque Daedalus potionem ferventissimam
haurit, Fortunata mola buxea piper trivit.

sumptis igitur matteis respiciens ad familiam Trimalchio 6
'quid? vos' inquit 'adhuc non cenastis? abite, ut alii
veniant ad officium.' subiit igitur alia classis, et illi quidem 7
exclamavere: 'vale Gai', hi autem: 'ave Gai.' hinc primum 8
hilaritas nostra turbata est; nam cum puer non inspeciosus
inter novos intrasset ministros, invasit eum Trimalchio et
osculari diutius coepit. itaque Fortunata, ut ex aequo ius 9
firmum approbaret, maledicere Trimalchioni coepit et pur-
gamentum dedecusque praedicare, qui non contineret libidinem suam. ultimo etiam adiecit: 'canis'. Trimalchio contra 10

---

deesse aliquid ante ergo *putat Reinesius*   suas *sic H*: *del. Buecheler*
ita ut supra *del. Müller*   *ante* lucernas *lacunam ind. Müller, post*
lucernas *Buecheler*   notavimus *Müller*: notaverim *H*   6 servus
meus *H*: *nomen servi excidisse videtur* (Croesus meus *Wehle*)
    74 4 de vicinia *del. Müller* (*cf. 74. 2*)   oenococtus (*cf. 47. 10*)
Orioli: aeno coctus *H*   5 qui...fecerat *del. Müller¹*   6 *aliquid
deesse ante* sumptis *susp. Friedlaender*   quid? *ita interpunxit Nisbet*
9 Trimalchioni *Buecheler, praeeunte Anton*: Trimalchionem *H*

11 offensus convicio calicem in faciem Fortunatae immisit. illa
tamquam oculum perdidisset exclamavit manusque tremen-
12 tes ad faciem suam admovit. consternata est etiam Scintilla
trepidantemque sinu suo texit. immo puer quoque officiosus
urceolum frigidum ad malam eius admovit, super quem in-
13 cumbens Fortunata gemere ac flere coepit. contra Trimalchio 'quid enim?' inquit 'ambubaiam non meminisse! de
machina illam sustuli, hominem inter homines feci. at inflat
se tamquam rana, et in sinum suum conspuit, codex, non
14 mulier. sed hic qui in pergula natus est aedes non somniatur.
ita genium meum propitium habeam, curabo domata sit
15 Cassandra caligaria. et ego, homo dipundiarius, sestertium
centies accipere potui. scis tu me non mentiri. Agatho unguentarius [here] proxime seduxit me et "suadeo" inquit "non
16 patiaris genus tuum interire." at ego dum bonatus ago et
17 nolo videri levis, ipse mihi asciam in crus impegi. recte,
curabo me unguibus quaeras. et ut depraesentiarum intel-
legas quid tibi feceris: Habinna, nolo statuam eius in monu-
mento meo ponas, ne mortuus quidem lites habeam. immo,
ut sciat me posse malum dare, nolo me mortuum basiet.'

75 post hoc fulmen Habinnas rogare coepit ut iam desineret
irasci et 'nemo' inquit 'nostrum non peccat. homines sumus,
2 non dei.' idem et Scintilla flens dixit ac per genium eius
3 Gaium appellando rogare coepit ut se frangeret. non tenuit
ultra lacrimas Trimalchio et 'rogo' inquit 'Habinna, sic
peculium tuum fruniscaris: si quid perperam feci, in faciem
4 meam inspue. puerum basiavi frugalissimum, non propter
formam, sed quia frugi est: decem partes dicit, librum ab
oculo legit, thraecium sibi de diariis fecit, arcisellium de
5 suo paravit et duas trullas. non est dignus quem in oculis

---

13 ambubaiam . . . illam *Nisbet*: ambubaia non me misit sede
machillam illam *H*   conspuit *H*: non spuit *Reiske*   15 here *del.*
Nisbet: hercle *Müller²*: herae proximae *Buecheler*
    75 1 inquit *om. Lφ*   nostrum non *Lφ*: non nostrum *H*   dei *Hφ*:
dii *L*   2 se frangeret *Heinsius*: effrangeret *H*   3 fruniscaris
patav.: frunis canis *H*   4 thraecium *Orelli*: thretium *H*

feram? sed Fortunata vetat. ita tibi videtur, fulcipedia? 6
suadeo bonum tuum concoquas, milva, et me non facias
ringentem, amasiuncula: alioquin experieris cerebrum
meum. nosti me: quod semel destinavi, clavo trabali fixum 7
est. sed vivorum meminerimus. vos rogo, amici, ut vobis 8
suaviter sit. nam ego quoque tam fui quam vos estis, sed
virtute mea ad hoc perveni. corcillum est quod homines
facit, cetera quisquilia omnia. "bene emo, bene vendo"; 9
alius alia vobis dicet. felicitate dissilio. tu autem, sterteia,
etiamnum ploras? iam curabo fatum tuum plores. sed, ut 10
coeperam dicere, ad hanc me fortunam frugalitas mea per-
duxit. tam magnus ex Asia veni quam hic candelabrus est.
ad summam, quotidie me solebam ad illum metiri, et ut
celerius rostrum barbatum haberem, labra de lucerna unge-
bam. tamen ad delicias [femina] ipsimi [domini] annos 11
quattuordecim fui. nec turpe est quod dominus iubet. ego
tamen et ipsimae [dominae] satis faciebam. scitis quid
dicam: taceo, quia non sum de gloriosis. ceterum, quemad- 76
modum di volunt, dominus in domo factus sum, et ecce cepi
ipsimi cerebellum. quid multa? coheredem me Caesari 2
fecit, et accepi patrimonium laticlavium. nemini tamen 3
nihil satis est. concupivi negotiari. ne multis vos morer,
quinque naves aedificavi, oneravi vinum—et tunc erat
contra aurum—misi Romam. putares me hoc iussisse: 4
omnes naves naufragarunt, factum, non fabula. uno die
Neptunus trecenties sestertium devoravit. putatis me defe- 5
cisse? non mehercules mi haec iactura gusti fuit, tamquam
nihil facti. alteras feci maiores et meliores [et feliciores], ut
nemo non me virum fortem diceret. sc⟨it⟩is, magna navis 6
magnam fortitudinem habet. oneravi rursus vinum, lardum,

---

6 facias *Mentel*: facies *H*   7 trabali *Scheffer*: tabulari *H*
8 corcillum *Scheffer*: coricillum *H*   10 summa *H*: *corr. Mentel*
metiri *Scheffer*: me uri *H*   11 femina *et* domini *et* dominae *del.*
Buecheler

76 2 accepi *Scheffer*: accepit *H*   4 putares me hoc iussisse
obscurum esse putat Delz   Neptunus *patav.*: neptunno *H*   5 et
feliciores *del. George*   6 sc⟨it⟩is *Buecheler*

7 fabam, seplasium, mancipia. hoc loco Fortunata rem piam
fecit; omne enim aurum suum, omnia vestimenta vendidit
et mi centum aureos in manu posuit. hoc fuit peculii mei
8 fermentum. cito fit quod di volunt. uno cursu centies sestertium corrotundavi. statim redemi fundos omnes, qui
patroni mei fuerant. aedifico domum, ⟨comparo⟩ venalicia,
coemo iumenta; quicquid tangebam, crescebat tamquam
9 favus. postquam coepi plus habere quam tota patria mea
habet, manum de tabula: sustuli me de negotiatione et
10 coepi ⟨per⟩ libertos faenerare. et sane nolentem me negotium meum agere exhortavit mathematicus, qui venerat
forte in coloniam nostram, Graeculio, Serapa nomine, con-
11 siliator deorum. hic mihi dixit etiam ea quae oblitus eram;
ab acia et acu mi omnia exposuit; intestinas meas noverat;
tantum quod mihi non dixerat quid pridie cenaveram.
77 putasses illum semper mecum habitasse. rogo, Habinna—
puto, interfuisti—: "tu dominam tuam de rebus illis fecisti.
tu parum felix in amicis es. nemo umquam tibi parem
gratiam refert. tu latifundia possides. tu viperam sub ala
2 nutricas" et, quod vobis non dixerim, etiam nunc mi restare
vitae annos triginta et menses quattuor et dies duos. praeterea cito accipiam hereditatem. hoc mihi dicit fatus meus.
3 quod si contigerit fundos Apuliae iungere, satis vivus per-
4 venero. interim dum Mercurius vigilat, aedificavi hanc
domum. ut scitis, †cusuc† erat; nunc templum est. habet
quattuor cenationes, cubicula viginti, porticus marmoratos
duos, susum cenationem, cubiculum in quo ipse dormio,

7 fit *Scheffer*: fio *H*   8 comparo *suppl. Sullivan* (paro *Buecheler*):
comparo *ante* iumenta *suppl. Müller in adn.*   9 per *add.*
Heinsius   10 nolentem *Scheffer*: nolente *H*   ał exhortavit *H*^m:
exoravit *H*   11 exposuit *Scheffer*: exposcit *H*   mihi *in textu
omissum suppl.* *H*^m

77 1 *post* tuam *aliqua periisse susp. Müller*   amicis *Scheffer*:
amicos *H*   2 quod *H*: quid *Scheffer*   4 cusuc *corruptum*: casa
patav.: casula *Heinsius*: casa adhuc *Corbett* (*cf.* CP *lxiv* (*1969*), *112 s.*)
marmoratos duos *Buecheler*: marmoratis duos *H*: marmoratas duas
patav.   cenationem *Scheffer*: lavationem *Salonius*: cellationem *H*

viperae huius sessorium, ostiarii cellam perbonam; hospitium hospites ⟨C⟩ capit. ad summam, Scaurus cum huc 5
venit, nusquam mavoluit hospitari, et habet ad mare pater-
num hospitium. et multa alia sunt, quae statim vobis
ostendam. credite mihi: assem habeas, assem valeas; habes, 6
habeberis. sic amicus vester, qui fuit rana, nunc est rex.
interim, Stiche, profer vitalia, in quibus volo me efferri. 7
profer et unguentum et ex illa amphora gustum, ex qua
iubeo lavari ossa mea.'

non est moratus Stichus, sed et stragulam albam et prae- 78
textam in triclinium attulit

⟨*⟩

iussitque nos temptare an bonis lanis essent confecta. tum 2
subridens 'vide tu' inquit 'Stiche, ne ista mures tangant aut
tineae; alioquin te vivum comburam. ego gloriosus volo
efferri, ut totus mihi populus bene imprecetur.' statim 3
ampullam nardi aperuit omnesque nos unxit et 'spero'
inquit 'futurum ut aeque me mortuum iuvet tamquam
vivum.' nam vinum quidem in vinarium iussit infundi et 4
'putate vos' ait 'ad parentalia mea invitatos esse.'

ibat res ad summam nauseam, cum Trimalchio ebrietate 5
turpissima gravis novum acroama, cornicines, in triclinium
iussit adduci, fultusque cervicalibus multis extendit se supra
torum extremum et 'fingite me' inquit 'mortuum esse.
dicite aliquid belli.' consonuere cornic⟨in⟩es funebri strepitu. 6
unus praecipue servus libitinarii illius, qui inter hos hone-
stissimus erat, tam valde intonuit, ut totam concitaret vici-
niam. itaque vigiles [qui custodiebant vicinam regionem] 7

C add. Heinsius: M Scheffer   5 summa H: corr. Scheffer
   78 1 lac. ind. Buecheler: quae (sc. vitalia) Trimalchio miratus est
Marmorale   3 ampullam patav.: appollam H   5 cornicines
patav.: cornicipes H   6 cornicines patav.: cornices H   libitinarii Scheffer: libertinarii H   qui ... erat secl. Delz   7 qui ...
regionem secl. Müller

rati ardere Trimalchionis domum effregerunt ianuam subito
et cum aqua securibusque tumultuari suo iure coepe-
8 runt. nos occasionem opportunissimam nacti Agamemnoni
verba dedimus raptimque tam plane quam ex incendio
fugimus.

COMMENTARY

IN the passage before the *Cena Trimalchionis* Petronius has made fun of trite views on the decline of rhetoric and morals, using as his mouthpiece the narrator Encolpius, and then the rhetorician Agamemnon. There follows a series of misadventures which already show up Encolpius as the luckless homosexual lover, falling out with his companion and rival Ascyltos over the boy Giton; some hints are given that the wrath of Priapus is an underlying theme of at least this part of the novel (see Introduction I D). Unfortunately there is a gap, which could be of considerable length, immediately before the *Cena*, so that it is impossible to tell what is referred to in the opening sections. It seems that Encolpius, Ascyltos, and Giton are in some kind of trouble, possibly connected with a stolen cloak. Agamemnon has arranged for them to come with him to have dinner with the wealthy freedman, Trimalchio.

Ch. 26

§ 7 id est expectatio liberae cenae : *libera cena* appears to have been a technical term for a meal provided for *bestiarii* (on these see note on 45. 11) before they had to face wild beasts in the arena; cf. *Passio S. Perpetuae* 17 'pridie quoque cum illa cena quam liberam vocant quantum in illis erat, non cenam liberam sed agapen cenarent', Tert. *Apol.* 42. 5 'non in publico Liberalibus discumbo, quod bestiariis supremam cenantibus mos est.' The meaning of *libera* here is doubtful. Probably it should be taken as 'open to all' (cf. Hor. *Od.* iii. 24. 12 f. *liberas fruges*) or else 'liberating', rather than 'extravagant, generous', a sense which is possible in itself (cf. E. Löfstedt, *Verm. Stud.* 105) but inappropriate here.

If the text in *H* is sound here, the *libera cena* cannot be Trimalchio's forthcoming dinner, since the depression of Encolpius and his companions is removed by the mention of that dinner. It must instead be a figurative description of some imminent danger, e.g. a lawsuit arising from the stolen cloak mentioned in chs. 12 ff.

Buecheler instead took the whole phrase *id est . . . cenae* as an interpolation, assuming that some reference had been made

earlier in the text to an actual, not a figurative, dinner for
gladiators. His argument is weakened by the fact that he takes
literally Ascyltos' abusive attack on Encolpius at 9. 8 ' "non
taces," inquit, "gladiator obscene, quem de ruina harena
dimisit?".' It must be admitted that *id est* is flat here, but
Buecheler's solution is too drastic. It would be simpler to suppose that *id est* has somehow replaced some other phrase, e.g.
cumque eo.

§ 8 quonam genere: = *quanam ratione*. This usage is common in
Silver Latin, and is found even in Cicero; cf. Cic. *Att.* ii. 20. 4
'novo quodam genere in summam gloriam venit', *de Orat.* ii.
185 'alio quodam genere'.

unus : this has clearly begun to serve as an indefinite article,
like the French *un*, Italian *uno*, etc. This development is certain
in later Latin (see, for example, H. Rönsch, *Itala* 425); but the
examples often cited from authors earlier than Petronius all seem
to show *unus* functioning mainly, if not entirely, as a numeral,
and fall into one or other of these categories: (i) *unus* = an ordinary, cf. Cic. *de Orat.* i. 132 'sicut unus paterfamilias his de
rebus loquor', Cat. 22. 10, (ii) *unus* with a superlative, cf. Plaut.
Truc. 250 'sed est huic unus servos violentissimus', Cic. *Fam.*
xv. 16. 3 'cum uno fortissimo viro', (iii) passages where *unus*
is either certainly or almost certainly a simple numeral, e.g.
Ter. *Andr.* 117 f. 'interea inter mulieres / quae ibi aderant forte
unam aspicio adulescentulam', Quadrig. ap. Gell. xv. 1. 7
'Sulla eduxit copias ut Archelai turrim unam, quam ille inter-
posuit, ligneam incenderet.' See E. Wölfflin, *ALL* xii. 191, A. H.
Salonius, *Vit. Patr.* 237 f., L.–H.–S. 193.

§ 9 quid? : 'look' or 'I say'; a regular device to prepare the way
for a following question.

hodie apud quem fiat : 'at whose place it'll be today', i.e. who
is going to be the host today.

lautissimus homo : 'he's the height of elegance.' *lautus* and
lautitia are several times used as comic descriptions of Trimalchio's tasteless vulgarity (cf. 27. 4, 32. 1); but note also that the
slave's brief indication of his extravagance is enough to arouse
the eagerness of Encolpius and his friends. Encolpius himself
is sometimes made to show a naïve vulgarity in his reactions
(see notes on 27. 2, 29. 1), even if more often Petronius makes
him express his contempt for the vulgarity and boastfulness of
Trimalchio and his friends.

horologium : presumably a water-clock rather than a sundial (see *OCD* s.v. 'Clocks'). Neither this nor the trumpeter is mentioned again in the *Cena* as we have it.

ut subinde sciat . . . : 'so that all the time he'll know how much of his life is behind him'. The ordinary person would have to send a slave to the forum to find out the time (cf. Juv. 10. 215 f. 'clamore opus est ut sentiat auris / quem dicat venisse puer, quot nuntiet horas', and see Mayor's note); in preferring to have a trumpeter all dolled up (*subornatum*) to give regular announcements of the time Trimalchio betrays here as elsewhere (cf. 77. 6–78. 8, the mock-funeral scene) a morbid, although whimsical, preoccupation with death.

§ 10 servile officium : Giton, who is being passed off as the slave of Encolpius and Ascyltos, carries out the normal servile duties of looking after his masters' clothing at the baths and attending them when they go out to dinner.

[usque hoc] : it is doubtful whether these words can yield the sense 'up till now'; even if they could, they are misplaced, since they must be taken with *libentissime*.

in balneum : *in balneo H* must be corrected. The narrative parts of the *Cena* are written in elegant Silver Age Latin, but a manuscript as faulty as *H* inevitably introduces apparent vulgarisms, e.g. 74. 9 'male dicere Trimalchionem'. The difficulties in assessing the soundness of *H* become much greater in the speeches of the freedmen, in which Petronius' attempt to represent lower-class idiom has to be allowed for as well as the scribe's normal carelessness.

Exercise followed by a bath was the normal routine before dinner; cf., for example, Plin. *Ep.* iii. 1. 8.

Ch. 27

§ 1 interim : the temporal meaning of this word becomes debased (cf. Ter. *Hec.* 177 f. *primo . . . interim . . .*, Hand, *Tursellinus* iii. 424), so the transition from the previous sentence is less abrupt than it might seem at first sight. Friedlaender and others take *interim* strictly in the sense 'meanwhile', and are in consequence tempted to suppose that something must have fallen out after *sequi*.

coepimus : from Plautus onwards *coepi* with the infinitive is used in place of the simple perfect; in Petronius this usage is particularly common, occurring both in narrative and in the language of the freedmen. Cf. Löfstedt, *Peregr.* 209 ff., L.–H.–S. 319.

iocari : 'jest'. Probably corrupt; it cannot bear any sense which would provide the contrast with *errare* implied by *immo*. Heinsius conjectured *otiari* 'idle around', a word rare enough to be readily altered but scarcely an improvement in sense. Nisbet's *morari* is further from the reading in *H*, but it gives a contrast between wandering around aimlessly and lingering close to one place. Alternatively *errare* may be corrupted from e.g. *hilarari*.

ludentium : *ludentem* appears to be a corruption influenced by *ludentem pila* at the end of the sentence. Buecheler is content to delete *ludentem*, but *circulis* seems rather vague by itself.

If *circulis* is sound, *accedere* is here used with the dative, a much rarer construction than with *ad* or the simple accusative (cf. 6. 4 *accedo aniculam*, 8. 2 *accessit ad me*).

cum subito videmus : an example of the *cum* 'inversum' construction, in which the less important idea, the specification of time or circumstances, is put into the main clause, and the more important thought comes in the second place in a subordinate clause introduced by *cum* (see K.–S. ii. 338 ff.). Petronius makes frequent use of this device, usually in the *Cena* to throw emphasis on some new inanity of Trimalchio, e.g. 32. 1 'in his eramus lautitiis, cum ipse Trimalchio . . .', 47. 1 'eiusmodi fabulae vibrabant, cum Trimalchio intravit.'

senem : several contrasts are used to make the picture of Trimalchio as absurd as possible. The bald old man stands out among the *capillati* (at 75. 10 f. he recounts how he had himself as a small boy won the favour of his master and mistress). His dress is brighter in colour than a normal man's; he sets himself up as a *paterfamilias*, yet appears in public wearing bedroom slippers; he still plays ball at an age when a respectable man would have given up such a pursuit (see the description of eccentric behaviour in Sidon. *Ep.* i. 8 'student pilae senes, aleae iuvenes, armis eunuchi'); he cheats, and he ensures his comfort by means of a comic luxury.

russea . . . prasina : there is a notable frequency of red and green in the description of Trimalchio and his surroundings; cf. 28. 4 'hinc involutus coccina gausapa', 28. 8 'ostiarius prasinatus, cerasino succinctus cingulo'.

capillatos : pages whose hair was kept long and whose physical attractions appealed to their masters; cf. Sen. *Ep.* 95. 24 'transeo puerorum infelicium greges quos post transacta con-

vivia aliae cubiculi contumeliae expectant; transeo agmina
exoletorum per nationes coloresque discripta ut eadem omnibus
levitas sit, eadem primae mensura lanuginis, eadem species
capillorum, ne quis cui rectior est coma crispulis misceatur.'
See Mayor's note on Juv. 3. 186.

§ 2 quamquam erat operae pretium : immediately after hinting
at Trimalchio's homosexual tendencies, Encolpius is made to
reveal his own.

nec amplius . . . : 'he didn't make any more effort to pick
up . . .'

§ 3 spadones : the possession of eunuchs is probably to be seen
as a claim to regal magnificence; cf. Suet. *Claud*. 28 'libertorum
praecipue suspexit Posiden spadonem, quem etiam Britannico
triumpho inter militares viros hasta pura donavit', Liv. ix.
17. 16, and see Mayor's note on Juv. 10. 307. Maecenas is said
to have been attended by two eunuchs (cf. Sen. *Ep*. 114. 6), but
it should not be taken for granted that Petronius had him in
mind here. See note on 32. 2.

in diversa parte circuli : probably 'on the opposite side of the
group', i.e. opposite Trimalchio.

matellam : there was nothing vulgar to a Roman in having this
kept at hand, but the use of gold or silver for this purpose was
somewhat ostentatious; cf. Mart. i. 37 'ventris onus misero,
nec te pudet, excipis auro, / Basse, bibis vitro: carius ergo
cacas.'

numerabat pilas : in his variation of a game in which the number of successful throws or bounces of the ball would be counted
by the *pilicrepus*, Trimalchio prefers to count the number of
times a ball is dropped. The game played here cannot be identified with certainty, but it might be *trigon*, in which three players
stood in a triangle and threw several balls to one another (see
Balsdon, *Life and Leisure*, 165, although he seems to regard
Trimalchio's system of scoring as normal). The verb *expellere*
appears to have had some technical meaning; possibly it was
used when a player did not catch the ball but punched it or
knocked it with the flat of his hand on towards another player
(cf. Mart. xiv. 46, where a *pila trigonalis* is made to speak: 'si
me mobilibus scis expulsare sinistris, / sum tua. tu nescis?
rustice, redde pilam'). But the reading in *H, lusu expellente*, is
unsatisfactory, while *luxu expellente L* is impossible. Perhaps
we should read *expellentes*, deleting *lusu* as a gloss.

§ 4 Menelaus : an assistant (cf. 81. 1 *antescholanus*) of the rhetorician Agamemnon.

cubitum : at a dinner-party it was customary to recline with the left elbow on one's couch, thus leaving the right hand free for eating and drinking with; Nisbet and Hubbard in their note on Hor. *Od.* i. 27. 8 cite Alciphron 3. 29 (65), where Πηξάγκωνος 'Elbow-propper' is the name of a parasite.

ponitis : for the use of the present rather than the future cf. 30. 3 *cenat*, 33. 1 *permittitis*, 58. 4 *cresco*, 71. 5 *aedificas*. The idiom is familiar, and is not confined to lower-class speech. Cf. L.–H.–S. 307 f.

principium : while he is still speaking, Menelaus is interrupted by the chamber-pot incident, which he calls the beginning of the dinner.

§ 5 digitos concrepuit : the gesture is imperious, if not necessarily discourteous; cf. Cic. *Off.* iii. 75, Mart. iii. 82. 15.

§ 6 in capite . . . tersit : for this use of the hair see Luke 7: 38 'His feet were wetted with her tears and she wiped them with her hair, kissing them and anointing them with the myrrh'; Stat. *Theb.* ix. 375. In these cases a voluntary act is described, so Trimalchio's behaviour, although it shows his absolute power within his household, may have seemed less grotesque to a Roman than it does to us.

Ch. 28

§ 1 longum . . . excipere : 'It would have taken too long to pick out all the details', *not* 'I cannot linger over details' (Heseltine). These opening words of ch. 28 look like a device used by Petronius to allow his narrator to move on to a new scene (cf. 30. 1 *non licebat . . . considerare*, even though the text there is doubtful). Here, however, we might have expected to find between *tersit* and *longum erat* some indication of the general scene which Petronius has chosen not to describe fully; note also that at § 6 below Agamemnon reappears in the narrative without warning, although this is not in itself a decisive argument in favour of a lacuna.

sudore calfacti : 'baked in sweat' (the form *calfactus* had become regular in place of *calefactus* by the time of Quintilian; cf. i. 6. 21). In this sentence Petronius suggests their rapid progress through the different stages of bathing—hot bath (see note on *balneum* at 73. 2), hot sweat-chamber (*laconicum*), and cold bath (*frigidarium*).

eximus : contracted form of the perfect.

§ 2 non linteis... : 'not with linen towels but with blankets of the softest wool'.

§ 3 iatraliptae : masseurs, but this hardly brings out their social status and importance. The younger Pliny relied on an *iatraliptes* when his life was in danger, and later recommended that he should be highly rewarded (cf. *Ep.* x. 5, with Sherwin-White's note).

suum propin esse : 'they were drinking a toast in his memory.' Unperturbed at the waste of valuable Falernian wine, Trimalchio regards it as a mark of respect to himself in the form of a premature funeral libation (for the practice of pouring drink-offerings to the dead into the ground cf. Virg. *Aen.* v. 77 f.). *propin*, Heraeus's conjecture for the almost impossible *propinasse* of *H*, is a contracted form of the Greek infinitive προπιεῖν (cf. *CIL* v. 5272. 13, 25 'oleum et propin').

§ 4 gausapa : shaggy woollen cloth. The word may be used here to suggest a rather effeminate luxury; cf. 21. 2 'cinaedus myrtea subornatus gausapa'.

phaleratis cursoribus : *cursores* were slaves who ran along in front of their master's carriage, to clear the way or at least to make his progress conspicuous. Here they have *phalerae*, metal discs worn by soldiers or by horses, often as a military distinction but sometimes merely as ornaments. For this ornamental use cf. Suet. *Nero* 30. 3 'numquam minus mille carrucis fecisse iter traditur, soleis mularum argenteis, canusinatis mulionibus, armillata phalerataque Mazacum turba atque cursorum'; the partial resemblance between Trimalchio's entourage and that of Nero should not, however, have led anyone to think that Petronius must have had Nero in mind.

chiramaxio : a small four-wheeled bath-chair or go-cart (cf. Greek χειράμαξα, χειραμάξιον, D.–S. s.v. *chiramaxium*).

puer : at 64. 5 Trimalchio's *deliciae* is called Croesus. The word *puer* is sometimes used of a slave without a precise reference to age, but here the contrast between *vetulus* and the ordinary meaning of *puer* brings out his repulsiveness.

§ 5 ergo : resumptive use after what amounts to a parenthesis; cf. K.–S. ii. 144.

symphoniacus : rich men quite often had their own group of musicians (cf. Cic. *Mil.* 55 'tum casu pueros symphoniacos uxoris ducebat et ancillarum greges'). By placing the word between *minimis* and *tibiis* Petronius adds to the effect of mock grandeur.

toto itinere cantavit : throughout the *Cena* the fondness of slaves and freedmen for music is emphasized: cf. 31. 4, 32. 1, 33. 4, 36. 1, 41. 6, 47. 8, 64. 5, 73. 3; at 53. 12 Trimalchio sums up his own tastes: 'ceterum duo esse in rebus humanis quae libentissime spectaret, petauristarios et cornicines.' Here, however, not content with having music provided for him during this short journey, he ostentatiously ensures that no one else can hear it.

§ 7 dominico : this adjective is found in Afranius, Varro, Seneca, etc., but remains infrequent until it is taken over by legal and ecclesiastical writers.

In late Latin, and to some extent in early Latin, the genitive of a name or noun denoting a relationship may be replaced by an adjective formed from the noun: thus *fraternus* for *fratris*, *Venerius* for *Veneris*, *erilis* for *eri*; cf., e.g., Tac. *Hist.* i. 17 *principale scortum*, and see Löfstedt, *Syntactica* i. 107 ff. Here the adjective helps to give a formal, official ring to the announcement.

foras exierit : pleonasms like this, wrongly described as vulgar by Perrochat, are not uncommon in ordinary language; cf. Cic. *Div.* i. 114 'evolant atque excurrunt foras.'

§ 8 ostiarius : the unduly colourful garb of this slave is contrasted with his menial position; cf. Sen. *de Ira* 3. 37. 2, where the janitor is referred to as *mancipium extremum*.

prasinatus : the colours seem to have been chosen merely for the sharp contrast. Some have seen in *prasinatus* a sign that the janitor was represented as a supporter of the green faction at the local circus (cf. 70. 10 'etsi prasinianus es famosus'), but this leaves his preference for a cherry-coloured belt a little odd.

§ 9 pica : talking magpies were by now familiar enough; cf. Plin. *NH* x. 118 'these birds get fond of uttering particular words, and not only learn them but love them, and secretly ponder with careful reflection, not concealing their engrossment. It is an established fact that if the difficulty of a word beats them this causes their death, and that their memory fails them unless they hear the same word repeatedly, and when they

are at a loss for a word they cheer up wonderfully if in the mean-
time they hear it spoken' (ib. 78). The *pica varia* may, however,
have still been quite rare, and a *salutatrix pica*, especially in
a golden cage, would no doubt be a little too much for the more
sophisticated (note Martial's disdain for the owners of such
pets at vii. 87. 6).

Ch. 29

§ 1 **paene resupinatus . . . :** 'I almost fell flat on my back and
broke my legs.' Comic exaggeration of his own reactions, so
that the reader's interest in the sequel may be aroused; cf. Cic.
Planc. 65 'concidi paene, iudices, cum ex me quidam quae-
sisset . . .'

canis... pictus : several such dogs have been found on mosaics
in Pompeii, the best-known being the one in the House of the
Tragic Poet, but artificial watch-dogs are mentioned in much
earlier times: see Homer, *Od.* vii. 91 ff. 'On either side of the
door there stood gold and silver dogs, which Hephaestus had
fashioned with cunning skill to guard the palace of great-
hearted Alcinous.' So, in exaggerating Encolpius' alarm at the
sight of something not particularly surprising, Petronius is
making him a somewhat simple-minded character (cf. 36. 7,
65. 5). Hence it is not altogether safe to assume that in various
references to the *lautitiae* of Trimalchio's establishment Encolpius is to be seen merely as the sophisticated observer making
ironical comments: cf. 30. 5 'his repleti voluptatibus', 31. 1
'obligati tam grandi beneficio', 32. 1 'in his eramus lautitiis',
34. 5 'laudatus propter elegantias', 39. 1 'interpellavit tam
dulces fabulas', etc.

§ 3 **titulis :** each slave offered for sale in the market (*venalicium*)
carried a placard (*titulus*) stating his price, origin, abilities, and
vices. This served as a warranty to protect the purchaser; cf.
Dig. xxi. 1. 1, Marq. *Prl.* 172.

caduceum : herald's wand; the word is derived from the Doric
Greek καρύκειον. Here, as often, applied to the wand of Mercury, the god of commerce, whom Trimalchio as a successful
trader regards as his patron deity; cf. 67. 7, 77. 4.

Minerva : an appropriate deity to preside over Trimalchio's
triumphal entry; cf. Liv. xlv. 33. 1 f. 'cetera omnis generis
arma cumulata in ingentem acervum, precatus Martem, Miner-
vam Luamque matrem et ceteros deos, quibus spolia hostium
dicare ius fasque est . . . succendit.'

Romam : the reading in *H* gives satisfactory sense. Trimalchio has commissioned a portrait of himself entering Rome in a novel kind of triumph, as a *capillatus* on his way to the slave-market. He is connected with Rome only twice elsewhere (70. 3 'attuli illi Roma munus cultros Norico ferro', 71. 12 'cum posset in omnibus decuriis Romae esse, tamen noluit').

§ 4 dispensator : the term is used of a steward, the slave or freedman in charge of the accounts, if not of the over-all management of an estate. See Marq. *Prl.* 155; also notes on 30. 1, 9.

curiosus pictor cum inscriptione : the painter (and through him Trimalchio) is derided for including too many explanations. Aelian (*VH* x. 10) criticizes early painters whose crude representations required identifying sub-titles: τοῦτο βοῦς, ἐκεῖνο ἵππος, τοῦτο δένδρον.

§ 5 levatum mento : 'lifted up by the chin'. The picture suggested by the text of *H* is absurd, but quite consistent with Trimalchio's tastes; thus there is no need for a conjecture such as Fraenkel's ⟨de pavi⟩mento excelsum ⟨eum⟩. Mercury appears here in his role as the patron of those engaged in commerce, but there is also a hint of his function as guide to the souls of the dead (ψυχοπομπός); in this connection note the heroic clausula *Mercurius rapiebat.*

§ 6 [copiosa] : the phrase *cornu copiae* had become familiar (see Nisbet and Hubbard on Hor. *Od.* i. 17. 16), so the scribe has added *copiosa* as an explanation of *abundanti.*

aurea pensa : gold threads spun by the Fates appear as a motif in accounts of the Age of Gold; hence they symbolize Trimalchio's blissful prosperity.

§ 8 armarium : here applied to a box or cupboard, the top of which was in the shape of a temple-front and contained the *lares* of the household.

pyxis : the cutting off of a boy's first beard was often marked by some ceremony, and the hair was preserved in a container and offered to a god. The same extravagance in the choice of a container is seen in Nero: see Suet. *Nero* 12. 4 'inter buthysiae apparatum barbam primam posuit conditamque in auream pyxidem et pretiosissimis margaritis adornatam Capitolio consecravit.' But it is most unlikely that this use of an expensive jewel-case was peculiar to Nero; if it was, those who think that

Petronius was writing for Nero and his circle of friends are forced to credit him with incredible boldness.

ipsius : *ipse* and *ipsa* are used colloquially by slaves in referring to their master or mistress; cf. Cat. 3. 6 f. 'suamque norat / ipsam tam bene quam puella matrem', Plaut. *Aul.* 356 'si a foro ipsus redierit'.

§ 9. The appearance of the *atriensis* is a little abrupt, and it may well be that some description of him and of the *atrium* has fallen out just before this. However, Buecheler's view that the missing passage dealt with other pictures (i.e. not merely those in the *atrium*) seems to assume that *in medio* means 'in the middle of the *atrium*' (a similar assumption lies behind *in media* sc. *porticu* in the margin of *t*); but the phrase is used more loosely in the sense of 'available' (cf., for example, Hor. *Sat.* i. 2. 108 'transvolat in medio posita et fugientia captat', *TLL* viii. 594 f.).

atriensem : used sometimes of the steward who supervised the entire household, including the accounts, and sometimes of a slave or freedman in charge of the *atrium* (or his underlings); cf. Marq. *Prl.* 142.

Iliada . . . munus : in Athenaeus v. 178 f the polite guest is advised not to rush in to dinner, but to pause first in order to admire his host's house. Here the pause to admire Trimalchio's paintings enables Petronius to slip in a comic juxtaposition of themes.

Laenas must be the name of the magistrate who had presided over a set of games held in the town, a man important locally but a nonentity to Petronius' readers. Maiuri is too specific in arguing that since it was a cognomen found among the Pompeii as well as other families it must here refer to the Pompeius whom Trimalchio by implication claims as his patron (cf. 30. 2 *C. Pompeio Trimalchioni*).

Ch. 30

§ 1. As the text stands in *H*, the sentence *nos iam . . .* is too abrupt after the words *non . . . considerare*, and *nos* is pointlessly emphatic, even if Petronius is by strict classical standards sometimes rather free in his use of personal pronouns. *multaciam* is certainly corrupt, although the general sense is likely to have been 'We could not make a more careful examination.' Anton's *multa iam* for *multaciam*, combined with Heinsius's *nam nos* (or simply *nam*) for *nos iam*, improves the text of *H* considerably; but Buecheler's postulation of a lacuna after *considerare* seems justified.

procurator : the word can be applied to anyone empowered to act on behalf of someone else in legal and financial business. Often it is used of a slave or freedman entrusted with substantial responsibilities in the management of his master's property. Here it is possibly a synonym for *dispensator* (see § 9 note, and Crook, *Law and Life of Rome* 60, 187).

in postibus . . . : the description of the door is not altogether clear. If *in postibus* means the same as *in utroque poste* below, each door-post must have on it the dedicatory inscription on the ship's-beak emblem underneath the rods and axes; another copy of the inscription is on the lintel, illuminated from below by a double lamp hanging from the ceiling. Alternatively *in postibus* might be used loosely to mean 'on the door'; the emblem and inscription would then occur once only, and would presumably occupy the space above the lintel. Apart from the strained explanation of *in postibus*, this interpretation makes *eodem* difficult to understand.

Note in any case various eccentricities of Trimalchio here: (i) It was the custom for Romans of high rank or ancestry to display trophies of war in the *vestibulum* of their houses, where passers-by could admire them (cf. Cic. *Phil.* ii. 68 'an tu in vestibulo rostra ac spolia quum aspexisti, domum tuam te introire putas?'; Plin. *NH* xxxv. 7); Trimalchio fixes his emblems at the entrance to his dining-room. (ii) The ship's beaks suggest success in a naval battle; Trimalchio's success has been through commerce. (iii) He flaunts the rods and, more important, the axes, which were the insignia of a Roman consul, although the highest office he has held is that of *sevir*.

§ 2 seviro Augustali : the *seviratus Augustalis* was established in various towns in Italy and elsewhere as a means of attracting the loyalty of wealthier citizens by appealing to their ambition. It consisted of a board of six, usually if not always freedmen, known as *Augustales* or *seviri Augustales*, who supervised the cult of the emperor and were granted in return various privileges and honours (see also 71. 12 note).

§ 3 bilychnis : 'two-branched'. A hybrid form found only here and in *CIL* x. 114, in each case qualifying *lucerna*. Each time this type of lamp appears to be mentioned as a rare luxury.

⟨erant⟩ **et duae . . . :** Buecheler's conjecture eliminates the awkward omission of a finite verb in *HL*.

C. noster : cf. 50. 1 'Gaio feliciter', 53. 3, 67. 1, 74. 7, 75. 2. The gratification felt by a freedman on acquiring a *praenomen* as a mark of his free status is also mocked in Hor. *Sat.* ii. 5. 32 'gaudent praenomine molles / auriculae', and Pers. 5. 79. As at 53. 3, the use of *noster* by an underling of Trimalchio is meant to bring out the over-familiarity of his household towards him.

foras cenat : it has been claimed that the accusative *foras* is here used in place of the classical *foris* because *cenare* is equivalent to a verb of motion, but this explanation cannot apply to the two other passages in the *Cena*, both Vulgar like this, where *foras* is used for *foris*: 44. 14 'domi leones, foras volpes', 47. 5 'omnia foras parata sunt.' Confusion between *foras* and *foris* is frequent in late Latin.

For the colloquial use of the present *cenat* in place of the future cf. L.–H.–S. 307 f.

§ 4 altera . . . notabantur : one door-post has an open notification to Trimalchio's household and to any visitors of the dates when he is dining out (if we could be sure that Petronius had already said that the *Cena* took place some time before December, the point would lie in the infrequency of his dinners away from home, but the fact that the dates are consecutive is puzzling); on the other post he shows his superstitious nature (for this see especially 74. 1–3) by displaying an astrological calendar to ensure that his activities fall on propitious dates.

stellarumque septem : i.e. the sun, earth, Mercury, Venus, Mars, Jupiter, and Saturn.

§ 5 [in triclinium]: *del. Müller*; apart from being superfluous, the words involve a construction not used elsewhere with *intrare* by Petronius (cf., e.g., 31. 1 'cum intrassemus triclinium').

qui supra hoc officium erat positus : deleted unnecessarily by Fraenkel as an interpolation modelled on 56. 8 'puerque super hoc positus officium'.

§ 6 dextro pede : it was thought lucky to start a journey or an enterprise by stepping off with the right foot, avoiding a stumble, which was regarded as particularly ill-omened if it occurred on the threshold. Vitruvius (iii. 3) has this superstition in mind when in his instructions for building the stairway up to a temple he advises the architect to provide an odd number of steps, so that the worshipper will be able to use his right foot both for the first step on the stairs and for entering the temple itself. Trimalchio, however, is made to surpass ordinary superstitiousness by having someone bark out *dextro pede* at the entrance to his dining-room.

sine dubio : for this weakened use of the phrase in a concessive sense ('of course', 'naturally'), followed by an adversative, see *TLL* v. 2122 ff.

§§ 7–11. The whole incident conveys indirectly the grandeur of Trimalchio's establishment, but not all the details are fanciful. For example, a slave could in fact own another slave as part of his *peculium* (cf. Mart. ii. 18. 7 'esse sat est servum, iam nolo vicarius esse'; *Dig.* xv. 1. 17 'si servus meus ordinarius vicarios habeat'). Again, the danger of having his clothes stolen while he was at the baths must have been familiar to any Roman or Greek (cf. Plaut. *Rud.* 385 'fur facile quem observat videt: custos qui fur sit nescit'; also *Dig.* xlvii. 17 'de furibus balneariis'), but an exotic flavour is given here by describing the stolen clothes as *Tyria*—the luxury of wearing clothes of Tyrian purple may even have been illegal at this time if the prohibition imposed by Nero (Suet. *Nero* 32) was in force.

§ 7 dextros gressus : Fraenkel deletes *dextros* here and in § 9, no doubt finding the joke too laboured; it should certainly be kept in § 9 and perhaps here also.

§ 8 X̄ sestertiorum : this larger figure given by *L* (= ten thousand sesterces) is absurd especially after *vix* but more appropriate to the context than *decem* (*H*)—even the slaves have extravagant notions. Martial (iv. 61. 4–5) mentions ten thousand sesterces as the price of an expensive cloak.

§ 9 in oecario : 'in a little room'. Heraeus's suggestion is based on οἰκάριον, a rare diminutive of οἶκος. Those who keep *in precario H* are forced to give it the unlikely sense 'in a place where requests are listened to'.

The *dispensator* need not be assumed to be identical with the *procurator* of § 1; he could instead be his superior.

§ 11 cubitoria : an alternative, found only here, for *cenatoria*, 'dinner-suit'.

cliens quidam : it was not unknown for a slave to have some right of ownership over another slave, his *vicarius*, but Trimalchio's steward goes further by claiming to be a *patronus* with his own clients paying their respects to him.

iam semel lota : a similar extravagance in dress is attributed to Nero (cf. Suet. *Nero* 30 'nullam vestem bis induit') and to

Heliogabalus (cf. SHA, *Heliog.* 26. 1). *lota* should probably be taken as 'cleaned'; the process of fulling clothes was perhaps more destructive than simple washing (see H. Blümner, *Technologie* 170 ff.). Martial (x. 11) refers contemptuously to a friend who boasts unduly of his generosity:

> 'donavi tamen' inquis 'amico milia quinque
> et lotam, ut multum, terve quaterve togam.'

quid ergo est? : a common colloquial phrase 'Oh well', 'What does it matter?'; cf., for example, Cic. *Att.* ii. 19. 5, Sen. *Ep.* 90. 46, and see Hof. *LU* 67.

Ch. 31

§ 1 humanitati nostrae : later Encolpius professes himself less ready to forgive a slave's misdemeanour (cf. 49. 7 'aliquis oblivisceretur porcum exinterare? non mehercules illi ignoscerem, si piscem praeterisset', although he criticizes Trimalchio for his inconsistencies (cf. 52. 11).

§ 2 ad summam : see 37. 5 n.

vinum dominicum ministratoris gratia est : the slave hints here at the habit of some hosts of not providing the same fare for all their guests, cf., for example, Plin. *Ep.* ii. 6: Pliny goes out to dinner and finds that the host has three different grades of wine, one for himself and a favoured few, another for the rest of the free-born guests, and a third for the freedmen. In rejecting this system Pliny claims that he invites his guests 'ad cenam, non ad notam'.

For the claim that the phrase is derived from an Oriental proverb 'The wine is the master's, the thanks the butler's' see M. Hadas, *AJP* l (1929), 378 ff.

§ 3 tandem ergo : Petronius' style often contains swift transitions from one scene to another. Friedlaender, however, suspected that phrases like *ergo, tandem ergo, autem tandem* were inserted by an interpolator after a passage had been omitted: cf. 53. 11 *petauristarii autem tandem* . . .; 61. 1 *postquam ergo* . . .; 64. 13 *repressus ergo.* . . . It should be pointed out that Buecheler and Friedlaender tended to be too bold in their assumption that *H* suffered from extensive lacunae.

pueris Alexandrinis : to the Romans the Alexandrians represented luxury and corruption: cf. Caes. *BC* iii. 110. 2 'in consuetudinem Alexandrinae vitae ac licentiae venerant', Quint. i. 2. 7 'verba ne Alexandrinis quidem permittenda deliciis'.

aquam ... nivatam : ice and snow were used in antiquity for chilling drinks (see R. J. Forbes, *Studies in Ancient Technology*, vol. vi, 108 ff., T. R. Glover, 'Iced Water', in *The Challenge of the Greeks*, 110 ff.) but even this practice, less ostentatious than Trimalchio's, earned the disapproval of moralists; cf., for example, Plin. *NH* xix. 55 'hi nives, illi glaciem potant poenasque montium in voluptatem gulae vertunt. servatur algor aestibus excogitaturque ut alienis mensibus nix algeat'; Sen. *Ep.* 78. 23.

paronychia : normally the care of finger- and toe-nails was one of the tasks of the barber; cf. Plaut. *Aul.* 312 'quin ipsi pridem tonsor unguis dempserat'; Mart. xiv. 36.

§ 7 pantomimi : the *pantomimus* was a solo performer who danced and mimed to an instrumental or choral accompaniment (cf. Balsdon, *Life and Leisure*, 274 ff.). This form of entertainment won extravagant acclaim, but stricter critics thought it tended to deprave audiences; cf. Sen. *Ep.* 47. 17 'ostendam nobilissimos iuvenes mancipia pantomimorum; nulla servitus turpior est quam voluntaria'; Plin. *Pan.* 46. 4 'effeminatas artes et indecora saeculo studia'.

§ 8 allata est ... lauta : although he seems to disapprove of the noise in Trimalchio's house, Encolpius is impressed with the quality of the hors-d'œuvre (*gustatio*) now set before him. The use of *lauta* here, followed so quickly by *lautitiis* in 32. 1, shows that at least at this point he is being credited with a naïve admiration (as at 29. 1–2 in the incident of the painted dog), and *tamen* should be given its normal adversative force.

locus novo more primus : the plan given below takes account of some of the guests, but does not find places for the freedmen introduced in chs. 41–6. It agrees in most respects with Sedgewick's plan, but he mistakenly describes the *locus libertinus* as *imus in imo* (see 38. 11 n.), and places Ascyltos beside Hermeros despite 57. 2.

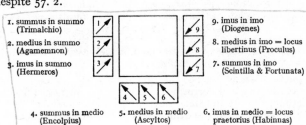

1. summus in summo (Trimalchio)
2. medius in summo (Agamemnon)
3. imus in summo (Hermeros)

9. imus in imo (Diogenes)
8. medius in imo = locus libertinus (Proculus)
7. summus in imo (Scintilla & Fortunata)

4. summus in medio (Encolpius)
5. medius in medio (Ascyltos)
6. imus in medio = locus praetorius (Habinnas)

The context seems to require *locus novo more primus* to mean
'according to a new fashion the first (i.e. the end or top) place
was being kept'. Plut. *Mor.* 619 shows that the top place on
each couch (nos. 1, 4, and 7 in the diagram) was referred to as
ὁ πρῶτος τόπος (i.e. *locus primus*), and the top place on the most
important couch (*summus in summo*) would naturally be
referred to simply as *locus primus*. The place thus kept for
Trimalchio (no. 1) instead of the host's normal place, *summus
in imo* (no. 7) is convenient for his late arrival and for his tem-
porary absence (41. 9). The word-order has persuaded some
translators to give misleading renderings (e.g. 'and the place
of honor—reserved for the host in the modern fashion'
(Arrowsmith); 'ein seltsamer Ehrenplatz' (Ehlers)); but the
place of honour is the *imus in medio*, the *locus consularis* or
locus praetorius (no. 6), which is here reserved, in accordance
with custom, for the most important guest, Habinnas.

§ 9 promulsidari : 'entrée-dish'. The main course in a Roman
dinner was preceded by hors-d'œuvre, the *gustatio* or *gustus*
(cf. 34. 1 *gustatoria*), sometimes referred to as *promulsis* from
mulsum, the drink served at this stage (cf. 34. 1). The *gustatio*
could consist of such items as vegetables, olives, eggs, and shell-
fish (see Balsdon, *Life and Leisure*, 41).

Corinthius : of Corinthian bronze (see note on 50. 1).

bisaccio : 'double pannier'. The word occurs elsewhere only in
glosses and in ps.-Acron on Hor. *Sat.* i. 6. 106 (in feminine form
bistacia).

§ 10 nomen Trimalchionis . . . pondus : Greek and Roman silver
articles often had the weight, and occasionally the owner's
name, inscribed on them, but such inscriptions were seldom
prominent; cf. D. E. Strong, *Greek and Roman Gold and Silver
Plate*, 19.

ponticuli . . . ferruminati : 'little bridges soldered on to the
plate' (Heseltine).

glires : dormice were regarded as a delicacy by the Romans,
but they were by no means rare (see Varro *RR* iii. 15 on how to
rear and fatten them). In these sections Petronius wants us to
see Encolpius' whole-hearted enjoyment of a succulent dish, as
well as Trimalchio's extravagance.

§ 11 fuerunt . . . mali : 'there were also sizzling sausages which
rested on top of a silver grill, and underneath were plums with

pomegranate seeds.' On the craze for food served extremely
hot see Sen. *Ep.* 95. 25 'quid? illa purulenta et quae tantum
non ex ipso igne in os transferuntur iudicas sine noxa in ipsis
visceribus extingui?' Unless it is thought to be purely ornamental, the silver grill sounds impractical, but is not without
parallel in real life in antiquity: a few cooking-vessels of silver
have been found (cf. Strong, loc. cit.).

Neither plums nor pomegranates would strike the reader of
Petronius' day as being unusual; in fact, the point of the
description may lie in the fact that very ordinary foods are
served on rather unusual dishes.

Ch. 32

Now that the reader's interest has been aroused by numerous
details concerning Trimalchio's household, Petronius goes on
in the next few chapters to give for the first time a fuller picture
of Trimalchio himself.

§ 1 **minutissima** *L* (**munitissima** *H* 'piled high'): this reading,
with its slightly comic flavour, is supported by Apul. *Met.* x. 20:
'ac desuper brevibus admodum sed satis copiosis pulvillis aliis
nimis medicatis, quis maxillas et cervices delicatae mulieres
suffulcire consuerunt, superstruunt.'

expressit imprudentibus risum : 'forced a laugh from the un-
wary'. One of the few incontrovertible signs of Encolpius'
hostility or contempt for Trimalchio. See Introduction.

§ 2. The picture of Trimalchio is certainly meant to suggest
vulgar luxury and perhaps effeminacy as well. For signs of
effeminacy note (i) his tiny cushions (in Apul. *Met.* x. 20, cited
in § 1, similar cushions are provided by the woman who has
fallen violently in love with Lucius the ass); (ii) his choice of
scarlet, cf. Mart. i. 96. 6 f. 'qui coccinatos non putat viros esse /
amethystinasque mulierum vocat vestes'; (iii) the fringe on his
napkin. The occurrence of *Maecenatianus* as part of Trimalchio's name at 71. 12 has, however, helped to persuade various
commentators that in the present passage there is a particular
reference to Seneca's description of Maecenas (*Ep.* 114): 'hunc
esse qui in tribunali, in rostris, in omni publico coetu sic
apparuerit ut pallio velaretur caput exclusis utrimque auribus,
non aliter quam in mimo fugitivi divitis solent.' But note that
Maecenas, with his head completely covered, apart from his
ears, is compared to characters in a mime, presumably runa-
ways who have to cover their foreheads to conceal the marks

branded on them in servitude. Trimalchio, on the other hand, has exposed his whole head, which, whether bald (27. 1 *calvum*) or close-cropped (32. 2 *adrasum*), suggests the shaven head of the newly-freed slave. It is true that Maecenas' retinue, like Trimalchio's, includes *duo spadones* (Sen. *Ep.* 114. 6; *Sat.* 27. 3; for some evidence on eunuchs see Mayor on Juv. 10. 307), but this coincidence is no more significant than the fact that Cicero's opponent Piso, like Trimalchio, wears sandals at the wrong time, as well as wrapping up his head like Maecenas (Cic. *Pis.* 13 'involuto capite soleatum'; cf. 27. 2 above, *soleatus*). In any case, even if Petronius were deliberately echoing details from *Ep.* 114, it should not be forgotten that Seneca was there himself expressing contempt for Maecenas, so there can be no question of Petronius satirizing Seneca. The same argument applies to any resemblance between Trimalchio and Pacuvius (see opening note on ch. 78) or Calvisius Sabinus (see 59. 4–5 n.), and may help to suggest that nowhere does Petronius satirize Seneca.

laticlaviam : his tasselled napkin has the broad stripe appropriate to a senator's *tunica*. Martial (iv. 46. 17) notes a *lato variata mappa clavo* at the end of a list of trivial gifts which gratified an upstart.

§ 3 anulum . . . : in the Empire the wearing of rings reached ridiculous extremes; cf. Sen. *NQ* vii. 31 'in omni articulo gemma disponitur'; Quint. xi. 3. 142 'manus non impleatur anulis, praecipue medios articulos non transeuntibus'; Mart. xi. 59; Plin. *NH* xxxiii. 23 ff. These passages show that in fact Trimalchio is credited with a certain restraint. On the smallest finger of his left hand he wears a ring which although large is merely gilt; since, strictly speaking, the right to wear a gold ring was mainly confined to equestrians of free birth, gilt rings were common among those who combined ostentation with some regard for the law (cf. Plin. *NH* xxxiii. 23). On the last joint of the next finger he wears a gold ring but one ornamented with iron stars; this gives it the force of an amulet, for which this finger is appropriate (cf. *Catalogue of Finger Rings, Greek, Etruscan and Roman, in the British Museum*, ed. F. H. Marshall, xxii f.). When giving instructions for his tomb Trimalchio is less restrained: 71. 9 'cum anulis aureis quinque'. See also R. Browning in *CR* lxiii (1949), 12–14.

§ 4 armilla aurea : gold armlets often suggest regal or effeminate luxury; cf. Nepos *Dat.* 3. 1 'atque armillis aureis, ceteroque regio cultu', Plaut. *Men.* 530 ff. It is sometimes assumed that

Petronius must have had Nero in mind here, but even if it had been safe to satirize Nero, he could not have done so by giving Trimalchio a plain arm-band instead of the more unusual one once worn by Nero: cf. Suet. *Nero* 6. 4 '(serpentis exuvias) tamen aureae armillae ex voluntate matris inclusas dextro bracchio gestavit aliquamdiu.'

eboreo . . . conexo : 'a circlet of ivory fastened by a shining metal plate'.

Ch. 33

§ 1 sed ne diutius . . . : *H* is badly muddled at this point. The text printed here assumes that the form *absentivus*, which occurs nowhere else, was glossed in *H* by *absens*, and that the incorporation of this in the text led to the dislocation of *morae vobis* (along with *absens*) in *H*, and the wrong division of *absentivus* into *absenti vos* (the ending *-ivus* is sometimes claimed to be 'plebeian', cf. F. T. Cooper, *Word-Formation in the Roman Sermo Plebeius*, 105 ff.; none of the other adjectives with this ending in Petronius supports this view: *aestivus, captivus, fugitivus, furtivus, intempestivus*). Müller castigates editors for their *admirabilis credulitas* in accepting *absentivus*, but his argument that *absentius* in *l r t Memm.* has merely arisen by dittography after *diutius* fails to account satisfactorily for the readings in *H*.

permittitis : the present and the future indicative are each used occasionally as a courteous alternative for the imperative, mainly in colloquial or Vulgar speech, e.g. *CIL* iv. 3494 'itis, foras rixsatis.' See L.–H.–S. 311, 327.

§ 2 tesseris : probably this means dice, in which case the game could be the popular *ludus duodecim scriptorum*, which resembled backgammon. See R. G. Austin, 'Roman Board Games', in *Greece & Rome*, iv (1934–5), 24 ff., 76 ff.

rem . . . delicatissimam : 'the height of refinement'; as often elsewhere in the *Cena*, Encolpius observes rather than criticizes explicitly.

§ 3 omnium †textorum dicta : usually taken to stand for *omnia textorum dicta*, but the parallels cited all involve the word *genus*: 69. 8 'omnium genera avium', *Bell. Alex.* 28. 3 'variis generum (v.l. genere) munitionibus', Suet. *Claud.* 46 'ex omnium magistratuum genere' (see Löfstedt, *Peregr.* 293 and *Synt.* ii. 109). The allusion to weavers has been explained in several ways. (i) They may have been notorious for their bad language. This view, however, has been supported only by the unsatisfactory evidence of Mart. xii. 59. 6 'hinc instat tibi textor, inde fullo.' (ii) The triviality of their conversation may be meant, cf. Arnob. v. 14 'textriculas puellas taediosi operis circumscribentes moras'. (iii) Gothein (*Sitzber. Heidelb. Akad.*, 1912, 4, 3–7), noting that gamblers as they shake the dice often mutter some regular formula in the hope of getting a lucky throw, suggests that Trimalchio intones a weaving-song for this purpose. As well as being over-ingenious, this explanation makes *dicta* unnatural and leaves *omnium* difficult. None of these interpretations inspires much confidence, but no certain emendation has been proposed. J. H. Simon's *tesserariorum* 'dice-players' (cf. *lusorum* Burmann, *aleatorum* Hildebrand ad Apul. *Flor.* 18) has the merit of making *omnium* easier to understand, and it is less devious than Gothein's interpretation discussed above.

§§ 4–5. The peacock and its eggs were delicacies, but their rarity should not be exaggerated. Varro gives the price of their eggs as five *denarii* each in his day (*RR* iii. 6. 6), and he also mentions that it was a common practice to have them hatched out by farmyard hens (iii. 9. 10). Trimalchio's ingenuity consists in his use of an imitation hen along with imitation eggs which are more exotic than they seem at first sight; furthermore the fig-peckers concealed under imitation egg-shell are served with real yolk.

   In the course of the *Cena* we find numerous examples of foods which turn out to be not quite what they had seemed. In particular various fancifully shaped pastries are mentioned: 40. 4 'porcelli ex coptoplacentis facti', 60. 4 'Priapus a pistore factus', 69. 6 'turdi siliginei'. Note also Apicius' boast at the end of his recipe for *patina de apua sine apua*: 'ad mensam nemo agnoscet quid manducet' (iv. 2. 12).

§ 5 scaenam : 'scene, tableau'. Trimalchio is portrayed as a kind of theatrical producer, eager to entertain his audience with a series of swift-moving scenes as in a comedy or mime.

§ 6 cochlearia : the *cochlear* was a spoon with a point at one end and a little cup at the other, used for eating snails, eggs, etc. It was normally very light—Martial complains (viii. 71. 10) that a friend is now so niggardly that he has sent him a *cochlear* lighter than a needle; in contrast, Trimalchio's spoons, weighing half a pound each, are enormous.

farina pingui : probably pastry made from flour and oil (Apic. vi. 5. 6 has *farina oleo subacta*, but that seems to mean a paste rather than pastry).

§ 8 persecutus putamen manu : 'I went over the shell with my hand'; cf. Cic. *Pis.* 53 'dum omnes solitudines persequeris'.

ficedulam : the fig-pecker (beccafico) is occasionally mentioned as a dainty morsel. Gourmets are said to have advised that this is the only bird which should be served up whole (Favonius ap. Gell. xv. 8. 2). It appears twice in the extensive lists of hors-d'œuvre for the sumptuous pontifical banquet described in Macrobius *Sat.* iii. 13. 11–12.

vitello : 'yolk of egg'.

Ch. 34

§ 1. Suetonius records (*Aug.* 74) that Augustus used sometimes to arrive at dinner after other people had begun (and to leave before they had finished), but he implies that this was a sign of his moderate tastes; by contrast Petronius hints here at a hold-up in the proceedings while the vulgar Trimalchio catches up with the others.

mulsum : wine with honey added, a drink usually taken along with the *gustatio* or *promulsis*.

§ 3 supellecticarius : Dousa, 'slave in charge of dishes and furnishings'. This word occurs in *Dig.* xxxiii. 7. 12. 31. *lecticarius HL* is suspected on the ground that a person as extravagant as Trimalchio could be expected not to use the same slave for such different functions. It is true firstly that he is shown elsewhere as displaying *inaequalitas* (see 52. 11), and secondly that occasionally even in comfortable households a similar doubling of functions is mentioned as occurring, sometimes as a sign of meanness: in Atticus' household every footman (*pedisequus*) could read or copy books (Nep. *Att.* 13), and Piso is accused of being so stingy that in his house 'idem coquus, idem atriensis' (Cic. *Pis.* 67). But here *lecticarius* would make the reader wonder how Encolpius could know that this slave was a litter-bearer, yet it would not have sufficient point to justify it (contrast Encolpius' description of a fellow guest as *veterem convivam* at 33. 8 although he has not been mentioned previously).

verrere : this verb sometimes has as its object the articles swept up rather than the place from which these are swept, cf. Mart. ii. 37. 1, Cic. ap. Quint. vi. 3. 55 'futurum ut omnia verreret'. The change to *everrere* (Goesius) is therefore not necessary, although it gives a double cretic ending.

§ 4 **Aethiopes capillati** : 'long-haired Ethiopian boys' (for *capillati* see note on 27. 1). This is probably meant to sound incongruous, Ethiopians normally having short curly hair; Herodotus, however, mentions straight-haired Ethiopians also (vii. 70). Encolpius is reminded of the attendants whose job it was to sprinkle the surface of the arena with water to keep down the dust and to freshen the air.

vinum : Plutarch (*Phocion* 20) tells of Phocion's distaste for a luxurious banquet at which the water for washing the guests' feet was mixed with wine and spices.

§ 5 **obiter et . . . facient** : 'incidentally even those stinking slaves won't make us so hot by crowding round.' In contrast, once the party has reached the maudlin stage, Trimalchio declares his sympathy for slaves: ' "amici," inquit "et servi homines sunt et aeque unum lactem biberunt" ' (71. 1).

§ 6 **Falernum Opimianum . . .** : Pliny (*NH* xiv. 55) states that some of the famous vintage of Opimius' consulship (121 B.C.) survived to his day but could be used only to give body to younger wine. B. Baldwin suggests (*AJP* lxxxviii (1967), 173–5) that Trimalchio's vulgarity here consists in serving as a choice beverage by itself an old wine normally used by then merely as a seasoning.
Everyday wines could bear an inscription showing their age rather than the date of production, just as whisky today may be labelled, for example, 'twenty years old' as a guarantee of its maturity. Roman inscriptions of this kind, however, relate to wine only a few years old. Both through the choice of *centum* and through the addition of the remote consular date the label on Trimalchio's wine extends this practice absurdly.

§ 7 **tangomenas faciamus** : this phrase, which recurs at 73. 6, must mean something like 'let's drink our fill' each time. No satisfactory explanation of *tangomenas* has yet been proposed, although the ending *-omenas* resembles a Greek middle or passive participle. As for the stem, two types of suggestion have been made: (i) the Greek τέγγω 'dip', 'soak', could fit (cf. Alcaeus *fr.* 39), if we supply some feminine noun, e.g. *epulas* or *potiones*. Presumably the word was confused with the familiar *tangere*. (ii) *tangere* itself may fit, cf. 66. 3 'de melle me usque tetigi', Apic. viii. 2. 1 'cervum coctum intro foras tanges'; but the use of a Greek ending then becomes puzzling. The best that can be claimed for such explanations is that they are not patently absurd. It should be added that the phrase may form part of a hexameter, so it may be that Trimalchio is quoting some familiar tag.

§ 8 larvam argenteam : Herodotus (ii. 78) and Plutarch (*Mor.* 357 f) describe an Egyptian custom of bringing out a skeleton or something similar at a feast as a reminder of the fragility of human life. A cup in the Bosco Reale treasure from Pompeii has several skeletons on it, with the inscription ζῶν μετάλαβε· τὸ γὰρ αὔριον ἄδηλον ἔστι, i.e. 'join in while you are alive, for tomorrow is uncertain' (for an illustration see M. Rostovtzeff, *Soc. and Econ. Hist. of the Roman Empire*, plate vii).

sic aptatam . . . : 'made so that its joints and backbone could be moved freely and turned in every direction'. Heinsius's conjecture *luxatae* gives better sense than *laxatae H.* The two words are sometimes confused in manuscripts, e.g. at Plin. *NH* viii. 179.

§ 10. This combination of two hexameters and one pentameter occurs occasionally in Greek and Latin epitaphs, e.g. Kaibel, *Epigrammata Graeca* 558, 5–7 (Rome), 309 (Smyrna), Buecheler and Lommatzsch, *Carm. Lat. Epigr.* 428, 13–15 (Stabiae). No doubt the material in these epitaphs is conventional, but the fact that the first of them comes from a physician's memorial to his wife is a warning not to assume that this combination necessarily betrays a striking lack of education.

esse bene : 'enjoy ourselves'. In familiar language *esse* is used with an adverb where the adjective would be regular, e.g. 59. 1 'suaviter sit potius'. See L.–H.–S. 170 f., Hof. *LU* 166.

Ch. 35

§ 1 laudationem : this is too bald to satisfy (contrast 48. 7 'haec aliaque cum effusissimis prosequeremur laudationibus'), and Müller is justified in suspecting a lacuna.

§ 2. For discussions of the astrological dish described in the following sections see S. Gaselee, *A Collotype Reproduction of the Codex Traguriensis*, 17 ff., J. G. W. M. de Vreese, *Petron 39 und die Astrologie*, and K. F. C. Rose and J. P. Sullivan, 'Trimalchio's Zodiac Dish', in *CQ* xviii (1968), 180–4. Despite Encolpius' assertion that *novitas tamen omnium convertit oculos*, the idea of having an astrological dish can hardly have been unknown to Petronius' readers, for Athenaeus (ii. 60) quotes from Alexis (fourth to third century B.C.): 'There was set before us a platter with a marvellous smell of the Seasons, shaped like the hemisphere of Heaven's vault. For all the beauties of the constellations were on it—fish, kids, the scorpion running between them, while slices of egg represented the stars' (tr. Gulick). The lack of originality is perhaps meant to emphasize the pretentiousness of Trimalchio's dish even more than Encolpius' naïvety.

§ 3 **cicer arietinum :** 'ram's head chick-pea'. Here the resemblance between the sign of the zodiac and the item of food is one of shape; cf. Plin. *NH* xviii. 124 'est enim [sc. one type of chick-pea] arietino capiti simile, unde ita appellant'; but an obscene sense of the phrase may also be hinted at; cf. Sophilus ap. Athen. ii. 54.

bubulae frustum : 'a slice of beef'. Here the item of food is so obvious that it warns us not to demand too much subtlety in the cases in § 4 where the text is doubtful.

super geminos testiculos ac rienes : the connection here is obvious enough, but it is made more obvious by the occurrence elsewhere of *gemini*, like the Greek equivalent οἱ δίδυμοι, in the sense of 'testicles'; cf. *Anth. Pal.* v. 105, LXX *Deut.* 25: 11.

coronam : Trimalchio explains this at 39. 8.

super leonem ficum Africanam : as in the preceding case, the link is astrological: figs ripen when the sun is under the sign of the Lion. The excellence of African figs is mentioned in Plin. *NH* xv. 69.

steriliculam : 'barren sow's womb'; dimin. of *sterilis* (sc. *vulva de porca virgine*). See Heraeus, p. 102. Apicius' recipes for this occur in book vii, which is reserved for extravagant dishes.

§ 4 **scriblita . . . placenta :** *placenta* was a kind of cake, of which, according to Cato *RR* 76, the main ingredients were flour, groats, cheese, and honey; *scriblita* had the same ingredients except that it had no honey (ib. 78).

[pisciculum marinum] : the most obvious article of food here would be the scorpion-fish, but *super scorpionem scorpionem* (Scheffer) would be too inane even for this context. It is possible that instead of naming this fish Petronius might have written 'the sea-fish named scorpion'; the diminutive *pisciculum*, however, would not suit this. It is simpler to assume that *pisciculum marinum* is a gloss which has replaced the name of some smaller scorpion-like fish.

oclopetam : for discussion of the reading here see Heraeus, pp. 98–100, 190 n., Rose and Sullivan, l.c. The first part of the word should be accepted (see note on 39. 11 for the astrological connection between Sagittarius and the eyes). *oclopetam* was plausibly interpreted by Heraeus as 'crow' (Rose and Sullivan wrongly claim that crow is inedible) on the evidence of Isid. *Etym.* xii. 7. 43 'corvus: hic prior in cadaveribus oculum petit' (cf. the use of ὀφθαλμοβόρος of the heron in Arist. *HA* 617ᵃ9). Buecheler suggested *oclopectam*, i.e. with fixed or staring eyes; this word occurs as the name of a racehorse (A. Audollent, *Defixiones* 459); in support of this conjecture see Heraeus, and also P. B. Corbett in *CP* lxiv (1969), 112 f. (who, however, suggests the meaning 'eye-jelly'). Rose and Sullivan prefer *oculatam*, the name of a fish occurring in Plin. *NH* xxxii. 149, but this seems too straightforward to have been corrupted.

locustam marinam : 'lobster'. The words *in quo cornua erant* must be a gloss on *locustam* which has been wrongly attached to *capricornum*. For the *cornua*, presumably claws, of lobsters cf. Plin. *NH* ix. 95.

Gaselee replaced *pisciculum marinum* with *locustam*, arguing firstly that the lobster is the marine parallel of the scorpion, and secondly that there may be a reference to the woman poisoner Locusta or Lucusta active during Nero's reign (note also 39. 11 'in scorpione venenarii et percussores'). Rose and Sullivan support this transposition, while apparently rejecting the alleged reference to Locusta. After *capricornum* they substitute *caprum et cornutam* (καπρός 'boar-fish', Arist. *HA* 535ᵇ18), but there seems to be no justification for their claim that a double *rebus* is required by the compound nature of the sign of Capricorn.

§§ 6–7. Some words must have fallen out after *panem*: *ipse* presumably refers to Trimalchio, but no warning is given of any change of subject after *circumferebat Aegyptius puer. ipse* = 'the master' occurs in the *Cena*, but only in the speech of the freedman guests; cf. 63. 3, 69. 3, 75. 11.

The missing words may also have contained an explanation of the puzzling phrase *ad tam viles . . . cibos*. This suits several of the items in the zodiac dish, but is quite inappropriate for others, especially *steriliculam* and *duos mullos*. Rose and Sullivan think that it may be another example of Encolpius' rather ponderous irony, but this interpretation would fit only if *all* the items of food were of great value. The missing words may have described Encolpius' disappointment at discovering that everything on the dish was made of pastry or something similar; cf. 40. 4 'porcelli ex coptoplacentis facti', and note on 69. 9. This would help to explain 39. 3 'rogo, me putatis illa cena esse contentum, quam in theca repositorii videratis?'

§ 6 **clibano** : a vessel in which bread was baked (cf., for example, Plin. *NH* xviii. 105), so we see here the same love of foods served extremely hot and the same affectation of impractical luxury as in the case of the silver grill in 31. 11.

Laserpiciario mimo : 'the mime called *The Silphium Gatherer*'. No mime of this name is recorded elsewhere, but similar titles occur, e.g. the *Centonarius* of Laberius. Mimes won enormous popularity through the exploitation of farcical, obscene, or melodramatic situations, and were the equivalent of today's 'Top Ten' popular tunes; cf. Balsdon, *Life and Leisure*, 276 ff., Beare, *The Roman Stage*, 149 ff.

§ 7 **ius cenae** : Trimalchio makes a feeble statement, 'This is the rule for dinner', but the reader is reminded of the familiar pun which depends on the other meaning of *ius* viz. gravy, juice; cf. Varr. *RR* iii. 17. 4 'hos piscis nemo cocus in ius vocare audet', Cic. *Verr.* i. 121 'ius Verrinum'. Friedlaender, following Reiske, rejected *ius* and interpreted *hoc est in(itium) cenae* in *H* as a gloss; this leaves *suadeo cenemus* without much point.

Ch. 36

§ 2 **[scilicet in altero ferculo]** : probably an explanatory gloss, although the deletion produces a hiatus and removes a double cretic clausula. For *scilicet* in other suspected glosses cf. 16. 3 'illa scilicet quae paulo ante cum rustico steterat', 63. 7 'quia . . . manus'.

sumina : 'sow's udders'. Pliny (*NH* xi. 211) shows the care taken to have these in prime condition for the table: the udder of a sow killed the day after farrowing is best, provided that it has not suckled its young.

leporem : praised by Martial xiii. 92:

> inter aves turdus, si quid me iudice certum est,
> inter quadrupedes mattea prima lepus.

§ 3 **Marsyas** : the serving-plate now revealed has representations of the satyr Marsyas with a wineskin over his shoulder, as in the well-known statue in the Roman forum (cf. Hor. *Sat.* i. 6. 120).

Water-spouts with figures on the ends were familiar in antiquity, with the water flowing from some convenient part of the body; cf. *Dig.* xix. 1. 17. 9 'et personas ex quorum rostris aqua salire solet'. But here the gravy flows from the wineskins (*utriculis* should be taken as a diminutive of *uter*, not *uterus*).

garum : a sauce made by pickling the entrails of fish until they putrefied (see André, *L'Alimentation*, 198 ff. for details). Since the preservation of meat, etc., in good condition was almost impossible, the Romans reacted by developing a taste for very highly seasoned dishes. For *garum piperatum* cf. Apicius vii. 15. 1, and note the occurrence of the word πιπερόγαρον in the sixth-century-A.D. writer Alexander Trallianus (i. 15).

euripo : the name Euripus, properly the straits between Boeotia and Euboea, came to be applied to any artificial canal, such as an ornamental channel in a garden, and here apparently to a channel running round the rim of the tray.

§ 4 damus omnes plausum . . . : another peculiarity of Trimalchio's household: the slaves give the cue to the guests when it is time to applaud. But Petronius manages here as elsewhere to hint at the enthusiasm, if not gluttony, with which Encolpius attacks the food.

§ 5 methodio : 'piece of ingenuity' (Sullivan); hap. leg., dimin. of μέθοδος, which sometimes means a trick or stratagem.

§ 6 scissor : see Juvenal 5. 120 ff. on the skill demanded of the carver:

> structorem interea, ne qua indignatio desit,
> saltantem spectes et chironomunta volanti
> cultello, donec peragat dictata magistri
> omnia; nec minimo sane discrimine refert
> quo gestu lepores et quo gallina secetur.

essedarium : 'chariot-fighter'. Experience of the British and Gallic practice of fighting from chariots had led to the introduction of this type of combat in gladiatorial shows at least as early as the reign of Caligula (cf. Suet. *Calig.* 35. 3).

hydraule : player of a water-organ, an instrument whose invention is ascribed to Ctesibios of Alexandria (third century B.C.); cf. Plin. *NH* vii. 125, Athen. iv. 174. Some have seen here an allusion to Nero's interest in water-organs (see Suet. *Nero* 41. 2 'quosdam e primoribus viris domum evocavit, transactaque raptim consultatione reliquam diei partem per organa novi

et ignoti generis circumduxit', cf. ibid. 54), but it is clear
from Suetonius, as well as from, for example, Cic. *Tusc.* iii. 43
and Vitr. i. i. 9 that these instruments had already become
popular and that no special reference to Nero is meant.

§ 7 'Carpe, Carpe' : the point here lies partly in Encolpius' inability to see the joke even where he suspected some *urbanitas*,
as well as in Trimalchio's feeble sense of humour (see, for
example, the *apophoreta* in ch. 56). P. Grimal (*Rev. Phil.* xv
(1941), 19 f.) thought that Petronius could expect his readers
to detect a reference to a particular Carpus named in *CIL* vi.
143 as Aug. lib. Pallantianus, who may have passed into Nero's
possession; the name occurs quite frequently, however, in
inscriptions; cf. *TLL* s.v.

The repetition of a word is often used as here to make an
address more emphatic or urgent; cf. 49. 4 'quid? quid? ... voca
voca', 25. 1 'ita ita'. This should be distinguished from repetition
intended to strengthen the basic meaning of the word; cf. 37. 3
'modo modo'. See E. Wölfflin, 'Die Gemination im Lateinischen',
in *Ausgew. Schr.* 285 ff., Hof. *LU* 58 ff., and L.–H.–S. 26, 808.

Ch. 37

Encolpius' failure to recognize his host's wife provides a drama-
tic motivation for the insertion of the next two chapters, with
their revelations of the life and language of Trimalchio's circle.
The situation imagined by Petronius may have resembled
reality more than we might think: Pliny (*Ep.* ix. 23. 4) shows
no surprise at the fact that at a dinner-party which he attended
at least one of his fellow guests had never met him before and
yet was not then formally introduced (see Sherwin-White ad
loc.).

§ 2 nummos modio metitur : proverbial expression for the possession of great wealth, cf. Xen. *Hell.* iii. 2. 27 Ξενίαν τὸν
λεγόμενον μεδίμνῳ ἀπομετρήσασθαι τὸ παρὰ τοῦ πατρὸς ἀργύριον, and Otto
s.v. *modius*.

§ 3 modo modo : 'just a little while ago'; cf. Sen. *Dial.* x. 18. 5,
Mart. ii. 57. 7. Here the repetition intensifies, taking the place
of a superlative, as with the Italian *pian piano* 'very softly',
Mod. Greek καλὸς καλός. See also note on 36. 7 *Carpe, Carpe*, and
E. Wölfflin, *Ausgew. Schr.* 285 ff.

ignoscet mihi genius tuus : the future is sometimes used as
a courteous alternative for the imperative, e.g. Cic. *Att.* ix. 6A

'festinationi meae brevitatique litterarum ignosces', cf. Hof.
LU 132. Here the courtesy is reinforced by the replacement of
the second person by the third person, used with an abstract
noun or at least its equivalent. This type of expression is rare
in classical Latin but it becomes more frequent amid the for-
mality of the imperial court, e.g. Plin. *Ep.* x. 1. 1 'tua quidem
pietas, imperator sanctissime, optaverat'; cf. L.–H.–S. 746 f.,
J. Svennung, *Anredeformen* 112 ff.

In popular belief each person had an individual attendant
deity, a *genius* in the case of a man, a *Iuno* in the case of a
woman. This belief may in earlier times have been shared by
Romans of high or low status; cf. Sen. *Ep.* 110. 1 'ita tamen
hoc seponas volo ut memineris maiores nostros qui crediderunt
Stoicos fuisse; singulis enim et Genium et Iunonem dederunt';
but by the time of Petronius it had become a sign of servile
origin to refer in conversation to someone else's *genius* or *Iuno*;
cf. 53. 3 'Gai nostri genio', 57. 10, 62. 14, 75. 2, Sen. *Ep.* 12. 2
(sc. vilicus) 'iurat per genium meum', Hor. *Ep.* i. 7. 94, Prop.
iv. 8. 69.

noluisses . . . accipere : a similar proverb occurs in Greek: παρ'
ἧς τὸν ἄρτον ἡ κύων οὐ λαμβάνει. Hermeros' way of using it might
seem rude, for he says 'You wouldn't have . . .' instead of
'(even) a dog wouldn't have . . .'. Hence comes the need for the
apologetic courtesy of *ignoscet mihi genius tuus.*

§ 4 nec quid nec quare : 'God knows how or why' (Arrowsmith).
Perrochat points out that this expression is characteristic of
vulgar speech both in its abridgement (the verb is omitted) and
in the alliterative pleonasm *quid . . . quare.*

in caelum abiit : 'she's on top of the world' rather than 'she
feels on top of the world'. See Shackleton Bailey's note on Cic.
Att. ii. 9. 1 'in caelo sum.'

Trimalchionis topanta est : 'she's Trimalchio's one and only',
cf. Hdt. i. 122 ἦν τέ οἱ ἐν τῷ λόγῳ τὰ πάντα ἡ Κυνώ, Liv. xl. 11. 4
'Demetrius iis unus omnia est.' The explanation of the change
from τὰ πάντα to *topanta* is unknown; Süss implausibly suggests
the influence of τόπος.

§ 5 ad summam : 'in short', cf. § 10. The recurrence of the phrase
at 57. 3, 9 and 58. 8 supports the conventional identification
of the present speaker with Hermeros, the freedman whose
tirades occupy chs. 57–8. See also note on 57. 1 'is ipse qui
supra me discumbebat'.

mero meridie : *meridius* is not formed from *merus* but from *medius*, but the repetition *mero meri-* was probably felt to have the same intensifying force as *modo modo* in § 3.

For the thought cf. Cic. *Att.* i. 1. 1 'si iudicatum erit meridie non lucere', Prop. iv. 1. 143 'illius arbitrio noctem lucemque videbis', Otto s.v. *sol* (4).

§ 6 saplutus : hap. leg., from the Greek ζάπλουτος 'very rich'. For the change from ζ to s cf. *CIL* i. 1047 (Setus from Zethus).

lupatria : almost certainly this is a hybrid formation from the Latin *lupa* (lit. 'she-wolf', but long familiar in the sense 'prostitute') with a Greek suffix. It may be formed on the analogy of the Greek πορνεύτρια from πόρνη.

est ubi non putes. est . . . : this text, suggested by Müller in his second edition, runs better than that of *H*, whether that is punctuated *et ubi non putes est.* (Burmann) or *et ubi non putes. est . . .* (Buecheler).

§ 7 sicca sobria : for this collocation cf. Sen. *Ep.* 18. 4, 114. 3, and Mart. xii. 30. 1

> siccus sobrius est Afer; quid ad me?
> servum sic ego laudo, non amicum.

So no doubt Petronius has deliberately made Hermeros use a cliché here.

tantum auri vides : bracketed by some editors and transposed by others to precede *nummorum nummos*. No change is necessary, however: in order to prove the prudence and wisdom of Fortunata the speaker remarks, 'You see all this gold', just as at 38. 5 he says, 'vides tot culcitas', before concluding, 'tanta est animi beatitudo.'

pica pulvinaris : perhaps 'a magpie on a couch'. This phrase, coming just after *est tamen malae linguae*, probably refers either to the chattering tongue of the *pica*, suggested by the use of alliteration, or to its ability to repeat what it has heard, cf. Plin. *NH* x. 118 (quoted in note on 28. 9), rather than to its acquisitive nature. The expression belongs to a type in which the adjective is used to give an unusual setting to the noun (often a proper noun); cf. Cic. *Pis.* 20 'lanternario consule' (and see Nisbet's note on 'barbaro Epicuro' in the same sentence).

§ 8 quantum milvi volant : proverbial expression for a great area or distance; cf. Pers. 4. 26 'dives arat Curibus quantum non milvus oberrat' (Schol. 'secundum proverbium, quantum milvi volant'). *H* has *qua*, but the form of the proverb given by the Persius scholiast justifies Scheffer's change to *quantum*.

nummorum nummos : this expression may provide another example of the Greek flavour given to Hermeros' speech (see note on *babae babae* below) cf. Soph. *OC* 1238 κακὰ κακῶν, Aesch. *Pers.* 681, etc., although these phrases refer to quality, not to amount as in the present passage. Less plausibly, Hebrew influence has been given as the explanation here; in Christian Latin, phrases of this type, including some which refer to amount or number rather than quality, e.g. *saecula saeculorum*, must originate from Hebrew idiom. A native Latin idiom cannot be altogether discounted here, but only unsatisfactory parallels have been cited: *Carm. Saliar.* ap. Varr. *LL* vii. 27 'divum deo', Virg. *Catal.* 5. 6 f.

> 'tuque, o mearum cura, Sexte, curarum
> vale, Sabine.'

For discussion see M. Hadas, *AJP* l (1929), 378 ff., Süss, p. 8, L.–H.–S. 55 f., and note on 43. 8 *olim oliorum*.

§ 9 **babae babae** : an expression of surprise and admiration which is used with *geminatio* in its Greek form as well; cf. Nauck, *Tragicorum Graecorum Fragmenta*, p. 746 (Achaeus). It is one of a number of Latin exclamations which have been taken over from Greek, both through popular borrowings and through translations of comedy (see Hof. *LU* 23 ff. on *attatae, sophos, papae, pax, euge*, etc.). Hermeros is credited with a fondness for Greek expressions: see note on *topanta* in § 4 above, also 57. 11 *haec sunt vera athla*, 58. 7 *Athana, deuro de* (cf. Süss, pp. 59 ff.).

§ 10 **babaecalis** : this seems to mean rich or dissolute; cf. Arnob. iv. 22 'an uxore contentus una, concubinis pelicibus atque amiculis delectatus, impatientiam suam spargebat passim, ut babaecali adulescentes solent, salax deus'. The derivation of *-calis* is doubtful (καλός, καλῶς, καλῆς, and καλεῖν have all been put forward, but it may simply give a diminutive force to *babae*). Whichever of these is correct, the word implies criticism of those who use the word *babae*, which had just been used by Hermeros himself in § 9; cf. Alexis 206 οὐχὶ τῶν μετρίων ἀλλὰ τῶν βαβαὶ βαβαί. The group referred to by Hermeros is not clear; perhaps he is shown as already beginning to quarrel with Ascyltos.

in rutae folium coniciet : the literal meaning of this appears to be 'beat up along with a leaf of rue'. Hermeros uses this expression again at 58. 5. Even if an exact explanation of it is impossible, two points are clear: (i) *conicere* occurs as a t.t. in recipes and in prescriptions, e.g. 49. 5 'putes illum piper et cuminum non coniecisse'; Cels. vi. 7. 7 'acetum et cum eo nitri paulum coniciendum est.' (ii) *ruta* (rue) occurs as an ingredient in many recipes, e.g. Apicius v. 2. 1 'adicies in mortarium piper . . . rutam', Mart. xi. 31. 16 f. 'ut condat vario vafer sapore / in rutae folium Capelliana', and also in medical and veterinary prescriptions for both external and internal use, e.g. Plin. *NH* xxix. 30 'quidam et salem admiscent luxatis, alii cum lana rutam tritam adipemque imponunt, item contusis tumentibusque', Cato *RR* 70 (here the prescription specifies that rue-leaves and other ingredients should be macerated). The use of *in* here (as in Mart. l.c.) is puzzling (elsewhere we find, for example, *conicere in caccabum* or *in acetum*). Presumably it means 'add to', i.e. beat up along with. At any rate we should reject M. Johnston's suggestion (*Cl. Wkly* xix (1926), 157) that the phrase refers to the configuration of the rue-leaf; Friedlaender's view that *in rutae folium* was proverbial for a very confined space lacks proper support.

Ch. 38

§ 1 **domi nascuntur :** a common expression originating from the widespread ambition in the ancient world to have a self-supporting household; cf. Fraenkel ad Aesch. *Agam.* 961.

laina : *lana H.* P. A. George argues plausibly (*CQ* xvii (1967), 130) that we require something more exotic than *lana*, which may have come in from § 2 below, and proposes *laina*, the lentisk or mastic tree, cf. Plin. *NH* xii. 72.

cedria : 'resin from cedar'. *credrae H* should be regarded as a vulgar corruption either of *cedria* or of *cedrium* 'cedar-oil'. Note the spellings offered by the manuscripts at Plin. *NH* xxix. 47 *cedria R² cedra V R¹d.* Müller accepts instead Jacobs's conjecture *citrea* 'citrons'; this fruit was in fact somewhat different from our citron (Plin. *NH* xxiii. 105 speaks of it as almost inedible, cf. André, *L'Alimentation* 79 ff.). This change seems unnecessary, however: the context demands something rare, but cedar-resin or cedar-oil is appropriate.

piper : Pliny mentions one type of pepper-tree as being acclimatized in Italy by his time (*NH* xii. 29), but pepper was normally imported from the East. Its popularity can be judged from its extremely frequent appearances in the recipes of

Apicius, although it may be that sometimes the word *piper* is used in a generic sense of 'spice' rather than 'pepper'.

lacte gallinaceum : proverbial for something rare and valuable; the Greek equivalent is γάλα ὀρνίθων. See Otto s.v. *gallina*. The form *lacte* occurs as an alternative at various periods for the more literary *lac*.

§ 2 a Tarento : in classical Latin the prepositions *ab* and *ex* are used with the ablative of a place-name instead of the simple ablative where the sense required is 'from the neighbourhood of'. This sense would fit here and in § 3 *ab Athenis*, but in any case Sallust and Livy use these prepositions even where the movement is from the town itself, and this usage becomes commoner from the first century A.D. onwards, cf. L.–H.–S. 102 f.

On the fame of Tarentine wool cf. Mart. xiii. 125, Hor. *Od.* ii. 6. 10.

culavit : 'got them to bash his ewes'; hap. leg., formed from *culus* (cf. French *reculer*, Italian *rinculare*, and *apoculare* at 62. 3, 67. 3).

§ 3 meliusculae : diminutive forms of the comparative of this type are found in Plaut., Ter., Cic. *Epp.*, etc. (cf. Hof. *LU* 140, L.–H.–S. 772). Here, along with *vernaculae* and *Graeculis* (and possibly also *babaecalis*), it adds to the colloquial flavour.

§ 4 illi : here and in § 16 'cum timeret ne creditores illum conturbare existimarent' a form of *ille* replaces the reflexive *sibi* or *se*. In § 16 this could be explained merely by the wish to avoid ambiguity, just as *is* is sometimes used in classical Latin as a reflexive in subordinate clauses; but here *sibi* would not be ambiguous. Often, too, in the language of the freedmen in the *Cena*, *ille* replaces *is*, e.g. §§ 1 and 2 above. See L.–H.–S. 175, 191 f., Süss, p. 33.

semen boletorum : the exaggeration in ordering this from India gives sufficient point here, but there could be an added irony at Hermeros' or Trimalchio's expense if Petronius, like the Elder Pliny, regarded mushrooms as spontaneously generated; cf. *NH* xxii. 94 'origo prima causaque e limo et acescente suco madentis terrae aut radicis fere glandiferae', and see André, *L'Alimentation*, 45.

nam : used here as a formula of transition, introducing another point to prove that *omnia domi nascuntur*; cf. 56. 4 *nam mutae* *bestiae* . . ., and see Austin on Cic. *Cael.* 4, L.–H.–S. 505, K.–S. ii. 117.

§ 5 culcit[r]as : the intrusive *r* should be treated as a scribal error, rather than as a Vulgarism (cf. Spanish *colcedra*, Italian *coltrice*) given by Petronius to an uneducated speaker. It is true that *H* has *frustrum* at 66. 5 (Habinnas), as well as *credrae* in § 1 above; but note also 35. 3 *frustrum H* (narrative); cf. 59. 7 *frustra H* (again narrative) and 66. 7 *frusta H* (Habinnas), 98. 5 *culcitra L* (narrative).

conchyliatum aut coccineum tomentum : for the use of purple and scarlet in unconcealed grandeur and regal pomp see Suet. *Nero* 30. 3 'piscatus est rete aurato et purpura coccoque funibus nexis.'

§ 7 sucosi : 'loaded' (lit. 'juicy'). The form found in *H*, *succossi*, should probably, like *dignitossus* at 57. 10, be treated as another scribal error. Such forms have also been seen as a mannerism given to Hermeros, but his speech (like that of the other freedmen) also contains examples of the normal spelling: 57. 7 *laboriosus*, 57. 8 *lacticulosus* (*laeticulosus H*). If the forms in *-ossus* here and at 57. 10 are regarded as sound, *laboriosus* and *lacticulosus* should presumably be altered to make Hermeros' usage consistent.

vides illum : cf. Plin. *Ep.* ix. 23. 4 'vides hunc?' (see note at beginning of ch. 37).

sua : see note on *suum* in § 12 below.

de nihilo crevit : cf. 43. 1 *ab asse crevit*, 71. 12 *ex parvo crevit*.

§ 8 quomodo : in later Latin *quomodo* and *quemadmodum*, probably because of their fuller sound, gradually replace *ut* in such clauses; cf. L.–H.–S. 649, Elcock, p. 150.

Incuboni : a kind of gnome who guarded hidden treasures; by taking his cap one could force him to say where the treasure was. As for the suffix *-o, -onis*, Swanson, pp. 78 ff., claims that this is the most undeniably Vulgar Latin suffix of the classical period. Note especially the comic formations in 60. 8 *Cerdonem*, *Felicionem*, *Lucrionem*, and 58. 11 *Occuponem*.

[et] thesaurum invenit : *et* here is more likely to be a dittography after *rapuisset* than an example of the superfluous *et* which occurs in later Latin at the beginning of the main clause when a subordinate clause has preceded it. See L.–H.–S. 482.

§ 9 **subalapa** : 'something of a boaster'. This form, like Heraeus's *subalapo*, does not occur elsewhere but is based on the existence of *alapari* 'boast', which occurs in glossaries (see Heraeus, p. 110). Unduly forced explanations have been put forward by editors who retained *sub alapa H*: (i) 'he has only recently been given his freedom (and so is rather ostentatious); cf. *alapa*, blow, often used of the symbolic blow given by a master when he manumitted his slave; (ii) 'he's a bit touched' (lit. 'he has been struck', sc. by a *daemon*).

non vult sibi male : 'he doesn't mean to harm himself.'

§ 10 **cenaculum hoc titulo proscripsit** : 'he used this notice to advertise a garret.' Buecheler's *cenaculum* (cf. *oecum* Gronovius) assumes that *proscribere* is used with an accusative and a simple ablative as in § 16 below. Fraenkel and Fuchs think that *cum* originally introduced a clause explaining Diogenes' straitened circumstances, but this way of regularizing the construction is too drastic.

ex kalendis Iuliis : for evidence that 1 July was a regular starting-date for leases cf. Mart. xii. 32, *Dig.* xix. 2. 60.

§ 11 **libertino loco** : for notes on the seating at table see 31. 8. *libertino* is a little more likely than *libertini*: 65. 7 *praetorio loco* and Plut. *Mor.* 619 are better parallels than Sen. *Contr.* ix. 2. 2 'meretrix uxoris loco accubuit, immo praetoris.' The 'freedman's place', a phrase not found elsewhere, appears to be a technical term for the *medius in imo*, for Hermeros has just mentioned Diogenes as *imus in imo*, and Fortunata must be in the *summus in imo*, next to Habinnas, who sits *imus in medio*.

impropero : 'condemn'. This form, found here for the first time, occurs frequently in late Latin, and appears to be a Vulgar variant of *improbo*. The dative *illi* (cf. Vulg. *Matth.* 27: 44 'latrones improperabant ei') is possibly influenced by the construction of *invidere*.

§ 12 **sestertium suum vidit decies** : millions of sesterces can be expressed (i) by a numeral adverb + *centena milia sestertium* (= *sestertiorum*), e.g. *deciens centena milia sestertium* = 1,000,000; (ii) as in (i), but with *centena milia* omitted, e.g. 71. 12 'sestertium reliquit trecenties' = 30,000,000. Hermeros' idea of a fortune is more modest than others': cf., for example, Sen. *Ben.* 2. 27. 1 'hic qui quater milies sestertium suum vidit'. *suum* here and in § 7, as well as in Sen. l.c., is presumably a colloquialism.

non puto illum capillos liberos habere : 'I don't think he can call his hair his own' (Sullivan). In his note on Ter. *Phorm.* 661 Donatus cites a Greek proverb εἰ δὲ ὤφειλε τὰς χεῖρας;

omnia ad se fecerunt : presumably 'have done everything to suit their own interests' (for *ad* with the accusative in place of the *dativus commodi* see L.–H.–S. 86. 3).

§ 13 sociorum olla male fervet : probably = 'a pot which belongs to partners does not boil well.' A Jewish proverb gives a similar sense: 'A pot which is the common property of partners is neither cold nor hot.' It is doubtful, however, whether M. Hadas (*AJP* 1 (1929), 378–85, 'Oriental Elements in Petronius') is justified in claiming that Petronius has tried to give an Oriental flavour to the speech of these freedmen of Asiatic origin.

amici de medio : 'away go your friends', sc. *recedunt;* cf. Cic. *Rosc. Am.* 112. For the sentiment see Otto s.v. *amicus* (7).

§ 14 quod illum sic vides : 'as for your seeing him like this', i.e. in such reduced circumstances. This type of *quod* clause is quite common (cf. L.–H.–S. 573), but here its position at the end of the sentence is unusual.

libitinarius : 'undertaker'. This profession did not normally enjoy much esteem: cf. Val. Max. v. 2. 10 'hunc tam contemptum gregem'.

§ 15 apros gausapatos . . . : the text in *H* poses several problems. (i) Even if we allow for some disjointedness in Hermeros' speech, the items of food in this list seem unsatisfactory. The words *sic cenare quomodo rex* lead the reader to expect either an unbroken list of exotic foods (or even comically plebeian items) or else a list ending in an anticlimax, but the text in *H* provides neither of these. (ii) *apros gausapatos* 'boars in blankets' appears to be a technical term, but we have no way of telling whether it means, for example, boars served whole in their skins (cf. 'potatoes in their jackets'), pork sausages (cf. American 'pigs in blankets'), or even some fancy pastry shaped like boars (in this case *opera pistoria* would have to be deleted as a gloss). (iii) *opera pistoria* seems too vague for the context, and may be a gloss on *apros gausapatos* (see above) or on some lost item. (iv) *vis* is corrupt. Scheffer's *avis* is an easy change, but it is not enough by itself. Immisch's conjecture *avis bis coctos Pistorenses*, however, has the disadvantage that it removes *cocos pistores*, for which cf. Cic. *Rosc. Am.* 134.

phantasia, non homo : probably 'He's not a man—he's ostentation personified.' For this sense of *phantasia* cf. Polyb. xv. 25. 22, *Act. Ap.* 25: 23.

For this type of phrase cf. 43. 3 *discordia non homo*, 44. 6 *piper non homo*, 58. 13 *mufrius non magister*, 74. 13 *codex non mulier*, also, for example, Cic. *Att.* i. 18. 1, Cat. 115. 8, and in Greek Krobylos fr. 8K (= Athen. i. 5 f) κάμινος οὐκ ἄνθρωπος. See also Fraenkel, *Elem. Plaut.* 49.

§ 16 conturbare: 'was bankrupt'; see Fordyce on Cat. 5. 11.

Iulius : Proculus' gentile name shows that we should not take too precisely the word *collibertos* in § 6, which ought to mean that all these guests had once been slaves of the same master as Trimalchio (cf. § 10 C. Pompeius Diogenes, 71. 12 C. Pompeius Trimalchio Maecenatianus). It is needlessly complicated to assume that Proculus had been under more than one master.

Ch. 39

§ 2 suave faciatis : lit. 'you must make the wine pleasant (by your drinking it)' (cf. 48. 1 'vos illud oportet bonum faciatis'); a polite formula whereby the host compliments his guests while apologizing for the humble fare offered to them (cf. Mart. v. 78. 16 'vinum tu facies bonum bibendo', *Anth. Pal.* xi. 44, Nisbet and Hubbard on Hor. *Od.* i. 20 'vile potabis').

pisces natare oportet : probably 'The fish (which you have already eaten, cf. 36. 3) must have something to swim in.' The phrase 'Fish must swim' is in fact used in Scotland in this sense. A less likely interpretation is 'You must enjoy this just as surely as fish must swim.'

§ 3 sic notus Ulixes? : Virg. *Aen.* ii. 44 (where Laocoon warns the Trojans that the Greek fleet has not gone for good; surely they know the crafty Ulysses better than to imagine that?).

inter cenandum philologiam nosse : similarly the Younger Pliny says of a dinner which a friend had failed to attend: 'quantum nos lusissemus risissemus studuissemus' (*Ep.* i. 15. 3).

inter with the gerund occurs as early as Ennius but is rare before the Silver Latin period; cf. L.–H.–S. 233.

§ 4 hominem inter homines: 'as good as the next man', a phrase used several times in the *Cena*; cf. 57. 5, 74. 13.

fer[i]culus : one of a number of masculines replacing the normal neuter; cf. 41. 11 *balneus*, 41. 12 *vinus*, 42. 5 *fatus*, 57. 8 *lorus*.

Such changes point towards the subsequent disappearance of
the neuter from Romance languages; see Palmer, p. 160.

The unsyncopated form *fericulus* found in *H* should not be
retained. Even in narrative *H* has *fericulum* at 69. 7, but *HL*
have *ferculum* at 35. 1.

†ta mel habuit praxim† : *habuit praxim* is taken to mean 'has
given proof', but *praxis* does not occur elsewhere in Latin, and
the Greek πρᾶξις (= success, result, etc.) does not offer close
parallels for the required sense. If Jacobs's *apodixin* 'demonstration, proof' (cf. 132. 10, Quint. v. 10. 7) is substituted, or
even *dixin* (= δεῖξιν), which is not found elsewhere, Heraeus'
iam semel would be plausible, and J. H. Simon's *praebuit*
(*p̄buit*) is a possible improvement on *habuit*.

§ 5 ff. For the details of this passage see de Vreese's book (cited
in ch. 35). Trimalchio's pedantic accuracy in astrology, con-
forming to conventional beliefs although embroidered in places,
is contrasted with his striking ignorance of literature, history, etc.

§ 5 duodecim dii : the number twelve had long been convenient
astrologically. As for the identity of the gods included, Ennius
lists them as:

> Iuno, Vesta, Minerva, Ceres, Diana, Venus, Mars,
> Mercurius, Iovis, Neptunus, Vulcanus, Apollo,

but controversy occurs as early as Herodotus (ii. 43 and 145).

et modo fit aries : Trimalchio has the astrological dish in front
of him as he gives this exposition. He is perhaps imagined as
turning it round as he proceeds, as if it were a celestial sphere
(for the use of these see *RE* vii. 1. 1428 s.v. *Globen*). Like astrological writers, Trimalchio begins with Aries, and he keeps the
signs in their correct order. Shepherds and shamelessness
normally go under Aries, but the next detail is eccentric:
scholastici, instead of being put under Pisces like *rhetores*, are
put here out of place so that Trimalchio can poke fun at his
better-educated guests, Agamemnon and his friends.

scholastici : 'rhetoricians'.

arietilli : 'ram-like'. This word, used only here and to describe
a variety of chick-pea in Columella, is obscure. Trimalchio
might be hinting that rhetoricians meet like charging rams, or
possibly some obscene sense lies hidden.

§ 6 mathematici : 'astrologer'; cf. Tac. *Hist.* i. 22 'urgentibus
etiam mathematicis, dum novos motus et clarum Othoni annum

observatione siderum adfirmant, genus hominum potentibus
infidum, sperantibus fallax, quod in civitate nostra et vetabitur
semper et retinebitur'.

calcitrosi : self-willed people are placed under Taurus because
in representations of the zodiac Taurus alone faces backwards
and appears to go unwillingly.

bubulci : 'ploughmen'.

qui se ipsi pascunt : probably 'those who can maintain themselves without the help of others', rather than 'gluttons' (who
come under Leo). Trimalchio hints at the contrast between
himself and his guests, who are glad to accept dinner at his
expense.

§ 7. On the face of it this sign includes several items which form
natural pairs—*bigae, boves, colei*—but these may each have
some underlying reference to a type of person; e.g. *colei*, as well
as meaning 'testicles', a sense sometimes borne by *gemini* (see
note on 35. 3), apparently stands for 'lecherous men' (in Greek
astrological writers μοιχικοί come under Gemini). Certainly
qui utrosque parietes linunt should be taken here as referring
euphemistically to those who are equally adept in homosexual
or heterosexual relationships (cf. 43. 8 'omnis minervae homo').

§ 8 cancro : under Trimalchio's own sign, the Crab, astrologers
usually put merchants and others engaged in making profits.

ne genesim meam premerem : 'so that I should not cause my
natal star to sink'. *genesis*, a technical term in astrology (see
Mayor on Juv. 14. 248), here refers back to 35. 3, where only
a garland was placed over Trimalchio's sign.

§ 10 mulierosi : 'fond of women'; Firm. Matern. viii. 24. 6 includes under Virgo 'erunt elegantes, qui virginum concubitus
saepe sectentur.' *mulieres H* has been interpreted as 'effeminates'
(Firm. Matern. viii. 11. 1 also has under Virgo 'muliebrium
artium studiis deditus'). However, this sense of *mulieres*, if it
is ever possible, would here be obscure.

fugitivi : the constellation Virgo had according to legend previously been Erigone, who fled from earth at the end of the age
of gold.

compediti : Virgo stood near one of the knots (*nodi*) or cardinal
points of the zodiac, and in pictorial representations the feet
of Virgo appeared to be bound by this knot.

libra : here the links are more straightforward: astrologers naturally associated with this sign those whose work involved weighing things. Hence Burmann's *expendunt* is a certain correction for *expediunt*.

§ 11 **scorpione :** cf. Firm. Matern. viii. 26. 14 'erunt . . . venefici, ad neces hominum venena vendentes, ut multos interficiant.'

sagittario : Sagittarius was associated with afflictions of the eyes, including squints (cf. Firm. Matern. viii. 27. 11 'erunt unioculi, strabi'), and also with thieves, i.e. men who look one way while their attention is concentrated in another direction.

§ 12 **capricorno :** Capricorn was in astrology the 'house' of Saturn, and hence associated with those who endure hardships. The significance of the words *prae mala sua cornua nascuntur* remains obscure, but they may mean 'are cuckolded' cf. L.–S.–J. s.v. κέρας vi. It is less likely that they refer to the *Campanus morbus* (cf. Hor. *Sat.* i. 5. 58 ff.), characterized by excrescences on the head which might resemble the scars left when horns had been removed.

For *prae* with the accusative cf. 46. 1 *prae litteras*. No earlier occurrences have been noted, but the construction is common in late Latin, cf. L.–H.–S. 269.

copones : contrast the use of the classical form *caupo* in narrative, 98. 1. Innkeepers were often accused of putting too much water in their wine. Contrast the unusual innkeeper in Mart. iii. 57. 1–2:

> callidus imposuit nuper mihi caupo Ravennae:
> cum peterem mixtum, vendidit ille merum.

But they do not seem to be found associated with Aquarius in astrological writers.

cucurbitae : apart from its literal meaning, viz. 'gourd', this word can also mean a cupping-glass for bleeding, an activity put under Aquarius in Greek astrology, or a blockhead, a person with water on the brain.

§ 13 **obsonatores :** this word usually has the general sense of 'caterer', although it is derived from ὀψωνέω, which normally refers to the purchase of fish in particular. Trimalchio's friends are assumed to be capable of recalling the meaning of the Greek word, just as they are expected to understand the pun in *argentum sceleratum* in 56. 8.

rhetores : cf. Firm. Matern. viii. 30. 7 'erit orator advocatus affluentia docti sermonis ornatus.'

aliquid mali facit : this should be taken in its normal sense 'is up to some mischief', even though this means that Trimalchio classifies birth as well as death as an evil. The sentiment is conventional and gives a philosophical air to Trimalchio's remarks. Friedlaender and others preferred 'works some magic' (cf. *maleficium*), but this sense does not fit the context so well.

§ 15 tamquam favus : the word *bona* is ambiguous, but Trimalchio takes it to mean primarily property, hence he adds *tamquam favus*, which for him and for Phileros is a symbol of growth (cf. 43. 1, 76. 8).

Ch. 40

§ 1 sophos : Martial several times pokes fun at the use of this Greek adverb as an exclamation of applause for a forensic or literary performance; e.g. i. 76. 9 f. 'praeter aquas Helicon et serta lyrasque dearum / nil habet et magnum sed perinane "sophos" ', also iii. 46. 7 f. O. Hirschfeld is unconvincing in his speculation (*Philol.* li (1896), 470) that Martial vi. 48 ('quod tam grande sophos clamat tibi turba togata, / non tu, Pomponi, cena diserta tua est') is a reminiscence of the present passage.

sublatis manibus : a gesture of prayer, hence used as an extravagant expression of approval; cf. Cic. *Acad.* ii. 63, id. *Fam.* vii. 5. 2.

Hipparchum Aratumque : Aratus (third century B.C.) was highly regarded for his *Phaenomena*, a poem, still extant, dealing with astronomy (cf. *Anth. Pal.* ix. 25. 5 f. 'Let us count him second to Zeus, in that he made the stars brighter'); but Hipparchus (second century B.C.) in his commentary on it, also extant, criticized Aratus' descriptions, and even Cicero, who himself translated the *Phaenomena*, described Aratus as *homo ignarus astrologiae* (*de Orat.* i. 69).

homines : 'had not been fellows you could compare with him'. The word is awkward here, and is perhaps corrupt; Heinsius' *homini* is only slightly better. Müller deletes *homines*, but it is an unlikely gloss.

donec : like *cum* 'inversum', *donec* enables Petronius to make a swift transition to a new detail or topic (see note on 27. 1). Sometimes wrongly taken as introducing another main clause

with the sense 'thereupon' 'next' (cf. French *donc*); on this see
L.–H.–S. 630, K.–S. ii. 379.

toralia : normally these were valances hanging between the
feet of the couches (see D.–S. s.v. *torus*, G. M. A. Richter, *Furniture of the Greeks, Etruscans and Romans*, 119 and fig. 598).

proposuerunt : 'displayed'. *toris* seems to have been inserted
by a scribe who took *proposuerunt* (*praeposuerunt* Mentel)
in the sense 'placed in front of'; but it is more appropriate that
the servants should enter flaunting valances which are not
fixed in place, rather than somewhat mysteriously attaching
them to the couches some time after the dinner has begun.

subsessores : t.t. in hunting. These lay in wait for game which
had been hemmed in by nets; hence they were equipped with
venabula, spears suitable for close-quarter fighting, not with
amenta, javelins for throwing; see J. Aymard, *Chasses romaines*,
61, 225.

§ 2 et ecce : familiar and not confined to lower-class speech
(cf. New Testament Greek καὶ ἰδού), although the other three
instances of this combination in the *Cena* occur in the speech
of the freedmen: 45. 4 (Echion), 66. 4 (Habinnas), 76. 1 (Trimalchio). See Hof. *LU* 34 f., L.–H.–S. 482.

canes Laconici : Spartan dogs are often praised, especially as
hunting-dogs; cf. Virg. *Georg.* iii. 405 'velocis Spartae catulos',
Varr. *RR* ii. 9. 5.

§ 3 aper : a boar served whole would in itself be of no special
interest by this period: Pliny (*NH* viii. 210), after mentioning
that this dish was first served by P. Servilius Rullus, whose
son was a tribune in 63 B.C., adds 'tam propinqua origo nunc
cottidianae rei est.' It takes a greater extravagance than this
to rouse Juvenal: cf. 1. 140 f. 'quanta est gula, quae sibi totos /
ponit apros, animal propter convivia natum.'

et quidem pilleatus : again at 59. 6 an animal is served in
human dress: 'vitulus . . . et quidem galeatus'. The *pilleus*, a felt
cap, was worn by newly-manumitted slaves and appears on some
coins as a badge of freedom, but Roman citizens normally wore
it only at the time of the Saturnalia. On the significance of the
aper pilleatus see note on 41. 4.

palmulis : here applied to the leaves or branches of the date-
palm, not to its fruit (*palma* and φοῖνιξ similarly fluctuate in
sense). Palladius (iii. 27) mentions a palm-leaf basket used as
a colander.

caryotis ... thebaicis : 'juicy dates ... dry Egyptian dates'; cf. Plin. *NH* xiii. 43 ff. *caryotae* are mentioned several times as trivial gifts given by poor clients at the New Year; cf. Mart. viii. 33. 11, xiii. 27, Stat. *Silv.* iv. 9. 26.

§ 4. A dish known as *porcus Troianus,* in which an animal was brought to the table 'quasi aliis inclusis animalibus gravidum', was mentioned by Titius (mid second century B.C.), when he proposed a sumptuary law (see Macrob. *Sat.* iii. 13. 13); and Apicius viii. 7. 14 has a recipe for *porcellus hortolanus* in which the stuffing includes thrushes. Trimalchio's ingenuity is more curious: his boar purports both to be suckling pastry piglets and to be pregnant with live thrushes. Note, however, that despite the surprising pregnancy details Encolpius and his companion still refer to the animal as a male at 41. 1 ff.

coptoplacentis : *coptoplacenta* (cf. Greek κοπτός 'pounded', κοπτή, κοπτοπλακοῦς) was a kind of hard pastry or biscuit, perhaps identifiable with the *copta Rhodiaca* described by Martial (xiv. 69 'peccantis famuli pugno ne percute dentes: / clara Rhodos coptam quam tibi misit edat').

On the *porcelli* formed from this pastry see note on 33. 4–5.

apophoreti : the practice of handing over small gifts for guests to take away with them was common; see note on 56. 8 *apophoreta.* Elsewhere, however, the form which occurs is the neuter plural, used as a substantive.

§ 5 fasciis cruralibus : leggings or puttees, a normal part of a huntsman's outfit (for illustration see D.–S. s.v. *venatio,* figs. 7360, 7375). Sometimes worn by invalids (cf. Hor. *Sat.* ii. 3. 254 f., Quint. xi. 3. 144); the wearing of specially whitened *fasciae* is mentioned as a sign of foppishness (see Shackleton Bailey on Cic. *Att.* ii. 3. 1).

alicula : apparently a diminutive form of the Greek ἀλλιξ 'cloak', here referring to the short hunting-cloak which allowed the wearer sufficient freedom of movement in the chase; cf. J. Aymard, *Chasses romaines,* 203 ff. An unusually ornate garment is suggested by the word *polymita* (lit. 'many-stranded'); J. P. Wild (*Textile Manufacture in the Northern Roman Provinces,* 53 ff.) thinks that *vestes polymiae* probably meant fabric on which patterns were worked freehand in a weft of various colours over the warp.

§ 6 **harundinibus** : reeds smeared with bird-lime were used to snare birds; cf. Varr. *RR* iii. 7. 7, Mart. ix. 54. 3.

§ 7 **et iam videte . . . :** 'and now see what fine acorns that woodland boar has been eating.' The prompt action of the slaves as described in the next sentence shows that he refers to the dates rather than to the thrushes. *glans* can in fact be used of fruit and not merely of acorns; its cognate in Greek βάλανος is specifically used of dates as well as acorns.

lotam : Muncker's conjecture for *totam H*, which sounds too feeble even for Trimalchio. For *lotam* in place of *lautam* cf. 39. 12 *copo*, 45. 13 *plodo*.

§ 8 **quae pendebant e dentibus** : in his first edition Müller deleted this phrase, regarding it as an interpolation based on § 3 'e cuius dentibus sportellae dependebant'; but the repetition is hardly suspicious in itself.

ad numerum : 'keeping time'; cf. Mart. xiv. 199 'hic brevis ad numeros rapidum qui colligit unguem'.

Ch. 41

§ 1 **qui privatum habebam secessum** : probably 'who was far away' sc. in my thoughts (cf. Sen. *Ep*. 25. 7 'tunc praecipue in te ipse secede cum esse cogeris in turba'), even though this makes *in multas cogitationes diductus* somewhat otiose. With a literal explanation, such as Heseltine's 'who had got into a quiet corner by myself', the point of the phrase is obscure.

§ 2 **postquam . . . consumpsi** : 'so after I had worked my way through every kind of wild idea'.

itaque : this is sometimes put second or even later in the sentence in various authors, especially Livy. See L.–H.–S. 514, K.–S. ii. 130.

bacalusias : found only here. The form, derivation, and precise meaning are uncertain. It may mean idle, foolish, or simple thoughts, according to whether we derive it from (i) βαυκάλησις 'lullaby' (cf. *nenia*, which can mean a dirge, a lullaby, or mere nonsense); (ii) *baceolus* (cf. Greek βάκηλος), a word which Suetonius (*Aug*. 87. 2) says was used by Augustus in place of *stultus*; (iii) βαίκυλος, glossed in Hesychius by προβατώδης. Many other suggestions have been put forward.

duravi . . . torqueret: 'I steeled myself to ask that mentor of

mine about what was tormenting me.' Note how flowery the
language is in the circumstances. The infinitive with *durare*
occurs as early as Plautus (*Truc.* 326), but not in prose before
Mela (i. 72); see *TLL* 2297. 78 ff.

quod me torqueret : a relative clause treated by the speaker
as if in indirect speech; *quid* in *H* shows that it was wrongly
assumed to be an indirect question.

§ 3 servus tuus : 'your humble servant (i.e. 'I') can explain this
as well'; cf. *Vulg. Gen.* 44: 18 'oro, domine mi, loquatur servus
tuus in auribus tuis et ne irascaris famulo.' At 77. 6 *amicus
vester* appears to be used in the same way. See J. Svennung
(*Anredeformen* 16 ff.), who ascribes this type of expression to
Oriental influence. The humility of this usage should, however,
not be exaggerated: see note on 57. 2 *domini mei*.

§ 4 cum heri summa cena . . . : perhaps 'although it had been
marked down as the *pièce de résistance* at yesterday's meal, the
diners let it go.' The text and interpretation present difficulties,
but *vindicasset*, if it is sound, is more likely to mean 'claimed'
than 'set free', which would leave *dimissus est* almost tauto-
logous.

§ 5 damnavi ego stuporem meum : on this occasion Encolpius is
credited with an affectation of stupidity, since even an intelli-
gent man could hardly have guessed why the boar was *pilleatus*:
as well as manumitted slaves, the soldiers of a triumphant
general, certain priests, and ordinary citizens at the Saturnalia
might all have been found wearing the *pilleus*. But elsewhere
he alludes to his own stupidity in situations where a sensible
person might have been expected to guess what Trimalchio
was up to. Petronius appears to be uncertain whether to make
Encolpius a naïve observer (as at 29. 1 in the painted-dog
episode, and at 36. 7 'Carpe, Carpe'), or an ironical critic.
P. Veyne ('Le "je" dans le *Satiricon*', in *RÉL* xlii (1964) 301 ff.)
deals with these passages, but he ignores, or at least seriously
underestimates, the stupidity of Encolpius' reactions to various
situations.

honestos : 'respectable'; cf. 38. 14 'et quam honestam negotiationem exercuit, quod illum sic vides. libitinarius fuit.'

§ 6. The guests and slaves at the dinner are fond of giving imitations as part of the entertainment; cf., for example, 64. 5,

68. 3. Dionysus is mentioned several times elsewhere as a subject for such imitations at festivities; cf. Xen. *Symp.* 9. 2–6, Vell. ii. 82. 4, and see W. Beare, *The Roman Stage*, 149 ff. At Trimalchio's dinner we may have a parody of the practice in Dionysiac ritual whereby the leader of the worshippers tended to be identified with the god himself. Hence the slave-boy, with the effeminate beauty by this time appropriate to Dionysus, is hailed by the god's titles: Bromius 'roarer' (βρέμω), Lyaeus 'loosener' (λύω), Euhius (from the Bacchic cry εὐοῖ); and he wears two of the conventional emblems of Dionysus, vine-tendrils and ivy (see Dodds on Eur. *Bacch.* 81, 115, 453–9).

§§ 7–8. Trimalchio puns on *liber* 'free' and Liber, the Roman equivalent of Dionysus: 'Be free' or 'Be (act the part of) Liber'. When the slave has pretended to interpret the words in the first sense and has taken up the freedman's cap from the boar, Trimalchio repeats the pun in a slightly different form: 'You won't deny that I have a father who is free' (an untrue claim with reference to any freedman), and 'You won't deny that I possess Father Liber' (Liber Pater was a standard title for the god), i.e. the slave Dionysus.

§ 8 rursus adiecit . . . inquit : for this pleonastic use of *inquit* cf. Sen. *Contr.* vii. 5. 9 'Cestius dixit, cum descripsisset quam leve vulnus esset: "nocueras" inquit "mihi . . ."', L.–H.–S. 418, *TLL* vii. l. 1773. 74 ff. It occurs frequently in later Latin.

laudavimus . . . sane perbasiamus : Encolpius is ironical at the expense of Trimalchio, but at the same time he reveals his own propensities. For illustrations in the *Cena* of his interest in handsome boys cf. 27. 2 'nec tam pueri nos, quamquam erat operae pretium, ad spectaculum duxerant', 74. 8 'puer non inspeciosus'. The intensifying use of *per* ('we kissed him heartily') is particularly common in colloquial speech. See Landgraf on Cic. *Rosc. Am.* 20 *perfacile*, L. Laurand, *Études sur le style des discours de Cicéron*, 271 ff.

§ 9 libertatem sine tyranno : the criticism of Trimalchio is perhaps less harsh than it might appear at first sight: the phrase looks as if it might be proverbial, and in addition *tyrannus* may be used in the sense of *arbiter bibendi*, like *rex, dominus*, and βασιλεύς (cf. Plut. *Mor.* 622 a, Lucian, *Sat.* 4).

invitare convivarum sermones : there are several grounds for suspicion here. Firstly, the sentence 'laudavimus . . . perbasiamus' seems to describe the behaviour of *all* the guests; but the text in *H* here implies that without any warning Encolpius is now referring to himself, Ascyltos, and Giton. Perhaps more important, Dama's brief speech does not sound like the response to any invitation. Editors do not agree, however, even on the general sense required by the context. Müller thinks we expect something like *coepimus intermissos repetere sermones*; Fuchs suggests that something like *coepimus nos ipsi ad bibendum invitare* is needed, the words *convivarum sermones* being an intrusive gloss. Possibly the original text here explained the presence of additional guests—the freedmen who appear in chs. 41–6, and who may have had places on a separate set of couches.

§ 10 **Dama** : (*clamat H*). Dama occurs in Hor. *Sat.* i. 6. 38 as a slave's name, and in Pers. 5. 76 as the type for a freedman of humble origin.

pataracina : Müller rightly suspects this reading. Heraeus explained it as a popular formation combining *patacinum* (from πάταχνον; cf. πεταχνόομαι, drink deep) and *patera* (sometimes written *patara*); alternatively it may be a scribal error for *patacina*. Dama may well be asking for larger wine-cups to be provided, a familiar enough request but one not usually made in the absence of the host; cf. Hor. *Sat.* ii. 8. 35 'et calices poscit maiores', Cic. *Verr.* i. 66 'mature veniunt, discumbitur. fit sermo inter eos, et invitatio ut Graeco more biberetur; hortatur hospes, poscunt maioribus poculis.'

dum versas te : cf. Sen. *de Ira* 3. 43. 5 'dum respicimus, quod aiunt, versamusque nos, iam immortalitas aderit.'

§ 11 **mundum frigus habuimus** : *mundum* here may mean 'fine' in an ironical sense; or else 'nothing but' (from the meaning 'pure, clean'; cf. August. *c. Petil.* ii. 26. 60 *munda fallacia*). *frigus* probably means 'frost'; but it could mean 'chill', 'fever' (for the alternation this would involve between plural and singular cf. K.–S. i. 88).

§ 12 **vestiarius** : probably used in its usual sense, 'clothes-dealer'. The alternative would be to suppose that Dama is allowed one more masculine form where a neuter would be expected (cf. *balneus, vinus*, and see note on 39. 4 *fer[i]culus*).

staminatas : hap. leg. If this reading is sound, it is probably a hybrid formation from the Greek στάμνος 'wine-jar', and *potiones* must be understood (cf. 34. 7 *tangomenas faciamus*). Thus the sense would be 'I've taken in drinks the size of a wine-jar.'

matus : presumably formed from mad(i)dus 'drunk', less probably a participial formation from *madere* (cf. *egretus = egressus*). In glossaries it occurs in association with *stultus* and with *tristis*, senses which could also fit here. See Heraeus, p. 63, Stefenelli, pp. 67 f.

Ch. 42

Dama, simple in mind and in expression, is followed by Seleucus, whose view of life is consistently gloomy. Notice that Petronius allows each of the freedmen after Dama to make a longer contribution to the conversation than his predecessor.

§ 1 **baliscus** : 'bath'. For the omission of *n* in other variants of *balneum* cf. *CGL* iv. 487. 43 *balastrum*, *CGL* iv. 600. 33 *belastrum*. Müller's suggestion in his second edition, *aliptes*, is much too drastic.

The comparison between bathing and fulling is found elsewhere: Clement of Alexandria (*Paed.* 3. 9) says of the baths that they used to be called places for fulling men (ἀνθρωπογναφεῖα).

§ 2 **cor . . . liquescit** : cf. ps.-Ambros. *Laps. Virg.* 8. 35 'cor . . . liquescens tamquam cera'.

laecasin : from the Greek λαικάζειν, i.e. *fornicari*; cf. Mart. xi. 58. 12 'λαικάζειν cupidae dicet avaritiae' (λαικάζειν Schneidewin for λαιτκζε *B*ᴬ *leicazin C*ᴬ). Actual obscenities like this are rarely found in the *Satyricon*, even in the speech of the freedmen.

fui in funus : *esse* is used in late Latin with *ad* or *in* and the accusative in place of a verb of motion; cf. *Peregr.* 7. 1 'id est qua primitus ad Aegyptum fueram'. A few examples of this construction occur in classical and early Latin; but some alleged examples involve merely *esse* in its normal sense along with *ad* = 'in the neighbourhood of', e.g. Cic. *Att.* vii. 17. 3 'ut essem ad urbem'. See L.–H.–S. 276, Hof. *LU* 166, Löfstedt, *Peregr.* 171 ff.

§ 3 **bellus** : this word was preferred in colloquial speech to *pulcher*. Although in origin it is a diminutive of *bonus*, Stefenelli (p. 70) is hardly justified in seeing an etymological play here in *bellus tam bonus*.

animam ebulliit : 'has breathed his last'. A colloquial expression; cf. 62. 10 (Niceros), Sen. *Apoc.* 4. 2. *ebullire* is used intransitively in Pers. 2. 9 f. 'o si / ebulliat patruus, praeclarum funus!'

modo modo : see note on 37. 3.

§ 4 **utres inflati** : the comparison of men with bladders occurs as early as the fifth century B.C. (cf. Sophron, *PSI*, xi. 1214d ἀσκοὶ πεφυσαμένοι, Epicharmus 246 Kaibel), and it must have been trite by this time: 'avete. utres sumus' was found written in a shop in Pompeii (cf. *Notizie degli scavi di antichità* 1927. 101). See Hof. *LU* 158, 202, Otto s.v. *uter*.

muscae : for the insignificance of the fly cf. Suet. *Dom.* 3. 1 'ut cuidam interroganti essetne quis intus cum Caesare non absurde responsum sit: ne musca quidem', Herod. *Mim.* 1. 15 ἐγὼ δὲ δραίνω μυῖ᾽ ὅσον, i.e. 'I have the strength of a fly.'

aliquam virtutem habent : proverbial, like 'even a worm will turn'; cf. *Paroem. Gr.* i. 74 ἔνεστι κἂν μύρμηκι χολή, i.e. 'even an ant can get angry', ib. ii. 433.

bullae : 'bubbles'. For this proverb cf. Schol. on Pers. 2. 10 'ex quo proverbialiter dicimus, homo bulla est.' The cliché is treated with ironical exhaustiveness in Lucian, *Charon* 19: 'In fact, I've thought of a simile to describe human life as a whole. I must tell you what it is. You know the bubbles that rise to the surface below a waterfall—those little pockets of air that combine to produce foam? . . . Well, that's what human beings are like. They're more or less inflated pockets of air . . . but sooner or later they're all bound to go pop' (Graves's translation).

§ 5 **et quid si non . . .** : 'if only he hadn't been so frugal!'; cf. § 7 'quid si non illam optime accepisset!' In these passages *quid si* seems to introduce an unfulfillable wish, 'if only . . .'; on the regular expressions for such wishes see L.–H.–S. 331, K.–S. i. 184.

abstinax : hap. leg. The ending *-ax* is found in Latin of every level, but more extensively in colloquial speech; note Plautus' comic exploitation of it in *Pers.* 410 'procax, rapax, trahax', and 421 'edax, furax, fugax', and see Cooper, pp. 109 f., Swanson, p. 141.

abiit ad plures : 'he's gone to join the great majority.' For *plures* = 'the dead' cf. Plaut. *Trin.* 291 'quin prius me ad plures penetravi', Ar. *Eccl.* 1073 ἀνεστηκυῖα παρὰ τῶν πλειόνων.

medici illum perdiderunt : the death-dealing physician was a literary commonplace; cf. Menander *fr.* 1112 πολλῶν ἰατρῶν εἴσοδοί μ᾽ ἀπώλεσαν, *Anth. Pal.* xi. 112–26, Mart. i. 47, vi. 53, Plin. *NH* xxix. 18 'discunt periculis nostris et experimenta per mortes agunt, medicoque tantum hominem occidisse impunitas

summa est; quin immo transit convicium et intemperantia culpatur ultroque qui periere arguuntur.' The standards of the
profession in reality may have been alarming enough; cf. *SG*[8] i.
342 ff.

immo magis : see Fordyce's note on Cat. 73. 4 'immo . . .
magis': 'examples like these . . . show how readily *magis* could
become in later Latin an adversative particle, the ancestor of
Ital. *ma* and Fr. *mais*', and cf. L.–H.–S. 492, 498, Elcock, p. 150.

fatus : for the disappearance of neuter forms in favour of masculines see note on 39. 4 *fer[i]culus*. This particular masculine
form, illustrating a superstitious tendency to personify fate,
occurs again at 71. 1 and 77. 2, as well as in inscriptions, e.g.
Buecheler and Lommatzsch, *Carm. Lat. Epigr.* 148. 2 'hoc
tempus voluit, hoc fuit fatus meus.'

§ 6. Sumptuary legislation appears to have been used from the
XII Tables onwards in attempts to control excessively luxurious
funerals. Two features of expensive funerals are referred to here:
firstly the ritual lamentations, often provided by hired mourners
(cf. Varr. *LL* vii. 70 '⟨praefica⟩ dicta, ut Aurelius scribit, mulier
ab luco quae conduceretur quae ante domum mortui laudes
eius caneret'); and secondly the *vitalis lectus*, a euphemistic
term (cf. 77. 7 *vitalia*) for the *lectus funebris*, the high funeral
couch. See Marq. *Prl.* 345 ff., *SG*[8] iii. 129 ff.

manu misit aliquot : the manumission of slaves by testament
was calculated to ensure an impressive attendance of enthusiastic mourners; cf. Pers. 3. 105 f. 'at illum / hesterni capite induto
subiere Quirites.' *Cod. Iust.* vii. 6. 5 mentions a parsimonious
variation whereby the slaves appeared at the funeral wearing
the *pilleus* but were not in fact manumitted. Testamentary
manumissions, whatever the motives involved, were regulated
by the *lex Fufia Caninia* of 2 B.C. and the *lex Aelia Sentia* of
A.D. 4; cf. Gaius, *Inst.* i. 18, 38–46.

§ 7 mulier quae mulier : this curious phrase is also attributed
to Varro (*Men.* 230 'pareutactae assunt, mulier quae mulier,
Venus caput'; Lindsay deletes *caput*). The usual rendering
'a woman who is a true woman' makes some sense in both passages, although here the words *milvinum genus* are added on
awkwardly, and we might also wonder at the absence of analogous phrases, e.g. 'vir qui vir'. Alternatively we might punctuate
with a comma after *mulier quae mulier*, and suggest something
like 'a woman is (does) what a woman is (does)', i.e. a woman

can't help being what she is. This rendering has the weakness, however, that it does not fit the Varro fragment.

neminem nihil : cf. 58. 5 (Hermeros) 'nec sursum nec deorsum non cresco nisi . . . non conieci', 76. 3 (Trimalchio) 'nemini tamen nihil satis est.' In these passages the double negative is used to strengthen the negation, not to cancel it out. The fact that this usage occurs once or twice even in Cicero (cf. *Verr.* ii. 60 'debebat Epicrates nummum nullum nemini', *QF* iii. 4. 1 'nullam in nullo nostrum dignitatem') shows that it is not restricted to the speech of the lower classes.

cancer : 'a festering sore'. This interpretation, rather than 'crab', is favoured by the equivalent Greek proverb ἕλκος ἔχω τὸν ἔρωτα (*Paroem. Gr.* ii. 393). This sense occurs not merely in medical writers but also in Cato *RR* 157. 3, Ov. *Met.* ii. 825.

Ch. 43

§ 1 vivorum meminerimus : 'what's past is past'; cf. Cic. *Fin.* v. 3. This phrase, used not very aptly by Trimalchio at 75. 7, is here ironically given to Phileros, whose remarks are largely concerned with the deceased Chrysanthus.

sibi : *se* and *sibi* are sometimes found in an indicative subordinate clause where a demonstrative would be regular (cf. K.–S. i. 613). Contrast the much greater frequency with which the freedmen in the *Cena* adopt the opposite change, viz. the use of a part of *ille* as a reflexive (for this see note on 38. 4).

honeste vixit, honeste obiit : the epitaph of a certain Beatilla (Diehl 2383) is similar: '. . . que beate vixsit, beate obiit. beati qui legunt.' It appears from *Rhetores Graeci* iii. 255. 17 Spengel καλῶς ἐβίωσε καὶ καλῶς ἐτελειώθη that an equivalent expression was frequently used in Greek. See Heraeus, p. 122.

ab asse crevit : see note on 38. 7 'de nihilo crevit', and cf. 71. 12 'ex parvo crevit'. Note also in *H* the monkish corruption *abbas secrevit*.

quadrantem . . . tollere : a more vivid form of the proverb 'aurum in luto quaerere'; cf. Lucilius 659M 'mordicus petere aurum e flamma expediat, e caeno cibum', and see Otto s.vv. *lutum* (6) and *mordicus*.

crevit quicquid tetigit : Delz's *tetigit*, based on 76. 8 'quicquid tangebam, crescebat tamquam favus', should be preferred to *crevit H*, which does not provide a repetition analogous to

'honeste vixit, honeste obiit' above or to 44. 3 'serva me,
servabo te.' Friedlaender appears to base his deletion of *quicquid
crevit* as a marginal gloss on his misquotation of 76. 8 *quicquid
tangebam* as *quicquid crevit*.

§ 2 solida centum : 'a clear hundred thousand sesterces'. This
use of *centum* (sc. *milia sestertium*) occurs in Mart. iv. 37. 1
'centum Coranus et ducenta Mancinus, / trecenta debet Titius.'
The abbreviation, perhaps a little affected (like the English
slang *thou* for a thousand pounds), is used by Petronius to mock
Phileros' modest notion of what constitutes a fortune. For
solida cf. Liv. v. 4. 7 *solidum . . . stipendium*, Mart. iv. 37. 4
triciens soldum, also id. i. 99. 1 'non plenum modo viciens
habebas.'

in nummis: this could mean money invested as well as ready
cash ; cf. Cic. *Att.* viii. 10 'respondit se quod in nummis haberet
nescire quo loci esset ; alios non solvere, aliorum diem nondum
esse.'

§ 3 linguam caninam : Friedlaender assumes that this puzzling
phrase must refer to a superstition, not recorded elsewhere,
that anyone who ate the tongue of a dog must speak the truth.
Other suggestions include (i) a reference to *canina facundia*,
shameless eloquence (cf. Quint. xii. 9. 9, and see Otto s.v. *canis*
(3)); or else to the outspokenness of the Cynics (cf. Plut. *Mor.*
69 c παρρησία κυνική); (ii) M. Pokrovskij (see Perrochat ad loc.)
cites a Russian expression 'I have eaten a dog', which means
'I know the matter thoroughly'; (iii) Müller follows Scheffer
and Heraeus in interpreting *lingua canina* as the plant κυνόγλωσ-
σος (lit. 'dog's tongue'), whose fragrance was thought to assist
the hard of hearing (cf. ps.-Apul. *Herb.* 97); Phileros' words
would then mean something like 'I've been able to hear what's
been going on.'

durae buccae : 'his tongue was rough' (but at Lucilius 417M *os
durum* and Cic. *Quinct.* 77 *ore durissimo* the sense is 'impudent,
brass-necked').

linguosus : a rare word. The sense 'garrulous' seems to fit the
context here and at 63. 1 'immo certus est et minime linguosus.'

discordia, non homo : see note on 38. 15 *phantasia, non homo*.

§ 4 amicus amico : a common proverbial expression; cf., for
example, Plaut. *Mil.* 660 'nec qui amicus amico sit magis', and
see Otto s.v. *amicus* (11), Heraeus, p. 121. Phileros shares the

opinion widely held in antiquity that benevolence should be restricted to a chosen group.

manu plena, uncta mensa : this rearrangement of the text in *H, manu uncta plena mensa,* improves the sentence considerably. *manu plena* is a common expression to indicate generosity (cf., for example, Cic. *Att.* ii. 25. 1, and see Otto s.v. *manus* (17)). For *uncta mensa* cf. Mart. v. 44. 7 'captus es unctiore mensa', Sid. *Ep.* ii. 9. 10 'cenas unctissimas'.

et inter initia . . . : although there is no explicit statement it gradually becomes clear that Phileros is once more speaking about Chrysanthus and not about his brother. Phileros' use of *ille* is unclassical and wayward, but Süss (pp. 66 f.) exaggerates a little in claiming that Petronius has deliberately confused the reader in these sections in order to convey the speaker's muddleheadedness.

malam parram pilavit : the *parra,* possibly a type of owl, is mentioned as a bird of ill omen in Hor. *Od.* iii. 27. 1 f. 'impios parrae recinentis omen / ducat', Plaut. *Asin.* 260. But, apart from the somewhat otiose use of *malam* (cf. Hor. *Sat.* i. 1. 77 *malos fures, TLL* viii. 220. 21 ff.), the phrase *parram pilare* is puzzling. It is said to mean 'to catch a Tartar', lit. 'to pluck a bad *parra*', but this sense of *pilare* is doubtful. P. A. George suggests *inter initia mala parra pipilavit.*

recorrexit costas illius : 'set him on his feet again' (lit. 'straightened his ribs again').

quantum : this may be retained, although no earlier examples are cited of the accusative of price, a construction found sometimes in late Latin even with precise amounts, and not merely, as here, with neuter pronouns; see L.–H.–S. 73.

ex qua plus involavit . . . : 'out of which he stole more than had been left to him'. The *heres* was responsible for paying out any legacies made under a will; thus an unscrupulous person who accepted the position of *heres* might have opportunities for enriching himself at the expense of the legatees.

§ 5 terrae filio : 'nobody'; cf. Cic. *Att.* i. 13. 4 'huic terrae filio nescio cui committere epistulam tantis de rebus non audeo', Min. Fel. 21. 7 'ut in hodiernum inopinato visos caelo missos, ignobiles et ignotos terrae filios nominamus', Otto s.v. *terra* (2).

longe fugit, quisquis suos fugit : 'you have to go a long way if you want to get away from your own kin.' Presumably proverbial: one ef Varro's Menippean Satires (244B) is entitled 'longe fugit qui suos fugit.'

§ 6 oracularios : this word, which is not found elsewhere, must mean something like 'oracle-mongers'. Reinesius's conjecture *oricularios*, which would be a colloquial spelling of *auricularios* 'counsellors' (cf. *Vulg. II Reg.* 23: 24) makes the sentence less effective.

cito credit : proverbial (cf. Ov. *AA* iii. 685 f. 'nec cito credideris: quantum cito credere laedat, / exemplum vobis non leve Procris erit', and see Otto s.v. *credere* (2)). By the addition of the words *utique homo negotians*, Phileros is made to introduce, with deliberate flatness, a long-familiar play on the two senses of *credere*, viz. 'believe' and 'lend'; cf. Cic. *Att.* i. 16. 10 ' "mihi vero" inquam "xxv iudices crediderunt, xxxi, quoniam nummos ante acceperunt, tibi nihil crediderunt" ', Sen. *Suas.* 7. 5 'credamus Antonio, Cicero, si bene illi pecunias crediderunt faeneratores.'

tamen verum quod frunitus est : *fruniscor* is archaic and Vulgar for *fruor*; Gellius (xvii. 2. 5) states that it was already rare in Cicero's time, adding 'dubitatumque est ab imperitis antiquitatis an Latinum foret.' The text as it stands seems to mean 'It is true that he enjoyed himself as long as he lived'; no parallel for this absolute use of *fruniscor* is cited, and any examples of the absolute use of *fruor* (e.g. Ter. *HT* 345 'datur, fruare dum licet', Plin. *Pan.* 34. 4 'agnoscebamus et fruebamur cum . . .') seem easier than the present passage. In any case, the doubts raised by the words after *vixit*, not to mention the omission of the copula with *verum*, suggest the possibility of corruption here.

§ 7 †cui datum est, non cui destinatum : the reading in *H* can hardly be sound. Muncker's insertion of *datum est* after *cui datum est* gives a plausible text, but cannot be regarded as certain.

Fortunae filius : 'Fortune's favourite'; cf. Hor. *Sat.* ii. 6. 49 ' "Fortunae filius" omnes [sc. clamant]', and see Otto s.v. *fortuna* (10).

quadrata currunt : 'everything's running along nice and shipshape.' *currere* is used figuratively of, for example, time passing, or events turning out in some way or other (cf. Amm. xvii. 9. 1 'cunctis . . . ex voto currentibus'), but here the collocation with *quadrata* (lit. 'squared', hence 'fitting, appropriate') must be meant to sound odd.

annos secum tulisse : *secum ferre* is often used on gravestones where a person's age is recorded: e.g. *CIL* vi. 12845 'quadraginta

duo mecum fero flebilis annos', *CIL* x. 2311 'scire laboras,
annos quot tulerim mecum.' The whimsical application of this
expression found in § 8 comes closer to Cic. *Fin.* ii. 106 'Sar-
danapalli epigramma . . . in quo ille rex Syriae glorietur se
omnes secum abstulisse libidinum voluptates'.

corneolus : cf. Plin. *NH* xxxi. 102 'cornea videmus corpora
piscatorum', Cat. 23. 12 'corpora sicciora cornu' (in his note
Fordyce refers to the belief that the *siccum corpus*, which is
free from noxious humours, is healthy).

§ 8 niger tamquam corvus : black hair as a sign of youthful
vigour was contrasted with the white hair of the aged; thus
Demosthenes (21. 71) says of a pancratiast ἰσχυρός τις ἦν, μέλας
. . . For the proverbial blackness of the crow cf. Apul. *Met.* ii. 9
corvina nigredine.

olim oliorum : presumably 'ages and ages ago'. This has sometimes been taken to be a repetition of the type seen at 37. 8
nummorum nummos. The form *oliorum*, however, is strange,
and can hardly be explained as a part of *olle*, the archaic form
of *ille*; possibly it is a comic formation loosely resembling some
Oriental phrase. Heraeus (see Buecheler[8], p. 364) compares
αἰνόθεν αἰνῶς, οἰόθεν οἶος and ἤδη ἤδωσιν (the last of these is from
one of the Seth *defixiones*; cf. Wünsch, *Sethian. Verfluch.* 24).

adhuc : this occasionally has the same sense as *etiam tum* or
even *tamen*; see *TLL* i. 660. 73 ff.

non . . . in domo canem reliquisse : this must be proverbial
(cf. SHA, *Aurelian.* 22. 6 'canem in hoc oppido non relinquam'),
but here it is given an obscene sense (*canem*, as the next sentence shows, must be taken to mean 'bitch').

pullarius : the words *omnis minervae homo* show that the sense
needed here is 'fond of boys'. Burmann's *pullarius* (cf. *CGL* ii.
392. 6 'pullarius παιδεραστής') is thus more likely than *puellarius*
H, even though it may be claimed that this might come from
puellus = puer as well as from *puella*. See Friedlaender's note.

omnis minervae homo : 'a jack of all trades'. Another phrase
which takes its tone from the context; cf. Cic. *Rosc. Am.* 120
'inter suos omnium deliciarum atque omnium artium puerulos',
also 68. 7 below 'omnis musae mancipium'.

Ch. 44

Ganymedes takes over, complaining bitterly about the cost of
living, the aediles, and the decline in politics and religion since

the time when he was a boy. Petronius has chosen for this upholder of old-time morality a name with absurd associations: in myth the handsome youth Ganymedes held a degraded position (this gives point to the poet Eumolpus' over-enthusiastic welcome to Giton at 92. 3 ' "laudo" inquit "Ganymedem. oportet hodie bene sit" ', and the reader could be expected to think of the word *catamitus* which is derived from this name).

§ 1 narratis : colloquial in tone (see Krebs, *Antibarbarus* s.v.); it can be used, as here, with a hint of impatience, 'go on about'; cf. Cic. *Fam.* ix. 15. 3 'Catulum mihi narras et illa tempora.'

nec ad caelum nec ad terram pertinet : proverbial for irrelevance; cf. *Paroem. Gr.* i. 444 οὔτε γῆς οὔτε οὐρανοῦ ἅπτεται, and see Otto s.v. *caelum* (2).

cum interim : 'yet all the time'. The main idea is subordinated as with the *cum* 'inversum' construction (see note on 27. 1, also L.–H.–S. 623, K.–S. ii. 341). For the adversative force here cf. Cic. *Verr.* v. 162 'caedebatur virgis in medio foro Messanae civis Romanus, iudices, cum interea nullus gemitus . . . audiebatur . . .'

nemo curat, quid annona mordet : 'no one cares how much the price of corn pinches you.' For the mood of *mordet* cf. 76. 11 'tantum quod mihi non dixerat quid pridie cenaveram'. Several times in the *Cena* the indicative is used in an indirect question, as sometimes in early Latin and occasionally later (see L.–H.–S. 537 ff.). Note, however, that generally these freedmen use the subjunctive as in classical Latin; cf., for example, 56. 2 'medicus, qui scit quid homunciones . . . habeant', and see Süss, p. 57.
Complaints about the dearness of food had always been good for a laugh: cf. Ter. *Andr.* 744 ff.:

di vostram fidem!
quid turbaest apud forum! quid illic hominum litigant!
tum annona carast . . . (*aside*) quid dicam aliud nescio.

So this outburst by Ganymedes should not be used as evidence for a precise date for the setting of the *Cena*.

§ 2 buccam : 'mouthful'. In an informal letter to Tiberius Augustus writes: 'in balineo demum post horam primam noctis duas buccas manducavi' (Suet. *Aug.* 76. 2). In this colloquial sense *bucca* by itself may stand specifically for a mouthful of bread (cf. Apicius' use of the diminutive *buccella*, e.g. at vii. 6. 4).

§ 3 esur⟨it⟩io : Buecheler's conjecture for *esurio* should be preferred. *esurio* has been defended on the analogy of several
passages where a word or short phrase of direct speech is inserted into the structure of a sentence (cf. 57. 11 'tam facile est
quam "accede istoc" ', 58. 7 'qui te primus "deuro de" fecit'.
Here, however, the abruptness would be still greater, and it
would be safer to ascribe the manuscript reading to mere carelessness.

aediles : as at Rome, the *aediles* in a *colonia* were subordinate
magistrates whose duties included the supervision of weights
and measures and the corn supply. In *CIL* iv. 429 a candidate recommends himself for the aedileship at Pompeii thus:
'C. Iulium Polybium aed(ilem) o(ro) v(os) f(aciatis). panem bonum fert.' The corruption hinted at by Ganymedes might arise
when they negotiated contracts with the bakers for the supply of
bread at fixed prices; see Marq. *Prl.* 415 ff.

aediles male eveniat : *aediles* could be either (i) an accusative
irregularly used instead of the dative (cf. 58. 13 'cave, maiorem
maledicas', 96. 7 'maledic illam'), or (ii) meant originally as the
subject or object of some other verb (or possibly as an exclamation), but followed by an anacoluthon in order to indicate his
indignation.

colludunt. 'serva me, servabo te' : in view of the fact that *collu-
dere* is normally used absolutely this punctuation is better than
that of Buecheler and others who treat 'serva me, servabo te'
as the object of *colludunt*.
Heraeus, p. 122, cites similar jingles from inscriptions on
ancient rings: 'ama me, amabo te', and 'memini tui, memento
mei.'

populus minutus : apparently a cliché, like the journalese 'the
little man'; cf. Phaedrus iv. 6. 13 *minuta plebes*, and Italian
popolo minuto, common folk, workmen. See also Heraeus,
p. 111.

isti maiores maxillae : various types of *constructio ad sensum*
are found even in classical Latin, but in Vulgar Latin much
greater freedom is allowed, and the incongruous forms often
occur closer to each other; cf. § 5 *larvas istos*, L.–H.–S. 430 ff.
For the metaphorical use of *maxillae* cf. Suet. *Tib.* 21. 2 'mise-
rum populum Romanum qui sub tam lentis maxillis erit'.

semper Saturnalia agunt : this is a variant of a proverb which,
as used by Seneca and Lucian, hints that a day of repentance

will come for those who now enjoy themselves immoderately: Sen. *Apoc.* 12 'dicebam vobis: non semper Saturnalia erunt', Luc. *Merc. Cond.* 16 οἴει γὰρ ἀεὶ Διονύσια ἑορτάσειν;

§ 4 leones : as in § 14 below, the lion represents the courageous man.

§ 5 illud erat vivere : another trite phrase: the inscription on a gaming-table reads 'venari lavari ludere ridere occ est vivere' (*Inscriptiones Latinae Selectae*, ed. Dessau 8626 f, cf. Sen. *Ep.* 123. 10 'esse, bibere, frui patrimonio, hoc est vivere').

⟨si⟩ **simila Siciliae inferior erat :** 'if the high-grade flour of Sicily was not up to standard'. The reading in *H*, *similia sicilia interiores et* is kept almost unchanged by G. C. Whittick (*CR* N.S. ii (1952), 11 f.), who, following Heraeus, takes *si milia si cilia* (= χίλια) to be a jingling popular phrase in which *cilia* is merely the Greek equivalent of *milia*: 'Come one, come all', i.e. however great the odds. He then interprets *interiores* as a metaphorical expression for boldness, from the tactics of the charioteer who risks everything by going close to the post as he turns at the end of the Circus. This seems too involved, however. The text printed here, the suggestion of J. H. Simon, seems more plausible than Whittick's, and it involves a less drastic alteration than, for example, the conjecture of Buecheler, *si milio silicia interesset* [sc. *fraude pistorum*], 'when fenugreek was put in with the millet (by rascally millers)'.

larvas . . . istos : see note on *isti maiores maxillae* in § 3 above.

percolopabant : 'beat up'. Formed from *per+colopus*, a colloquial variant of *colaphus* (κόλαφος) 'punch', the form used in narrative at 34. 2. See Ernout–Meillet s.v. *colaphus*, Swanson, pp. 196, 201.

§ 6 piper, non homo : 'a regular firebrand'. See note on 38. 15 *phantasia, non homo*. For *piper* used figuratively of sharpness in a person or thing cf. Hier. *Ep.* 31. 2 'ut te aliquid et piperis mordeat', Sidon. *Ep.* 5. 8, 8. 11 *piperata facundia*, Mart. viii. 59. 4 *piperata manus*, also the Italian 'è tutto di pepe'.

§ 7 amicus amico : see note on 43. 4.

in tenebris micare : *micare* is applied to a method of sortition in which one person suddenly held up a number of fingers for another to guess. No precise details can be given of the procedure used, nor is it at all clear that it was usually a children's game (ps.-Acro on Hor. *Sat.* ii. 3. 248 took this view, although he thought it was played with nuts, not with fingers). See Pease on Cic. *Div*. ii. 85, Holden on Cic. *Off*. iii. 77, Marq. *Prl*. 836, Otto s.v. *micare*.

§ 8 [**vel pilabat**] **tractabat** : *tractare* here seems to be used metaphorically in the sense 'pull them about', 'savage them', a possible development from the sense of *trahere* in, for example, Sall. *Cat*. 11. 4 'rapere omnes, trahere'. This might have induced a scribe to add the gloss *vel pilabat* (for *pilare* = 'plunder' in late Latin, cf. Amm. Marc. xxxi. 2. 8 *castra pilantes*). Scheffer instead took *vel tractabat* as a gloss on *pilabat*.

nec schemas loquebatur sed derectum : 'he didn't use figures of speech, but spoke straight out.' The feminine *schema* used here by Ganymedes occurs in early Latin and also in Suet. *Tib*. 43. 2 'exemplar imperatae schemae' (note that at 126. 8 Encolpius has the classical form *schema -atis*, neuter). Other examples in the *Cena* of a feminine replacing a regular neuter form are 45. 9, 69. 1 *stigmam*, 66. 7 *rapam*, 76. 11 *intestinas*, 78. 1 *stragulam*. See Palmer, pp. 159 ff., Elcock, pp. 56 ff.

§ 9 **expuit** : Quintilian (xi. 3. 56) criticizes this and similar failings in orators: 'iam tussire et expuere crebro et ab imo pulmone pituitam trochleis adducere et oris humore proximos spargere . . . potissimum huic loco subiiciantur.' Ganymedes may of course be expressing his admiration for Safinius' behaviour in general, but the obscurity of the latter part of the sentence leaves this uncertain.

assi a dis habuisse : 'the gods had given him some kind of dryness.' Burmann's slight alteration of *asia dis H* gives a simple enough explanation for the words *nec sudavit umquam nec expuit*, but it should not be regarded as certain. Buecheler preferred to read *Asiadis*, a form which does not occur elsewhere; it would have to be taken either as equivalent to *Asiae* or else as a partitive genitive adjective used irregularly (see L.–H.–S. 57 f. on the rarity of third-declension adjectives in this construction). If *Asiadis* is sound, Ganymedes, an Asiatic himself, is suggesting that the fastidious habits of the Campanian orator 'had something Asiatic' about them. It is true that the Persians in particular were noted for their avoidance of spitting (cf. Varro ap. Non. 394M 'Persae eam sunt consecuti corporis siccitatem ut neque expuerent neque emungerentur', Xen. *Cyr*. i. 2. 16, viii. 8. 8), and that other Eastern races may have resembled them in this respect; but *Asiadis*, quite apart from the oddness of the form, seems to require too esoteric a knowledge of Asiatic habits.

§ 10 pro luto : 'dirt-cheap'. This phrase is also used by Trimalchio
at 51. 6 and by Habinnas at 67. 10. See Otto s.v. *lutum* (5).

§ 11 oculum bublum : the syncopated form is used here, but
note that *bubulae* is found in narrative at 35. 3. The context
demands that 'bull's eye' should denote some small object other
than bread: 'Nowadays I've seen bigger buns [say] than the
loaves they sell' (the literal meaning 'bull's eye' cannot altogether be excluded, but Friedlaender is certainly on the wrong
lines when he suggests that 'bull's eye' might have been the
name for round loaves of the kind discovered at Pompeii). In
Greek βούφθαλμον is used of several types of flower, and βούφθαλ-
μος is a kind of fish, but here we require some article of food
which is round, as well as being normally smaller than a loaf.

§ 13 ⟨non⟩ trium cauniarum : lit. 'not worth three Caunian
figs'. Buecheler's postponement of *non* should be preferred to
Mentel's *nos* (see Otto s.v. *triobolus*, where similar pejorative
expressions are cited both with and without a negative, e.g.
Nicophon *fr.* 12 οὐκ ἄξιος τριωβόλου, *Paroem. Gr.* ii. 667 τεττάρων
ὀβολῶν ἄξιος).

alter : in later Latin *alter* was used more and more frequently
in place of *alius*; cf. French *autre*, Ital. *altro*, and see Elcock,
pp. 97 f., L.–H.–S. 208, *TLL* i. 1736. 5, 30.

§ 14 denarios mille aureos : i.e. 100,000 sesterces, apparently
chosen here as the property qualification for the aedileship;
this amount is the qualification demanded of *decuriones* elsewhere (cf. Plin. *Ep.* i. 19 and Sherwin-White ad loc., R. Duncan
Jones, 'An Epigraphic Survey of Costs in Roman Italy', *BSR*
xxxiii, N.S. xx (1965), 226 ff.).

si nos coleos haberemus : cf. Pers. 1. 103 f. 'si testiculi vena ulla
paterni / viveret in nobis', Quint. i. 10. 31 'si quid in nobis virilis
roboris manebat'.

domi leones, foras vulpes : cf. Ar. *Pax* 1189 f. ὄντες οἴκοι μὲν
λέοντες / ἐν μάχῃ δ᾽ ἀλώπεκες.

foras : instead of *foris*; see note on 30. 3.

§ 15 casulas : here and at 46. 2 this should probably not be
taken as a true plural; cf. Juv. 9. 60 f. 'rusticus infans / cum
matre et casulis et conlusore catello'.

§ 16 a diibus : this abnormal form, which occurs often in inscriptions (see *TLL* v. 886. 39), was conjectured by Buecheler in place

of the pointless *aedilibus* in *H*. Forms like *deabus* and *filiabus* were devised to distinguish the feminine from the normal masculines *dis* and *filiis*; thereafter irregular masculines like *diibus* and *filiibus* were formed on the analogy of these feminines.

§ 17 f. Ganymedes condemns his fellow citizens for neglecting even the outward forms of religion and thus bringing drought upon themselves. Tertullian complains (*Apol.* 40. 14 f.) that pagans still practise such antique rites ('aquilicia Iovi immolatis, nudipedalia populo denuntiatis, caelum apud Capitolium quaeritis'), although ironically, when Christians by their fasting induce God to send rain, the pagans give the credit to Jupiter.

§ 17 Iovem : the deity in control of rain and the weather in general; see Flower Smith's note on Tib. i. 7. 26 *pluvio . . . Iovi*.

opertis oculis : everyone pretends to pray, with eyes covered, but in reality they are inwardly counting their possessions. *opertis oculis* must be taken as equivalent to *capite velato* (on the Roman practice of veiling the head during prayer cf. Cic. *ND* ii. 10 with Pease's note). This is more plausible than to take the phrase in a figurative sense 'blindly' (*clausis oculis* is so used in late authors; see Otto s.v. *oculus* (7)).

§ 18 stolatae : this must stand here for married women in general, who were by custom allowed to wear the *stola*, a long dress. Later the term *femina stolata* was used as a title for a more exclusive group, viz. women who had been granted the *ius trium liberorum*. See Marq. *Prl.* 575.

nudis pedibus : those taking part in religious or magic ritual went in bare feet (see Pease's exhaustive collection of examples in his note on Virg. *Aen.* iv. 518). Two main explanations are given for this practice: (i) the taboo on the wearing of leather was thus observed, (ii) the worshipper was in direct contact with the earth and its powers.

passis capillis : women making supplication are often described as wearing their hair free from any fastening; cf., for example, Virg. *Aen.* i. 480, Liv. i. 13. 1. See also J. G. Frazer, *The Golden Bough* abr. version, 234 ff., on the use made of cut or combed-out hair by various peoples to produce rain.

urceatim : 'by the bucket'; not found elsewhere. Adverbs in *-im* are a feature of Vulgar language, but of the dozen or so in Petronius only *urceatim* and one or two others are not in general use. See Swanson, pp. 66, 206 f., Cooper, pp. 196 ff.

plovebat : Vulgar form for *pluebat*. The epenthesis of [*w*] after a back vowel to avoid hiatus is well attested in the Pompeian graffiti; cf. Väänänen, *Pcmp*. 48, Stefenelli, p. 88, Swanson, pp. 197, 254.

udi tamquam mures : this may be even closer to the English 'like drowned rats' than one might think, for the term *mus* includes rats as well as mice.

pedes lanatos : this phrase refers to the anger of the gods, but other relevant passages suggest that even in antiquity its precise significance was not clear; cf. Schol. on Hor. *Od*. iii. 2. 31 'deos iratos pedes lanatos habere quia nonnumquam tarde veniunt nocentibus', Macrob. *Sat*. i. 8. 5 'cur autem Saturnus ipse in compedibus visatur, Verrius Flaccus [first century A.D.] causam se ignorare dicit, verum mihi Apollodori lectio sic suggerit. Saturnum Apollodorus alligari ait per annum laneo vinculo et solvi ad diem sibi festum, id est mense hoc Decembri, atque inde proverbium ductum deos laneos pedes habere. significari vero decimo mense semen in utero animatum in vitam grandescere, quod donec erumpat in lucem mollibus naturae vinculis detinetur.'

Ch. 45

The next speaker, Echion, is not an attractive character, although he looks at life less pessimistically. He is materialistic in his views on the importance of education and of various vocations, and he is sadistic, whether in killing off a young boy's pet birds or in watching the death-struggles of gladiators (even if we have to admit that the Romans accepted cruelty more readily than we do today; see A. W. Lintott, *Violence in Republican Rome*, ch. iii, M. Grant, *Gladiators* (1971 edn.), 102 ff.). His Latin is less 'classical' than that of the other speakers, a fact which stands out all the more clearly because of the greater length of his contribution.

§ 1 **oro te** : a colloquial formula often found at the beginning of a sentence. It is used here, as *quaeso* sometimes is, to introduce a euphemistic warning; cf. Fronto 59N 'sed meliora quaeso fabulemur', Hof. *LU* 128 ff.

centonarius : this may mean merely a clothes-dealer (cf. Cato *RR* 135. 1 'Romae tunicas, togas, saga, centones, sculponeas'). Alternatively it has been taken to mean a fireman or else a supplier of *centones* as fire-fighting equipment (cf. Caes. *BC* ii. 9. 4, Vitr. x. 14. 3). Numerous inscriptions in Italian towns and in some of the Western provinces associate *collegia* of *centonarii* with *fabri* and *dendrophori* as part of an organized fire-brigade; see Marq. *Prl.* 585, 719, Sherwin-White on Plin. *Ep.* x. 33. 1. Note, however, that Puteoli (in which the *Cena* appears to be set) and Ostia do not seem to have had such *collegia*, although they had fire-fighting *vigiles* from the time of Claudius (see Ruggiero s.v. *centonarius*).

melius loquere : euphemism, = 'avoid saying what is of ill omen'; cf. Cic. *Brut.* 329 'melius, quaeso, ominare, inquit Brutus.'

§ 2 modo sic . . . perdiderat : an unusual form of expression in which a general remark becomes amusing when put into some particular setting. Otto *Spr.*, introd. xxx, notes some parallels, e.g. Lucilius 531M 'hoc aliud longe est, inquit qui cepe serebat.' In the equivalent type of expression in English parataxis is not used: '. . . , as the bishop said to the actress.'

quod hodie . . . truditur : the whole sentence perhaps formed a popular epitaph. Wouweren cites an epitaph 'vixi ut vivis. morieris ut sum mortuus. sic vita truditur' (cf. Sen. *Brev. Vit.* 17. 6 'per occupationes vita trudetur') and Heim, *Incant. Mag.* 556, has 'hodie quod est, cras non est' (cited by Heraeus, p. 124). See also R. Lattimore, *Themes in Greek and Latin Epitaphs*, 250 ff.

§ 3 patria : town or home-town. Similarly the Greek πατρίς should not always be rendered as 'country' or 'native land'; cf. *Ev. Marc.* 6: 1, 4.

homines : cf. 39. 4 *hominem inter homines*, and see Shackleton Bailey on Cic. *Att.* xiii. 52. 2: 'Basically the implication of *homo, ἐμφατικῶς*, is "a man like other men", with ordinary sense and sympathies, as opposed to the more or less than human.'

delicati : fastidious, hard to please; cf. Sen. *Contr.* 10. 1. 1. 'non offeres delicatis oculis sordidam vestem.'

ubique medius caelus est : i.e. heaven is just as near to us wherever we are. In other words, 'it's the same for everybody'; cf. Cic. *Tusc.* i. 104 'undique enim ad inferos tantundem viae est.' For the form *caelus* see note on 39. 4 fer[i]culus.

§ 4 porcos coctos ambulare : Athenaeus 268–9 cites even more imaginative descriptions of an ideal land: roast thrushes served on the wing appear on menus from two fifth-century comic poets, Teleclides and Pherecrates, along with such items as fish which come to the house and bake themselves, then serve themselves on the tables.

habituri sumus : both here and at § 6 and § 10 *daturus est* Echion uses the periphrastic future when he is describing forth-coming entertainments. This form, used in these instances by Echion where his eager anticipation is evident, may be a more emphatic form than the normal future, rather than a pointless variant for it such as becomes common in late Latin; see L.–H.–S. 312, E. B. Lease, *AJP* xl (1919), 270 ff.

excellente : cf. 66. 3 (Habinnas) *excellente Hispanum*. Since most adjectives have a separate form for the neuter nomina-tive and accusative singular, there is sometimes a tendency to devise one for those few adjectives in which all genders share the same form of nominative. See Grandgent, p. 153.

in triduo die festa : 'within three days at the festival' (cf. *CIL* vi. 4. 2. 33929 'in triduo ereptus est rebus humanis'). The singu-lar *dies festus* is sometimes used of a festival lasting several days (cf. Liv. xxv. 23. 14 'nuntians diem festum Dianae per triduum agi', *TLL* s.v. *festus* 627. 48 ff.), but this scarcely justifies taking *in triduo* as 'lasting three days'.

familia non lanisticia, sed plurimi liberti : the freedmen re-ferred to here could be experienced gladiators who had won manumission after a period of service as slaves in the training-school of the *lanista*. See Balsdon, *Life and Leisure*, 289–91, *SG*[8] ii. 370 f.

§ 5 Titus noster : Echion claims familiarity with some local magistrate by using his *praenomen*. See note on 30. 3 *Gaius noster*, H. T. Axtell, *CP* x (1915), 398 ff.

caldicerebrius : 'hot-headed, impetuous'; only here, although restored by conjecture at 58. 4 for *caldus cicer eius*. Heraeus notes Dares, *B. Troi.* 16. 21 ed. Meister, *cerebro calido*, and cf. French *cerveau brûlé*.

non est mixcix : 'he does nothing by halves.' The word *mixcix* does not occur elsewhere, but the reduplication (cf. English 'shilly-shally') can be paralleled in other popular formations, e.g. *tuxtax*. See Hof. *LU* 60 f.

§ 6 ferrum : gladiatorial fight. For this sense cf. Suet. *Nero* 12. 1 'exhibuit autem ad ferrum etiam quadringentos senatores', Gaius in *Dig.* xxviii. 1. 8. 4 'qui ad ferrum aut ad bestias . . . damnantur'.

sine fuga : financial considerations rather than humanity usually ensured the survival of a defeated gladiator. Contests were fought to the death only if the person giving the show wished to display unusual generosity towards the spectator. Gaius iii. 146 cites a contract whereby the show-giver pays 20 *denarii* for hiring a gladiator if he survives, but is deemed to have 'bought' him for 1,000 *denarii* if he is killed or disabled.

carnarium in medio : 'butchery for all to see'; a special treat. What little evidence there is on the subject suggests that any gladiators not destined to survive were normally dispatched off-stage in the *spoliarium* (cf. SHA, *Comm.* 19. 1 'impuri gladiatoris memoria aboleatur. gladiatorem in spoliario', Sen. *Ep.* 93. 12 'numquid aliquem tam stulte cupidum esse vitae putas ut iugulari in spoliario quam in harena malit?').

amphitheater : Buecheler's conjecture is based on the occurrence of *amphiteater* (*CIL* vi. 31893 f) and similar forms in glossaries and late writers, e.g. *raster* for *rastrum*, *candelaber* for *candelabrum*. See Heraeus, p. 136.

unde : 'the wherewithal'; cf. Plaut. *Capt.* 850 'scis bene esse, si sit unde', Philetaer. 7. 3 Kock ἡδέως ζῆν . . . ἐὰν ἔχῃ τις ὁπόθεν.

sestertium trecenties : 30,000,000 (see note on 38. 12 for ways of expressing large sums of money). This is the amount mentioned in Trimalchio's proposed epitaph in 71. 12.

†male† : the text of *H* gives an implausible word-order, whether it is punctuated '. . . pater male.' (cf. *Pass. Perp. et Fel.* 7 'per infirmitatem . . . male obiit'), or '. . . pater. male . . .' 'even though he mis-spends 400,000 sesterces' (cf. *male vendere, male emere*). Müller in his second edition punctuates after *pater*, but takes *male* as an exclamation: 'what a pity!' 'too bad!'.

§ 7 nannos : dwarfs. Buecheler's conjecture provides a suitable special attraction for Titus' show (dwarfs are sometimes mentioned as a way of winning popular favour; cf. SHA, *Sev. Alex.* 34. 2, Marq. *Prl.* 152). The reading *Manios* is just possible. Festus (128L) cites a proverb 'multi Mani Ariciae' (cf. Otto s.v. *Manius*), but shows that there was some doubt whether it meant famous men or ugly men. Either of these categories might have formed the special attraction, but it is doubtful whether *Manios* would suggest anything sufficiently specific in this context.

essedariam : see note on *essedarius* at 36. 6. The feats of British women charioteers during the invasion of A.D. 43 and subsequently may have led to a demand for *essedariae* in the arenas of Italy. Women gladiators of other types are, however, mentioned as early as the time of Augustus: Nicol. Damasc. in Athen. 154 a claims that some Romans ordered in their wills that their most beautiful women slaves should fight as gladiators. It is true that Tacitus (*Ann.* xv. 32) thinks it worth including in his account that women gladiators fought in the arena in A.D. 64, but Nero's enormity consisted in forcing or allowing women of noble birth to do what some women of lower status had long been accustomed to do. See Balsdon, *Life and Leisure*, 167 f.

delectaretur : this verb is again used as a deponent at 64. 2 (Trimalchio). In early Latin certain verbs fluctuate between deponent and active, but in later Latin the number of such verbs is greatly increased. In the *Cena* note also 47. 4 *pudeatur*, 48. 4 *fastiditum*, 57. 3 *rideatur*. See L.–H.–S. 292, Palmer, p. 163. Süss (pp. 44, 70) argues that Petronius wishes to represent here the kind of error made by an uneducated person striving unsuccessfully to speak correctly (as in English 'between you and I').

In real life the slave might be intellectually or culturally superior to his master or mistress, although marriage between them was forbidden by law, but in literature such liaisons became a favourite topic because of the piquant contrasts they provided; see Sullivan, *Petronius*, 121.

videbis . . . amasiunculos : 'you will see the crowd quarrel, jealous husbands against Casanovas.'

§ 8 sestertiarius : this word occurs only here, but cf. 74. 15 *homo dipundiarius*, Cic. *Fam.* v. 10a. 1 *semissis homo*.

ad bestias dedit : G. Bagnani (*Arbiter of Elegance*, pp. 14 ff.) argues that Glyco must here have been acting *suo arbitrio*, and that such a condemnation of a slave would have been contrary to the *lex Petronia de servis* of A.D. 60 or 61; hence the supposed incident must be placed before that date. But Petronius should not be expected to make Echion report a fictional case with such precision that the reader can work out the legal implications; and Bagnani is unwise to base his argument on the assumption that in a real case in the reign of Nero all the facts would necessarily be brought out in court, even if the magistrate had been 'fixed'.

facere : probably a *double entendre*; cf. 87. 5, 9, and see note on 47. 4 'sua re causa facere'. When a freedman client was attacked on the ground that he had been the *concubinus* of his patron, Haterius replied: 'impudicitia in ingenuo crimen est, in servo necessitas, in liberto officium' (Sen. *Contr.* iv *praef.* 10).

illa matella : i.e. Glyco's wife. For this use of *matella* cf. Plaut. *Pers.* 533 'numquam ego te tam esse matulam credidi.'

§ 9 **filicem** : lit. 'fern' (cf. Hor. *Sat.* i. 3. 37 'neglectis urenda filix innascitur agris'), hence used figuratively of some worthless person (cf. Paul. Fest. 86M 'filicones mali et nullius usus, a felice dicti').

milvo volanti...ungues resecare : proverbial for accomplishing the impossible. For the kite as a type for avarice cf. 42. 7 *milvinum genus*, Otto s.v. *milvus* (1).

Glyco, Glyco : for this kind of repetition see note on 36. 7 *Carpe, Carpe*.

dedit suas : the most plausible solution here is to supply *poenas* (Burmann). Löfstedt, *Synt.* ii. 251 ff. cites other elliptical phrases with *suus*, although none of these is exactly parallel with this passage.

stigmam : for the feminine form see note on 44. 8 *schemas.*

§ 10 **subolfacio quia** : the accusative with infinitive after verbs of saying and perceiving is replaced more and more in late Latin by clauses introduced by *quod*, *quia*, or *quoniam* (cf. Elcock, p. 150). No indisputable examples of this usage with *quia* and few with *quod* are found before Petronius; cf. 46. 4 (Echion) 'dixi quia mustella comedit', 71. 9 (Trimalchio) 'scis quod epulum dedi', 131. 7 (Proselenos) 'vides quod aliis leporem excitavi?' (At 43. 3 Delz conjectures 'de re tamen ego verum dicam quia linguam caninam comedi'.) Note, however, that even the freedmen in the *Cena* normally have the classical accusative with the infinitive, e.g. 46. 1 'scimus te prae litteras fatuum esse.' See L.–H.–S. 572, 576 ff., 586 f., Löfstedt, *Peregr.* 116 ff.

epulum daturus est...binos denarios : cf. 71. 9. The phraseology is conventional; cf., for example, *CIL* ix. 2553 'epulum dedit decurionibus et Augustalibus sing(ulis) HS VIII' (= two *denarii* each). *epulum* often stands for a money payment rather than an actual dinner; see Marq. *Prl.* 209 ff. In some of these distributions every citizen was allowed a share, but often special categories such as *decuriones* or *Augustales* (and occasionally their children) were selected. By analogy, therefore, *meis* probably means 'my fellow members of the *collegium* of *centonarii*'. See R. Duncan-Jones, 'An Epigraphic Survey of Costs in Roman Italy', *BSR* xxxiii n.s. xx (1965), 189 ff., esp. 210–21, 257–73.

Mammea ... Norbano : these must be rival candidates for a magistracy in the *colonia* (*hunc* in § 10 = Mammea, *ille* in § 11 = Norbanus). Mammea is elsewhere a woman's name (see Friedlaender's note). The name Norbanus was borne by several notable Romans during the Republic.

plenis velis : 'at a canter' (Sullivan); cf. Quint. *Decl.* 12. 16 'plenis velis mors venit', Otto s.v. *velum* (2).

vinciturum : Vulgar form of the future participle of *vincere*, in the place of *victurus*, which also had to serve as the participle of *vivere*. Similar peculiar forms, if not this particular one, occur in glossaries and late writers (e.g. *disciturus, cresciturus, solviturus*), but an educated reader of Petronius' time might find *vinciturum* almost as odd as the infinitive *loquere* at 46. 1. See Heraeus, pp. 130 f., Süss, pp. 71 f.

§ 11 bestiarios : these are often said to have been criminals sent unarmed into the arena to be killed by wild beasts, in contrast with the *venatores*, whose skill and weapons gave them some chance of surviving; but the existence of a *ludus bestiariorum* shows that they too were not altogether untrained and defenceless. Undoubtedly, however, they did not enjoy the same esteem as the successful gladiator: Claudius was despised for taking pleasure in watching *bestiarii* and the inferior, lunch-interval gladiators (*meridiani*); cf. Suet. *Claud.* 34. 2, Cic. *Sest.* 135 'praeclara aedilitas! unus leo, ducenti bestiarii', and see Balsdon, *Life and Leisure*, 308 ff.

de lucerna equites : perhaps something like 'pint-sized knights'. Lamps decorated with figures of gladiators have frequently been found in graves (cf. *SG*8 ii. 529); possibly, therefore, *equites* should be taken here as a t.t. for mounted gladiators (cf. *SG*8 ii. 542, Galen xiii. 601 ed. Kuehn θεασάμενος γάρ τινα μονομάχων τῶν καλουμένων ἱππέων).

burdubasta : hap. leg. The first part of this word must come from *burdo*, 'mule'. The second part may be connected with *bastum* 'stave' (cf. SHA, *Comm.* 13. 3). *burdubasta* may then mean 'a stick to drive a mule', and could possibly have been used figuratively as the equivalent of our phrase 'as thin as a rake'. See also Stefenelli, pp. 91 f., Swanson, pp. 103 f.

tertiarius : a gladiator kept in reserve to meet the victor from an earlier contest in the show; cf. Plin. *Ep*. viii. 14. 21, *CIL* iv. 1179 'gl(adiatorum) par(ia) XXX et eor(um) supp(ositicii) pugn(abunt) Pompeis.' In Sen. *Ep*. 7. 4 the newcomer fights armed against the unarmed survivor of the previous bout, and then fights unarmed against an armed opponent, but this refinement need not have been typical. See *SG*[8] ii. 391 n. 3.

nervia : 'hamstrings'. Normally the masculine *nervus* is found, but the neuter (*nervia*) occurs in Varro *Men*. 368, and in glosses and other late sources. See Heraeus, p. 137.

§ **12 flaturae** : 'the only fighter of any quality'. The metaphor here seems to be connected with the use of bellows in metal-casting; cf. *flaturarius* 'metal-caster'.

Thraex : gladiator armed with a sabre and a small shield. See *SG*[8] ii. 539 f., Grant, *Gladiators* (1971 edn.), 56.

ad dictata pugnavit : Echion criticizes the over-drilled style of fighting; cf. 36. 6 'ut putares essedarium hydraule cantante pugnare', Suet. *Iul*. 26. 3 'ut disciplinam singulorum susciperent ipsique dictata exercentibus (sc. gladiatoribus) darent'.

plane fugae merae : (sc. the fights were) 'an absolute rout'. Less plausibly Sedgwick takes *fugae* as abstract for concrete.

§ **13 inquit** : sc. Norbanus. Sometimes the subject of *inquit* must be supplied from the context, especially where it introduces the words of an imaginary opponent. See L.–H.–S. 417 f., *TLL* vii. 1. 1779. 44 ff.

plodo : Vulgar for *plaudo*.

manus manum lavat : 'one good turn deserves another.' The same proverb is ascribed in Plat. *Axioch*. 366 c to Epicharmus ἔθος ἐστὶν αὐτῷ φωνεῖν τὸ ’Επιχάρμειον "ἁ δὲ χεὶρ τὰν χεῖρα νίζει·" δός τι καὶ λάβε τι; cf. Sen. *Apoc*. 9. 6.

Ch. 46

§ **1 argutat** : this active form is also used by Hermeros at 57. 8 'nec mu nec ma argutas', cf. Prop. i. 6. 7 'illa mihi totis argutat noctibus ignis.'

loquere . . . loquis : (*loqui H*, corr. Burmann) : very unusual active forms (see Heraeus, p. 127). When Echion turns to address the rhetorician Agamemnon, his Latin becomes strikingly in-correct (see notes below on *pauperorum, prae,* and *persua-deam*).

non es nostrae fasciae : the general sense is clear enough: 'You aren't one of us' (cf. Pers. 5. 115 'cum fueris nostrae paulo ante farinae'). The precise meaning of *fascia,* however, is uncertain. It is found as a measurement of length or area (*TLL* vi. 1. 298. 15 ff. cites for this sense *CIL* xii. 6032a 'fines fasciae fundi Pacatiani'), cf. Fronto 187N 'nostrae mensurae hominibus'.

pauperorum : this form in place of *pauperum* may show simply the shift of adjectives with stems in -*r* from third to second declension (see Väänänen, *Introd.,* p. 114); but there could be a more complicated development, analogous to that of *diibus* (see note on 44. 16): a distinctive feminine *paupera* is formed (cf. Plaut. *Vid.* fr. 3 *paupera res*) which subsequently gives rise to a second-declension paradigm for the masculine on the analogy of *tener, liber,* etc.

prae litteras fatuum : 'crazy along of (on account of) reading'; cf. note on 39. 12 *prae mala.* As in §§ 7–8, Echion's grammatical errors are most noticeable when he talks about education.

§ 2 quid ergo est? : see note on 30. 11.

te persuadeam : Niceros also has the accusative with *persuadere* at 62. 2. No certain example of this construction occurs before this, although the perfect participle passive is used personally in *Rhet. ad Herenn.* i. 9 f., Caecina in Cic. *Fam.* vi. 7. 2, and in poetic and late Latin. See L.–H.–S. 32 f.

casulas : for the plural see note on 44. 15.

manducemus : this word gradually replaces *comedo* in later Latin (cf. French *manger,* Ital. *mangiare*), but it is not exclu-sively Vulgar: it is used by Trimalchio (56. 4), but also collo-quially by Augustus (Suet. *Aug.* 76. 2 'duas buccas manducavi'). Note, however, that *comesse* is used seven times in the *Cena,* mostly in the speech of the freedmen (e.g. 44. 15).

belle erit : for the adverb with *esse* see note on 34. 10 'dum licet esse bene'.

disparpallavit : 'scattered'. Cholodniak's conjecture (see *Rh. Mus.* lxiv (1909), 330), based on the existence of French *épar-piller* and Ital. *sparpagliare,* is the most likely improvement of *dispare pallavit* in *H*; see Meyer-Lübke s.v. **disparpallare,* no. 2674a. Other suggestions include (i) *dispare pullavit* Reiske.

This would have to mean 'has made everything grow at the wrong time', just as *pullulare* can be used transitively as well as intransitively; (ii) *depravavit* Müller². This gives a satisfactory sense, but assumes a greater corruption in *H*.

§ 3 **cicaro** : again used of a small boy at 71. 11. The meaning and derivation are unknown.

Friedlaender thought that Echion's use of the word *servulus* is meant to reveal his inability to forget his own servile origin, but the phrase *habebis ad latus servulum* may be proverbial. On the other hand, Echion's concern for the boy's education does not prove that a boy of free birth is meant (on the education of Roman slaves see H.-I. Marrou, *History of Education in Antiquity*, 359 f., 554).

quattuor partes dicit : 'he can divide by four'; cf. 58. 7, 75. 4. Division into various fractions was a regular exercise for Roman schoolboys. The absurdity of Echion's pride in his boy's accomplishment is shown by, for example, Hor. *A P* 325 f. 'Romani pueri longis rationibus assem / discunt in partes centum diducere', *CIL* xi. 1236 'Attico ser. qui vixit ann. XX litteratus Graecis et Latinis librarius partes dixit CCC'.

caput de tabula non tollit : in colloquial and late Latin there is an increasingly frequent use of *de* at the expense of *a* and *ex* (cf. Elcock, pp. 36, 148); note also the quite different usage at 46. 7 *aliquid de iure*.

bono filo : 'there's good stuff in him' (Sullivan). *filum*, lit. 'thread', is sometimes in its metaphorical use applied to the texture of oratory, but here it is more general.

in aves morbosus : 'mad about birds'. This kind of passion was quite common among Roman children. Fronto writes of his grandson (181N): 'avicularum etiam cupidissimus est; pullis gallinarum columbarum passerum oblectatur, quo studio me a prima infantia devinctum fuisse saepe audivi ex eis qui mihi educatores aut magistri fuerunt.' Pliny (*NH* x. 116) describes the attractions of *cardueles* (finches) as pets: 'minumae avium cardueles imperata faciunt nec voce tantum sed pedibus et ore pro manibus. est quae boum mugitus imitetur, in Arelatensi agro taurus appellata.' See Balsdon, *Life and Leisure*, 91, 151 f.

§ 4 **dixi quia mustella comedit** : see note on 45. 10 *subolfacio quia*. One type of *mustella* (weasel) appears to have been treated as a household pet (cf. Plin. *NH* xxix. 60 'haec autem quae in domibus nostris oberrat'; some confirmation of this is to be found in the fact that in fables the *mustella* takes the place of our cat in encounters with mice, and in its use as a girl's name (cf. *RE* xvi. 902 ff.).

nenias : the sense 'trifles, nonsense' would fit here and at 47. 10 (see note). In an exhaustive study of the word (*TAPA* lxxiv (1943), 215–68) J. L. Heller argues that the central meaning was much closer to 'plaything' than to 'dirge' (the sense which it has in various authors).

§ 5 Graeculis calcem impingit : 'he's giving Greek the boot', i.e. he has finished with it, rather than 'he's putting his foot on Greek', i.e. he is making a start on it. For the order of study cf. *CIL* vi. 4. 2. 33929, where the epitaph of a seven-year-old boy has 'qui studens litteras Graecas non monstratas sibi Latinas adripuit et in triduo ereptus est rebus humanis'. Quintilian (i. 1. 12–14) advises that a boy's education should begin with Greek, but that he should not study Greek exclusively for too long, in case his pronunciation of Latin should begin to suffer. His advice, however, applies to boys from upper-class Roman families, and need not be typical of the educational system in other towns in Italy, even those which were Greek in origin. See Marrou, pp. 346 ff.

fit : *fit* and *est* have both been suggested in order to supply the required indicative (cf. § 4 'etiam si in aves morbosus est'). Süss (p. 72) retains *sit* as another example of 'hyperurbanism' (see note on 45. 7 *delectaretur*), but the indicative *consistit*, apparently also governed by *etiam si*, counts against the subjunctive here.

scit quidem litteras : *venit dem litteras H* is open to two objections: (i) *dem litteras* must be taken as an indirect command introduced awkwardly by *venit*, and the meaning of *litteras* is obscure (suggestions have included a cheque in payment for his services (cf. Ov. *AA* i. 428), books, exercise-books, or even letters of the alphabet formed out of ivory, cf. Quint. i. 1. 26); (ii) the contrast between the two teachers is not made altogether clear: the satisfactory teacher demands nothing for himself ('et quicquid dederis, contentus est'), but we expect a mention of the cupidity of the unsatisfactory teacher (H. Lamer, *Philologische Wochenschrift* (1927), 831 tries to supply this by interpreting *litteras* as a cheque). The text printed here assumes a lacuna after *venit* in which the first teacher's demands might have been stated; thereafter Jacobs's attractive conjecture *scit quidem* is accepted (for *scire litteras* cf. 10. 5 'et tu litteras scis et ego').

§ 6 feriatis diebus : schools closed frequently for holidays and festivals, on some of which occasions it was the custom for teachers to receive gifts from pupils or parents (see Marq. *Prl.* 92 ff.); but over-frequent holidays perhaps held dangers for the teacher: Theophrastus (*Char.* 30. 14) alleges that a parent might through stinginess keep his children away from school for the month of Anthesterion to avoid paying their fees for a month with so many interruptions for festivals.

§ 7 libra : Echion's use of neuter forms of words normally masculine (cf. § 8 *thesaurum*) conveys the impression of uneducated speech even more vividly than does the converse phenomenon.

rubricata : since the opening words on the official copy of the text of a law were written in vermilion, *rubrica* came to mean the title of the law or else the law itself (see Mayor on Juv. 14. 192). So here *libra rubricata* means law-books.

artificium : in view of the accusatives 'aut tonstrinum aut praeconem aut certe causidicum' it is safer to regard *artificii H* as a mere slip rather than as a deliberate solecism modelled on the genitive sometimes found after *doctus* and *docilis*. For a defence of *artificii* see Hofmann, *Syntax*, 390; cf. H. L. W. Nelson, *Petronius en zijn 'vulgair' Latijn*, 142.

aut tonstrinum aut praeconem aut certe causidicum : 'either a barber or an auctioneer or at any rate an advocate'. Echion first chooses two callings which were despised by Romans in comfortable circumstances. Juvenal (1. 24) sneers at an ex-barber who has made a fortune; the *praeco* too was a target for ridicule, even if he was successful in his trade (cf. Juv. 3. 157 f., Mart. v. 56. 10 f.). But the words *aut certe causidicum*, added on as if to refer to a second best, become comic only on the assumption that *causidici* in general were no more impecunious than the average barrister today.

The use of *praeconem* and *causidicum* instead of abstract nouns like *tonstrinum* is presumably colloquial; cf. Amm. Marc. xvi. 8. 10 'Dionysius . . . tonstrices docuit filias', Mart. v. 56. 9 'discat citharoedus aut choraules', *TLL* v. 1. 1731. 45 ff.

§ 8 Primigeni : this name is borne by numerous slaves and freedmen (see, for example, index to *CIL* iv).

modo modo : see note on 37. 3.

collo suo : the insertion of a possessive pronoun with a part of the body occurs in Vulgar writers (*Bell. Afr.*, Nepos, Vitruvius), and with increasing frequency in later times. In Petronius it is found in narrative (cf. 67. 9 *de cervice sua*, 74. 11 *ad faciem suam* and *sinu suo*) as well as in the speech of the freedmen.

thesaurum : Echion ends in style with another irregular gender at a striking point (see note on § 7 *libra*), and two misapplied proverbs. For less materialistic versions of these proverbs cf. Xen. *Mem.* i. 6. 14 καὶ τοὺς θησαυροὺς τῶν πάλαι σοφῶν ἀνδρῶν, οὓς ἐκεῖνοι κατέλιπον ἐν βιβλίοις γράψαντες, *CGL* iii. 39. 15 'ars enim transfertur ab homine et propterea ars non moritur.'

Ch. 47

Petronius could not afford to let the inane conversation of the freedmen guests drift on for too long. Trimalchio as the main character in the episode must be allowed more scope, but even he does not dominate the proceedings for too long at any one time.

§ 2. The disgusting man (ἀηδής) in Theophr. *Char.* 20. 6 also enlivens the conversation at dinner with an account of the workings of his digestion: 'When you sit next to him at a meal he will describe to you how he took a dose of hellebore which gave him a thorough clean-out; "You should have seen the colour of the bile in my excreta," he says, "darker than that gravy you've got." '

respondit : probably at least semi-technical with reference to excretion; cf. Cels. iv. 17 'solvere alvum, si aliter non respondit, etiam ducere'. Similarly ἀποκρίνεσθαι and ἀπόκρισις in Greek medical writers; cf. Arist. *PA* 665ᵇ24 ᾗ τὰ περιττώματα ἀποκρίνεται, Hipp. *Vict.* 4. 93 ἀπόκρισις σιτίων.

nec medici se inveniunt : 'the doctors don't know where they are.' For *se invenire* in a medical context cf. Plin. med. 40. 15R 'multi medici se [medicos] adversus hoc malum non inveniunt'; Seneca (*Contr.* iii. *praef.* 13) says of schoolroom declaimers when they are faced with real cases in the Senate or Forum 'non imbrem ferre, non solem sciunt, vix se inveniunt.'

The mention of more than one *medicus* in attendance might be taken as another piece of boastfulness on the part of Trimalchio, but the term is applied to various medical auxiliaries as well as to medical practitioners in our sense.

malicorium : 'pomegranate-rind'. The ailment which has baffled his doctors yields (like that of Theophrastus' disgusting man quoted above) to a standard remedy (for pomegranate-rind as a laxative cf. *Brit. Pharmacopoeia* s.v. *granati fructus cortex*), combined with pinewood boiled in vinegar (*taeda ex aceto*), a concoction more suitable for external use (Plin. *NH* xxiv. 41 notes *taeda decocta in aceto* as a remedy for toothache).

ex is often used like this in recipes and prescriptions: e.g. Cels. iii. 18. 8 'rutam ex aceto contritam', Apic. vi. 8 'anserem elixum calidum ex iure frigido Apiciano'; see L.–H.–S. 266.

§ 3 **veterem :** 'I hope that now it (i.e. my stomach) is behaving itself again.' Heinsius conjectured *veterem* for *ventrem H.* Müller deletes *ventrem*, no doubt regarding it as having been interpolated because of *venter* just before this, but the intrusion of the ungrammatical accusative is then hard to explain.

Note that here Trimalchio, while showing lack of taste in describing his constipation at all, uses euphemistic rather than coarse language.

imponit : altered unnecessarily by some editors to *imponet*; see note on 27. 4 *ponitis*.

§ 4 **sua re causa facere :** 'relieve himself'; cf. 66. 2 'et cum mea re causa facio, non ploro' (also 62. 4 'coepit ad stelas facere', although there *facere* has sometimes been taken to mean 'make for'). The construction of *sua re causa* has not been satisfactorily explained. It is conceivable that *sua re facere* 'to act in one's own interest' acquired also a euphemistic sense (see Lindsay on Plaut. *Capt.* 296 'tua re feceris') but even so *causa* is neither needed in the text nor is it a likely gloss on *sua re*. Asyndeton of *re causa* is implausible, and perhaps the least unlikely solution is to assume that *sua re* represents a genitive *suae rei*.

pudeatur : another non-classical deponent; see Neue iii³. 651 and note on 45. 7 above.

nemo nostrum solide natus est : at 102. 10 Eumolpus suggests that to avoid capture on board ship Encolpius and Giton should be hidden in bundles, but Encolpius notes a compelling objection to the plan: ' "ita vero" inquam "tamquam solidos alligaturus, quibus non soleat venter iniuriam facere?"' The resemblance may be a mere coincidence, yet it serves as a reminder that Encolpius is not to be placed far above Trimalchio and his circle in sophistication. On the other hand his revelation of his own greed at 60. 7 looks like a deliberate insertion in order to affect our response to his report of Habinnas' conversation in ch. 66.

continere : Trimalchio's remarks here have too readily been taken to be a parody of the behaviour attributed to Claudius in Suet. *Claud.* 32: 'dicitur etiam meditatus edictum quo veniam daret flatum crepitumque ventris in convivio emittendi, cum periclitatum quendam prae pudore ex continentia repperisset.' Philosophizing on this kind of *continentia* must have been long familiar: Cicero writes (*Fam.* ix. 22. 5) 'sed illi (sc. Stoici) etiam crepitus aiunt aeque liberos ac ructus esse oportere', and Nicarchus, perhaps a little later than Petronius, tells of its dangers (*Anth. Pal.* xi. 395): πορδὴ ἀποκτείνει πολλοὺς ἀδιέξοδος οὖσα.

vetare : the sense does not quite fit what has preceded, and the sentence runs too ponderously for such a colloquial remark. On the assumption that a scribe wrongly felt the sentence to be incomplete, Kaibel deleted *vetare*, thus giving a racier sense as well as improving the rhythm.

ne : 'not even'. This use of *ne* for *ne . . . quidem,* noted as a barbarism in Quint. i. 5. 39, occurs also at 9. 6, where, according to *L,* Encolpius says to Ascyltos 'quid dicis . . . muliebris patientiae scortum, cuius ne spiritus purus est?'. The manuscript reading should probably be accepted in both passages; see G. Bendz, *Eranos* xxxix (1941), 35, who argues that the stylistic differences between the speech of the freedmen and Encolpius' narrative should not be exaggerated.

Iovis : this form of the nominative is found in early and late Latin; see Neue i³. 293 f.

§ 5 desomnem : found only here.

vetui : changed unnecessarily by Buecheler to the irregular present *vetuo* (*vetuo* occurs at 53. 8, but there it provides bathos at the end of Trimalchio's lofty utterance).

foras : see note on 30. 3 *foras cenat.*

lasani : Buecheler. This unparalleled masculine, rather than Scheffer's *lasanum,* must lie behind the meaningless *lassant* of *H.* See note on 39. 4 for the change of gender.

minutalia : 'bits and pieces'; probably a euphemism for sponges (cf. Sen. *Ep.* 70. 20). In one glossary the word *minutal* is noted as meaning 'illud quod ponitur in latrinis ad purgandum anum' (*CGL* v. 621. 26). Heraeus, pp. 68 f., thinks that this gloss is derived from precisely this passage, and does not point to a technical expression in general use.

§ 6 **anathymiasis** : 'exhalation', 'vapours' cf. *fluctum* 'flux'. Galen (*UP* xi. 14 = 901 K) speaks of an exhalation from the humours being drawn up towards the head: ἡ ἐκ τῶν χυμῶν ἀναθυμίασις ἐπὶ τὴν κεφαλὴν ἀναφέρεται.

§ 7 **castigamus . . . risum** : 'we put a restraint on our laughter'; an unusually recherché expression.

§ 8 **lautitiarum** : rightly deleted by Fraenkel. It comes in awkwardly here, since *quod aiunt* must be taken with *in medio clivo laborare*; and in any case it labours the point a little (cf. 27. 5, where *L* inserts *lautissimus homo*). There are signs elsewhere that an interpolator has inserted an explanatory genitive, e.g. 137. 5 *tristitiae* (see the list in Müller[1] xliii, although he has changed his mind over some of the instances given there).

Ovid uses two variants of the phrase *in medio clivo laborare*: *Rem. Am.* 394 'principio clivi noster anhelat equus', *Her.* 20. 41 'mille doli restant, clivo sudamus in imo.'

commundatis : Heinsius' conjecture allows a new sentence to begin at *ego putabam* (cf. 65. 4). *cum mundatis H* gives us one sentence of unlikely length.

nomenculator : a slave who has to aid his master's memory by announcing the names of those whom he meets in the street, or who come to his house to a *salutatio*. He may well have had other functions at dinner, for example, assigning the guests to their places at table (cf. Athen. 47); and see Martial's caricature (x. 30. 23 f.) 'nomenculator mugilem citat notum / et adesse iussi prodeunt senes mulli.' The vulgarity of Trimalchio's *nomenculator* appears to lie in his over-detailed description of the next course.

§ 9 **petauristarios** : spring-board or trapeze artistes. See Mayor on Juv. 14. 265 f.

circulis : 'side-shows'; cf. 68. 6 *circulatores*, 'showmen'.

§ 10 **penthiacum** : found only here. Pentheus was torn to pieces by the Bacchae, so this word may have been used for a dish in which the ingredients were divided into pieces and stewed.

nenias : probably 'nonsense, trivialities' (see note on 46. 4). The word appears in a list of pork dishes in the *Notae Tironianae* (103. 78), and it seems to mean something like sausage in Arnob. 7. 24; but J. L. Heller (*TAPA* lxxiv (1943), 215 ff.) suggests that these and similar passages are derived ultimately from misinterpretations of Plautus *Bacch.* 889 *sovicina nenia* and *Poen.* 231 *facere neniam.*

oenococtos : 'cooked in wine' (*eno cocto H*; cf. 74. 4 *aeno coctus H*). *oenococtus* occurs several times in the recipes of Apicius, where it is corrupted in one or two manuscripts into *enococtus* and *aenococtus* (cf. André on Apic. v. 1. 2, viii. 7. 11). It has been restored here and at 74. 4 on the assumption that the same technical term was used as in Apicius. *aeno coctus* 'pot-roasted' would be attractive here, where it is used of calves, but less so at 74. 4, where it is used of a cock; Heraeus (p. 118) defends it on the analogy of e.g. *Acta Arval.* 1. 21 *exta aulicocta,* Varr. *LL* v. 104 *exta ollicoqua.*

§ 11 **decuria** : a squad of ten slaves. Columella (i. 9. 7 f.) says that for work on the land a group of this size was easier to control than a number of dispersed individuals, yet small enough for each slave to feel that his work mattered.

§ 12 **empticius** : cf. *Decl. Min.* 224R 'servus aut domi natus est aut relictus hereditate aut emptus.'

§ 13 **viatorum** : sometimes used technically for the attendants of magistrates; here perhaps equivalent to *cursores* (on whom see note on 28. 4).

cocum quidem potentiae admonitum : *potentiae* (*potentia H*) is suspiciously vague, and some word like *domini* has perhaps fallen out. The picture of the cook, by convention a comic figure, being led away by the pig, here referred to by anticipation as *obsonium,* is a little abrupt, but not impossible. For the personification of a dish cf. Juv. 4. 64 'exclusi spectant admissa obsonia patres.'

Ch. 48

§ 1 **bonum faciatis** : see note on 39. 2 'hoc vinum vos oportet suave faciatis.'

§ 2 **ad salivam facit** : 'makes your mouth water'. See *OLD* s.v. *facio* 30 on *facere ad* 'be effective in producing'.

Tarraciniensibus et Tarentinis : Trimalchio's boastfulness—Tarentum is about 150 miles from Tarracina—is pointed by the alliteration and by the choice of the Vulgar form *Tarraciniensibus* for *-nensibus* (see Heraeus, p. 146), as well as by *suburbano* and the mock-modest diminutive *agellis.*

On the use of names of peoples as place-names see L.–H.–S. 753.

§ 3 Africam . . . ire : the preposition is omitted before the name of a country in verse and in Vulgar writers, and occasionally in classical prose. See L.–H.–S. 50, K.–S. i. 481.

§ 4 controversiam : the technical term for a popular type of rhetorical exercise in which opposing speeches were delivered in a mock trial, with the issue turning on some quirkish point of law, usually imaginary. In the next sentence *causas* should also be taken in a technical sense: cf. Sen. *Contr.* i *praef.* 12 'declamabat autem Cicero non quales nunc controversias dicimus, ne tales quidem quales ante Ciceronem dicebantur, quas thesis vocabant. hoc enim genus materiae quo nos exercemur adeo novum est ut nomen quoque eius novum sit. controversias nos dicimus: Cicero causas vocabat.' See S. F. Bonner, *Roman Declamation*, 1 ff., A. Gwynn, *Roman Education*, 163 ff.

litteras didici : 'I've learned to read and write', not 'I've learned literature' (Loeb); cf. Varr. *Men.* 517 'Diogenem litteras scisse, domusioni quod satis esset, hunc quod etiam acroasi bellorum hominum', Sen. *Clem.* 2. 1. 2 'vellem litteras nescirem'.

fastiditum : on the use of the deponent form see note on 45. 7 *delectaretur*.

II bybliothecas : the point here may be simply that Trimalchio boasts of possessing what a better-educated person would take for granted (*bybliotheca* sometimes means little more than a bookcase with its contents; cf. Plin. *Ep.* ii. 17. 8 'parieti eius in bybliothecae speciem armarium insertum est'). With the reading *tres H* Trimalchio's failure to describe the third of his libraries would produce a bizarre effect somewhat different from that of his extravagant boasts elsewhere.

peristasim : a Greek technical term in oratory, defined by Quintilian (iii. 5. 17 f.) as *negotium*, the facts of a case. Its Latin equivalent *circumstantia* is defined by Victorinus (i. 1) thus: 'accepto igitur themate primum circumstantiam sectari debes, cuius partes sunt septem haec: quis, quid, quando, ubi, cur, quemadmodum, quibus adminiculis.'

§ 5 pauper et dives : a familiar pair of characters in *controversiae*; e.g. Sen. *Contr.* v. 2 is concerned with the complications which arise when the son of a poor man wants to marry the daughter of his father's enemy, a rich man, and cf. id. ib. ii. 1, v. 5, viii.

6, x. 1. Trimalchio's interruption 'quid est pauper?' combines a pretence at being too wealthy to understand the meaning of the word *pauper* with an aping of the rhetoricians' custom of starting from a careful definition of terms.

§ 6 si factum est . . . : Heinsius rightly took *controversia* in its technical sense: 'If this happened, it can't be a *controversia* (i.e. a debate which normally used a fictitious case); if it didn't happen, it's nonsense.' Friedlaender instead took *controversia* as non-technical: 'If this actually happened, there is nothing to have an argument about . . .', but this gives a less likely contrast between *controversia non est* and *nihil est*.

§ 7 duodecim aerumnas Herculis : the adoption of Hercules as the hero of the Stoics had helped to make the story of his twelve labours one of the most hackneyed in Roman culture by this period; cf. Juv. 1. 52 with Mayor's note.

pollicem †poricino† extorsit : Trimalchio purports to be drawing on his knowledge of Homer; but whereas in *Od.* ix. 318 ff. Odysseus pierced the eye of the Cyclops Polyphemus with a blazing stake, here there is a different version, either invented by Petronius for the occasion, or perhaps taken from one of the farcical comedies about Polyphemus which must by now have become familiar (C. Stöcker, *Humor bei Petron*, 80 ff. sees traces of a non-Homeric version in which the blind giant presents his victim with a magic ring which betrays where he is; the victim is able to escape only by cutting off his own finger). No certain explanation can be given to account for the meaningless *poricino*. Fuchs and Müller[2] delete it as a dittography after *pollicem*, but it is more likely to be a corruption of some genuine word. An ablative here would give more point to *pollicem extorsit* (suggestions have included *forcipe*, 'pincers', *circino*, 'compasses', as well as Buecheler's *porcino*, which has to be assumed to stand for some instrument shaped like a hog's head).

§ 8 Cumis : since it can be taken as certain that the *Cena* was set in a Campanian town, it is natural to assume that Trimalchio is referring to the Campanian Cumae rather than to Cumae in Greece or Lydia. Several commentators have favoured the Lydian Cumae on the evidence of Ampelius (second/third century A.D.), who describes something not altogether unlike Trimalchio's Sibyl, but with reference to Bargylia, a Carian town not far from the Lydian Cumae: 'Bargylo est . . . et Herculis aedes antiqua; ibi e columna pendet cavea ferrea rotunda,

in qua conclusa Sibylla dicitur' (viii. 16); but each of the various
shrines of the Sibyl may well have had similar curiosities to
display to visitors (see *SG*[8] ii. 180).

in ampulla pendere : in legend the Sibyl was said to have
been granted immortality but not everlasting youth (cf. Ov.
Met. xiv. 130 ff.). The layout of the grotto at Cumae, revealed
in excavations since 1932, suggests that the visitor passed
through a series of doors in the long, impressive gallery, before
reaching the *adyton* at the end, where some relic might be kept
in convenient semi-darkness (see A. Maiuri, *The Phlegraean
Fields*[3], 123–32).

The decrepit Sibyl and her longing for death find parallels in
German folk-tales. Frazer's note on Ov. *Fast.* iii. 534 is worth
quoting at length:

'Once upon a time there was a girl in London who wished
to live for ever, so they say:

London, London, is a fine town.
A maiden prayed to live for ever.

And still she lives and hangs in a basket in a church, and every
St. John's Day about noon she eats a roll of bread. Another
story, taken down near Oldenburg in Holstein, tells of a jolly
dame that ate and drank right merrily and had all that heart
could desire, and she wished to live for ever. For the first
hundred years all went well, but after that she began to shrink
and shrivel up till at last she could neither walk nor stand nor
eat nor drink. But die she could not. At first they fed her as if
she were a little child, but when she grew smaller and smaller,
they put her in a glass bottle and hung her up in the church.
And there she still stands in the church of St. Mary at Lübeck.
She is as small as a mouse, but once a year she stirs.'

Σίβυλλα, τί θέλεις ... ἀποθανεῖν θέλω : 'Sibyl, what do you want?'
'I want to die.' Despite their Greek origins Trimalchio and his
friends are nowhere credited with any more than a smattering
of Greek; cf. 58. 7 *deuro de*, and note 59. 3 'ille canora voce
Latine legebat librum.'

Ch. 49

§ 1 **nondum efflaverat omnia** : 'he was still griping away';
efflare, which is not found elsewhere in this sense and is presumably slang, adds a racy touch to Encolpius' narrative.

§ 3 **apparuerat** : Heinsius's conjecture, which means that the
pig now served is compared with what it had been at 47. 8,

gives better sense than *aper fuerat H*, which compares it with the *primae magnitudinis aper* of 40. 3. The deletion of *quam paulo ante aper fuerat* would leave the end of the sentence too abrupt.

§ 4 **exinteratus** : the same spelling *exint-* recurs at §§ 5, 7, 8, and at 54. 3. Perrochat claims that in the later passages Encolpius is either quoting Trimalchio or the cook, or mocking their language, and hence each time uses the Vulgar form *exinterare* in place of *exenterare*. But note that Apicius uses *exenterare* (or *extenterare*), although his language can more easily be called Vulgar than that of Pliny, who uses *exinterare*. See Süss, p. 9, Heraeus, p. 132 n. 1.

in medio : ablative for accusative. This, like the complementary irregularity, the accusative in place of the ablative (see note on 30. 3 *foras cenat*), is not introduced wholesale by Petronius into the speech of the freedmen: the ablative here points forward to the use of *in medio* (cf. ἐν μέσῳ) as a standard expression for *in* or *inter* (see L.–H.–S. 275, 277).

§ 5 **piper et cuminum** : pepper and cumin were highly popular seasonings by this time (see André, *L'Alimentation*, 203, 209), and are often mentioned together in the recipes of Apicius (e.g. iii. 2. 1). For the use of *conicere* as a technical term in cookery see note on 37. 10 'in rutae folium coniciet'.

§ 6 **tortores** : Trimalchio's household is so grand that it has functionaries usually possessed only by the state. When Juvenal wants to condemn the extreme cruelty of some Roman ladies towards their slaves, he adds (6. 480) 'sunt quae tortoribus annua praestent.'

solet fieri : a trite phrase in support of an entreaty; cf. Donatus on Ter. *Phorm.* 245 'quod a precatoribus dici solebat *communia esse* et *posse fieri*', Sen. *Contr.* ii. 4. 10 'nihil, inquit, peccaverat; amat meretricem; solet fieri.'

§ 7 **ego, crudelissimae severitatis** : the genitive of quality is rarely found with a personal pronoun; cf. Plin. *Ep.* ii. 1. 9 'me huius aetatis', L.–H.–S. 70. Note also the somewhat commoner use of this genitive with a proper noun (cf. 57. 1 'Ascyltos, intemperantis licentiae').

Encolpius is shown again here with the naïvety seen in the 'cave canem' episode of 29. 1, having temporarily abandoned his attitude of superiority to Hermeros (39. 1) and to Trimalchio (e.g. 40. 1 and 47. 7).

debet : 'must'. *debere* is occasionally used where the necessity is logical rather than moral (see *OLD* s.v. *debeo* 6b). Cf. 33. 8 'hic nescioquid boni debet esse', 67. 7; at 7. 2 'hic debes habitare' there is a play on the two senses, as well as a *double entendre* on *habitare*.

obliviscemetur : the subjunctive marks a rhetorical question in which an idea already mentioned is indignantly repudiated; cf. L.–H.–S. 338, K.–S. i. 182.

§ 8 palam : rare as a preposition; cf. Ov. *AA* ii. 549 *me palam*, Liv. vi. 14. 5 *palam populo*, L.–H.–S. 268.

§§ 9–10. This kind of dish would hardly have surprised a gourmet of Petronius' day. From Macrob. *Sat.* iii. 13. 13 it appears that by mid second century B.C. there was a dish known as *porcus Troianus*, so called because the pig was served 'quasi aliis inclusis animalibus gravidum ut ille Troianus equus gravidus armatis fuit'.

Ch. 50

In chs. 50–2 Petronius will unfold Trimalchio's absurd ignorance of history and mythology, as well as his pretensions to good taste. These themes are linked to the incident of the cook through the mention of the plate of Corinthian bronze on which stands the cup presented to the cook for his final trick.

§ 1 automatum : 'trick' (cf. 140. 11). This sense arises from the application of the word to something which appears to work without external agency (cf. Hero, *Aut.* passim, Suet. *Claud.* 34. 2, and 54. 4 below). Clearly not an adjective here (as Lewis and Short and Heseltine take it).

Gaio feliciter : see note on 30. 3 *Gaius noster* for the use of the praenomen, and cf. 60. 7 'Augusto patri patriae feliciter' for the form of acclamation.

argentea corona : at 60. 3 the guests are given gold crowns. Trimalchio's generosity is remarkable, although the Romans had, like the Greeks, long since acquired the habit of presenting gold or silver crowns, often for quite trivial services; see Marq. *Prl.* 685 f.

Corinthia : the craze for Corinthian bronze is mocked by various writers, including Martial and Seneca, e.g. *Brev. vit.* 12. 2 'illum tu otiosum vocas qui Corinthia, paucorum furore pretiosa, anxia subtilitate concinnat et maiorem dierum partem

in aeruginosis lamellis consumit?' Strictly the term was applied
to articles made from an alloy of bronze and a precious metal.
In § 5 below Trimalchio gives a garbled account of the conventional view, itself incredible, which claimed that Corinthian
bronze was first produced as an accidental consequence of the
burning of Corinth after its capture by the Romans in 146 B.C.;
cf. Plin. *NH* xxxiv. 6, *RE* s.v. *Bronze.*

Whereas Encolpius uses the form *Corinthius* here and at
31. 9, Trimalchio uses the form *Corintheus* in §§ 2, 4, 5, 6 below;
the form in *-eus* occurs also in inscriptions (e.g. *CIL* vi. 8686)
and in Isid. *Etym.* xvi. 20. 4. See Heraeus, p. 144.

§ 4 Corinthus : this is the third joke of Trimalchio's to depend
on the play on a name, and a name familiar enough to add to
the feebleness; cf. 36. 7 *Carpe, Carpe,* 41. 7 *Dionyse, Liber esto,*
TLL Onom. s.v. *Corinthus.*

nisi quis Corinthum habet : the sense required from this must
be 'unless one has a Corinthus to make it', but Müller with some
justification doubts whether this can be got from the Latin,
hence his suggestion *nisi quis a Corintho.*

§ 5 nesapium : an adjective formed from *ne+sapio,* on the
analogy of *nescius.* The grammarian Terentius Scaurus (second
century A.D.) has the form *nesapus (Orth.* vii. 12. 4 'nesapus qui
non sapit'), but this does not prove that Petronius has chosen
to give the less correct form to Trimalchio.

stelio : in its literal sense a type of lizard with a star-shaped
marking; if Plin. *NH* xxix. 90 is to be believed, it was venomous
and capable of terrifying even scorpions. On the use of the word
as a term of abuse cf. Plin. *NH* xxx. 89 'nullum animal fraudu-
lentius invidere homini tradunt, inde stelionum nomine in
maledictum translato.'

factae sunt in unum : *in unum* had already begun to develop
from a purely local sense into a substitute for *una*; cf. *CGL*
v. 571. 21 'inunum pro simul'. See Löfstedt, *Verm. Stud.* 205,
Stefenelli, pp. 104 f.

§ 6 catilla . . . statuncula : 'plates . . . statuettes'. The forms
usually found are *catillus,* masc., and *statuncula,* fem.

nec hoc nec illud : 'neither one thing nor another'; cf. 45. 5 'aut
hoc aut illud, erit quid utique.'

§ 7 quod dixero : *quid H. quis* and *qui* are often confused in late
Latin, but *quid* here in *H* is probably a scribal error. Müller

lists a number of similar errors, including 41. 2 'duravi interrogare illum interpretem meum quod me torqueret' (*quod* Buecheler: *quid H*), 115. 3 'mirati ergo quod illi vacaret in vicinia mortis poema facere' (*quod tp*: *quid lr*); both of these passages come in the narrative of Encolpius, where an unclassical usage would be surprising.

malo mihi : this use of the dative with *malle* occurs occasionally at all periods, e.g. Cic. *Brut.* 256 'malim mihi L. Crassi unam pro M'. Curio dictionem quam castellanos triumphos duo'; see *TLL* viii. 205. 29 ff.

non olunt : (*nolunt H*) this third-conjugation form is found occasionally in early Latin (cf. Plaut. *Poen.* 268); at 105. 3 the poet Eumolpus has the usual second-conjugation form.
The belief that a connoisseur could identify Corinthian bronze by its smell is mocked by Martial: 'consuluit nares an olerent aera Corinthon' (ix. 59. 11; cf. Plin. *Ep.* iii. 6. 1).

nunc autem vilia sunt : probably 'but as it is, they're not worth having'; if so, *nunc autem* will contrast the actual facts with an unreal situation (cf. Greek νῦν δέ, Cic. *Rosc. Am.* 104 'huc accedit quod paulo tamen occultior atque tectior vestra ista cupiditas esset. nunc quid est quod quisquam ex vobis audire desideret . . .?').

Ch. 51

§ 2 f. The story of the unbreakable glass: Pliny (*NH* xxxvi. 195) mentions sceptically a story that in the time of Tiberius when a certain craftsman had discovered how to make unbreakable glass his workshop was destroyed in order to prevent bronze, silver, and gold from losing their value. Dio Cassius gives a more picturesque version: a certain architect had already aroused the jealousy of Tiberius by his ingenuity in restoring a large portico in Rome which was threatening to collapse. Tiberius rewarded him with money, but through envy expelled him from Rome. Later the architect came to Tiberius to ask for pardon, and, as he did so, purposely let fall a crystal goblet; although it was bruised or bashed in he at once made it whole again by passing his hands over it. For this feat the Emperor put him to death (lvii. 21. 5–7).
The text in *H* is unreliable here. Marmorale suspects that the reference to the dish as a *munus* comes in too abruptly. In addition, something seems to have fallen out after *munere*. John of Salisbury (twelfth century) gives a paraphrase of Trimalchio's

story (see Testimonia) which, despite obvious stylistic alterations, gives several hints at what Petronius must have included.
From John of Salisbury's version it would seem that the inven-
tor first handed the dish to the Emperor, then asked him to
hand it back for a moment so that its properties could be
demonstrated. Perrochat and Marmorale follow Ernout in
believing that *fecit reporrigere Caesari* in *H* can be made to
yield a sense consistent with that situation: they take *Caesari*
as a dative of agent, although the verb *reporrigere* is active
(cf. French 'je lui ai entendu chanter cette romance', Italian 'fece
dare da Antonio una lira a Marco'); but this construction lacks
support in Latin. Scheffer's *Caesarem* gives the required sense:
'caused Caesar to hand it back' (cf. John of Salisbury's 'petitam
de manu Caesaris phialam recepit'); for *facere* in this sense
cf. Varr. *RR* iii. 5. 3 'desiderium marcescere facit volucres',
L.–H.–S. 354 f. However, the change to *Caesarem* is not
enough by itself, for it seems likely that a sentence has fallen
out which told of the Emperor's admiration for the gift.

§ 3 non pote valdius quam expavit : 'he couldn't have been more
terrified.' *pote* (sc. *est*) was probably originally a neuter, but it
occurs also with masculine and feminine subjects (see Fordyce
on Cat. 45. 5). *valde quam*, like *mire quam*, *nimis quam*, etc.,
may at first have been an exclamatory formula, but it became
so fossilized that the comparative *valdius quam* is used here
despite the possibility of confusion with the normal use of
quam after a comparative. See L.–H.–S. 164, K.–S. i. 14.

expavit : this suggests that the Romans had some superstition
similar to the modern fear of breaking mirrors.

§ 4 martiolum : the forms regularly used are *martulus* and
martellus. See Heraeus, p. 143.

§ 5 solium : cf. Stat. *Silv*. iii. 1. 25 f. 'sive tui solium Iovis et virtute parata / astra tenes', Hor. *Ep*. i. 17. 34 'attingit solium
Iovis.' *caelum tenere* would in itself be possible (cf. Sen. *Ben*.
1. 13. 2 'tamquam caelum, quod mente vanissima complecte-
batur, teneret'), but *caelum Iovis tenere* (as in John of Salisbury)
remains unconvincing. *coleum*, the reading in *H*, has in recent
years not been treated with sufficient scepticism (Warmington
calls it 'a glorious piece of blasphemy'): elsewhere in the *Cena*
the gods may be referred to frivolously (cf. 44. 17 f.), but not
blasphemously. There is in fact remarkably little coarseness to
be seen. Furthermore, the difficulty arising from the use of the

singular *coleum* should not be ignored (cf. 39. 7 'in geminis . . . nascuntur bigae et boves et colei').

condituram : probably 'way of making' (from *condere*; cf. Plin. *NH* xxxv. 163 'condidit patinam, cui faciendae fornax in campis exaedificata erat'), rather than 'method of tempering' (from *condire*), a sense which is closer to the normal meaning of the word.

§ 6 vide modo : stereotyped phrase used as an interjection even where more than one person is addressed. See Hof. *LU* 38, L.–H.–S. 289.

quia enim : 'because of course'. Colloquial; see L.–H.–S. 575, *TLL* v. 2. 589. 26 ff.

Ch. 52

§ 1 in argento studiosus : this construction with *studiosus* has a colloquial ring; cf. Cic. *Phil.* v. 22 'avidum in pecuniis'. For a much bolder example cf. *Bell. Afr.* 54. 5 'magis in seditione . . . quam . . . pudoris studiosiores'. See L.–H.–S. 274.

plus minus ⟨*⟩ : two arguments justify the indication of a lacuna here: (i) a numeral is called for after *plus minus*. Scheffer instead explains *plus minus* as qualifying *urnales*, i.e. 'more or less the size of an *urna*' (= about three gallons); the *scyphus* could often be quite large (see Nisbet and Hubbard on Hor. *Od.* i. 27. 1 on its convenience as a missile in a drunken brawl). As a parallel, although not a close one, one might cite Mart. viii. 71. 4, where *plusve minusve duae* (sc. pounds of silver) is contrasted with four pounds of silver. Scheffer's interpretation is, however, open to the objection that, apart from the doubtful use of *plus minus* and its position after *urnales*, the word to which it is said to refer, Trimalchio is left insufficiently boastful. (ii) The clause *quemadmodum* . . . introduces too abruptly the subject depicted on the cups. Two passages cited as parallel (see Delz, p. 683, on 71. 6) are less harsh: 48. 7 'tenes . . . de Ulixe fabulam, quemadmodum illi Cyclops pollicem poricino extorsit?', Rom. *Fab.* 91 'ubi erat pictura quomodo leo ab homine suffocabatur'. There might at first sight appear to be a satisfactory parallel in § 2 below ('capidem . . . ubi . . . includit'), but note that the text before *ubi* is certainly corrupt.

In the light of the latter argument for a lacuna it becomes clear that there is no particular reason for preferring to supply *C* (Wehle) after *plus minus*.

Cassandra : Priam's daughter, the prophetess who was fated always to be disbelieved. Pausanias ii. 16. 7 says that she had twin sons by Agamemnon, Teledamus and Pelops, who were murdered along with their parents by Aegisthus; but it is obvious that Trimalchio simply confuses her with Medea, whose murder of her own two children was a much more familiar story.

sic ut vivere : Heinsius' brilliant correction for *sicuti vere H.* Petronius makes fun of excessive admiration for realism in art; cf. Plin. *NH* xxxv. 66 'fertur et postea Zeuxis pinxisse puerum uvas ferentem, ad quas cum advolassent aves, eadem ingenuitate processit iratus operi et dixit "uvas melius pinxi quam puerum; nam si et hoc consummassem, aves timere debuerant" '; and see Douglas on Cic. *Brut.* 70.

§ 2 capidem quam : no doubt in order to balance *scyphos urnales plus minus ⟨C⟩,* Buecheler alters *capidem quas H* to *capides ⟨M⟩ quas.* This remedy would probably be found to be unnecessary if we had the true reading behind the corrupt *patronorum meus,* giving point to this item in Trimalchio's catalogue. Buecheler's own conjecture, *patrono ⟨meo⟩ Mummius* would credit Trimalchio with a name-dropping reference to L. Mummius, the conqueror of Corinth in 146 B.C. Müller rejects this, wrongly looking for consistency between Trimalchio's notions of history here and at 50. 5 'cum Ilium captum est, Hannibal . . .'; in his second edition he conjectures *patrono meo rex Minos,* assuming that an abbreviation standing for *rex* was mistaken for one for *-rum,* presumably after *meo* had already been lost.

Daedalus : Trimalchio here runs together three different legends: (i) Daedalus, who constructed a wooden cow for Pasiphae; (ii) Niobe, the sorrowing mother whose children were killed by Apollo and Artemis; and (iii) the Trojan Horse.

§ 3 Hermerotis pugnas et Petraitis : Hermeros (*hemerotis H*) occurs as the name of a gladiator on a first-cent.-A.D. lamp from Puteoli (cf. H. B. Walters, *Catalogue of the Greek and Roman Lamps in the British Museum,* no. 787). The name Petraites, however, has been claimed to supply proof of the Neronian setting of the *Cena* (see H. T. Rowell, *TAPA* lxxxix (1958), 12–25). A number of commemorative cups have been discovered which contain representations of pairs of gladiators. Several of these link a Petraites (or Tetraites or Petrahes) with a Prudens. Rowell identifies this pair with a pair of gladiators mentioned in a Pompeian inscription, and he assigns all the cups

to the Neronian period, mainly on the basis of his identification
of Spiculus, who is paired with a Columbus on two of the cups.
Rejecting the possibility that this might be the Columbus who
was poisoned by Caligula (cf. Suet. *Calig.* 55), he argues that
Spiculus must be the gladiator of that name whose career appears to have fallen entirely within the reign of Nero (cf. Suet.
Nero 30, *CIL* iv. 1474); but it is equally possible that the cups
refer to a pair active in the reign of Caligula. This alternative
possibility is based (as indeed is Rowell's dating) on the fact
that, like doctors and actors, gladiators quite often adopted
the names of their predecessors (see *SG*⁸ ii. 634 ff., L. Robert,
Les Gladiateurs dans l'Orient grec, 297 ff.). Besides, even if the
Petraites mentioned here is held to be associated with gladiators who were prominent in Nero's reign, it does not follow with
certainty that he himself could not have been prominent before
—or for that matter after—Nero.

meum . . . intellegere : the present infinitive active used as a
substantive along with *ipsum, totum*, etc., or with a possessive
pronoun, occurs in Latin with a colloquial flavour, e.g. Plautus,
Cicero's letters to Atticus, but not in Sallust, Caesar, or Livy.
See L.–H.–S. 343, K.–S. i. 666.

When he adds what appears to be a triumphant conclusion
'for I would not sell my expert knowledge for any money', the
point may be that such commemorative cups could be collected by anyone with sufficient money; the more fastidious
collector perhaps looked for something more out of the ordinary.

§ 4 cito . . . te ipsum caede : cf. Ter. *Andr.* 255 'abi cito et sus-
pende te.'

§ 5 labro ⟨ora⟩re ⟨coepit⟩ : Scheffer proposed *labro orare* for
labrore H. However, the only narrative passage in the *Cena*
which, on the evidence of *H*, uses a historic infinitive is 72. 4
'consurrexit . . . et . . . subsequi', where the fact that the finite
verb *consurrexit* has preceded strongly suggests that *coepit* has
fallen out.

§ 6. A lacuna between *percucurrit* and *et* must be postulated:
the subject of *percucurrit* is the boy, whereas Trimalchio must
be the subject of *clamavit* since it is he who is immediately
praised for the *urbanitas* of 'aquam foras, vinum intro'. Some
scribe may have found too coarse for his taste a phrase which
described Trimalchio as suiting his action to the words *aquam
foras* without retiring from the room (note his invitation to his
guests at 47. 5).

aquam foras, vinum intro : for the form of expression Heraeus (p. 122) compares *CIL* iv. 4278 (Pompeii) 'fures faras frugi intro', Tert. *in Valent.* 10 'malum, quod aiunt, foras'.

§ 7 excipimus : cf. Sen. *Contr.* ii. 1. 28 'haec in hoc loco cum diceret, excepta sunt.' See Summers on Sen. *Ep.* 21. 6: 'The elder Seneca often uses *excipere* to mean "hail with applause" in reference to the reception of a "point" by a declamation audience. It may have been a technical term in that sphere.'

Agamemnon has several of the characteristics of Theophrastus' flatterer; cf. *Char.* 2. 4 'Then he will tell the company to keep silent while the great man is speaking; he will praise him when he is listening; and when he pauses in his talk he will back him up with "hear, hear!".' When his patron makes a feeble joke he laughs, stuffing his cloak into his mouth as if he couldn't contain his merriment' (Vellacott's trans.). In an earlier passage he had himself attacked flatterers who hunt for dinner invitations from the rich (3. 3), and he returns to the theme in verse (5, v. 5).

§ 8 cordacem : the precise nature of this dance is more doubtful than its obscenity. In Theophr. *Char.* 6. 3 the man who suffers from ἀπόνοια dances the *cordax* even when sober. For *cordacem ducit* cf. Ar. *Nub.* 540 οὐδὲ κόρδαχ' εἵλκυσεν.

§ 9 Syrum histrionem : no actor of this name has been identified.

madeia perimadeia : various interpretations and conjectures have been put forward. Ribbeck, and later de Lorenzi *Rivista indo-greco-italica di filologia* xiii (1929), fasc. 3–4, 10 f.), have suggested that the text originally contained the names Medea and Perimede, possibly used as a magic incantation in some mime. For the two names in association cf. Theocr. 2. 14 ff.

καὶ ἐς τέλος ἄμμιν ὀπάδει
φάρμακα ταῦτ' ἔρδοισα χερείονα μήτε τι Κίρκας
μήτε τι Μηδείας μήτε ξανθᾶς Περιμήδας,

Prop. ii. 4. 7 f. 'non hic herba valet, non hic nocturna Cytaeis, / non Perimedaeae gramina cocta manus.'

§ 11 nam modo . . . : the text in *H* provides no verb for *Fortunatam*, and if *revertebatur* is changed to *verebatur* to supply this, the latter part of the sentence is left incomplete. Among a number of ingenious attempts (see app. crit.) to improve the text, Müller's is perhaps the most plausible, but the word-play *verebatur . . . revertebatur* is hardly characteristic of Petronius' style. The existence of lacunae elsewhere in this part of the work (e.g. §§ 1 and 6 above) suggests that the true reading may be irrecoverable.

Encolpius, whose conduct in the extant portions of the novel does not make him appear a model of consistency, readily condemns the absence of this virtue in Trimalchio. On *aequabilitas* as a moral duty see Fraenkel's comments (*Horace*, 86) on Hor. *Sat.* i. 3. 9 'nil aequale homini fuit illi.'

Ch. 53

The fantastic pretensions of Trimalchio have already been conveyed through his own words in ch. 48; now they are shown even more vividly when a clerk proceeds to read out a report of events in his estates. The immensity of his wealth is shown directly (§§ 2, 4) and indirectly (§§ 5 ff.), and his quasi-imperial power is implied in § 3 'in crucem actus est quia Gai nostri genio male dixerat', and in § 9 'cum elogio exheredebatur'.

The events here relate to a single day, 26 July, hence the comparison with the *urbis acta*, the daily gazette published at Rome from 59 B.C. onwards which contained reports of official and unofficial events (cf. Suet. *Iul.* 20. 1). Petronius has chosen outrageous figures to indicate the size of Trimalchio's *familia* and estates (to get some notion of the exaggeration involved, note that on the present U.K. birth-rate Trimalchio's Cumaean estate would have had a population of one and a half millions; and Friedlaender calculates that the grain listed in § 4 would feed 10,000 people for a year). Friedlaender tried rather misguidedly to tone down the absurdities by supposing that the clerk was reading out a report dealing with the first six months of the year which had taken several weeks to prepare; but the execution of the slave in § 3 and the fire in § 5 are expressly detailed as being events belonging to a single day.

It would likewise be dangerous to use this chapter as an indication of the time of year in which Petronius set the action of the *Cena*. Despite its entertainment value, disjointed material such as we find in 53. 1–10 would eventually bore the reader, so it is abandoned with characteristic abruptness at 53. 11 'petauristarii autem tandem venerunt . . .'. Thus Petronius is not forced to decide whether the *acta* would continue with the events of a succession of days. Common sense might seem to suggest that the events of 26 July would be recounted on 27 July or soon after that; but the same common sense would suggest that the notice at 30. 3 ('III. et pridie kalendas Ianuarias C. noster foras cenat') must be displayed towards the end of the year. Difficulties like this, however, arise from the demand for precision where it is not relevant to the comedy.

§ 1 **recitavit** : the presentation of a report by a clerk of records (*actuarius*) during the course of dinner may not in itself have seemed altogether unusual to a Roman, but some of our evidence on this is ambiguous: cf. Suet. *Galb*. 12. 3 '. . . adposita lautiore cena ingemuisse eum, et ordinario quidem dispensatori breviarium rationum offerenti paropsidem leguminis pro sedulitate ac diligentia porrexisse'.

§ 2 **sextiles** : since 8 B.C. this month had been officially named *Augustus*; hence the use here of the older name must be meant to sound a little quaint, especially when it is followed by the precision of 'in praedio Cumano quod est Trimalchionis'.

quod est Trimalchionis : these words are wrongly deleted by Müller; it is true that elsewhere, even in § 3 just below, Trimalchio is always referred to as Gaius within his household, but a *praenomen* would be out of place in this parody of legal jargon (for the use of the relative in documentary formulas cf. *CIL* ii. 5042 (= Riccobono, *Fontes* iii, no. 92) 'fundum Baianum qui est in agro qui Veneriensis vocatur', Cic. *Mur*. 26 'fundus, inquit, qui est in agro qui Sabinus vocatur').

§ 3 **Gai nostri genio male dixerat** : 'he had insulted the guardian spirit of our Gaius.' See note on 30. 4 on the use of the *praenomen*, also note on 37. 3 'ignoscet mihi genius tuus.' Apart from the absurd severity of the punishment inflicted, the slave's own behaviour is meant to strike us as unusual; normally a slave or freedman would swear by his master's *genius* as a kind of deity (cf. Hor. *Ep*. i. 7. 94 f., 'quod te per genium dextramque deosque penatis / obsecro et obtestor').

§ 4 **collocari** : 'invested'.

sestertium centies : ten million sesterces (on the form of expression see note on 38. 12). Notice that the sum amounts to one third of the total Trimalchio wants to be specified on his tombstone (71. 12).

§ 5 **hortis Pompeianis** : these words, corresponding to *praedio Cumano* above, appear to refer to an estate or villa at Pompeii (*horti* frequently stands for a suburban house; e.g. Cic. *Att*. ix. 13a 'cui Gnaeus noster locum ubi hortos aedificaret dedit'). If the town of Pompeii is meant, this is in itself almost indisputable evidence that the artistic setting of the *Cena* should be placed before A.D. 79, the date of the destruction of the town. The view that *Pompeianis* refers to some person, Trimalchio's patron perhaps, is much less likely, although it is not rendered impossible merely by Trimalchio's affected ignorance of the *horti* and his assertion at 76. 8 'statim redemi fundos omnes qui patroni mei fuerant.'

aedibus : a pretentious word to apply to an overseer's home: cf. Plaut. *Asin.* 430 'erus in hara, haud aedibus, habitat', 74. 14 below 'hic, qui in pergula natus est, aedes non somniatur.'

§ 8 intra sextum mensem : Trimalchio is allowed several pseudo-legal touches (*quicumque . . . , nisi . . .*). Six months is chosen as a standard period for legal notification (cf. Riccobono, *Fontes* i. 326, iii. 329), and this phrase should not be taken to prove that the *acta* read out here are the same as his *rationes* or that they must themselves cover a six-month period. See introductory note to this chapter.

§ 9 edicta aedilium : this reference to the aediles (see note on 44. 3) comes in a little strangely. Probably it is meant to imply that Trimalchio's household is large enough to require its own police organization, just as it has its own law-courts (cf. § 10 'iam reus factus dispensator et iudicium inter cubicularios actum'). *edicta aedilium* could possibly be taken in its normal sense as a reference to the enactments of the local magistrates; the juxtaposition of public magistrates and private employees would then have to be seen as an anticlimax.

saltuariorum testamenta : if these *saltuarii* (foresters) were slaves, they could make wills only in an informal sense; cf. Plin. *Ep.* viii. 16. 1 f. 'permitto servis quoque quasi testamenta facere . . . dividunt donant relinquunt, dumtaxat intra domum; nam servis res publica quaedam et quasi civitas domus est' (note also in § 10 the quasi-legal dispute between Trimalchio's bedroom attendants). Trimalchio shows his indifference to wealth by allowing the *saltuarii* to leave none of their property to him; contrast the tyrannical insistence of emperors on receiving forced bequests from their subjects (cf. Suet. *Calig* 38. 2). The word *elogium* was used of a clause or codicil in a will, especially one which disinherited someone (cf. Cic. *Cluent.* 135).

§ 10 nomina vilicorum : probably 'debts incurred by the over-seers' (or possibly 'accounts kept by the overseers').

circ[um]itore : patrol, inspector; cf. Frontinus *Aq.* 117

'utraque autem familia in aliquot ministeriorum species diducitur: vilicos, castellarios, circitores.'

balneatoris : this can mean either a slave employed at the baths or the manager in charge. Even the manager of the baths was regarded as scarcely respectable; cf. *Dig.* iii. 2. 4. 2, Juv. 7. 4. In Greece the bath-man had the reputation of being a busybody; cf. *Paroem. Gr.* i. 227 βαλανεύς· ἐπὶ τῶν πολυπραγμόνων. οὗτοι γὰρ σχολὴν ἄγοντες πολυπραγμονοῦσιν.

atriensis : see 29. 9. The penalty imposed on him gains its absurdity from the reputation of Baiae as a centre of pleasure (cf. Cic. *Cael.* 35 'accusatores quidem libidines, amores, adulteria, Baias, actas, convivia, comissationes, cantus, symphonias, navigia iactant', Sen. *Ep.* 51. 3 ff.), and from its closeness to the town in which the *Cena* is set.

§ 11 **baro :** cf. 63. 7, where the word is used of the 'hominem Cappadocem, longum, valde audaculum et qui valebat'. It occurs several times in Cicero, also in Pers. 5. 138. It seems to indicate physical strength or the stupidity sometimes associated with such strength. See Heraeus, pp. 72 f.

odaria saltare : 'dance to a song accompaniment'. The word *odarium* is not found elsewhere in Latin, but note *magister odariarius* (Dessau 5229).

trans⟨il⟩ire : Heinsius. *transire* H is possible, but *transilire* is more likely. For the feat involved cf. Manilius v. 437 'membraque per flammas orbesque emissa flagrantes'.

§ 12 **cornic⟨in⟩es :** Heinsius. Here and at 78. 6 H has *cornices*, a Vulgar form found in glossaries; see Heraeus, p. 148.

Trumpeters and other wind-players gave concerts and provided fanfares for gladiator-shows and funerals (cf. Juv. 3. 34, Sen. *Ep.* 84. 10). Their popularity is mocked by Juvenal in his story of the marriage of a Gracchus to a trumpeter he admired (2. 117 ff.).

reliqua [animalia] acroamata : the word *acroama* is used of different types of entertainment, or of the entertainer; cf. Cic. *Sest.* 116 'non solum spectator sed actor et acroama', Polyb. iv. 20. 10. The term would include trumpeters (cf. 78. 5 'novum acroama, cornicines'), whereas the text in *H* seems to imply a distinction between *cornicines* on the one hand and *animalia* and *acroamata* on the other. Hence Buecheler deletes *animalia* as a mistaken attempt to explain *reliqua acroamata*.

tricas meras esse : 'were just stuff and nonsense'. The origin
and precise meaning of *tricae* are doubtful (see Ernout–Meillet
s.v. on popular etymologies); the general sense of it is clear
enough (cf. Mart. xiv. 1. 7 'sunt apinae tricaeque et si quid
vilius istis').

comoedos : entertainers who specialized in reciting passages
from New Comedy (see Sherwin-White on Plin. *Ep*. i. 15. 2
and v. 19. 3). Trimalchio shows his lack of breeding by using
his *comoedi* to perform Atellan farces, which were often coarse
in tone.

choraulen : the flute-player who accompanied and directed a
chorus; his profession was lucrative (cf. Mart. v. 56. 9), but not
always appreciated; cf. Mart. ix. 77. 5 f. 'quod optimum sit
quaeritis convivium? / in quo choraules non erit.'

Ch. 54

§ 1 eo : Müller. If *Gaio* (*H*) is sound, it must express Encolpius'
contempt for the upstart freedman's pride in his acquired
praenomen (see note on 30. 3); but even if we allow for the
lacuna after *puer*, the change from *Gaio* to *Trimalchionis* is
harsh. As part of the missing phrase Buecheler suggests *in
lectum*, preceded by a reference to the cause of the boy's acci-
dent, e.g. *scalis subito perfractis*.

hominem : this must be taken to refer to the boy, if we are
to make sense of *alienum mortuum plorare*. For *homo* used of
a boy cf. 73. 6 'hodie servus meus barbatoriam fecit, homo
praefiscini frugi et micarius.' If Trimalchio were meant, the
other guests would be credited with a dislike for their host
which is scarcely evident elsewhere, and *ipse Trimalchio* at the
beginning of the next sentence would be pointlessly emphatic.

alienum mortuum plorare : cf. Sen. *Ep*. 12. 3 'quid te delectavit
alienum mortuum tollere?'. In each case the expression may be
taken literally but looks like a proverbial phrase for doing what
is not strictly part of one's duty, hence wasting one's time or
money. Burial rites were not lightly granted to those not
entitled to them; see the restrictive regulations of a burial
club in Lanuvium (*CIL* xiv. 2112 = Riccobono, *Fontes* iii, no.
35), cf. J. M. C. Toynbee, *Death and Burial in the Roman
World*, 54 f.
Some commentators have felt sure that this incident of the
acrobat's fall must be derived from Hor. *Sat*. ii. 8. 71 'adde hos

praeterea casus, aulaea ruant si'; see J. Révay, *CP* xvii (1922), 202 ff., Sullivan, pp. 126 ff., Stöcker, pp. 56 f. Yet it hardly seems necessary to assume that Petronius was influenced here by Horace. Acrobatic performances both on the stage and in private theatricals may well have been full of mishaps like this. Thus Suetonius (*Nero* 12) reports the fall of an actor playing the part of Icarus 'iuxta cubiculum eius (i.e. Nero's) decidit ipsumque cruore respersit'; any theory, however, which sees this as a unique incident and as the source of the present episode must accept that Nero was bound to be seen as the counterpart of Trimalchio here.

§ 3 pessime mihi erat . . . : 'I was very worried in case these entreaties meant that some trick would be used to bring about a surprise.' For this use of an adverb with *esse* see note on 34. 10.

§ 5 livoratum: Delz. *liberatum* (*H*) in its usual meaning will not fit here, and the rare sense 'cross over' (cf. 136. 9 'necdum liberaveram cellulae limen', Apul. *Met.* ix. 20 'pro limine liberato', Stefenelli, p. 148) would be impossibly forced. Delz, p. 682, suggests *livoratum* 'beaten black and blue', although the earliest occurrence he can cite is in the *Liber Historiae Francorum* (*Script. Rer. Merov.* ii. 269 Krusch). *vulneratum* (Heinsius, Scheffer) is as easy palaeographically, but the context perhaps calls for something less common.

Ch. 55

§ 2 non diu cogitatione distortus : 'without racking his brains for long'. If *distorta H* is retained, it must presumably be taken as an ablative, but no adequate parallel for this is cited (cf. Quint. xii. 1. 7 'sollicitudine, paenitentia . . . torquetur mens', Sen. *Ben.* 7. 2. 4 'curis distorquentibus mentem').

§ 3. The text in the manuscripts is faulty, but it appears that Trimalchio has been credited with the same combination of lines as at 34. 10, viz. two hexameters and a pentameter (e.g. 'fit ⟨ubique⟩ / ⟨nostra⟩ et' Heinsius). Less plausibly it could be argued that the greater feebleness of the unaltered text gives more point to *non diu cogitatione distortus*.

§ 4 Mopsum : Petronius hints at a long discussion with muddled recollections of the legendary Thracian singer Orpheus. Mopsus is the name of the seer for the Argonauts (cf. Stat. *Theb.* iii.

521) and of a shepherd in Virgil's fifth Eclogue (addressed as *divine poeta* in line 45).

§ 5 Ciceronem et Publilium : as at 48. 4 Trimalchio is made to air his pretensions to education; his comparison of Cicero and Publilius no doubt parodies trite themes for literary discussions (for later examples of such themes see Quint. x. 1. 106, where Demosthenes and Cicero are compared, also Macrob. v. 1, where Virgil and Cicero are compared).

Publilius Syrus was a writer of mimes in the time of Julius Caesar. We possess no sizeable extracts from his work, and even the 700 or so single lines, mainly epigrammatic in form, traditionally attributed to him could well be spurious; if no written text of his mimes was available in his own day, much less in later times, it would be easy for collectors of apophthegms to hand them on under his name. It is clear on other grounds that Petronius is not quoting genuine verses of Publilius. It would be out of character for an ignoramus like Trimalchio to recall a passage of this length; more important, an accurate quotation would be inartistic in this context. It is not even certain that Petronius is parodying Publilius; the content and style of this passage do not remotely resemble the extant aphorisms of Publilius. The resemblances to Varro's *Menippeae* might even suggest that Petronius was parodying Varro in order to make Trimalchio appear even more ignorant in attributing these lines to Publilius. Sullivan (pp. 192 f.), although regarding the verses as a parody of Publilius, notes that as well as the heavy alliteration and the archaizing vocabulary 'there are certain signs of a later age and style, e.g. the woven breeze (*ventus textilis*) ... such precious turns of phrase as *titulus tepidi temporis* (but see below). It should be added, however, that, as well as any element of parody in them, these lines serve to show Trimalchio as a hypocrite, denouncing luxurious living in the middle of his own lavish banquet, just as the fawning Agamemnon declaims a poem in praise of frugality and independence (ch. 5).

§ 6, v. 1 : mock-epic opening, with its archaic alliteration and somewhat bizarre imagery.

v. 3 plumato ... Babylonico : *Babylonico* stands for Oriental tapestry; the word is regularly plural (cf. Plaut. *Stich.* 378 'Babylonica et peristroma tonsilia et tappetia'). Although peacocks were usually associated with India or Persia, Fraenkel proposed to read *Babylonicus* on the strength of a mention of

Babylonian peacocks in Diod. ii. 53. 2; but this would entail taking either *plumato* or *aureo* as a noun (see Nisbet, p. 230).

plumato provides a deliberately feeble play: (i) plumed, (ii) embroidered in a feather-stitch (*plumarius* = embroiderer) cf. Marq. *Prl.* 537 ff.

v. 6. 'devotion-filled, slender-footed castanet-player'. The piling-up of compounds here is reminiscent of older writers, who sometimes use the device for comic effect (e.g. Plaut. *Trin.* 1021 'oculicrepidae, cruricrepidae, ferriteri mastigiae').

Petronius manages to combine adjectives which are appropriate on one level (storks are cited by Cicero along with ants and bees as models of altruistic behaviour (*Fin.* iii. 63, cf. Plin. *NH* x. 63), and they appear along with *Pietas* on some Roman coins; and *crotalistria* suggests the rattling sound made by the stork's mandibles), while on another level they clash with each other: *pietas* is not the quality a Roman would associate with castanet-players (cf. Prop. iv. 8. 39).

v. 7 titulus tepidi temporis : 'token of torrid temperatures'. This use of *titulus* points to an author later than Publilius (cf. Sen. *Suas.* vi. 19 'brevi ante princeps senatus Romanique nominis titulus') and is rather different from occurrences in Republican authors (e.g. Cic. *Pis.* 19 'sed qui tamquam truncus atque stipes, si stetisset modo, posset sustinere tamen titulum consulatus').

v. 8. 'has made her nest in the cooking-pot of your iniquity'.

tuae : the reading *meo* cannot be defended. We look for something to balance *tuo* in v. 2 and *tibi* in vv. 4 and 9; hence Fraenkel's *tuae* (or less probably Heinsius's *tuo*) is more effective than Buecheler's *modo*.

v. 9 quo . . . tibi : 'what use is it to you (to acquire) . . . ?' For the accusative with this construction cf. Hor. *Ep.* i. 5. 12 'quo mihi fortunam, si non conceditur uti?' (with Wilkins's note).

v. 10. 'so that a matron decked out in maritime medals may open her legs, unconquerable on her extra-conjugal couch'. The obscene phrase *tollat pedes* (cf. Cic. *Att.* ii. 1. 5, Mart. xi. 71. 8) is contrasted with *matrona*, which in itself implies respectability.

v. 14 carbunculis : the term covers rubies, garnets, etc.; cf. Plin. *NH* xxxvii. 92 'principatum habent carbunculi a similitudine ignium appellati, cum ipsi non sentiant ignes, a quibusdam ob hoc acaustoe appellati. horum genera Indici et Garamantici quos et Carchedonios vocavere propter opulentiam Carthaginis magnae . . .'

v. 15 ventum textilem : the wearing of transparent garments, expecially those of Coan silk, was a favourite theme for moralists and poets, who often regarded them as the uniform of the courtesan, cf., for example, Sen. *Contr.* ii. 7. 10 'infelices ancillarum greges laborant ut adultera tenui veste perspicua sit et nihil in corpore uxoris suae plus maritus quam quilibet alienus peregrinusque cognoverit', K. F. Smith on Tib. ii. 3. 53.

Ch. 56

From literature Trimalchio turns to inane and garbled generalizations. His remarks on the difficulties involved in being a doctor or a money-changer are a parody of another popular topic, the comparison of various professions in terms of their usefulness to the community. See Pease on Cic. *Div.* i. 24, who notes that the stock figures chosen are frequently the physician, the pilot, and the farmer; also Nisbet and Hubbard on Hor. *Od.* i. 1 on the development of the topic whereby philosophy is compared with other occupations. Once again, as at 55. 5 *inter Ciceronem et Publilium*, Petronius produces an anticlimax by putting the absurd feature second.

§§ 1–2 artificium . . . medicum et nummularium : for the variation between abstract and personal expression cf. 46. 7 'destinavi illum artificium docere, aut tonstrinum aut praeconem aut certe causidicum.'

§ 3 odi pessime : *male, peius,* and *pessime* are used in colloquial speech to intensify an expression which could loosely be called pejorative; cf. Ter. *HT* 664 'quam timui male', Hof. *LU* 74, 192. The distinction between this use and the use of *male* with a negative force is illustrated in Austin's note on Virg. *Aen.* ii. 23 *male fida.*

anatinam : Petronius may have chosen duck here partly because we expect some repulsive remedy to be specified (a modern equivalent might be 'My doctor insists that I must drink whisky'), and partly because, besides being a common remedy for digestive ailments (on account of its digestibility the younger Cato is said to have included it in his little book of prescriptions for his family; cf. Plut. *Cat. Min.* 23. 3), duck also figures in bizarre remedies of folk-lore: Columella (vi. 7. 1) says that pain in the stomach and the intestines of oxen is eased if the patient catches sight of swimming creatures, especially a duck, and the sight of a duck is even more successful in curing mules and horses; the elder Pliny reports a little incredulously (*NH* xxx. 61) that if someone suffering from colic has a duck placed beside his stomach the ailment disappears and the duck perishes.

§ 4 **laboriosissimae** : this picks up the sense of *difficillimum* in § 1. Trimalchio, not hitherto a conspicuous vegetarian, turns now to a Pythagorean theme, the services of different animals to mankind. Ov. *Met.* xv. 116 ff. expresses a similar thought by means of the same jingle (116 'quid meruistis oves' . . . 120 'quid meruere boves').

§ 6 **apes enim ego divinas bestias puto** : he now explains why he did not include bees as *mutae bestiae*. Bees could be regarded as divine because they passed on honey, the food of the gods and in some way produced by the air of heaven, for the benefit of mankind; cf. Virg. *Georg.* iv. 1 'aerii mellis caelestia dona', Plin. *NH* xi. 30, K. F. Smith on Tib. i. 3. 45. *vomunt* might look like a piece of vulgarity on the part of Trimalchio, but note Columella ix. 2. 4 'et utrum evomant liquorem mellis, an alia parte reddant', Plin. loc. cit. 'ore enim eum vomunt.'

Trimalchio concludes with an extremely trite sentiment. See Otto s.v. *mel* (3) : the notion was proverbial by the time of Plato (cf. *Phileb.* 46 c τὸ δὴ λεγόμενον πικρῷ γλυκὺ μεμιγμένον), which adds to the irony of the comment 'iam etiam philosophos de negotio deiciebat.' The way in which, despite his grand manner, he has drifted from topic to topic gives a sharp picture of the uneducated speaker, but Petronius, realizing as usual that the faithful representation of a bore will itself soon become boring, moves on at § 7 to another subject.

§ 7 **philosophos de negotio deiciebat** : Sullivan (pp. 209 f.) includes this in a list of resemblances between Petronius and Seneca, comparing it with *Ep.* 88. 44 'Zenon Eleates omnia negotia de negotio deiecit.' Seneca's pointed sentence must, however, be based on a regular expression *aliquem de negotio deicere*, even if no exact parallel can be cited (cf., for example, Cic. *Mur.* 79 'consulem . . . deici de urbis praesidio . . . volunt').

pittacia : here used of tickets which entitled the recipients to particular gifts to be taken away (*apophoreta*). At first the ticket would give a simple identification of the gift, but sometimes, as here, it contains some kind of pun, with a contrast between the actual gift and the expectation aroused. For a similar playfulness on the part of a host cf. Suet. *Aug.* 75. 1 'Saturnalibus et si quando alias libuisset, modo munera dividebat,

vestem et aurum et argentum, modo nummos omnis notae, etiam
veteres regios et peregrinos, interdum nihil praeter cilicia et
spongias et rutabula et forpices atque alia id genus titulis
obscuris et ambiguis.'

The recurrence of a number of Trimalchio's gifts among the
apophoreta in Book xiv of Martial may mean that these gifts
were of familiar types. If so, it is possible that the inane rebuses
were likewise familiar, and that in consequence there is more
irony than meets the eye in the words used to move on to
another topic: 'diu risimus: sexcenta huiusmodi fuerunt, quae
iam exciderunt memoriae meae' (§ 10 below).

§ 8 **'argentum sceleratum'** : the gift includes *perna* (leg of ham),
so *sceleratum* must be a pun on the Greek σκέλος (Heraeus, p. 74
cites *CGL* iii. 14. 46 for the equivalence of σκέλος and *perna*).
This pun is not meant to suggest fluency in Greek in Trimalchio's circle, any more than an English speaker's use of the
word *pomme de terre* implies mastery of French (see also notes
on 48. 8, 59. 2).

acetabula : originally the word *acetabulum* stands for a
vinegar-dish, often made of silver (see Heraeus, p. 74).

'cervical' : the guest expects a cushion (lit. 'neck-piece'), but
receives instead only a piece of neck-end.

'serisapia et contumelia' : *serisapia*, not used elsewhere, is
apparently a rendering of the Greek ὀψιμαθία (late learning),
a failing criticized in, for example, Theophr. *Char.* 27, but the
gift suggests another meaning: ξηρός 'dry', and *sap-* 'taste'.

The first part of the sentence describing the answering gifts
has been corrupted in *H* to the meaningless *aecrophagie*. Reiske
conjectured *xerophagiae* (herbs eaten raw), along with Burmann's *e sale*. Buecheler–Heraeus has the much less likely
aeclophagiae ⟨te⟩sellae.

The second gift, *contus cum malo*, a pole along with an apple,
could possibly be something like our toffee-apple, although
there is no evidence available. On this interpretation the feeble
play on *contumelia* must be taken as sufficient justification.
Studer suggested that the words are used *sens. obsc.* (*contus* =
phallus in *Carm. Priap.* xi. 3; cf. E. K. Borthwick in *CR* N.S.
xix (1969), 271; for sexual senses of *malum* see W. Goldberger,
Glotta xviii (1929), 35 (who cites *CGL* iii. 175. 8, 247. 60), *Priap.*
72, and Serv. on Virg. *Ecl.* ii. 51). H. D. Rankin rightly objects,
however (*Rh. Mus.* cvii (1964), 361–4), that there are no overt
verbal references to sexual impropriety in these *apophoreta*.

§ 9 'porri et persica' : leeks and peaches; the gifts are a whip and a knife. The connections appear to be: (i) one type of leek is the *porrum sectivum*, from *secare* to cut or beat; (ii) *persica* also suggests *sica* (sword), *persecare* (cut through), and even perhaps a Persian sword.

'passeres et muscarium' : sparrows and a fly-stopper. *muscarium* 'fly-whisk' occurs as a gift in Mart. xiv. 67, 68, but it might also suggest a place where flies gather, on the analogy of words like *apiarium*, hence the gift of Attic honey. *uvam passam* (raisins) is chosen simply for the pun.

'cenatoria et forensia' : again the neuter is convenient for its ambiguity between the general sense 'things for dinner and things for the Forum' and the more specific: *cenatoria* = clothes for dinner (the word is found in Martial's *apophoreta* at xiv. 136), and *forensia* = clothes for the Forum (cf. Suet. *Aug.* 73).

Here the guest received a chop or piece of meat (*offla*) and *tabulas*, writing-tablets (Martial's *apophoreta* include *pugillares* at xiv. 3 ff.).

'canale et pedale' : when altered to the neuter forms these suggest firstly in general terms something for a dog and something for the foot; but also more specifically a splint (cf. Celsus viii. 10. 5. A) and a bandage or puttee for the foot or else a cloth for wiping the foot (cf. *CGL* ii. 144. 18, 19). The forms in *H*, *canalem et pedalem*, could mean a pipe and a foot-rule, but they lack the necessary ambiguity provided by the neuters. See Heraeus, p. 75.

solea, when taken in conjunction with *lepus*, hare, must mean the fish, and an appropriate pun is thus introduced.

murem cum rana alligata : the gift recalls the fable of the frog which had a mouse tied to it but was itself seized by a kite (Aesop. *Fab.* 302, Phaedr. *Appx.* 6).

fascemque betae : a bundle of beet. The list thus ends suitably with a worthless item (cf. Mart. xiii. 13 'fabrorum prandia, betae'); beet is several times mentioned as a laxative, cf. Mart. iii. 47. 9, Apicius iii. 2. 3, Plin. *NH* xx. 69 f.

If Buecheler's addition of *accepit* here is accepted, the text in *H* provides a regular alternation between better and worse gifts than the recipient would anticipate from the rebus; cf. Mart. xiv. 1. 5 'divitis alternas et pauperis accipe sortes' (and see Friedlaender's note). Fraenkel obviates the need for any supplement by putting the words 'canale . . . allata' immediately after *mel Atticum*, but is forced to dislocate the alternation between better and worse gifts.

§ 10 diu risimus . . . : in his final sentence Petronius manages to convey to the reader the suspicion that the unrecorded witticisms were even more imbecile than the sample which he has given; but he does so without compromising the deliberate and delicate ambivalence of his narrator's attitude to what is described. By contrast, Ascyltos and Giton are immediately contemptuous of Trimalchio's wit.

Ch. 57

§ 1 Ascyltos, intemperantis licentiae : the genitive of quality attached to a proper noun occurs rarely in Cicero, Sallust, and Horace, but becomes more frequent in Livy and especially in the Elder Pliny. See L.–H.–S. 69 f., and cf. 49. 7 *ego crudelissimae severitatis.*

is ipse . . . discumbebat : in his first edition Müller followed Fraenkel in deleting these words as an explanatory gloss inserted by a scribe who identified Hermeros, the speaker in chs. 57 and 58 (cf. 59. 1), with Encolpius' neighbour at table (cf. 36. 7 'non erubui eum qui supra me accumbebat hoc ipsum interrogare'). Müller claimed that *discumbebat* was used here instead of *accumbebat* because the interpolator found *discumberem* in § 2 below. But the identification of Encolpius' neighbour with Hermeros, as well as being reasonable in itself, gains support from the recurrence of such mannerisms as the phrase *ad summam* at 37. 5, 10 and 57. 3, 9, 58. 8.

vervex : the stupidity of sheep was proverbial (cf. *Paroem. Gr.* ii. 189 μωρότερος προβάτου), but here there is also a suggestion of impotence (cf. Apul. *Met.* vii. 23), just as *maialis* (= *sus castratus*) is sometimes used as an insult (see Nisbet on Cic. *Pis.* 19). The form *berbex* in *H* may be genuine rather than simply a scribal error; see Heraeus, p. 147.

§ 2 domini mei : cf. 66. 5, where, referring to his wife, Habinnas says: 'bene me admonet domina mea' (also 67. 9 'domini mei beneficio'). Such forms of address do not indicate absentminded servility on the part of an ex-slave, for note that at *Ep.* 104. 1 Seneca refers to his elder brother as *domini mei Gallionis.* They are perhaps, however, more courteous than a person of higher social status would use in the same circumstances. See *SG*[8] i. 449 ff., Svennung, *Anredeformen*, 18, Sherwin-White on Plin. *Ep.* x. 2. 1.

convivare : active for deponent (see note on 45. 7, *delecta-retur*). It occurs also in Titinius, Ennius, and Pomponius.

ita . . . ut : on the use of this formula in asseverations see note on 58. 12.

tutelam : tutelary deity in the household *lararium*; cf., for example, *CIL* vi. 216 *tutela huius loci*, v. 3304 *tutela domus*.

clusissem : 'I'd have stopped his bleating by now'; this is more effective than *duxissem H* 'I'd have made him bleat by now.'

§ 3 rideatur : the irregularity of this deponent is emphasized by the proximity of § 2 'quid rides?', § 4 'ridet . . . rideat'.

larifuga : hap. leg. 'runaway' used pejoratively like *fugitivus*. For *lares* as household deities cf. 29. 8 *Lares argentei*. Sometimes the word means little more than 'home'; here, however, the more precise sense is appropriate: Hermeros, an ex-slave, thinks of *lares* because slaves were allowed to take part in their worship.

non valet lotium suum : 'isn't worth his own piss'.

si circumminxero illum : the figurative use here (= 'beat him up') must be connected with the reliance on urination as part of magic ritual (see 62. 6).

sed in molli carne vermes nascuntur : 'it's in rotten flesh that worms breed'. These words are best taken thus as a reference to Ascyltos. The alternative is to take *molli* as 'tender (cf. Wander, *Deutsches Sprichwörterlexicon* s.v. *Fleisch* (30) 'das süsseste Fleisch wird zuerst madig'); the phrase would then be an unflattering reference to Hermeros himself.

§ 4 numquid pater fetum emit lamna : 'Did your father have to pay money for his offspring?', i.e. 'Do you think you are entitled to give yourself airs?' *fetum* is not altogether convincing in this interpretation, but it is even more difficult in the alternative, 'Did your father buy a calf (or a lamb) for (sc. a little) money?' Otto s.v. *lamna* wrongly renders it, 'In your father's case does money reproduce itself?'

lamna means a piece of metal, and hence metal (cf. Sen. *Ben.* 7. 10. 1 'nunc volo tuas opes recognoscere, lamnas utriusque materiae', also 58. 8 below, and 57. 6 *lamellulas*).

eques Romanus es : et ego regis filius : is Hermeros accepting Ascyltos as a genuine knight but making an even grander claim for himself, or is he ridiculing Ascyltos' pose by making a boast which is patently incredible? The first interpretation is preferable: he asserts his royal origins, like, for example, Claudius' freedman Pallas (cf. Tac. *Ann.* xii. 53). Two objections can be made against this view. Firstly, at 58. 10 Hermeros is not prepared to regard Ascyltos as really being a knight: 'nisi si me iudicas anulos buxeos curare, quos amicae tuae involasti'. Secondly, at § 9 below he mentions that he had been a slave for forty years, an admission which makes nonsense of his account of his enslavement in § 4. Neither objection is fatal: Petronius characterizes him as a man so indignant that he is inconsistent both in attack and in defence. The alternative is to take the words *et ego regis filius* as ironical, like our 'well, if that's so, then I'm the Emperor of China'; but this makes him implausibly flat-footed when he immediately goes on to answer an imaginary question how he came to be a slave.

malui civis Romanus esse quam tributarius : in certain circumstances a free non-Roman might decide to sell himself into slavery to a Roman citizen on the understanding, no doubt backed by suitable safeguards, that he would at once be set free as a Roman citizen (see J. A. Crook, *Law and Life of Rome*, 59 f.). But in the rest of his account of his life Hermeros shows himself behaving like an ordinary slave gradually working his way towards freedom.

§ 5 homo inter homines : cf. 39. 4.

capite aperto : i.e. undisguised and unashamed; cf. Plaut. *Capt.* 475, Otto s.v. *caput* (3).

constitutum : a technical term for an agreement to repay a debt on a fixed date. The sense would thus appear to be 'I've never been in debt', rather than 'I've never been taken to court for not paying my debts.' *redde quod debes* is a formula for demanding payment of a debt; cf. Sen. *Ep.* 18. 14, Mart. ix. 92. 7.

§ 6 glebulas . . . lamellulas : the diminutive can be used with modesty, genuine or feigned.

viginti ventres pasco : cf. Sen. *Ep.* 17. 4 'facile est pascere paucos ventres.'

contubernalem : it was common for a freed slave to buy freedom for his *contubernalis*, his partner in the informal union which was permitted to slaves, legal marriage being forbidden; but this procedure would hardly be necessary for a person entering into the unusual type of slavery implied by Hermeros in § 4.

mille denarios : 4,000 sesterces, by no means a high price to pay for an ordinary slave (see Marq. *Prl.* 173 ff.). Ehlers (in Müller[2]) suggests that this amount represents here not the full price of the slave but merely the 5 per cent manumission tax (see note on 58. 2 *vicesimam*); but Petronius sometimes makes his point by revealing the comparatively modest ambitions or achievements of Trimalchio's circle; cf., for example, 65. 10 'quinquaginta enim millibus aestimant mortuum', 68. 8 'illum emi trecentis denariis.'

sevir gratis factus sum : on the sevirate see note on 30. 2. Appointment to various local magistracies and *collegia* regularly involved the payment of a fixed sum of money, the *summa honoraria*; for the sevirate in certain towns 2,000 sesterces was the standard amount (see R. Duncan-Jones, *BSR* xxxiii, N.S. xx (1965), 226 ff., 284 f.). As an exceptional honour this payment might be waived; cf., for example, *CIL* x. 3959 'sevir Aug(ustalis) decr(eto) decur(ionum) gratis factus' (see Ruggiero, *Dizionario epigrafico*, iii. 592 s.v. *gratuitus*, *gratis*).

§ 8 maior natus : possibly a vulgarism; cf. Commod. *Instr.* 2. 29 'maioribus natis dico.' Expressions like *annos natus maior quadraginta* (Cic. *Rosc. Am.* 39), where the actual age is specified, are common.

lacticulosus : 'just weaned'; the word is glossed by λιπογάλακτος and *lac desinens habere* (see Heraeus, p. 76).

nec mu nec ma argutas : 'You can't squeak out *mu* or *ma*' (Heseltine). For a similar proverbial expression cf. Ennius in Varr. *LL* vii. 101 'neque, ut aiunt, mu facere audent', and see Otto s.v. *mu*. After learning the alphabet, children went on to learn various combinations of letters, e.g. 'mi ma mu me' (see Mayor on Juv. 14. 209, Marrou, *History of Education in Antiquity*, 212, 364).

vasus fictilis : 'earthenware pot'. As well as the obvious insult there may be a *double entendre* here; cf. Plaut. *Poen.* 863 'refero vasa salva', Hesychius βασά· αἰσχύνη. ὅ ἐστι δρῦς (see Heraeus, p. 136). This would help to explain the transition to *lorus in aqua*, a proverbial expression used in patently obscene contexts; cf. 134. 9, Mart. vii. 58. 3.

For the masculine forms *vasus* and *lorus* see note on 39. 4.

lentior non melior : cf. Tac. *Hist.* ii. 38 'post quos Cn. Pompeius, occultior non melior' (see Heraeus, p. 125).

§ 9 annis quadraginta servivi . . . puer capillatus : if the explanation given on § 4 above is sound, Hermeros now reveals a past which is quite inconsistent with his earlier boasts.

§ 10 malista [et] : i.e. Greek μάλιστα; '*tout à fait* the gentleman'. George's conjecture *malista [et]* for *mali isto H* is more plausible than *maiesto* Muncker or *maiestoso* Immisch; *maiestus* and *maiestosus* are not found elsewhere, but cf. Italian *maestoso*.

dignitos[s]o : not found earlier; cf. *CGL* ii. 49. 38 'dignitosus ἀξιωματικός', Heraeus, pp. 75 f.

See note on 38. 6 *sucos[s]us* for a discussion of the view that the ending *-ossus* is a vulgarism deliberately given by Petronius to Hermeros. The occurrence of the normal ending in the case of *laboriosus* (57. 7) and *lacticulosus* (57. 8) shows the need for caution.

pluris erat unguis quam tu totus es : Porphyrio uses a similar expression in his attempt to explain Hor. *Sat.* i. 4. 14: 'solemus namque dicere *minimo digito provocat* cum volumus quem intellegere tantum valere minimo digito quantum alium totis viribus.' See Otto s.v. *digitus* (6).

§ 11 haec sunt vera athla : the plural ἆθλα sometimes has the sense of contest or struggle, which fits better here than 'prizes' (see L.–S.–J. s.v. ἆθλον II). For the form of expression Heraeus (p. 122) compares *CIL* iv. 3525 'Puteolos, Antium . . . Pompeios —hae sunt verae coloniae'.

[in] ingenuum nasci : *in* has been defended on the analogy of 62. 10 *in larvam intravi*, but the likelihood of its insertion by dittography is very great.

'accede istoc' : for the replacement of a noun by a short direct utterance see note on 44. 2 *esur⟨it⟩io*. Like 58. 7 *deuro de, accede istoc* is probably chosen as a familiar order by a master to a slave.

tamquam hircus in ervilia : 'like a goat in a field of vetch'. *ervilia* is probably ablative (cf. 58. 9 'curris, stupes, satagis, tamquam mus in matella', and see Heraeus, pp. 21 ff., Süss, pp. 41 f.). As for the sense, the expression seems to denote an *embarras de richesses*; for a somewhat different explanation see H. B. Gottschalk (*CP* lxvi (1971), 187 f.): just as Hermeros had begun by hinting that Ascyltos and his friends are unaccustomed to a fine dinner like this, so now he insults him by asserting that he is like a goat which, through an excess of vetch, a wholesome food when taken in normal amounts, is suffering from a flatulent disorder.

Ch. 58

The boy Giton cannot contain his hilarity at this tirade of Hermeros, who now feels obliged to turn on him. The reader should not assume that Petronius' sympathies are necessarily with Giton; certainly at 117. 12 f. Giton's limited sense of humour is indicated: 'nec contentus (sc. mercennarius Corax) maledictis tollebat subinde altius pedem et strepitu obsceno simul atque odore viam implebat. ridebat contumaciam Giton et singulos crepitus eius pari clamore prosequebatur.'

§ 1. Giton is passed off as the slave of Encolpius and Ascyltos; cf. 26. 10 'libentissime servile officium tuentem'. At 91. 1 he is, in Encolpius' opinion, less happy as the slave of the poet Eumolpus.

§ 2 tu autem : *autem* is often used to introduce an angry question (cf. K.–S. ii. 94); probably so here rather than merely as an indication that a new opponent is now being addressed.

io Saturnalia : the Saturnalia in mid December was the one time in the year when slaves were allowed some licence, sometimes even to the extent of temporarily changing places with their masters, just as in the army today it is customary for officers and N.C.O.s to serve Christmas dinner to their men; cf. Sen. *Ep.* 18, Plin. ii. 17. 24, Balsdon, *Life and Leisure*, 124 ff.

It would be unwise to inquire too closely what time of year Petronius had in mind for the *Cena*; but it can be seen that if Hermeros' ironical question 'mensis December est?' is to make sense, some month other than December must be meant.

vicesimam : as at 71. 2 'Carioni (lego) insulam et vicesimam et lectum stratum', this stands for the 5 per cent tax on manumissions; cf. *CIL* x. 3875, where a man is described as *soc(ius) vices(imae) liber(tatis)*. According to Liv. vii. 16. 7 it was first introduced in 357 B.C.

⟨*⟩ quid faciat : the change from the second person *numerasti* to the third person *faciat* points towards a lacuna. Buecheler's *nescit* may be on the right lines, but something more forceful would help.

crucis offla, corvorum cibaria : crucifixion, as the standard capital punishment for slaves, provides material for epithets

and threats in comic contexts; cf. Hor. *Ep.* i. 16. 48 'non pasce
in cruce corvos', Otto s.v. *corvus* (3).

curabo : also introduces threats at § 5 and 6, 69. 1, 74. 15, 17,
75. 9, Phaedr. v. 2. 6 'iam curabo ut sentiat.'

Iovis : this nominative occurs also at 47. 4.

§ 3 ita . . . dono : 'as sure as I hope to get my bellyful, I'll let
your behaviour pass, out of respect for my fellow freedman'
(i.e. Trimalchio). For *donare* with dat. = forgive (a person) for
the sake of some person or thing cf. Sen. *de Clem.* i. 1. 4 'alium
dignitati donavi, alium humilitati', *OLD* s.v. 5b.

depraesentiarum : 'under the present circumstances'; only
here and at 74. 17. It is formed on the analogy of *inpraesen-
tiarum* (= *in praesentia rerum*), which occurs as early as Cato
RR 144. 4 and in a number of later authors (see Butler and
Owen on Apul. *Apol.* 48).

eug' euge : no certain correction of *geuge* in *H* has been made.
Salonius' conjecture assumes that it is a corruption of the
reduplicated Greek exclamation εὖγε 'bravo!' hence *isti eugeuge*
would mean 'those who shout "bravo!" '. Süss punctuates less
plausibly 'isti—euge! qui . . .', with *euge* interjected ironically.
Both these solutions are based on the frequency of Greek words
and phrases in Hermeros' speeches; cf. 37. 9 *babae babae*, 37. 10
babaecalis, 58. 7 *deuro de*. Buecheler instead proposes *nugae* (for
nugae used personally cf. Cic. *Att.* vi. 3. 5).

[qui tibi non imperant] : this looks like a gloss borrowed from
qui tibi non imperat in § 2 and inserted here in an attempt to
explain the preceding words. It might be defended as a deliberate repetition meant to give the impression of a naïve man's
indignation, but it is less convincing than other mannered
repetitions in Hermeros, e.g. *curabo, recte, ad summam.*

qualis dominus, talis et servus : in Greek οἶαπερ ἡ δέσποινα τοία χἠ
κύων (*Paroem. Gr.* ii. 44, cf. Cic. *Att.* v. 11. 5, Otto s.v. *dominus*).

§ 4 caldicerebrius : restored by Jahn from *caldus cicer eius H* on
the strength of 45. 5.

recte : cf. § 6 'recte venies sub dentem', 74. 17. In each case
recte indicates ironical agreement and precedes a future expressing a threat. See Hof. *LU* 40.

in publicum : for the accusative in place of the ablative see
note on 30. 3 *foras cenat.*

terrae tuber : apparently the literal meaning of this is a toad-stool or mushroom. For its use as an insult compare Neapolitan *tartufolo*, Triestine *tartufo* 'dolt' (see Hof. *LU* 88).

§ 5 **nec sursum nec deorsum . . . non conieci** : this sentence contains two double negatives which reinforce instead of cancelling (see note on 42. 7). It also has unusual tenses: present for future in the apodosis, perfect for future perfect in the protasis.

in rutae folium non conieci : see note on 37. 10.

curabo . . . : 'I'll see to it that your worthless (*besalis* in its literal sense means two-thirds, usually of an *as*) curls and that no-good master of yours are no help to you.' For *longe esse* 'be far away', i.e. of no assistance, cf. Virg. *Aen.* xii. 52 'longe illi dea mater erit.'

§ 6 **venies sub dentem** : Gellius vi. 9. 4 quotes from Laberius 'sub dentes mulieris veni, bis ter memordit.'

barbam auream : some parts, and in particular the beards, of statues of certain gods were in some cases gilded; cf. Pers. 2. 55–8, Varr. *RR* i. 1. 4. Caligula was occasionally seen wearing a golden beard as well as other symbols of divinity (cf. Suet. *Calig.* 52).

§ 7 **deuro de :** = Greek δεῦρο δή '(come) here.' No doubt a normal command by a master to his slave, but here it has acquired an obscene meaning: 'first made you his come-hither', i.e. his *deliciae* (see 44. 2 for note on the insertion of a short direct utterance).

geometrias, critica : these plurals are not cited elsewhere in Latin (in Greek γεωμετρίαι is sometimes used in the sense of geometric problems; cf. Plat. *Men.* 76 a). These solecisms support Hermeros' confession of ignorance.

†**et alogias menias†** : *et* is suspicious here, and it may conceal something like *aetia* 'causes'. Even if *alogias* is accepted, a number of alternative explanations are possible: (i) it could be taken as a substantive in the sense of absurdities (cf. Sen. *Apoc.* 7. 1 'ne tibi alogias excutiam'), in asyndeton with *menias* 'wraths', i.e. poems like the *Iliad* (from the opening words of the *Iliad*, μῆνιν ἄειδε, θεά). This leaves *alogias* awkwardly, however, as the only real pejorative in the list; possible alterations include Scheffer's *nenias* 'trivialities' (cf. 46. 4 'invenit tamen alias nenias'), which produces a peculiar asyndeton after *et*. (ii) If *alogias* is taken as a solecistic form of the adjective

alogas (Scheffer in fact read *alogas*), *menias* is plausible, but *nenias* allows the sentence to run smoothly.

§ 8 exi : after Hermeros' offer to make a little wager (*sponsiuncula*; see note on 70. 13 *sponsione*) this word is obscure. Probably it is merely an exhortation to his opponent 'Come on'; alternatively it has been regarded as a technical term taken over from dicing (cf. *CIL* iv. 3494).

Hermeros rattles off his first riddle, then, leaving no time for any answer, he recites two more. It looks as if each of the riddles has an obscene solution (for this type of riddle cf. *Anth. Pal.* xiv. 43) and also a respectable solution (foot, eye, and hair have been proposed). This line of interpretation seems preferable to that of Schultz (see *RE* iA. 116 f.), who thinks that the first line is not actually part of the riddle but is merely an introductory formula; see also F. Scheidweiler, *Philol.* lxxx (1924), 204 ff., *Anth. Pal.* xiv *passim*.

Hermeros' interest in riddles must be meant to appear vulgar: Plutarch (*Mor.* ii. 988 a) says that as part of their after-dinner entertainment the uneducated turned to riddles; but note that some of the numerous examples in *Anth. Pal.* xiv demand at least a modicum of education.

§ 9 tamquam mus in matella : the mouse figures in similar mishaps in several proverbs; cf. Herodas 2. 62 f. κἠμ πίσσηι μῦς, *Paroem. Gr.* i. 275.

§ 10 qui te natum non putat : 'thinks you don't exist'; cf. Sen. *Apoc.* 3. 2 'nemo enim umquam illum natum putavit', Otto s.v. *nasci* (2).

nisi si : colloquial; as well as being common in early Latin it is found in, for example, Cicero's letters and early speeches. See L.–H.–S. 668.

anulos buxeos : 'rings made of box-wood'. Hermeros now hints that Ascyltos is an impostor in wearing a gold ring (the plural could be taken as a comic exaggeration), the badge of an *eques Romanus* (see notes on 32. 3, 57. 4).

§ 11 Occuponem : the name, possibly Petronius' own coinage, suggests some popular deity; cf. 60. 8 *Cerdonem, Felicionem, Lucrionem*. The suffix *-o, -onis*, is common in Vulgar Latin (see Cooper, pp. 53–8).

ferrum : the iron ring worn by Romans other than knights and senators; cf. Plin. *NH* xxxiii. 30.

§ 12 **vah !** : a word often used in comedy to express joy or (as here) disgust or anger; cf. Hof. *LU* 14 f.

bella res : 'a fine thing'; ironical here but not always so (cf. Sen. *Ep.* 69. 6, where a popular saying is quoted: 'bella res est mori sua morte').

ita . . . persecutus : 'as sure as I hope to make a fortune and die well off or have the people swear by my death, if I don't put my toga on the wrong way round and hound you everywhere'. This is a conflation of two different constructions: (i) *ita . . . ut . . .* 'As surely as I want *x* to happen, so true is *y*.' (ii) 'May *x* not happen unless I do *y*.' Hermeros starts with two clauses of type (i), the second of these being put in disjunctive form with *aut*, then instead of a correlative *ut* clause he moves over to a *nisi* clause as in (ii). An even greater incoherence is expressed if we adopt Jahn's *ut* for *aut*, but *ita . . . et ita . . . ut . . .* now becomes a consecutive construction: 'May I make such a profit and die so well off that the people swear by my death, if I don't . . .'

toga perversa : it would seem from Sen. *de Ira* 1. 16. 5 that where a capital charge was involved the presiding judge customarily wore his toga reversed, possibly only at the passing of sentence (as with the black cap in former British procedure).

§ 13 **mufrius :** not found elsewhere. Its meaning and derivation are unknown; Ernout (*Elements*, 200) connects it with *mufro* 'mountain-sheep', a word attested in Polemius Silvius and occurring in Sardinian and other dialects (cf. Ernout–Meillet s.v. *mufro*, Meyer-Lübke, no. 5715).

⟨**nos aliter**⟩ : some such supplement as this (or simply *nos*) is called for. Even when punctuated as in Süss, 'didicimus— dicebat enim magister—"sunt vestra salva?" ', the text of *H* can hardly be defended.

maiorem maledicas : the accusative with *maledicere* is Vulgar (cf. 96. 7 (Bargates) 'maledic illam versibus'), whereas the dative is used in narrative at 53. 3, 117. 11, 132. 13 (although at 74. 9 *H* has 'maledicere Trimalchionem coepit').

§ 14 **at nunc mera mapalia :** this is Heraeus' certain conjecture for *aut numera mapalia H. mapalia* appears to be a Punic word for huts (cf. Virg. *Georg.* iii. 340, and see Austin's note at *Aen.* i. 421 on *magalia*, a word of similar meaning but possibly unconnected in origin), but the phrase *mera mapalia* must have acquired some wider sense. A rendering like 'it's all an utter

shambles' gives a coherent explanation of the phrase here and
at Sen. *Apoc.* 9. 1 ' "ego" inquit "patres conscripti, interrogare
vobis permiseram, vos mera mapalia fecistis" ', as well as
suiting Festus 132. 9L 'mapalia casae Punicae appellantur, in
quibus quia nihil est secreti solet solute viventibus obici vocabulum.' See E. Mueller-Graupa, *Philol.* lxxxv (1930), 303 ff.

dupondii evadit : 'ends up worth twopence'. Buecheler–
Heraeus understand *e schola* with *evadit*, but this is too specific.

Ch. 59

§ 1 **scordalias :** 'wrangling'; not found elsewhere. It is derived
from the Greek σκόροδον, garlic. According to Xen. *Symp.* iv. 9,
fighting-cocks were sometimes fed on garlic to fit them for
battle.

For the use of *de medio* cf. 38. 13 *amici de medio.*

sanguen : this neuter form is found frequently in early Latin
and also occasionally in later authors (e.g. Stat. *Theb.* iv. 464).
Probably a Vulgar form, although the regular accusative *sanguinem* occurs at 62. 11, a passage with a number of undoubted
Vulgarisms. See Stefenelli, pp. 117 f., for the argument that
sanguen should instead be taken as an archaism, and that the
various Romance forms, e.g. Italian *sangue*, Rumanian *sînge*,
are derived from a popular form of the accusative, viz. *sanguem*,
rather than from *sanguen*.

§ 2 **qui vincitur vincit :** proverbial; cf. Cato *Monost.* 42 'qui
vinci sese patitur pro tempore, vincit', Publ. Syr. 398 Ribb.
'non vincitur sed vincit, qui cedit suis', Otto s.v. *vincere* (2).

capo : here apparently means rascal or rogue, from *capo* in the
sense of a young cock.

cocococo : the call of a cock is used here as a boisterous interjection (see Hof. *LU* 60), but it also possibly sounded obscene
(cf. Greek κωκώ in *Anth. Pal.* xii. 3. 4 and κόκκους ib. 222. 3).

a primitiis : perhaps 'anew' (cf. Greek πάλιν ἐξ ἀρχῆς) ; if so, the
sense will be 'Let's go back to the beginning and enjoy ourselves', i.e. 'Let's forget about this little unpleasantness.'

Homeristas : instead of the old rhapsodists who merely recited
passages from Homer these *Homeristae* combined to give
theatrical performances (see *SG*[8] i. 429).

Note that Trimalchio follows the Greek with the help of a
Latin translation, a detail consistent with the very limited
Greek with which he is credited in 48. 8.

§ 3 canora voce : 'in a full-throated voice'. In an article entitled 'Silent Reading in Antiquity', in *Greek, Roman, and Byzantine Studies* ix (1968), 421 ff., Bernard M. W. Knox refutes the conventional notion that in antiquity the ability to read silently was regarded as extraordinary.

§§ 4–5. Trimalchio's wild version of the story is entertaining precisely because each detail distorts some identifiable part of the normal version. In place of Helen's brothers Castor and Pollux he puts the Greek warrior Diomedes and the Trojan (or Cretan) boy Ganymedes, who are linked only by having a similar ring to their names. Agamemnon for a moment replaces Paris as the ravisher of Helen, but he then goes on to sacrifice a hind to Diana in her stead, a detail which is based on the fate of Iphigenia in the normal version: just before the start of the Trojan War, when the Greek fleet lay becalmed at Aulis, Agamemnon was on the point of sacrificing Iphigenia when a hind was miraculously substituted for her. The Iphigenia story is further distorted a little later. In the usual version she is tricked into coming to Aulis by the false promise that she is to marry Achilles; Trimalchio, however, says that the marriage actually took place, but at the end of the war, not the beginning. Again, the hero Ajax is usually said to have gone mad when the arms of the dead Achilles were given to Odysseus rather than to himself; Trimalchio makes him a lover jealous of Achilles the successful suitor.

Some of the features of Trimalchio's character here have been thought to be based on the description Seneca gives (*Ep.* 27. 5–8) of a Calvisius Sabinus, a wealthy noble of limited ability (the words 'et patrimonium habebat libertini et ingenium' are too often taken as a proof that he was a freedman, despite his far from servile name; see *RE* s.v. Calvisius, nos. 12–16). Calvisius used his wealth in a vain effort to make up for his intellectual shortcomings: 'hanc itaque compendiariam excogitavit: magna summa emit servos, unum qui Homerum teneret, alterum qui Hesiodum; novem praeterea lyricis singulos adsignavit.' The resemblances between Trimalchio and Calvisius are not necessarily more than coincidental, and even if they are, we have no reason to assume that Petronius could have learned about Calvisius only through Seneca. See also note on ch. 78.

§ 4 Tarentini : Scheffer's conjecture gives an attractive alliteration (cf. 48. 2 *Tarraciniensibus et Tarentinis*). *H* has *Parentini*, i.e. the inhabitants of Parentium, a town about 30 miles north of Pola; this would give a possible play on Paris.

§ 6 ducenaria : 'of two hundred pounds weight'. Pliny (*NH* xxxiii. 145) asserts that a slave of Claudius, his *dispensator* in Hispania Citerior, had a silver plate weighing 500 pounds, with eight others of 250 pounds each.

§ 7 modo versa modo supina gesticulatus : 'making now forehand, now backhand sweeps'; sc. *manu* with *versa* and *supina*.

frust[r]a : *H* has the Vulgar form *frustrum* in narrative here and at 35. 3.

Juvenal ridicules the flourishes with which food was carved and arranged on plates at a banquet:

> structorem interea, ne qua indignatio desit,
> saltantem spectes et chironomunta volanti
> cultello . . .   (5. 120 ff.)

Ch. 60

§ 1 strophas : 'flourishes'; in Latin this plural comes to mean tricks or *tours de force*, but here it does not seem to have lost completely the original sense of the Greek στροφή viz. 'turn' or 'twist'.

lacunaria : Suetonius (*Nero* 31) says that Nero's palace had dining-rooms with movable ceiling-panels from which flowers and unguents were showered down upon the guests. Elagabalus, it is said (SHA, *Heliog.* 21. 5), went even further: his guests were smothered to death when they were unable to crawl out from under the violets and other flowers showered down upon them. Similar features were not unknown in earlier times: see Sallust's account of a banquet given in honour of Metellus Pius: 'simul croco sparsa humus et alia in modum templi celeberrimi. praeterea tum sedenti in transenna demissum Victoriae simulacrum cum machinato strepitu tonitruum coronam ei imponebat' (Macrob. *Sat.* iii. 13. 8); cf. Val. Max. ix. 1. 5 '(Metellus Pius) demissas lacunaribus aureas coronas velut caelesti capite recipiebat', Marq. *Prl.* i. 311.

§ 2 de caelo nuntiaretur : light-hearted use of a technical expression from augury; cf. Varr. *LL* vi. 86 *de caelo nuntium*.

§ 3 [de cupa videlicet grandi excussus] : this fatuous reference to a *cupa*, a wooden barrel used for storing wine, has presumably been interpolated by some scribe in late antiquity or in the Carolingian period. It is not appropriate to Encolpius nor is it likely to have been inserted by any commentator close to Petronius' own time.

alabastris : small globular vases of alabaster, used especially for perfumes or unguents.

Crowns or garlands and unguents were often presented to guests at the close of a dinner when the *comissatio* began; see Marq. *Prl.* 331. Thus when Habinnas arrives from the other dinner which he has attended he comes 'oneratus aliquot coronis et unguento per frontem in oculos fluente' (65. 7).

§ 4 Priapus : pastry figures in human or animal shape are mentioned at 40. 4 *minores porcelli*, 69. 6 *turdi siliginei*, etc. Martial has a pastry Priapus among his *Apophoreta* (for the obscene possibilities of pastry see also Mart. ix. 2. 3). Priapus often appears as the god of gardens, hence the fruit in his lap here. *more vulgato* is skilfully reserved for the end of the sentence: Priapus' dress, lifted up to hold the fruit, reveals his *phallos* (see illustration in Roscher, *Lex. d. gr. u. röm. Mythol.* iii. 2. 2983).

§ 5 pompam : 'splendid array'; the word is used of rich food by Martial as well: 'mullus tibi quattuor emptus / librarum cenae pompa caputque fuit' (x. 31. 3 f.).

commissio : 'start, opening'; cf. Cic. *Att.* xv. 26. 1, Delz, p. 682, Nisbet, p. 230. *remissio H* 'relaxation' is all but impossible, even though *ludorum* could be taken as a genitive of definition (cf. Cic. *de Orat.* ii. 212 *remissio lenitatis*), and the association of *ludi* and *remissio* is paralleled in Cic. *Cael.* 39 'quem non quies, non remissio, non aequalium studia, non ludi delectarent'. Buecheler's *missio* does not suit: the natural meaning of it in this context would be 'end' (cf. Cic. *Fam.* v. 12. 8 *ante ludorum missionem*), not 'release' (of the saffron), despite such uses of *missio* and *mittere* as Ov. *Fast.* v. 360 'accidere in mensas ut rosa missa solet'.

§ 6 crocum : cf. 68. 1 'scobemque croco et minio tinctam sparserunt'. Saffron was sprinkled in public places, especially in theatres, on account of its fragrance (cf. Mart. v. 25. 7 f.). Here it is unpleasant only because it is squirted into the guests' faces; cf. Plin. *NH* xxi. 32 'altera probatio (sc. of Cilician saffron), si manu relata ad ora leniter faciem oculosque mordeat.' In general see Balsdon, *Life and Leisure*, 258.

usque ad os ⟨nobis⟩ : Delz suggests that *os* was left out; *ad nobis* would then be altered to *ad nos H*.

§ 7 **tam religioso apparatu perfusum** : saffron was used in sacrifices as well as in theatres; cf. Ov. *Fast*. i. 75 f. 'cernis, odoratis ut luceat ignibus aether / et sonet accensis spica Cilissa focis?'

Augusto, patri patriae, feliciter : according to Dio li. 19. 7, as early as 30 B.C. it was decreed that everybody in Rome should pour a libation to Augustus at all banquets, public and private. From Hor. *Od*. iv. 5, addressed to Augustus, it would seem that this acclamation normally came during dessert: 'hinc ad vina redit laetus et alteris / te mensis adhibet deum' (vv. 31 f.). At Trimalchio's dinner, however, the dessert has not yet been reached (cf. 68. 1), so the acclamation of Augustus at this point might be equivalent to our drinking a toast to the Queen during the main course of a dinner.

The title *pater patriae*, granted to Augustus and other Julio-Claudian emperors, was declined by Tiberius (Suet. *Tib*. 26. 2), but this fact by itself would not necessarily count against a Tiberian setting for the *Cena*: for all we know, the acclamation of Augustus may have continued to be customary even after his death, or the point might lie in the guests' ignorance of Tiberius' refusal to accept the honour for himself.

mappas : handkerchiefs or napkins. Guests usually brought their own to dinner, using them both to wipe their hands and to remove *apophoreta*; often, at least in satire, they preferred to remove the *mappae* brought by their neighbours at table or those provided by the host; cf. Mart. xii. 28. 21 f. 'ad cenam Hermogenes mappam non attulit umquam, / a cena semper rettulit Hermogenes', Cat. 12, Marq. *Prl*. 313 f.

ego praecipue... : thefts of food by dinner guests form another conventional topic; Martial rebukes an over-acquisitive diner (ii. 37. 10 f.) 'ullus si pudor est, repone cenam: / cras te, Caeciliane, non vocavi.' In portraying Encolpius' greed on Giton's behalf Petronius also wants to create a resemblance between him and Habinnas, perhaps the most repulsive of Trimalchio's guests: cf. 66. 4 'ego tamen duo (sc. mala, the traditional gift of the lover) sustuli . . . nam si aliquid muneris meo vernulae non tulero, habebo convicium.'

§ 8 **Lares bullatos** : the free-born child was given a *bulla*, a round or heart-shaped amulet, at birth; when he assumed the *toga virilis*, the *bulla* was dedicated to the *lares*; cf. Pers. 5. 31 'bullaque succinctis laribus donata pependit', Marq. *Prl*. 84 ff.

dii propitii : according to Servius' note on *Aen*. i. 730, after the main course had been removed at a normal dinner there was customarily a solemn silence until some food was burned as an offering and a boy proclaimed the words 'dii propitii'; here, however, these words are preceded by a scramble for *apophoreta* and followed by the announcement of the comic, materialistic names of the *lares*.

clamabat . . . aiebat autem : we would expect Trimalchio, rather than the boy, to give the quaint names of the *lares*. This requires a lacuna to explain the change of subject after *unus . . . clamabat*. The first two boys bring on four statuettes between them, the representations of Cerdo, Felicio, Lucrio, and Trimalchio; the statuette of Trimalchio was probably first mentioned in the missing passage, perhaps in such unflattering terms that *veram* (= *verisimilem*, cf. Plin. *NH* xxxv. 52) was more effective than it seems to be as the text now stands. The kissing of his image looks like another travesty of imperial ritual.

Cerdonem . . . Felicionem . . . Lucrionem : 'Gain', 'Luck', 'Profit'. For names in *-o, -onis*, see note on 38. 8 *Incuboni*. These three all occur elsewhere as names of slaves in literature or inscriptions: Cerdo (from Greek κέρδος = *lucrum*) occurs in *Dig.* xxxviii. 1. 42, cf. Juv. 4. 153, 8. 182, Felicio in *CIL* iv. 3163 ff., Lucrio in *CIL* ii. 3501. See Heraeus, p. 77.

Ch. 61

The urge for variety is a sufficient explanation of the inclusion of the two supernatural stories in chs. 61–3. Sullivan, however, in his chapter 'The Sexual Themes of the *Satyricon*', thinks that these stories, like the more obviously sexual incidents in the novel, may illustrate the pervasive theme of scopophilia.

§ 1 bonam mentem bonamque valetudinem : cf. 88. 8 'ac ne bonam quidem mentem aut bonam valetudinem petunt.' The prayer is conventional; cf. Sen. *Ep.* 10. 4 'roga bonam mentem, bonam valetudinem animi, deinde tunc corporis', Juv. 10. 356 'orandum est ut sit mens sana in corpore sano' and see Nisbet and Hubbard on Hor. *Od.* i. 31. 17.

§ 2 muttis : Scheffer's conjecture for *mutes H*; only here in Petronius, but it occurs in Ennius, Plautus, and Terence, mostly with a negative.

Warmington in his revision of Heseltine's translation renders this sentence thus: 'Something or other makes you dumb now, and you do not utter a sound.' This seems more likely than to take *taces* and *muttis* as indicatives in an indirect question (as at 44. 1 'nemo curat quid annona mordet').

sic felicem me videas : cf. 72. 3 'sic vos felices videam.'

§ 3 gaudimonio : apart from two common legal terms, *patrimonium* and *testimonium*, the only other noun with this characteristically Vulgar ending used by Petronius is *tristimonium* at 63. 4. See Cooper, pp. 36 f.

dissilio : 'I'm simply bursting'; a colloquial usage, cf. 75. 9 'felicitate dissilio', Sen. *Ep.* 113. 26 'dissilio risu.'

§ 4 viderint : 'they'd better watch it.' A warning; cf. Ov. *Her.* 12. 211 'viderit ista deus qui nunc mea pectora versat.'

§ 5 'haec ubi dicta dedit' : a formula from early Latin (cf. Lucilius 18 'haec ubi dicta dedit, pausam ⟨dedit⟩ ore loquendi'), taken over by Virgil (see Austin's note on *Aen.* ii. 790), by Livy (cf. xxii. 50. 10, where it introduces a hexameter 'haec ubi dicta dedit, stringit gladium cuneoque'), and by Silver Latin poets.

§ 6 quomodo dii volunt : see note on 38. 8 *quomodo*. Heraeus (p. 113) cites *CGL* iii. 111. 25, where *quomodo di volunt* is given as the answer to the question 'quo modo res tuae ? omnia bene ?' Ogilvie comments on Liv. i. 39. 4 'evenit facile quod dis cordi esset': 'This moralizing generalization reflects a commonplace, often colloquial, practice of adding a touch of mock-seriousness to a story by adding *quomodo di volunt* and the like.'

uxorem Terentii coponis : this gives more than a hint of her character: inns were notorious for prostitution; cf. *Cod. Iust.* iv. 56. 3 'eam quae ita venit ne corpore quaestum faceret, nec in caupona sub specie ministrandi prostitui, ne fraus legi dictae fiat, oportet', Marq. *Prl.* 471 f., *SG*⁸ ii. 45.
Both her name and her origin are carefully chosen. Melissa is found as the name of a courtesan in, for example, Athen. 578 c. Tarentum was noted for its honey (cf. Hor. *Od.* ii. 6. 13 ff.) as well as for its vicious luxury (cf. Juv. 6. 297 'coronatum et petulans madidumque Tarentum').

bacciballum : not found elsewhere; presumably a term of endearment or approbation. It has a comic ring to it, even if the etymology is obscure. Orioli sees a connection with *bacca*; the word would then refer to Melissa's plump shape, although the ending *-ballum* would remain unexplained. See also K. Sittl, *ALL* ii. 610.

§ 7 ⟨illam⟩ [autem] : the combination *sed autem* is sometimes found (see L.–H.–S. 488, 525), but here *autem* seems to have come in by dittography before *aut* (cf. 73. 4 *autem* [*aut*]). This may in turn have led to the loss of *illam*, although an object is not absolutely necessary (see Bendz, pp. 28 f.).

benemoria : the corrupt reading in *H*, *bene moriar*, is possibly influenced by 58. 12 'ita bene moriar.' Hadrianides proposed *bene morata*, but Orelli's *benemoria* is closer; cf. *CGL* iii. 333. 41 ἀνέντροπος: *malemorius*, Heraeus, pp. 104 ff.

§ 8 ⟨*⟩ **in illius sinum demandavi** : the text is almost certainly incomplete here. Petronius may have wanted to bring out the incredibility of Niceros' tale by showing him as too gullible to realize that he has been paying Melissa much more than he has received from her. Even so, Buecheler's ⟨*quicquid habui*⟩ is not necessarily the right supplement; some conjecture with no particular justification (e.g. *omnia* Jacobs) may be right. Delz on the other hand follows Fuchs in assuming an asyndeton at *assem semissem* (see app. crit.): 'If I had a penny or a halfpenny, I entrusted it to her pocket.' A lacuna must then be postulated before *fecit* to give it a construction, unless perhaps *negatum fecit* is a Vulgarism, not attested elsewhere, for *negavit*.

fefellitus sum : an irregular, reduplicated form derived from the perfect *fefelli* in place of the regular participle *falsus*. Similarly *pepercitum* and *pepertum* are both found as formations from *peperci* in late sources. See Heraeus, p. 130.

§ 9 **contubernalis** : see note on 57. 6. The word is probably used accurately here: Melissa is the *contubernalis* of the unnamed slave whose death is described in the story; later she becomes the *uxor* of Terentius, whose gentile name shows him to be a free man. The alternative is to assume that *contubernalis* represents the absent-mindedness of Niceros, an ex-slave himself, in referring to the death of Terentius.

per scutum per ocream : lit. 'through shield and through greave', = 'by hook or by crook'.

aginavi : 'schemed'. Only here in literature, but confirmed by glosses, e.g. *CGL* ii. 11. 34 'aginat: διαπράσσεται, στρέφει, μηχανᾶται'. See Heraeus, p. 77.

⟨**scitis**⟩ **autem** : *autem* as the first word could be defended here: Quintilian (i. 5. 39) gives examples of solecisms in word-order: 'quoque ego, enim hoc voluit, autem non habuit'; but *scitis*, supplied by Buecheler, may have fallen out of place and been changed to *scita* in the next line.

in angustiis amici apparent : Cic. *Amic.* 64 quotes Ennius 'amicus certus in re incerta cernitur'; see Otto s.v. *amicus* (6).

Ch. 62

§ 1 Capuae : 'to Capua'. Donatus mentions this use of the locative as a solecism: 'si interrogati quo pergamus respondeamus Romae' (*Gramm.* iv. 393. 12); cf. Vulg. *II Tim.* 1: 17 'venisset Romae'. See Süss, p. 34, L.–H.–S. 150 f.

scruta : 'odds and ends', syn. of Greek γρύτη; cf. Lucilius 1282M 'quidni? et scruta quidem ut vendat scrutarius laudat / praefractam strigilem soleam improbus dimidiatam.'

[scita]: kept by most editors, e.g. Sedgwick 'pretty trumpery', but rightly challenged by P. A. George, *CQ* N.S. xvii (1967), 130. George regards it as a dittography of *scruta*, but see note on 61. 9 ⟨*scitis*⟩ *autem*.

§ 2 persuadeo hospitem : see note on 46. 2 *te persuadeam*.

§ 3 apoculamus nos : 'arsed off'; cf. 67. 3 (Habinnas) 'ego me apoculo.' Probably a Vulgar hybrid from ἀπό and *culare* (cf. 38. 2 (sc. arietes) 'culavit in gregem', French *reculer*, English *recoil*).

§ 4 inter monimenta : just out of town they would begin to see tombs built on either side of the road, like those still standing along the Via Appia outside Rome. Graveyards were said to be favourite haunts of werewolves; cf. K. F. Smith on Tib. i 5. 54.

homo meus : cf. § 13 *miles meus*, 63. 7 *baro noster*, Phaedr. v. 7. 32 'homo meus se in pulpito . . . prosternit.' In this idiom the speaker indicates his sympathy, usually with a hint of irony. See Hof. *LU* 137, 200.

facere : euphemistic 'do his business' (cf. 47. 4 'sua re causa facere'; at 9. 9 *facere* is used euphemistically but in a different sense: 'qui ne tum quidem, cum fortiter faceres, cum pura muliere pugnasti'). Note also Trimalchio's concern for the protection of his monument at 71. 8 'praeponam enim unum ex libertis sepulcro meo custodiae causa, ne in monumentum meum populus cacatum currat.' The alternative interpretation of *facere* here as 'make for' (cf. Tert. *Pall.* 3 'ad illum ex Libya Hammon facit') does not fit the context so well.

secedo ego cantabundus : Delz objects to Scheffer's *sedeo ego*
on the ground that *respexi* implies that Niceros has moved
a little way off while his companion relieves himself; he also
proposes *cunctabundus* for *cantabundus H*, but he is not per-
suasive in claiming that singing does not suit here.

§ 5 **mihi [in] anima in naso esse :** the expression describes
extreme fear: the soul of a dying person was thought to leave
through his mouth or his nose.

The historic infinitive is quite often found in colloquial language: Cicero, for example, uses it in his early speeches and in
his letters. It is, however, rare in Petronius (cf. note on 52. 5
⟨ora⟩re. See L.–H.–S. 367, Hof. *LU* 50 f.

§ 6 **subito lupus factus est :** although belief in werewolves was
widespread, Petronius perhaps indicates by his choice of Magna
Graecia as the setting for this tale that, like the elder Pliny (cf.
NH viii. 80 ff.), he regarded it as an illustration of *Graeca
credulitas*. For detailed analyses of Niceros' story see K. F.
Smith, 'An Historical Study of the Werwolf in Literature', in
Publications of the Modern Languages Association of America
ix (1894), 1 ff., M. Schuster, 'Der Werwolf und die Hexen', in
Wien. St. xlviii (1930), 149 ff. Before changing into a wolf the
werewolf must first take off all his clothes, and his resumption
of human form depends on safeguarding them. Hence the
circle of urine is probably to be seen as a magic device for pro-
tecting them rather than for effecting his transformation into
a wolf. In any case Schuster is surely right in emphasizing the
element of parody in Petronius' selection of this particular
ritual.

§ 8 **primitus :** 'at first'. Only here in Petronius, but found in
Lucilius, Varro, and Lucretius, as well as in late Latin.

lapidea facta sunt : apparently another precaution against the
loss of his clothes; Schuster (loc. cit., p. 162) suspects that this
detail is related to another version in which the werewolf left
his clothes under a stone for safety.

§ 9 †**matauitatau**† : the text cannot be restored here. Commentators are divided between (i) those who think that the reading
in *H* represents some magic incantation or formula, like our
abracadabra (see Butler and Owen on Apul. *Apol.* 38. 20 for the
use of strange names and words in magic, also L.–S.–J. s.v.
'*Εφέσια*), and (ii) those who assume that some Latin words have
been corrupted; e.g. *in tota via* Scheffer, *meta vitata* Rankin,

matutinas Heinsius, *matavi tetavi*, 'I killed and slaughtered'
G. R. Watson (*CP* lx (1965), 118).

umbras cecidi : the superstition that iron was feared by dead
men and spirits is mentioned by a scholiast on Hom. *Od.* xi. 48
(cf. Norden's note on Virg. *Aen.* vi. 260). See also J. G. Frazer,
The Golden Bough (abr. version), 226: 'Thus in the Highlands
of Scotland the great safeguard against the elfin race is iron,
or, better yet, steel. The metal in any form, whether as a sword,
a knife, a gun-barrel, or what not, is all-powerful for this
purpose.'

§ 10 in larvam : 'like a ghost'. The reading in *H* should be kept;
cf. Schol. Juv. 2. 147 'pugnavit in gladiatorem', August. *Civ.*
xx. 19 'dicimus "sedet in amicum" id est "velut amicus" .' See
L.-H.-S. 275, also Süss, p. 35, who defends the reading *in
ingenuum nasci* at 57. 11.

undabat : Nisbet, p. 230, makes this palaeographically easy
conjecture for *volabat*, suspecting that *sudor volabat* is not possible Latin (despite Heinsius' citation of Sen. *Oed.* 922 'gelidus
volat (sic *A*; *fluit E*) sudor per artus').

oculi mortui : an obscure phrase which possibly means 'my
eyes were glazed.' See also note on 68. 8.

§ 11 omnia pecora : some word indicating violent action is
needed; a compound in *per-*, e.g. *perculit* Buecheler, would
help to explain the omission after *pecora*. Various editors,
including Ernout and Marmorale, have accepted the text of *H*
as it stands, assuming an anacoluthon; but this seems a less
plausible solution than at 44. 3 'aediles—male eveniat'.

§ 12 †hac nostri† : Ehlers's suggestion, *maturius*, is much better
than *Gai nostri* of Buecheler.

tamquam copo compilatus: 'like the innkeeper who was robbed'.
The phrase is paradoxical in itself: innkeepers had an evil reputation for robbing and even killing their guests. Theophrastus
(*Char.* 6. 5) says of the man suffering from ἀπόνοια, 'He is very
likely, too, to go in for inn-keeping or brothel-keeping or tax-
farming . . . he gambles and lets his mother starve' (Vellacott's
translation; see also Ussher's note ad loc.). But there is a
further point to the expression: Aesop. *Fab.* 196 Halm tells of
an innkeeper who is cheated of a fine suit of clothes by a guest
who, by claiming to be a werewolf, terrifies him into running
away. See Rogge, *Philologische Wochenschrift* (1927), 1021–3.

§ 13 **bovis** : cf. 47. 4 *Iovis.*

§ 14 **exopinissent** : not found elsewhere. If sound, it is a hybrid, with an ending based on Greek verbs in -ίζειν (for the Latinization of -ίζειν cf. 67. 10 *excatarissasti*, Plaut. *Men.* 11 f. 'graecissat . . . sicilicissitat'). The dislocation of the preceding words in *H*, however, leaves doubt over the genuineness of this form.

Ch. 63

§ 1 **salvo tuo sermone** : 'with all respect for your story'. Sedgwick points out that Trimalchio begins as if he were about to cast doubt on it.

si qua fides est : 'if you'll take my word for it', a stock formula apologizing for something far-fetched (cf. 65. 1 'si qua est dicenti fides', Ov. *Met.* ix. 55, 371). The exclamatory *ut* which introduces *mihi pili inhorruerunt* adds to the disjointed effect already created by the odd use of *salvo tuo sermone.*

§ 2 **asinus in tegulis** : apparently a proverbial expression for something remarkable. Similar escapades are reported of a horse and two oxen respectively in SHA, *Pertinax* 1, and Liv. xxxvi. 37. 2. Even closer is the fable (Babr. 125) in which an ass climbs to the top of a house; when punished for breaking a tile, he exclaims that the monkey had done it before him and got away with it. Friedlaender presses the connection too far, however, in suggesting that the end of this fable is the clue to the proverb, and that Trimalchio means: 'I cannot tell as good a story as Niceros; compared with him I am like the ass on the roof.'

§ 3 **vitam Chiam** : Chians had a reputation for effeminacy as well as luxurious living. According to *Paroem. Gr.* i. 230 the proverbs 'Ionian laughter' and 'Chian laughter' were applied to *cinaedi.*

ipsimi : cf. 69. 3 *ipsumam meam*, 75. 11 *ipsimi, ipsimae*, 76. 1 *ipsimi*; a Vulgar superlative of ipse = 'the master'. Heraeus, pp. 78 f. quotes an analogous form of the superlative: *CGL* v. 179. 17 *clarimum: clarissimum.*

delicatus : 'pet'. Like *deliciae*, the word does not necessarily refer to a sexual relationship, although it clearly does here; cf. *CIL* vi. 17416 'Eutycheti puero delicato b. m. L. Fufidius Sporus dominus fecit', Sen. *Ep.* 12. 3 'ego sum Philositi vilici filius, deliciolum tuum.' See Ruggiero, *Dizionario epigrafico* s.v. *delicium.*

†caccitus† : corrupt. Jacobs's *catamitus* is perhaps too un-complimentary but it might fit if there is a *double entendre* in *omnium numerum*. H. Rönsch ([*Neue*] *Jahrbücher für Philologie und Pädogogik* cxxv (1882), 424–6) conjectures *zacritus* = διάκριτος, i.e. excellent.

omnium numerum : i.e. complete in all respects. The idiom may be connected with the technical use of *numerus* in wrestling = 'throw'; e.g. Quint. x. 1. 4 'athleta, qui omnes iam perdidicerit a praeceptore numeros', xii. 2. 12, Sen. *Ben.* 7. 1. 4. If it is, it may contain a *double entendre* here: 'a lad who knew all the positions'. See Pease on Cic. *de Div.* i. 23, L.–S.–J. s.v. ἀριθμός I. 4.

§ 4 nostrum plures : Heinsius' conjecture for the unacceptable reading in *H*, *nos tum plures*, is sharper in sense than *comploratores* Delz or *plorantes* Müller[2], as well as being an easier change.

tristimonio : the feminine form *tristimonia* occurs in *Bell. Afr.* 10. 3. See also note on 61. 3 *gaudimonio*.

strigae : 'witches'. On *striga* as a Vulgar form for *strix* 'screech-owl' see Heraeus, p. 134. K. F. Smith writes of the *strix*: 'For the Romans it belonged as much to the kingdom of dreams as to the kingdom of birds . . . hence one can never be sure in any given instance whether the *strix* is a real *strix* or a witch in the form of one' (note on Tib. i. 5. 52).

§ 5 Cappadocem : the Cappadocians were noted for their physi-cal strength; cf. Martial vi. 77. 4 'quid te Cappadocum sex onus esse iuvat?' See also note on 69. 2 ' "adcognosco" inquit "Cappadocem." '

valde audaculum : the addition of *valde* illustrates the decline of the original sense of smallness in the diminutive. See Hof. *LU* 140 f.

On adjectives in *-ulus* see Cooper, p. 186.

bovem iratum tollere : *Iovem* in *H* is a scribe's untimely reminiscence of 58. 2 'curabo, iam tibi Iovis iratus sit.' The ability of the famous athlete Milo of Croton to lift up a heifer became proverbial; cf. Quint. i. 9. 5.

§ 6 involuta sinistra manu : cf. Liv. xxv. 16. 21 'paludamento circa laevum bracchium intorto—nam ne scuta quidem secum extulerant—in hostes impetum fecit.'

salvum sit quod tango : before adding that the *strigae* were invisible Trimalchio is able to tell his audience precisely in which part of the body one *striga* was struck by the imprudent Cappadocian. He at once adds an apotropaic formula 'salvum sit quod tango' so that he should not himself be wounded in the same place; cf. English 'God save the mark.' See M. Schuster, *Wien. St.* xlix (1931), 86, F. Skutsch, *Kl. Schr.* 328 ff.

§ 7 **baro** : cf. note on 53. 11. *noster* is used like *meus* in 62. 4.

[**quia . . . manus**] : these words hold up the story a little, and are probably a scribal interpolation rather than an attempt by Petronius to convey Niceros' naïvety.

§ 8 **cluso** : for *clauso*; cf. 62. 12 *copo* for *caupo.*

amplexaret : this active form occurs also in early Latin and in glosses. See note on 46. 1 for other substitutions of active forms for deponents.
The subjunctive is not found in early Latin after *dum* as a purely temporal conjunction, but it is so used in *Bell. Afr.* 23. 2, 25. 1, occasionally in verse, and frequently in Livy and in late Latin. See L.–H.–S. 613 f.

manuciolum : 'a tiny handful'; hap. leg., but cf. *manipulus*, sometimes corrupted in manuscripts to *maniculus*. See Heraeus, p. 142.

vavatonem : the derivation and meaning are unknown; it is perhaps formed from a word like **baba*, spoken by or to a young child (see Heraeus, p. 178).
In other tales the victim's skin is left as an empty shell after his flesh and blood have been removed from within; see M. Schuster, *Wien. St.* xlviii (1930), 174 ff., ib. xlix (1931), 87 ff.

§ 9 **plussciae** : hap. leg., formed on the analogy of *nescius* and *conscius.*

et quod sursum est, deorsum faciunt : a common proverbial expression; cf., for example, Sen. *Ep.* 44. 4 'omnia ista longa varietas miscuit et sursum deorsum fortuna versavit'; on the idea see Nisbet and Hubbard on Hor. *Od.* i. 34. 12 f. 'valet ima summis / mutare.'

§ 10 **numquam coloris sui fuit** : 'he never looked the same again.' Trimalchio describes the continuing effect on the soldier of the attack related in §§ 6–7.

post paucos dies phreneticus periit : M. Schuster (*Wien. St.* xlviii (1930), pp. 169 f.) cites similar medieval tales in which the

victim gains a short respite before the power of evil spirits
proves fatal.

Celsus (iii. 18) distinguishes *phrenesis* (delirium) from melan-
choly and insanity proper; see Pease on Cic. *de Div.* i. 81.

Ch. 64

§ 1 **osculatique mensam :** clearly an apotropaic observance.
In Plut. *Mor.* 704 b a Roman recalls hearing his grandmother
say 'The table is sacred'; see Blümner, *Philol.* lxxvi (1920),
345 f.

ut suis se teneant : cf. Hor. *Sat.* ii. 3. 324 'teneas, Damasippe,
tuis te.'

Buecheler appears to be justified in expecting after § 1 a
reference to the growing tipsiness of the guests.

§ 2 **lucernae . . . plures :** double vision of the lamps in a dining-
room during the later stages of a party became a commonplace;
cf. Juv. 6. 304 f. 'cum iam vertigine tectum / ambulat et geminis
exsurgit mensa lucernis', Hor. *Sat.* ii. 1. 24 f. 'saltat Milonius,
ut semel icto / accessit fervor capiti numerusque lucernis', Sen.
Ep. 83. 21, *Anth. Pal.* xii. 199 (Strato).

tibi dico : a formula intended, like σοὶ λέγω, to make someone
pay attention to what is about to be said; e.g. Plaut. *Curc.*
516 f. 'CA. heus tu! tibi ego dico. / CU. eloquere, quid vis?
CA. quaeso ut . . .'. It frequently expresses indignation; see
Hof. *LU* 125, Heraeus, p. 113.

delectaris : deponent as at 45. 7.

solebas suavius esse : (*suavis H*) this echo of Trimalchio's words
to Niceros at 61. 2 'solebas suavius esse in convictu' helps to
convey that the party is approaching the sentimental or even
maudlin stage.

canturire : despite the desiderative form this can be taken to
mean the same as *cantare* (see Heraeus, p. 80, Wölfflin, 'Die
Verba Desiderativa', in *ALL* i. 408 ff.). In sense it might seem
to go better with *melicam* 'song' than with *deverbia*, the spoken
dialogue in a play, hence Buecheler's interchange of *canturire*
and *dicere* (*adicere H*); but Petronius may have deliberately
misplaced the verbs in order to show up Trimalchio's ignorance.

melicam is not found elsewhere as a feminine.

§ 3 **abistis dulces caricae :** (*dulcis carica H*) lit. 'You are de-
parted, sweet Carian figs'; presumably the sense is something
like 'the good times are past.' Trimalchio seems to be quoting

from some comedy or mime; the quaintness of this phrase is matched by Plocamus' high-flown opening 'My chariot has now run its course', which leads into the anticlimax 'ever since I began to suffer from gout'.

podagricus : gout was assumed to be a consequence of wealth; cf. Juv. 13. 96 f. 'pauper locupletem optare podagram / nec dubitet Ladas' (with Mayor's note). In *Anth. Pal.* xi. 403 Lucian ends his address to the goddess Gout thus: 'Therefore thou fliest the brassless threshold of poverty and delightest to come to the feet of wealth.'

tisicus : consumptive; variant of phthisicus (Gk. φθισικός), but not necessarily a Vulgarism (cf. Süss, p. 30 n. 28).

§ 4 tonstrinum : 'my barber's shop imitation'. As centres for gossip barbers' shops provided good material for the entertainer, and Theophrastus (Plut. *Mor.* 679 a) called them 'wineless symposia'.

Apelletem : most probably a reference to the tragic actor, Asiatic in origin like a number of the guests at the *Cena*, who was prominent in the reign of Caligula; cf. Suet. *Calig.* 33, Dio lix. 5. But even if this identification is sound, we are not entitled to adduce it as a clear proof that the setting of the *Cena* must be put in Nero's reign, still less that it must be put in any particular part of Nero's reign.

§ 6 semesum : 'half-eaten'. Burmann's conjecture gives a plausibly disgusting picture. *semissem H* 'half a pound in weight' would contrast the large loaf with the small dog, but the contrast is not great enough to be convincing.

§ 7 quo admonitus officio : 'reminded by this act of duty'. In support of the reading in *H* Delz notes Cic. *Lig.* 36 'huius admonitus officio'. As well as removing the gentle irony of *officio*, Buecheler's *officii* gives an awkward construction; Müller's *quo ⟨adspectu⟩ admonitus officii* is equally awkward, and is not really parallel to Cic. *de Div.* i. 79 'quo adspectu exterrita'.

'praesidium domus familiaeque' : this phrase appears to be a formula or quotation (note that *-que* does not occur elsewhere in the speech of the freedmen in the *Cena*). Theophrastus (*Char.* 4. 10) says that it is characteristic of the boorish man to answer the door himself, and, calling his dog and holding it by the muzzle, to say οὗτος φυλάττει τὸ χωρίον καὶ τὴν οἰκίαν 'This fellow guards the estate and the house.' The resemblance should not, however, be exaggerated. The high-flown phrase used by Trimalchio may be a parody (cf. *CRF* 53 'te tutamen fore sperarat familiai, domuique columen'), especially when used of Scylax (the name Scylax 'puppy', found in Columella's list of dogs' names (vii. 12. 13) is here absurdly applied to a mastiff); but it cannot be taken as a parody of the Theophrastus passage.

cubaret : the word is used of a dog lying down in Plaut. *Stich.* 620, and (with a play on different senses) on gravestones for dogs, e.g. *CIL* vi. 29896. See Heraeus, p. 113.

§ 9 taeterrimo : cf. 35. 6 *taeterrima voce*, 64. 5 *nescioquid taetrum exsibilavit*, 70. 7 *tremula taeterrimaque voce cantavit*. Petronius must have meant this to stand out as a mannerism of Encolpius, but such an effect is not assisted by the accidental, or at any rate less obviously deliberate, repetition in § 7 above: *quo admonitus officio . . . admonitusque ostiarii calce*.

§ 10 candelabrum : this can refer to a tall lamp-stand, the equivalent of a standard lamp, or to a smaller type, the equivalent of a table lamp (cf. 75. 10 'tam magnus ex Asia veni quam hic candelabrus est'), often consisting of a plinth supporting a short column from whose capital several lamps hung down (see illustrations in H. Blümner, *Röm. Privatsalt.* 141 ff.

§ 12 plana : Scheffer's conjecture for *plena H* is supported by Sen. *Ep.* 56. 1 'audio crepitum inlisae manus umeris, quae prout plana pervenit aut concava, ita sonum mutat'; cf. Juv. 13. 128 *plana . . . palma*.

bucca bucca quot sunt hic? : the game described here resembles *micare digitis* (see note on 44. 7) in that a player has to try to guess the number of fingers held up by his opponent; but to judge from the many related modern versions it differs in that the opponent mounts on his back before asking him to guess (see B. L. Ullmann, *CP* xxxviii (1943), 94–102, P. G. Brewster, ib. 134–7). Ullmann observes that in several modern versions of this game the question chanted by the opponent includes a word cognate with the Old English bucca = he-goat; e.g. German 'Bock, Bock, wieviel Hörner hab' ich?', English 'Buck, buck, how many fingers do I hold up?' If *bucca* could bear only senses related to the meaning 'cheek', the use of these expressions must be either a coincidence or a case of phonetic borrowing without borrowing the meaning. Ullmann, however, argues plausibly that there may have been a Latin word *bucca* = goat; this involves a slight difficulty with the words *usus equo*, but he suggests that this may have been a general term for riding on someone's back.

Ch. 65

§ 1 **matteae :** tit-bits served after the main course of a dinner; they were not placed on the tables but passed round among the guests (note *circumlatae sunt* below; cf. *CGL* iii. 14. 54 περιφορὰ *mattia*, Athen. 245 f περιφέρειν ματτύην and see Heraeus, pp. 80 f.). Martial (xiii. 92) expresses his preference for a thrush as a suitable delicacy at this late stage in a meal.

Petronius' familiar ambivalence is apparent here, hinting at Encolpius' gluttony as well as Trimalchio's lack of taste ('singulae gallinae pro turdis').

§ 2 **ova... pilleata :** the use of this phrase here and at 66. 7 without further explanation shows that, unlike *aper pilleatus* at 40. 3, it must have been a technical term. Perhaps it refers to some covering to keep the eggs warm (see note at 31. 11 on the Roman passion for hot foods). If, however, as most commentators have assumed, it is applied to some way of cooking eggs, Sullivan's 'eggs in pastry hoods' looks quite possible.

§ 3 **valvas lictor percussit :** the arrival of the late-comer Habinnas parodies that of a magistrate at Rome with his retinue of lictors; cf. Plin. *NH* vii. 112 'Cn. Pompeius ... intraturus Posidonii sapientiae professione clari domum forem percuti de more a lictore vetuit et fasces litterarum ianuae submisit', Stat. *Silv.* i. 2. 48.

Attempts have been made to link the arrival of Habinnas with the arrival of Alcibiades after the other guests in Plato's *Symposium* (see note by A. L. in *Philologische Wochenschrift* (1900), 925 f., Averil Cameron, *CQ* N.S. xix (1969), 367 ff.). It is true that Habinnas, like Alcibiades, has come on from another party and is therefore wearing garlands and smothered in scent; but whereas his greed and gluttony are made prominent by Petronius, Plato emphasizes Alcibiades' tipsiness. Furthermore, the theme of the arrival of the late or uninvited guest must by Petronius' time have become so familiar that any relationship with Plato was now very faint (see R. Hirzel, *Der Dialog*, ii. 46). It was in any case an obvious device for an author like Petronius who takes such pains to introduce variety into the structure of his scenes.

veste alba : Habinnas wears white, the appropriate colour for a festive occasion, even one in honour of the dead (see note on *novendiale* in § 10 below). Cicero (*Vat.* 30 ff.) affects to be scandalized by Vatinius' appearing in mourning dress at a funeral banquet.

§ 4 praetorem : strictly the chief magistrates in a *colonia* would be *duumviri*, but the term *praetor* was sometimes loosely applied to them. In the *de Lege Agraria* (ii. 93) Cicero sneers at the magistrates of Capua for taking the title of *praetor*.

Encolpius' alarm might, if we had a full text of the *Satyricon*, prove to be connected with the episode of the cloak whose ownership was disputed (chs. 12 ff.); but it could be merely one more incident where he shows himself more stupid than his companions.

nudos pedes : on reaching his couch for dinner the guest would remove his sandals, handing them over to his slave until it was time to depart; see Balsdon, *Life and Leisure*, 40 f.

§ 5 idemque lapidarius : these words give Agamemnon an effective ending, a mixture of snobbery and sycophancy (for *idemque* and *et idem* cf., for example, Cic. *Rosc. Am.* 152 'sicarium eundemque accusatorem', and see *TLL* vii. 191. 27–67). The clause *qui . . . facere*, despite its good clausula (noted by Nisbet, p. 229), is much too feeble to justify retention, and is presumably an interpolation based on 71. 5, where Trimalchio addresses Habinnas: ' "quid dicis" inquit "amice carissime? aedificas monumentum meum, quemadmodum te iussi?" '

§ 7 unguento per frontem in oculos fluente : scented oil was often put on the hair for a festivity (cf. Tib. i. 7. 51 'illius et nitido stillent unguenta çapillo'). Here Habinnas' appearance suggests that he has rushed eagerly just as he was, flowers, scent, and all, from one dinner to the other; certainly in the next chapter his greed is made apparent.

praetorio loco : the place of honour is kept for Habinnas, a *sevir* still in office. This is presumably the end place on the middle couch (*imus in medio*), referred to elsewhere as *locus consularis* (Plut. *Mor.* 619 b τόπος ὑπατικός). See also note on 31. 8.

caldam : the addition of hot water to wine was usual (see Marq. *Prl.* 332); but the well-mannered guest was not expected to make these immediate demands without any invitation from the host, hence the ironical 'delectatus hac hilaritate'.

§ **8 capaciorem poposcit scyphum :** the call for larger wine cups is frequently mentioned in carousals, but it is normally a question of a larger cup for each person present, not for one individual alone; cf. Cic. *Verr.* i. 66 'fit sermo inter eos et invitatio ut Graeco more biberetur; hortatur hospes, poscunt maioribus poculis', Hor. *Epod.* ix. 33 'capaciores adfer huc, puer, scyphos.'

§ **9 oculi enim mei hic erant :** i.e. those most dear to me. Sullivan's 'the apple of my eye was here' would be satisfactory as an approximation to the Latin idiom, but it implies that Habinnas is referring only to one person. For this sense of *oculus* cf. Plaut. *Pseud.* 179 f. 'ubi isti sunt quibu' vos oculi estis, / quibu' vitae, quibu' deliciae estis, quibu' savia, mammia, mellillae?', Cic. *Att.* xvi. 6. 2 'cur ocellos Italiae, villulas meas, non video?', Cat. 31. 2 (and Fordyce's note). The sentence is taken differently by several translators, e.g. Friedlaender 'denn in Gedanken war ich hier', Heseltine 'my eyes were here with you.'

§ **10 novendiale[m] :** after nine days of mourning, offerings were made to the spirit of the dead person, and a banquet was held for the mourners; see Marq. *Prl.* 379 f., J. M. C. Toynbee, *Death and Burial in the Roman World*, 51.

misello : this diminutive was often used of the dead; cf. Tert. *Test. An.* 4 'cum alicuius defuncti recordaris, misellum vocas eum', Cat. 3. 16 'o, miselle passer'.

quem mortuum manu miserat : the owner who manumitted a slave in normal circumstances would retain some rights over him; even if he manumitted him by will, he could have the satisfaction of knowing that his own funeral would be more impressive (cf. 42. 6). But the master who manumitted a dying slave was more likely to be moved by affection (Martial says (i. 101) that he set free his nineteen-year-old scribe so that he would not have to die a slave) since he would still have to pay the *vicesima*, the 5 per cent tax on manumissions, without enjoying any of the usual advantages. In the present case *mortuum* causes a little difficulty. Possibly it is a false reading influenced by *mortuum* at the end of § 10. If it is sound, it can be taken either (i) in the sense of *moribundum* or *morientem* (cf. L.-H.-S. 391), or (ii) in its normal sense; the transaction would then be quite irregular (although compare the irregular transactions in 53. 9–10), but the point might be that Scissa, while wanting the satisfaction of a sentimental gesture, grudged paying the tax.

cum vicensimariis magnam †mantissam habet : *vicensimarii*, not recorded elsewhere, must mean here the collectors of the *vicesima* (see note on 58. 2).

The word *mantissa* is more difficult. It is cited once from Lucilius (*'mantisa* additamentum dicitur lingua Tusca quod ponderi adicitur, sed deterius et quod sine ullo usu est. Lucilius *mantisa obsonia vincit'*, Paul. ex Fest. 103. 1). But the context in Petronius seems to require something like 'She has a right battle on with the liberation-tax men'; if so, *mantissam* appears to be corrupt (P. A. George suggests *antistasim* 'conflict'). Certainly renderings like Sullivan's 'And I think she'll have a pretty penny to pay in liberation tax' hardly tally with Festus or with Lucilius, and they take *cum* in a strained sense.

§ 11 potiones . . . effundere : offerings of wine were customarily made to the dead at later commemorative celebrations as well as immediately after the cremation of the corpse; see R. D. Williams on Virg. *Aen.* v. 77 f.

Ch. 66

Habinnas' enthusiastic recollections of the menu at the other dinner employ commonplace material. Theophrastus says of the ἀδολέσχης, the chatterer (*Char.* 3. 2), 'He is the sort of man who sits down beside someone he doesn't know and begins by delivering a panegyric on his own wife; continues with an account of his dream of the night before; then describes in detail what he had for supper.' In the fourth book of his *Deipnosophistae* Athenaeus cites from various Greek writers inordinately lengthy menus which exploit the comic possibilities of the theme; cf., for example, 131, 136, 146 f. Even Habinnas' difficulty in remembering all the details (§ 5 'bene me admonet domina mea') is a familiar device; cf. Athen. 147 c).

§ 2 botulo : sausage. Corrected by Iac. Gronovius from *poculo* H. Marmorale defends the reading in *H* as being analogous with 40. 3 *aper pilleatus*, 59. 6 *vitulus . . . galeatus*, and also 36. 2 *leporem . . . pinnis subornatum*; but Habinnas' gluttonous recollections should not be assumed to contain the absurd *elegantiae* seen in the banquet offered by Trimalchio.

sangunculum : possibly a blood sauce rather than a blood sausage or black pudding; see L.-S.-J. s.v. αἱμάτιον, Heraeus, pp. 228 ff.

gizeria optime facta : 'giblets superbly cooked'; cf. Paul. ex Fest. 95. 7 'gizeria: ex multis obsoniis decerpta', Lucilius 309M.

betam : a suitably plebeian item; cf. Mart. xiii. 13 'ut sapiant fatuae, fabrorum prandia, betae, / o quam saepe petet vina piperque cocus.'

panem autopyrum : whole-meal bread.

de suo sibi : 'pure'. See W. M. Lindsay, *Syntax of Plautus*, 41 on the pleonastic use of *sibi* along with *suus* in colloquial Latin. He suggests that it could be formed on the model of, for example, Plaut. *Bacch*. 994 'tuus tibi servus tuo arbitratu serviat', i.e. the dative originally was part of the construction of the sentence, but later became fossilized (cf. L.–H.–S. 94); *de* was then combined with this idiom, giving the literal sense 'made of nothing but its own' (cf. Apic. viii. 8. 6 'ius de suo sibi').

mea re causa facio : Trimalchio had used the same idiom at 47. 4 in expressing a similar preoccupation with constipation.

§ 3 sc[i]rib[i]lita : see note on 35. 4. Cold *scriblitae* may suggest an eccentricity on the part of Scissa; cf. Plaut. *Poen*. 42 f. 'nunc dum occasio est, / nunc dum scriblitae aestuant, occurrite', Mart. iii. 17. 1 f. 'circumlata diu mensis scriblita secundis / urebat nimio saeva calore manus.' Note also that in his recipe for *scriblitae* (*RR* 78) Cato expressly says that they are not made with honey, so the warm honey served here along with them may well be another oddity.

me . . . tetigi : 'I soaked myself in the honey'; cf. Apic. vii. 10 'petasonem . . . melle contingis.' Heraeus, p. 125, also cites Heim, *Incant. Mag*. 558. 4 'lingulae praecantatio: duabus manibus tangis de melle et dicis haec . . .'

§ 4 cicer et lupinum : chick-peas and lupines. These two items occur together in a meagre dinner offered by Martial (v. 78. 21 'et fervens cicer et tepens lupinus'); Columella says of lupines (ii. 10. 1) 'boves per hiemem coctum maceratumque probe alit; famem quoque, si sterilitas annorum incessit, hominibus commode propulsat.'

calvae : possibly hazel-nuts, sometimes called *nuces Abellanae* from Abella in Campania. See Heraeus, p. 82.

arbitratu : i.e. as many as you wanted.

mala singula : in rebuking a friend for failing to attend a modest dinner-party to which he had invited him Pliny seems to poke fun at this habit of allocating a fixed portion for each guest: 'paratae erant lactucae singulae, cochleae ternae, ova bina, halica cum mulso et nive' (*Ep.* i. 15. 2).

ego tamen duo sustuli : for the resemblance between Encolpius and Habinnas see note on 60. 7 *ego praecipue*. Note also Habinnas' criticism of those who made off with more than he did: (§ 7) 'unde quidam etiam improbe ternos pugnos sustulerunt'.

§ 5 bene me admonet : similar phrases occur occasionally in colloquial speech: e.g. Cic. *Verr.* iv. 5 'sed earum artificem quem? quemnam? recte admones: Polyclitum esse dicebant.' Theophrastus says (*Char.* 7. 3) that εὖ γε, ὅτι με ὑπέμνησας 'I'm glad you reminded me' is one of several phrases used by the garrulous man to prevent anyone else from taking over the conversation. See Heraeus, p. 114.

domina mea : this might be used by a man of any class when referring to his wife: cf. Suet. *Claud.* 39 'occisa Messalina, paulo post quam in triclinio decubuit, cur domina non veniret requisiit', *CIL* v. 4438 (Brixia) 'et coniuge huius, domne meae sanctissimae et amicae carissimae' (cited in *SG*[8] i. 454); but it has none the less a formal sound (cf. 'my good lady'). See note on 57. 2 *domini mei*.

in prospectu habuimus : if these words are sound, they presumably mean 'we had . . . to look forward to', or even 'we had on the menu' (P. A. George). Heinsius seems to see a reference to a dish already visible on a side-table before it is actually served; cf. Sen. *Ep.* 78. 24 'non iacebit in conspectu aper ut vilis caro a mensa relegatus.'

ursinae : despite the opportunities offered by the wholesale slaughter of bears in the arena, bear-meat does not seem to have been much eaten (cf. Galen vi. 666 Kühn), although Plutarch mentions bear-paws as a delicacy (*Mor.* 917 d).

frust[r]um : see note on 59. 7.

§ 7 catillum †concagatum : possibly through fear of seeming guilty of bowdlerizing the text, most commentators have welcomed Burmann's *concacatum* a little uncritically. It is claimed that it means something like a ragoût, on the analogy of the Greek ὀνθυλεύω = dress with forced meat. *catillum concacatum* sounds impossible as a technical term, and if it is merely an obscenity used non-technically it fits its context badly, even if we take *pax Palamedes* as equivalent to an apology for its coarseness. A possible reading here would be *catillum* *ornatum*: Athenaeus (xiv. 647 c) quotes from the culinary writer Chrysippus κάτιλλος ὀρνᾶτος ὁ λεγόμενος παρὰ ῾Ρωμαίοις; cf. Heraeus, p. 83.

pax Palamedes : *pax* (Greek πάξ) is used as an exclamation to end a discussion: 'Enough!' *Palamedes* remains obscure. G. Bendz plausibly suggests (*Eranos* xxxix (1941), 44–6) that *pax Palamedes* may be an alliterative catch-phrase from some comedy dealing with the misfortunes of Palamedes, a Greek warrior falsely accused of treachery during the Trojan expedition and hence a likely character to indulge in interminable complaints.

oxycomina : 'pickled cummin'. Heraeus, p. 84, cites a gloss 'oximinum acetum mixtum cum cumino' also 'acetum ĉuminatum'. Alternatively from *cominia* (plur.), a kind of olive, Pallad. *Agric*. 3. 18. In any case these pickles are passed round in a generously sized container, an *alveus*, a tub or trough.

pernae missionem dedimus : even this dinner of no great pretensions had items held in reserve; cf. 41. 4 'hic aper cum heri summa cena eum vindicasset, a convivis dimissus est.'

Ch. 67

§ 2 quomodo nosti inquit illam : this appears to be a confusion between 'As you know' and 'You know her', rather than an ironical exclamation 'How (well) you know her!'

§ 3 me apoculo : see note on 62. 3 *apoculamus nos*.

§ 4 galbino : greenish-yellow; certainly not a respectable colour when worn by a man (cf. Juv. 2. 97, Mart. i. 96. 9 'galbinos habet mores'); perhaps it should be included among the colours denounced by Seneca: 'colores meretricios, matronis quidem non induendos, viri sumimus' (*NQ* vii. 31. 2).

phaecasiae : a type of shoe worn by Athenian gymnasiarchs, Egyptian priests, homosexuals, and others; at 82. 3 Encolpius is contemptuously addressed by a centurion: '"age ergo" inquit ille "in exercitu vestro phaecasiati milites ambulant?"' See Mayor on Juvenal 3. 218.

§ 5 est te … videre? : 'Can it really be you?' (For *est = licet* see L.-H.-S. 349, *ALL* ii. 135 ff.) A formula for greeting someone after a long interval; cf. Donatus on Ter. *Hec*. 81 'set videon ego Philotium?', *CGL* iii. 211. 23 ff. 'ἔστιν σε ἰδεῖν; τί πράττεις;: est te videre? quid agis?' Tiberius' veterans greeted him with

the words 'videmus te, imperator? salvum recepimus?' (Vell. ii.
104. 4). See Heraeus, pp. 114 f.

§ 6 reticulum : a coif of network, sometimes made of gold
thread (see illustrations in Smith's *Dict. of Antiqq.* s.v. *coma*).
Fortunata claims that hers is of *obrussa*, 'pure gold' (cf. ὄβρυζα,
'assaying of gold').

§ 7 barcalae : the context points to the sense 'fools, simpletons',
but the word is of doubtful derivation; cf. *bargus*, dull (*CGL* ii.
569. 25 'bargus: ingenio carens') and *bardus* (Plaut. *Bacch.* 1088 f.
'qui fuerunt . . . stulti, stolidi . . . bardi'), and see Buecheler,
Rh. Mus. xxxv (1880), 70 f., A. Nehring, *Glotta* xvii (1929), 117.

ex millesimis Mercurii factam : this is usually taken to mean
that he has diverted to his own use gold which he had vowed
to give to his patron deity, Mercury, as the thousandth part of
his gains. His off-hand way of implying that he possesses ten
thousand pounds weight of gold is acceptable, even if his
exaggeration is more unrestrained than sometimes elsewhere;
but the suggestion that he has robbed Mercury seems out of
character, and it may be that the phrase contains a technicality
whose significance is unknown to us.

§ 9 crotalia : ear-rings with pearl pendants which rattled like
castanets (*crotala*). This type of ear-ring appears to have been
a recent innovation, if we may judge from Pliny's disparaging
remarks (*NH* ix. 114): 'crotalia appellant, ceu sono quoque
gaudeant et collisu ipso margaritarum; cupiuntque iam et
pauperes, lictorem feminae in publico unionem esse dictitantes.'

domini mei : see note on 57. 2.

§ 10 excatarissasti : 'cleaned me out'. Latinized form from
ἐκκαθαρίζω.

fabam vitream : Habinnas refers to his wife's expensive jewels
in depreciatory terms. Romans in Petronius' day would be
familiar with the use of glass to imitate precious stones, sometimes for fraudulent purposes; cf. Plin. *NH* xxxvii. 112, 197 ff.

omnia pro luto haberemus : cf. 44. 10 'annona pro luto erat.'

caldum meiere et frigidum potare : i.e. to lose what is of greater
value than what is received in exchange. The expression
reflects the Roman fondness for drinking wine with warm water
added (see Mayor on Juv. 5. 63).

§ 11 **sauciae :** tipsy, reeling; cf. Mart. iii. 68. 5 f. 'hinc iam deposito post vina rosasque pudore / quid dicat, nescit saucia Terpsichore', Just. xxiv. 8. 1 'Galli hesterno mero saucii'.

indulgentiam : i.e. she complains that he is much too friendly with his *deliciae*. *indulgentiam*, the reading in the first edition of the *Cena*, takes up the sound of *diligentiam* more pleasingly than *indiligentiam*, the rather frigid reading in *H*.

§ 13 **au au :** '*au* interiectio est perturbatae mulieris', Donatus on Ter. *Eun.* 899.

Ch. 68

§ 1 **secundas mensas :** when Trimalchio asks for *secundae mensae* (dessert), his slaves pretend to misunderstand him and merely bring in a second set of tables. One suspects that this was among the most familiar inane Roman jokes.

scobemque croco et minio tinctam : see 60. 6 on the use of saffron for its fragrance. In the Circus powdered mica (here described as 'ex lapide speculari pulverem tritum') was sometimes used for its glitter, while vermilion (minium) contributed to spectacular colour-effects (cf. Plin. *NH* xxxiii. 90, xxxvi. 162, Suet. *Calig.* 18. 3). Trimalchio's unusual extravagance consists in having these luxuries in a private dining-room. The words *quod numquam ante videram* may be merely a comment on this eccentricity; but Petronius may wish to represent the limited experience of Encolpius as well as Trimalchio's vulgarity.

§ 2 **si quid belli habes, affer :** immediately after his feeble pun on *secundae mensae* (for the level of humour cf. 35. 7 'hoc est ius cenae'), Trimalchio plays on the word *bellus*: (i) its ordinary use, = 'nice' (cf. 78. 5 'dicite aliquid belli'); (ii) its connection with dessert; cf. Donatus on Ter. *Ad*. 590 'proprie *bellissimum* dixit, unde et huiusmodi ad irritandam gulam cibi bellaria dicuntur', Gell. xiii. 11. 6 f.

§ 3 **Alexandrinus :** see note on 31. 3.

subinde : probably = *saepius* (cf. L.–H.–S. 280) 'while Trimalchio kept calling out "Let's have something different" '. If *subinde* is taken to mean *deinde*, the present participle *clamante* must refer to an action subsequent to that of the main verb. In either case it looks as if *muta* is possibly a topical catchphrase or conceals some obscure joke.

§ 5 praeter . . . miscebat : 'apart from the way he raised or lowered his voice in his barbarous meandering, he mixed up Atellane verses with it.' Quintilian regards the proper control of the volume of the voice when reading as a matter to be taught in an elementary school (i. 8. 1).

miscebat : followed by Delz (p. 683) in place of Buecheler's *immiscebat*; for this use of *miscere* cf. Claudian. *in Rufin.* ii. 143 'et Arcadium mixto terrore precatur', *TLL* viii. 1088. 41.

§ 6 adiecit : see note on 41. 8 for the combination of this with *inquit* (but note that here *inquit* is an emendation).

§ 7 desperatum valde ingeniosus : 'desperately clever'. *ingeniosus* is strengthened, not by being put in the superlative, but by the colloquial *valde*, which itself is intensified by the addition of *desperatum* used adverbially; cf. Plaut. *Mil. Glor.* 24 'estur insanum bene', id. *Nervol.* fr. 6 'insanum valde uterque deamat', L.-H.-S. 163, Löfstedt, *Peregr.* 35 f.

omnis musae mancipium : cf. 43. 8 *omnis minervae homo*. For *omnium numerum* (§ 8) see note on 63. 3.

§ 8 strabonus : the usual form is *strabo*, which stands for a greater degree of squint than *paetus*; cf. Hor. *Sat.* i. 3. 44 f. 'strabonem / appellat paetum pater.'

vix oculo mortuo umquam : cf. 62. 10 'oculi mortui, vix umquam refectus sum.' The occurrence of *vix umquam* along with this obscure phrase here and immediately after it at 62. 10 gives grounds for suspicion. Delz reads 'ideo nihil latet vix †oculo mortuo† umquam illum. emi trecentis denariis.'

trecentis denariis : a very modest price, especially for a talented slave; 100,000 sesterces is given as the price of a boy in Mart. i. 58. 1, xi. 70. 1.

Ch. 69

§ 1 agaga : not found elsewhere. Probably = 'pander', a sense which would explain Scintilla's jealousy, as well as Trimalchio's remark 'nihil sibi defraudat.' The diminutive *agagula* is often glossed with *lenocinator* (pander), and once with *fornicator*, a sense which hardly suits here. *agaga* has sometimes been taken to mean *catamitus*, a sense which would make the words 'tu autem Scintilla, noli zelotypa esse' easily comprehensible, but would perhaps make less of 'nihil sibi defraudat.'

stigmam : feminine as at 45. 9.

§ 2 **Cappadocem** : as well as being noted for brawn (see note on 63. 5), the Cappadocians were sometimes accused of making money by disreputable means; cf. *Anth. Pal.* xi. 238 'The Cappadocians are always bad, but when they get a belt (i.e. become soldiers) they are worse, and for the sake of gain they are the worst of all' (tr. Paton), Suidas s.v. κάππα διπλοῦν: τρία κάππα κάκιστα· Καππαδοκία Κρήτη καὶ Κιλικία. This helps to explain why the *leno* in Plautus' *Curculio* is identified as *Cappadox*.

hoc enim nemo parentat : Sullivan's 'You can't take it with you' is the nearest colloquial equivalent in English, although strictly the sense of the Latin is rather different: if you don't enjoy these pleasures during life, you're making a mistake, since no one will give you them at the *parentalia* after your death. For the *parentalia* see note on 78. 4.

§ 3 **ipsumam meam** : see note on 63. 3.

debattuere : 'knock'. Cicero notes *batuere* as a word which, although not in itself obscene, may be used in an obscene sense (*Fam.* ix. 22. 4).

sed tace, lingua, dabo panem : clearly proverbial, but no other examples are cited in Otto. It seems to be used as a formula for dropping a subject.

§ 5 **harundinibus quassis** : using these broken reeds he pretends to be playing a pipe made from reeds of various lengths so as to produce different notes; cf. Virg. *Ecl.* 2. 36 f.

mulionum fata : the text and interpretation are obscure. *mulionum* is a simple conjecture for *molionum H*. It fits *lacernatus cum flagello* and *dono tibi caligas*, although it introduces a contrast between *choraulae*, professional entertainers of some standing (cf. 53. 13), and muleteers (for their low status even among manual labourers see Sen. *Ep.* 47. 15 'erras si existimas me quosdam quasi sordidioris operae reiecturum, ut puta illum mulionem et illum bubulcum. non ministeriis illos aestimabo sed moribus'). P. A. George tentatively suggests *morionum*, clowns. This would link *choraules* with another kind of entertainer, and it might explain why the slave is humorously addressed by the name Massa (cf. Schol. on Juv. 1. 35 'Massa morio fuisse dicitur'); but would remove any obvious explanation for the outfit worn by the slave. In any case *fata* is doubtful. Some claim that a mime 'Lives of the Muleteers' is referred to, but this does not sound altogether plausible as a title. George conjectures *fatua*.

tanto melior : 'bravo!' a stereotyped expression of praise, frequent in colloquial speech; e.g. Sen. *Ep.* 31. 4 'admirabor et clamabo "tanto melior, surge et inspira et clivum istum uno si potes spiritu exsupera." ' See Haupt, *Opuscula*, ii. 323.

dono tibi caligas : ironical contrast between the effeminate slave and the sturdy, clod-hopping muleteer. *caliga* is often applied expressly to the boots worn by soldiers, but *Ed. Diocl.* 9. 5a has *caligae mulionicae*.

§ 6 epidipnis : dessert (cf. Mart. xi. 31. 7, Athen. xiv. 664 e) is now brought in and placed on the *secundae mensae* (cf. 68. 2), which have remained empty during the interlude of 68. 3–69. 5.
Encolpius expresses disgust at the arrival of still more examples of foods dressed up to imitate something else; thrushes made of wheaten loaves (cf. 40. 4 'minores porcelli ex coptoplacentis facti'), quinces done up as sea-urchins (quinces were a very ordinary fruit in Italy by this time; cf. André, *L'Alimentation*, 76), as well as imitation fish and fowl.

§ 8 omnium genera avium : for this expression, where we might expect *omnia genera avium*, cf. Suet. *Claud.* 46 *ex omnium magistratuum genere*, *Bell. Alex.* 28. 3 *variis generum munitionibus* (these passages have with less justification been cited sometimes as being parallel to 33. 3 *omnium textorum dicta*). See Löfstedt, *Peregr.* 293.

amici : supplied by Buecheler on the analogy of 33. 1, 5, 47. 2, 71. 1, 73. 6.

§ 9 de ⟨*⟩ facta sunt aut certe de luto : as well as disguised but edible dishes, the guest who was entertained by a host with a liking for practical jokes might find himself faced with something quite inedible; the philosopher Sphaerus was offered wax pomegranates by Ptolemy Philopator (Diog. Laert. vii. 177, cf. SHA, *Heliog.* 25. 9, 27. 4), and some such practical joke may have been described in the passage lost at 35. 6. But while the general sense here is clear enough, the exact reading is doubtful. *aut certe* implies that in the lacuna before *facta sunt* something more repulsive than *lutum* must be supplied; hence Heinsius' *cera* is not ideal (although it could stand if *certe* is deleted). P. A. George points out the possibility that *aut certe de luto* might be an inept gloss, and that, if it is, *farre* could be inserted before *facta sunt*.

Ch. 70

§ 1 **patrimonio, non corpore :** this qualification illustrates the superstitious fear of being misunderstood or taken too literally by the gods. Friedlaender cites the tale in Phaedrus of the *meretrix* who, on being granted by Mercury her wish that whatever she first touched might follow her, was imprudent enough to scratch her nose (Phaedr. *Appx.* 3).

§ 2 **colepio :** possibly knuckle of pork; cf. Plaut. *Pers.* 92 *colyphia*, Mart. vii. 67. 12 *coloephia*.

Daedalus : a legendary figure who became the type for inventiveness and skill. The name was common enough in later times, so once again, as with Carpus (36. 5 ff.) and Corinthus (50. 4), Petronius is poking fun at Trimalchio's fondness for the overobvious; and see Nisbet and Hubbard on Hor. *Od.* i. 16. 9 for evidence that the excellence of steel from Noricum (modern Carinthia, etc.) was by now a hackneyed theme.

§ 4 **tamquam qui :** cf. Sen. *Ben.* 2. 24. 2 f. 'alius accipit fastidiose, tamquam qui dicat . . .' This usage is found mainly in late Latin; see L.–H.–S. 597.

lacum : small reservoir from which water had to be carried to individual buildings, and hence a natural meeting-place for slaves (cf. Hor. *Sat.* i. 4. 37).

§ 8 **pudet referre quae secuntur :** Petronius is ironical at the expense of Encolpius, who is made to seem almost as distressed at this incident as at his much more alarming misadventures in the scene before the opening of the *Cena*.

The practice of putting perfumed oil on the feet is attributed to luxury-loving Athenians by the Old Comedy writer Cephisodorus (Athen. 553, cf. *Ev. Luc.* 7: 36 ff., *Ev. Johann.* 12: 1 ff.), whereas Pliny says (*NH* xiii. 22) 'vidimus etiam vestigia pedum tingui, quod monstrasse M. Othonem Neroni principi ferebant.' K. F. C. Rose (*Arion* v (1966), 292 f.) maintained that in referring to the use of unguents here as *inaudito more* Petronius must in fact be 'making a sly dig at Otho by attributing the custom to Trimalchio'. But if, as Rose himself argues elsewhere, the *Satyricon* was written in A.D. 65–6, at a time when Otho had been in virtual banishment in Spain since A.D. 58 (see Tac. *Ann.* xiii. 46), this sly dig, which would surely depend on topicality, came apparently at least seven years after the event; and, if the connection with Otho was recognized at all, Nero might easily have thought that he himself, rather than Otho,

was being ridiculed. It is true that the enforced suicide of
the Tacitean Petronius in A.D. 66 (see Appendix IA) may be
said to prove that the author had miscalculated how forbearing
Nero would be, but the miscalculation here attributed to him
is so obvious as to be incredible. Sullivan takes the same general
line, albeit more cautiously, as Rose: 'Petronius might be ready
to play in literature the dangerous game Plutarch tells us he
played in real life' (*Petronius*, 149). For what it is worth, however, Plutarch implies (*Mor.* 60 d, see *Testimonia*) that the
Petronius he is talking about flattered Nero's taste for luxury
by pretending to rebuke him for his stinginess. Several alternatives to the interpretation of Rose and Sullivan ought, then, to
be at least mentioned. Firstly, if we have an in-joke of the type
favoured by them, it might fit more comfortably into the
period before A.D. 58, when a reference to Otho would not be
so dangerous. More important, it could be held that the passage
in Pliny has been misunderstood. He seems to remark particularly on the use of perfumed oil on the *soles* of the feet (*etiam
vestigia pedum*), whereas Petronius seems to be drawing attention not merely to the anointing of the guests' feet but also to
the absurdity of their wearing garlands round their ankles.

§ 9 **in vinarium :** Pliny is also shocked at the use of unguents in
wine: 'at hercules iam quidam etiam in potus addunt, tantique
est amaritudo ut odore prodigo fruantur ex utraque parte
corporis' (*NH* xiii. 25).

§ 10 **coeperat . . . velle saltare :** cf. 9. 4, 98. 8. Often *velle* in such
expressions is used to give a more rounded phrase and does not
add much to the meaning. See Löfstedt, *Peregr.* 209.

[et Cario] : at 71. 2 the *contubernalis* of Philargyrus is mentioned, so Kaibel believes that here the reference to Cario is a
gloss based on the later passage. If *et Cario* is sound, the words
'et Cario . . . famosus' must be seen as a rather awkward aside.

prasinianus : a supporter of the Green faction at the Circus;
see Carcopino, *Daily Life*, 238, Balsdon, *Life and Leisure*, 314 ff.

§ 13 **Ephesum tragoedum :** not known elsewhere.

sponsione : the cook challenges Trimalchio by offering to pay
if the Greens win (not, as Heseltine, 'invited him to make a bet
on the green winning . . .'). *sponsio* can be used technically of
a form of procedure whereby an opponent could be challenged
to prove the truth of something he had said or to disprove the

truth of something said by the challenger; the matter at issue is specified in a *ni* or a *si* clause.

Ch. 71

§ 1 et servi homines sunt : in *Ep.* 47 Seneca commends his friend Lucilius for inviting his slaves to dine along with him : ' "servi sunt." immo homines. "servi sunt." immo contubernales. . . . "servi sunt." immo conservi, si cogitaveris tantundem in utrosque licere fortunae. itaque rideo istos qui turpe existimant cum servo suo cenare.' But he himself notes in § 15 the dangers of carrying this liberality too far: ' "quid ergo? omnes servos admovebo mensae meae?" non magis quam omnes liberos.' Hence Sullivan (*Petronius*, 135) is rather unfair in asserting: 'The chaos and the exhibition of bad taste that follow the seating of the slaves at the dinner table [in the *Cena*] naturally reflect on the unsoundness of Seneca's advice.' Petronius is not satirizing Seneca; he is making fun of those who had been less judicious than Seneca in their advocacy of generosity towards slaves.

lactem : a rare masculine form; the word is normally neuter, whether as *lac* or in the less common form *lacte* (as at 38. 1).

me salvo : 'as long as I'm spared'; used illogically here in connection with benefits which cannot be enjoyed until he is dead (cf. 57. 6 'spero, sic moriar, ut mortuus non erubescam').

aquam liberam : proverbial; cf. Ov. *Am.* i. 6. 26 'nec tibi perpetuo serva bibatur aqua', Antiphanes fr. 25 Kock μηδέποθ' ὕδωρ πίοιμι ἐλεύθερον, Xenarchus in Athen. 440 ἐλεύθερον πιοῦσαν οἶνον ἀποθανεῖν.

omnes . . . manu mitto : the wholesale testamentary manumission of his slaves which Trimalchio appears to promise would be illegal if the *lex Fufia Caninia* (see note on 42. 6) was still in force.

§ 2 insulam : block of apartment-houses. See Carcopino, pp. 35 ff.

vicesimam : cf. 65. 10 *vicensimariis*. The slave manumitted by testament would lose his *peculium* unless this was expressly granted by his master (cf. *Frag. Vatic.* 261); a more generous master would waive this payment to himself by granting *gratuita libertas* (cf. Suet. *Vesp.* 16. 3, *CIL* vi. 2211), or, better still, he might also pay on the slave's behalf the *vicesima* due to the state (cf. Riccobono, *Fontes* iii, no. 47, 31 ff. (A.D. 142)

'Cronionem servom meum post mortem meam . . . tunc liberum volo esse vicesimamque pro eo ex bonis meis dari volo').

§ 4 oblitus nugarum : 'now in a serious mood'; cf. 136. 5, Sen. *Apoc.* 7. 3.

§ 5 quid dicis? : a phrase used like *quid ais?* to attract the listener's attention and to prepare the way for a genuine question. See Hof. *LU* 43 f.

aedificas : this looks like another example of the present for the future. See note on 27. 4 *ponitis*.

§ 6 fingas : Scheffer's correction of *pingas H*, which looks odd when applied to the work of a monumental sculptor (although Delz, p. 683, compares Rom. *Fab.* 91 'cum venissent ad monumentum ubi erat pictura quomodo leo ab homine suffocabatur', where the equivalent passage in Greek, *Aesopica* 63 Halm, has γλύφειν).

Petraitis : cf. 52. 3 for this gladiator. Gladiatorial contests were first introduced into Rome as a tribute to the memory of *nobiles* (see Balsdon, *Life and Leisure*, 248 f.). The representation of such contests on sepulchral monuments (although on a more modest scale than Trimalchio demands here) was thus a natural development, and a useful second-best for those who could not afford to give actual shows in memory of their relatives; see *SG*[8] ii. 530.

in fronte . . . in agrum : a formula used to give the dimensions of a burial-ground by its frontage on the road and its depth; it occurs with minor variations in numerous inscriptions, e.g. IN AG P XII IN FR P XXIV (cf. Hor. *Sat.* i. 8. 12). The size prescribed for Trimalchio's tomb is not without parallel; see *SG*[8] iii. 137.

§ 7 omne genus : *quod genus, id genus,* and *omne genus* were at first used appositionally with the nominative or the accusative, but later also along with other cases; see K.-S. i. 306b, L.-H.-S. 47.

poma : Greek and Roman tombs were often set in orchards or gardens (*cepotaphia*), which, as well as giving the dead the kind of surroundings they might be expected to continue to enjoy in death as in life, could produce a return to pay for the regular commemorations held at the tomb. In the instructions for his tomb a Gaul, Publicius Calistus, lays down that it should have 'a vineyard one third of an acre in area, from whose yield I wish libations of no less than fifteen pints of wine to be poured for me each year' (*CIL* xii. 1657, cf. J. M. C. Toynbee, *Death and Burial in the Roman World*, 95 ff.).

vinearum largiter : *largiter* occurs with the genitive in early and late Latin; see L.–H.–S. 52.

hoc monumentum heredem non sequatur : this or some similar formula was often added in an effort to prevent alienation of the tomb and its surroundings by a grasping heir (see J. A. Crook, *Roman Law and Life*, 135, 137, Toynbee, *Death and Burial in the Roman World*, 75).

non is occasionally employed in prohibitions instead of *ne*; see L.–H.–S. 337.

§ 8 ne in monumentum meum populus cacatum currat : this danger is frequently mentioned in inscriptions and in literature, presumably because the tombs lining the roads just outside towns proved too convenient for passers-by; cf. Buecheler and Lommatzsch, *Carm. Lat. Epigr.* 838 (Rome) 'hospes, ad hunc tumulum ne meias ossa precantur / tecta hominis. set si gratus homo es, misce, bibe, da mi', R. Lattimore, *Themes in Greek and Latin Epitaphs*, 120, Jahn on Pers. 1. 112–14.

§ 9 in tribunali . . . quinque : Trimalchio's monument will show him at the high point in his career, the time when he served as a *sevir Augustalis*. As an ex-*sevir* he does not wear a proper gold ring during the dinner (cf. 32. 3); the five gold rings which he now demands are probably grander than even a *sevir* in office was entitled to wear. The use of gold rings to adorn statues is, however, not unknown in Greece and Rome; see *Catalogue of Finger Rings, Greek, Etruscan and Roman, in the British Museum*, ed. F. H. Marshall, xxvii n. 8, xxviii n. 7.

scis . . . quod : cf. 45. 10 *subolfacio quia*, 46. 4 *dixi quia*.

binos denarios : on the amount see note on 45. 10.

§ 10 faciantur : Goesius's correction is to be preferred to *faciatur* H, which has been defended either (i) as a singular predicate used with a neuter plural subject through the influence of the regular Greek construction (Löfstedt, *Peregr.* 292 rejects the idea of Greek influence but accepts *faciatur* as a simple Vulgarism), or (ii) as a normal singular verb, with *triclinia* taken as an abnormal feminine (Süss, pp. 14 f. compares 76. 11 *intestinas meas*, and *armentas, membras*, and the like in glosses).

populum : Marmorale notes in *CIL* vi. 10234 (= Riccobono, *Fontes* iii, no. 36) the phrase 'in quo populus collegi s(upra) s(cripti) epuletur'; but the normal meaning of *populus* is more natural here.

§ 11 cicaronem meum : used similarly by Echion at 46. 3.

unam : despite his injunction that the *amphorae* must be *gypsatas ne effluant vinum*, Trimalchio wants one of them to be broken; the weeping boy will then be part of this scene. Iac. Gronovius's *urnam* would mean that as well as the *amphorae*, all unbroken, there is to be a broken urn and weeping boy, a more clearly symbolic scene. Funerary monuments sometimes contained the motif of the weeping child, but the broken urn is perhaps unclassical (at Prop. iv. 5. 75 an old wine-jar with broken neck is to serve as a tomb for a *lena*, but that is a part of a curse, not a description of a standard motif). A further objection to *urnam* is that it makes the word-order of the phrase *u. licet fractam sculpas* less likely for a speaker like Trimalchio.

§ 12 Maecenatianus : this name, not claimed at 30. 2 'C. Pompeio Trimalchioni', gives an impression of immense wealth and patronage of the arts, and perhaps also a hint of effeminacy (cf. Sen. *Ep.* 114. 6 'spadones duo, magis tamen viri quam ipse'). In real life an *agnomen* might indicate the ex-slave's original master, while the *praenomen* and *nomen* were taken over from the owner by whom he was eventually manumitted.

huic seviratus absenti decretus est : this appears to parody the appointment of a candidate in his absence to some loftier position in Rome or elsewhere: cf., for example, Sall. *Iug.* 114. 3 'Marius consul absens factus est', *CIL* x. 5394 'ei honorem IIIIvir(atus Veronenses ratione habita) absentis eius extra or(dinem)'. See Th. Mommsen, *Hermes* xiii (1878), 118 f.

decuriis : the better-off freedman could buy membership of one or more *decuriae*, i.e. guilds of subordinates of magistrates and priests. In practice he might remain a member for the rest of his life; see *SG*[8] i. 375.

pius, fortis, fidelis : *fortis fidelis* is a common collocation in the description of loyal soldiers or allies (e.g. Liv. xxi. 44. 2); *pia fidelis* is the title of two legions named by Claudius.

sestertium reliquit trecenties : 30,000,000 sesterces. Some sepulchral inscriptions state the amount left by the dead man; e.g. *CIL* xi. 5400 (520,000 sesterces). Here Trimalchio claims an amount which is large but by no means incredible: fortunes of several hundreds of millions of sesterces are known (see *SG*[8] i. 248 for details). More remarkable is the fact that, after announcing here the precise amount of his estate, Trimalchio later (77. 2) assures his guests that he still has thirty years to live and will shortly inherit more money.

nec umquam philosophum audivit : this may simply make fun of the ignorant glorying in his ignorance, but possibly it is more subtle, a parody of the distrust shown by the upper classes, even in the provinces, towards philosophers: cf. Tac. *Agr.* 4. 3 'memoria teneo solitum ipsum narrare se prima in iuventa studium philosophiae acrius, ultra quam concessum Romano ac senatori, hausisse, ni prudentia matris incensum ac flagrantem animum coercuisset' (see note ad loc. by Richmond and Ogilvie), *SG*[8] iv. 293 ff.

vale : et tu : 'farewell to you, Trimalchio: and farewell to you, passer-by.' The custom of burying the dead by the side of the highways leading out of towns helped to give rise to the convention whereby through his epitaph the dead man addressed the passer-by and even engaged sometimes in an extended dialogue with him; see R. Lattimore, *Themes in Greek and Latin Epitaphs*, 230 ff.

Ch. 72

Trimalchio himself breaks down as he comes to the end of his epitaph, and the whole company, including the slaves, give way to tears. J. Révay (*CP* xvii (1922), 202 ff.) sees here one more sign that Petronius has been greatly influenced by Horace's *Cena Nasidieni*; cf. *Sat.* ii. 8. 58 f. 'Rufus posito capite, ut si / filius immaturus obisset, flere.' The resemblance is, however, extremely tenuous: in Horace the host weeps when some hangings fall down, and a guest moralizes on Fortune; in Petronius everyone, including the host, weeps on hearing the host's epitaph (a feature nowhere to be found in Horace), and the host moralizes. See also introduction, IIB.

§ 3 sic vos felices videam : cf. 61. 2 'sic felicem me videas'.

coniciamus nos in balneum : moralists and physicians were armed at the practice of taking a hot bath immediately after a heavy meal, or even during the course of it; e.g. Plin. *NH* xxix. 26 'balineae ardentes quibus persuasere in corporibus cibos coqui, ut nemo non minus validus exiret, oboedientissimi vero efferrentur', cf. Marq. *Prl.* 290 nn. 8 f., Mayor on Juv. 1. 143.

meo periculo : 'I'll guarantee'; cf. Plaut. *Poen.* 878 'crede audacter meo periclo', Cic. *Att.* iv. 7. 2 'tibi nummi meo periculo sint.'

§ 4 ⟨coepit⟩ : G. Bendz (*Eranos* xxxix (1941), 30 f.) argues that *coepit* is unnecessary; but the text in *H* here connects the historic infinitive and the finite verb more harshly than at 62. 5 'mihi [in] anima in naso esse, stabam tamquam mortuus', or, for example, Tac. *Ann.* iii. 26 'postquam exui aequalitas et pro modestia ac pudore ambitio et vis incedebat' (see L.–H.–S. 815, K.–S. i. 137 f.).

§ 7 canis catenarius : a chained watch-dog at the door is frequently mentioned (cf., for example, Sen. *Contr.* x. 1. 13 'si canem ad ostium alligasses'); in Trimalchio's house the dog harasses those already inside but does not seem to challenge those approaching from outside (cf. 29. 1). The painted dog described in ch. 29 is now referred to in the irrelevant and awkward interpolation *qui . . . canem*.

§ 9 ratione acutissima : in over-praising a not particularly clever device of Giton Encolpius seems to be stupid rather than ironical. As elsewhere, Petronius is not always consistent in his placing of Encolpius' character and intellectual level.

Ch. 73

§ 2 balneum intravimus . . . : *balneum* is often used of the hot bath as opposed to the cold (cf. Cels. i. 1 'prodest etiam interdum balneo, interdum aquis frigidis uti'), and the bather would normally sit down in it (see illustration in Smith's *Dict. of Antiq.*² s.v. *balneae*, p. 187), hence the emphasis here on *rectus stabat*.

The words *angustum . . . simile* are difficult: we do not expect the baths in Trimalchio's house to be small, yet *scilicet* ('of course') implies such an expectation. Sullivan deletes the whole phrase, but it looks like an unlikely interpolation. George suggests more plausibly that only the words *angustum scilicet et* should be deleted; they could be seen as an unsuccessful attempt to explain *cisternae frigidariae simile*. If so, Encolpius must be referring to Trimalchio's extravagance: his hot bath was as big as the main cold-water reservoir (cf. Sen. *Ep.* 86. 4 'cisternam aedificiis ac viridibus subditam quae sufficere in usum vel exercitus posset'); and when he remarks how pleasant it is *sine turba lavari* he indicates that in his eyes the present company is too small to be regarded as a crowd.

§ 3 invitatus balnei sono : Theophrastus includes singing in the bath as a characteristic of the boorish man (*Char.* 4. 13); cf. Hor. *Sat.* i. 4. 76 'suave locus voci resonat', Sen. *Ep.* 56. 2 'adice nunc scordalum et furem deprensum et illum cui vox sua in balneo placet.' As usual, however, it should not be assumed that Petronius was incapable of drawing his material from contemporary life as well as from literary sources.

[usque ad cameram] : Nisbet, p. 230, suggests that an interpolator may have taken *diduxit os* 'opened his mouth' (cf. Gell. v. 9. 2 'diduxit adulescens os clamare nitens') to mean 'raised his voice', then adding *usque ad cameram* (cf. 40. 1 'sublatis manibus ad cameram'), which would otherwise make little sense, even if we allow for exaggeration. The deletion also has the advantage of producing a double cretic clausula.

Menecratis : almost certainly the man of this name rewarded by Nero whom Suetonius (*Nero* 30) refers to as a *citharoedus*.

§ 4 labrum : abbreviated form of *lavabrum*; t.t. for a large tub or cauldron in the *caldarium* (cf. Vitr. v. 10 'labrum sub lumine faciendum videtur ne stantes circum suis umbris obscurent lucem', Cic. *Fam.* xiv. 20 'labrum si in balineo non est'). Less probably, *labrum* = 'lip', 'edge'.

gingilipho : not found elsewhere; perhaps connected with γιγγλισμός, tickling, or γίγγλυμος, kissing. *clamore* or *ingenti clamore* may be an interpolator's attempt to explain an unfamiliar word.

ceteri . . . alii autem : as the text stands, all the other guests (*ceteri*) are running round the *labrum* with arms linked to form a ring (*manibus nexis*); yet at the same time some of them (*alii autem*) are performing acrobatic feats with their hands tied behind their backs (*restrictis manibus*). Since it is clear that this is impossible, we are left with two types of solution: (i) words indicating some lapse of time and the actions of another group to balance *alii* must have fallen out; e.g. 'Before long most of them sank down exhausted, *alii autem* . . .'. If the missing section contained *alii*, the sentence here might continue *alii aut* (rather than *alii autem*); (ii) the sentences *ceteri convivae* . . . and *alii autem* . . . describe two distinct groups. Such a contrast can hardly be found in the present text, so some corruption has to be postulated; e.g. 'ceterorum convivarum alii . . . alii [autem] aut . . .'.

With either (i) or (ii) Buecheler's change to *illi* in place of *alii* H has to be accepted in the clause 'dum illi sibi ludos faciunt'.

§ 5 **solium** : a tub in which the individual bather took a hot bath (cf. Fest. 298b 22M 'alvei quoque, lavandi gratia instituti, quo singuli descendunt, solia dicuntur', Marq. *Prl.* 286).

servabatur : (*pervapatur H*) cf. 31. 8 'cui locus novo more primus servabatur'. Heraeus, p.116, prefers Heinsius's *temperabatur*, and compares *CGL* iii. 287. 30 'bene temperatum est solium', Plin. *NH* xxviii. 183.

ergo : Friedlaender claims several times that *ergo* is inserted by an interpolator after a passage has been abbreviated; cf., for example, 27. 4, 31. 3, 64. 13. Elsewhere he perhaps fails to allow for Petronius' desire not to labour a point, but it must be admitted that here the preceding sentence gives a weak conclusion to the scene in Trimalchio's bath.

suas [ita ut supra]: Müller regards *ita ut supra* as a gloss, noting a similar interpolation in Caes. *BG* i. 24. 2. Buecheler's deletion of *suas* is less attractive, however, even if the fact that it is written *suas* in *H* suggests uncertainty on the part of a scribe. Note that in any case the text is unsatisfactory in that *lucernas* is not specific enough to fit the context.

piscatores : fishermen occur occasionally as a motif on lamps, terracotta figures, etc. One might suspect that Encolpius expresses contempt (cf. diminutive *aeneolos*, and see note on *vinum . . . defluens* below) for a type of object fashionable among the less sophisticated (like little plastic gnomes in gardens today).

vinum in conspectu sacco defluens : 'wine being strained through a cloth where everyone could see'. A hint at Encolpius' snobbery: high-quality wines were thought to suffer if strained through a linen-cloth; cf. Hor. *Sat.* ii. 4. 53 f., D.-S. s.v. *saccus* (4).

§ 6 **servus meus** : the vagueness of this phrase is surprising. Wehle (p. 39) emends to *Croesus meus*, identifying the slave with the *puer lippus sordidissimis dentibus* of 64. 6; but if Croesus is also the 'puer vetulus, lippus, domino Trimalchione deformior' of 28. 4, he is rather old to be celebrating his *barbatoria* (for the ceremony of the first beard see note on 29. 8).

praefiscini : 'so help me'; used superstitiously to avoid the evil consequences of praise; cf. Plaut. *Asin.* 491 'praefiscini hoc nunc dixerim: nemo etiam me accusavit / merito meo . . .', Hof. *LU* 131.

micarius : hap. leg., 'penny-pinching' (from *mica*, crumb).

tangomenas faciamus : see note on 34. 7.

Ch. 74

Petronius has already mentioned Trimalchio's superstitiousness
in passing (e.g. 30. 6 *dextro pede*), but here he emphasizes it by
putting close together a number of illustrations of it. It was
ominous if a cock crowed earlier or later than usual (cf. Plin.
NH x. 49). Fearing that here it is an omen either of a fire or
of a death in the neighbourhood, Trimalchio, with the same
kind of extravagance as at 34. 4, pours wine under the table
and splashes the lamp with neat wine (this was done to produce
a lucky omen when the lamp sputtered or 'sneezed'; cf. *Anth.
Pal.* vi. 333 ἤδη, φίλτατε λύχνε, τρὶς ἔπταρες); whereas Pliny
merely says 'incendia inter epulas nominata aquis sub mensam
profusis abominamur' (*NH* xxviii. 26). Pliny also mentions
(*NH* xxviii. 57) that most people change their ring from the
left hand to the longest finger of the right hand in response to
hiccups or sneezes, which were often taken to be ominous.

§ 3 corollarium : 'bonus'. Used in general of a tip or gratuity;
on its origin cf. Varr. *LL* v. 178 'corollarium, si additum praeter
quod debitum; eius vocabulum fictum a corollis, quod eae,
cum placuerant actores, in scaena dari solitae', Cic. *Verr.*
iv. 49.

§ 4 oenococtus : see note on 47. 10.

§ 5 haurit : while Daedalus consumes the wine-based liquid in
which the cock has been cooked (rather than 'drew off the
scalding liquid', as Sullivan takes it), Fortunata grinds pepper
as a finishing touch for the dish (Apicius ends many recipes
thus; e.g. iv. 2. 12 'super aspargis piper tritum et inferes'). As
at 49. 1 ff., the joke consists in the incredible speed of preparation
of the dish, but this time the cooking is done instantaneously
and there is no explicit comment by Encolpius. On the repetition
of types of joke by Trimalchio see note on 50. 4 *Corinthus*.

§ 7 Gai : see note on 30. 3.

§ 9 ut . . . approbaret : lit. 'in order to establish her rights in
accordance with equity'.

Trimalchioni : (*Trimalchionem H*). Another of the relatively
rare passages where the manuscript reading credits Encolpius

with a Vulgarism. For the construction with *maledicere* cf. note on 58. 13 *cave maiorem maledicas*.

§ 10 canis : often a term of abuse, as a symbol either for shamelessness or for backbiting; see Hof. *LU* 88, Lilja, p. 33. Here, however, it is the ultimate insult so it may be more specific: cf. Hesych. s.v. κύων: δηλοῖ δὲ τὸ ἀνδρεῖον αἰδοῖον.

calicem . . . immisit : see Nisbet and Hubbard on Hor. *Od.* i. 27. 1 on the use of drinking-cups as weapons in drunken brawls.

§ 13 ambubaiam : Syrian flute-girl, but the word implies more than just music-making; cf. Hor. *Sat.* i. 2. 1 'ambubaiarum collegia', Suet. *Nero* 27 'scortorum . . . et ambubaiarum ministeria'.

machina : the platform on which slaves were exposed for sale; cf. [Q. Cicero], *Comment. Petit.* 8 'amicam quam domi palam haberet de machinis emit.'

in sinum suum conspuit : cf. *Paroem. Gr.* ii. 112 εἰς κόλπον πτύεις· ἀντὶ τοῦ μεγαλορρημονεῖς, ' "You spit in your breast" means "you are boastful" ' (*conspuit* has sometimes been changed unnecessarily to *non spuit* on the analogy of *Paroem. Gr.* i. 245 εἰς κόλπον οὐ πτύει· ἐπὶ τῶν μεγαλαύχων, ' "He doesn't spit in his breast" is said of those who are vainglorious'). Here he may mean merely that she literally spits on her breast as she rants on (this appears to be the sense in Juv. 7. 112 'conspuiturque sinus'); but note that spitting on the breast is frequently mentioned as an apotropaic device (see K. F. Smith on Tib. i. 2. 54, 96, Mayor on Juv. 7. 112).

codex, non mulier : cf. Ter. *HT* 877 'quae sunt dicta in stulto: caudex, stipes, asinus, plumbeus'. Wrongly rendered 'an animated ledger' by F. A. Todd, *CQ* xxxvii (1943), 105.

For the form of phrase see note on 38. 15 *phantasia, non homo*.

§ 14 hic qui in pergula . . . non somniatur : presumably he refers to Fortunata: you can't expect a woman of such a lowly origin to adapt herself to better society. If he refers to himself, the sense would be slightly different: 'If you come from a humble background like me, you can't hope for everything.'

hic qui is often used by first century A.D. writers where classical usage would call for *is qui*; cf. L.–H.–S. 181, K.–S. i. 621.

Cassandra caligaria : 'jack-booted Cassandra', or, more freely, a military Moaning Minnie; the phrase suggests a domineering woman who rants and nags perpetually. This interpretation

provides the contrast usually present in such expressions, e.g.
Cael. *fr.* 37 *Pelia cincinnatus*, Cic. *Cael.* 18 *Palatina Medea.*
Delz, p. 683, considers deriving *caligaria* from *caligo* (cf. August.
Civ. iii. 20 'fallacium divinationum caligine decipientes'), but
this is obscure and less effective.

§ 15 **homo dupundiarius** : cf. 58. 5.

unguentarius: perfume-selling could be highly profitable, even
though Cicero includes it in a list of *artes illiberales* (*Off.* i.
150).

[here] **proxime** : if both words are sound, this must mean 'just
yesterday'; but Nisbet, p. 231, suggests that *here* could be a gloss
on *proxime. herae proximae* (Buecheler) and *tabernae proximae*
(Leo) seem forced.

§ 16 **bonatus** : 'good-natured'. Hap. leg., but other adjectives
of this type are found. Friedlaender notes *CGL* ii. 126 *malatus*:
στυγνός, Plaut. *Cas.* 854 *belle belliatula*, and French *bonace.*

mihi asciam in crus impegi : 'I've cut my own throat'
(Sullivan), lit. 'I've stuck the axe into my own leg' (Heseltine).
Otto s.v. *crus* (1) cites a number of variants of this proverb,
e.g. Apul. *Met.* iii. 22 'meque sponte asciam cruribus meis
inlidere compellis?', Cic. *Mur.* 48.

§ 17 **recte ... quaeras** : 'all right, I'll make you want to dig me
up with your finger-nails.'

depraesentiarum : see note on 58. 3.

Ch. 75

§ 1 **nemo ... nostrum non peccat ...** : see Otto s.v. *homo* (2) and
(3) for more examples of these commonplace sentiments; e.g.
130. 1 'fateor me, domina, saepe peccasse; nam et homo sum et
adhuc iuvenis', Menander, fr. 499 Kock ἄνθρωπος ὢν ἥμαρτον
οὐ θαυμαστέον.

§ 2 **appellando** : the ablative of the gerund sometimes replaces
the nominative of the present participle; cf. Tac. *Ann.* xv. 38
'in edita adsurgens et rursus inferiora populando', Virg. *Aen.*
ii. 6 (with Austin's note). This usage was the source of the
present participle in Romance languages. See L.–H.–S. 380,
Löfstedt, *Peregr.* 159 f.

§ 3 **fruniscaris** : used with the accusative as at 43. 6.

§ 4 decem partes dicit : see note on 46. 3.

ab oculo legit : 'he can read at sight.' Heraeus, p. 116, cites *CGL* iii. 381. 63 ff. 'legi lectionem meam: quam mihi exposuit (magister) diligenter, donec intelligerem et personas et sensum verborum autoris: deinde ab oculo citatim ignotum et quod rare legitur.'

thraecium : if Orelli's conjecture for *thretium* is correct, the boy has saved enough from his daily allowance (*diaria*) to acquire a set of toy armour resembling the kind worn by the gladiators known as Thracians (cf. 45. 12). Playing at gladiators was a Roman equivalent of the modern 'Cowboys and Indians'; see Balsdon, *Life and Leisure*, 91 f.

arcisellium : probably a chair with rounded back (see Richter, *Furniture of the Greeks, Etruscans, and Romans*, figs. 507, 509, 511); cf. *CGL* iii. 366. 6 'sella arcuata: θρόνος'. It has also been taken to be the name for a litter with arching canopy (see D.–S., fig. 4378), cf. Tac. *Ann.* xv. 57 *arcum sellae*.

trullas : the *trulla* can be equivalent to a ladle, a strainer, or a trowel.

§§ 5 ff. Sullivan, p. 125, argues that, just as Habinnas' entry at 65. 3–8 (see notes ad loc.) is based on Alcibiades' drunken entrance in Plato's *Symposium* (212 c ff.), so Trimalchio's sketch of his own life and character parallels Alcibiades' description of Socrates at *Symp.* 215 a ff., where he compares him to the figures of Silenus to be seen in the statuary's shops. This parallel seems even less convincing than the earlier one.

in oculis feram : 'Doesn't he deserve to be the apple of my eye?' (Sullivan); cf. Cic. *Att.* vi. 2. 5 'publicanis in oculis sumus', Otto s.v. *oculus* (2).

§ 6 fulcipedia : presumably 'high-heeled' (cf. *fulmentum*, heel), but with the added sense 'high-stepping'; see Buecheler, *Rh. Mus.* xxxix (1884), 425 ff.

bonum tuum concoquas : probably 'think over what's good for you' (cf. Cic. *Rosc. Com.* 45 'tibi diu deliberandum et concoquendum est utrum . . .'), rather than, as Friedlaender took it, equivalent to Ter. *Phorm.* 318 'tute hoc intristi, tibi omnest exedendum' (cf. English 'you have made your own bed, now you must lie on it').

amasiuncula : cf. 45. 7 *amasiunculos*. Here used to wound: 'my little darling'.

erebrum : 'temper' (cf. 45. 5 *caldicerebrius*).

§ 7 clavo trabali fixum : 'fixed with a twelve-inch nail' (Sullivan). Scheffer's *trabali* for *tabulari* H assumes that the normal form of this expression was used here; cf. Cic. *Verr.* v. 53 'ut hoc beneficium quemadmodum dicitur trabali clavo figeret', Otto s.v. *clavus* (1), Nisbet and Hubbard on Hor. *Od.* i. 35. 18. *tabulari* (i.e. suitable for a plank rather than for a beam) is less appropriate, although the rendering in Warmington, 'drawing-pin', exaggerates the difference.

vivorum meminerimus : cf. note on 43. 1.

§ 8 corcillum : 'it's the old brain-box that . . .'; diminutive of *cor*, the heart being sometimes regarded as the seat of intelligence.

§ 9 sterteia : hap. leg., 'snorer'.

§ 10 candelabrus : another unusual masculine (cf. Caecilius, *CRF* 111); see note on 39. 4. For the sense see note on 64. 10 *candelabrum*.

rostrum : Nonius (455 M) quotes Plautus, Novius, Lucilius, and Varro for the use of *rostrum* with reference to a human being; Varro in fact has *barbato rostro*.

Ch. 76

§ 1 cepi ipsimi cerebellum : 'I was the only thought in master's mind.'

§ 2 coheredem me Caesari fecit : the emperor was sometimes named as joint heir to an estate in the hope that he would thus be ready to allow the rest of the property to be distributed according to the true wishes of the testator; cf. Tac. *Ann.* ii. 48. 1, xiv. 31. 1, xvi. 11, id. *Agr.* 43. 4. So here Trimalchio hints that his master was wealthy enough to have to beware of imperial disfavour. It should be added, however, that if Petronius was writing for Nero and his closer friends, he must have been sailing close to the wind in reminding them of a type of avarice to which Nero himself is said to have been particularly prone; cf. Suet. *Nero* 32. 2 'ante omnia instituit . . . ut ingratorum in principem testamenta ad fiscum pertinerent, ac ne impune esset studiosis iuris qui scripsissent vel dictassent ea.'

patrimonium laticlavium : i.e. the fortune of a senator, who was entitled to wear the *latus clavus*, a broad purple band down the centre of his *tunica*. Strictly the amount indicated should be at least a million sesterces; cf. Tac. *Ann.* i. 75, Dio liv. 17.

3 nemini . . . nihil : for the double negative see note on 42. 7.

contra aurum : 'worth its weight in gold'. For similar expressions see Otto s.v. *aurum* (1). *contra* is occasionally found in the sense of 'weighed against'; cf. Varr. *RR* i. 2. 10 'ubi poma veneunt contra aurum', K.–S. i. 541, L.–H.–S. 130.

§ 4 putares me hoc iussisse : Delz, p. 683, finds this remark incomprehensible; but possibly Trimalchio is merely seen as anticipating the fortunate consequences of his initial set-back.

§ 5 non mehercules mi haec iactura gusti fuit : i.e. it meant nothing to me. *non gusti* is analogous to *non flocci, non pili*, etc.; so taken by Heraeus, p. 135, who notes Rumanian *nagutta = nec gutta*, and old Venetian *nemiga*, French *ne . . . mie* (both = *ne mica*), all with the same meaning as *nihil*.

et feliciores : George deletes these words mainly on the ground that they anticipate the outcome of the story.

§ 8 cito fit quod di volunt : cf. note on 61. 6 'quomodo dii volunt'.

centies sestertium corrotundavi : 'I rounded off a million sesterces.' *corrotundare* does not seem to occur elsewhere in this slang use, but cf. Hor. *Ep.* i. 6. 34 f. 'mille talenta rotundentur, totidem altera, porro et / tertia succedant et quae pars quadret acervum'.

quicquid tangebam . . . : see note on 43. 1.

§ 9 manum de tabula : 'stop working!' Plin. *NH* xxxv. 80 might make us think that in this expression *tabula* means a painting: 'dixit enim (Apelles) omnia sibi cum illo (Protogene) paria esse aut illi meliora, sed uno se praestare, quod manum de tabula sciret tollere'; but Cicero's use of the phrase in *Fam.* vii. 25. 1 shows that it is originally a command by a schoolmaster to his pupils when he wishes to see how much work they have now done: 'sed heus tu, manum de tabula! magister adest citius quam putaramus; vereor ne in catomum Catonianos.'

§ 10 exhortavit : cf. active *cohortare* in Quadrigarius ap. Non. 472. 19.

mathematicus : astrologer; see note on 39. 6.

Graeculio : hap. leg. for *Graeculus*. For Vulgar formations in *-o, -onis*, see note on 38. 8 *Incuboni*. As with *Graeculus*, a pejorative sense need not be assumed.

consiliator deorum : there are various similar expressions, often used contemptuously, to describe surpassing cleverness; e.g. ps.-Sall. *in Cic.* 2. 3 'tamen Cicero se dicit in consilio deorum immortalium fuisse, inde missum huic urbi', cf. Otto s.v. *deus* (6), Pease on Cic. *ND* i. 18 'tamquam modo ex deorum concilio et ex Epicuri intermundiis descendisset'.

§ 11 ab acia et acu : lit. 'from thread and needle', i.e. in great detail; cf. Titin. *CRF* 5 'reliqui acus aciasque ero atque erae nostrae.'

intestinas : see Heraeus, pp. 131 ff., on this feminine, which occurs occasionally in Vulgar sources, e.g. *CGL* iii. 86. 11 *intera*: *intestinae*. Note that even Habinnas uses the normal form *intestina* (neut. pl.) at 66. 5.

cenaveram : see note on 44. 1 for the indicative in indirect questions.

Ch. 77

§ 1 tu dominam . . . fecisti : probably 'you acquired your good lady by using that wealth of yours'; but *de rebus illis* has something of the professional vagueness of the fortune-teller: 'using we all know what resources'. There may also be a trace of a euphemism; cf. Mart. xi. 43. 11 'parce tuis igitur dare mascula nomina rebus', Arnob. iii. 10 'Priapum inter deas virgines atque matres circumferentem res illas'. *domina* has also been taken to refer here to Trimalchio's former master's wife, but this seems too remote. Müller suggests that something may have fallen out after *tuam*, but any addition would detract from the balanced conciseness of the prophecies.

§ 3 fundos Apuliae iungere : this makes Trimalchio appear a little absent-minded in view of his earlier boast 'nunc coniungere agellis Siciliam volo, ut cum Africam libuerit ire, per meos fines navigem' (48. 3).

satis vivus pervenero : 'I shall have gone far enough in my lifetime.'

§ 4 cusuc : very unlikely, although Sedgwick defends it, connecting it with Persian *Kúshk* and Turkish Kiöshk, a little summer pavilion (*CR* xxxix (1925), 117). Corbett's *casa adhuc* (*casa* patav., *casula* Heinsius) is possible.

porticus…duos : *porticus* occurs occasionally in inscriptions as a masculine, e.g. *CIL* vi. 11913. 8 'porticus … qui'; see Heraeus, p. 135.

cenationem : preferable to *cellationem H*, a word not found elsewhere, which Heinsius defends in the sense of a row of rooms. Even *cenatio* is open to the objection that it is neither grandiose nor eccentric, and Salonius' suggestion of an up-stairs washroom (*lavationem*) is attractive.

viperae : on the use of this as a term of reproach for a woman cf. ἱματισμένη ἔχιδνα Secund. *Sent.* 8. E. K. Borthwick (*CR* n.s. xvii (1967), 250 ff.) notes various passages where courtesans are likened to vipers.

sessorium : apparently 'sitting-room' rather than 'den'. The word means 'seat' in Cael. Aurel. *Acut.* i. 11. 84.

ostiarii : as at 28. 8, the point lies in the lowly status of the door-keeper in the normal household.

hospitium hospites ⟨C⟩ capit : Heinsius's supplement is the simplest way of dealing with the impossible flatness of the text in *H*.

§ 5 Scaurus : the great family of Aemilii Scauri had died out in A.D. 34 with the suicide of Mamercus Scaurus (cf. Sen. *Suas.* ii. 22), so if one of them is referred to, we should have to assume that the *Cena* is placed in a setting not too long after that date. In any case the name is surely chosen here for its aristocratic associations. Maiuri suggested instead A. Umbricius Scaurus, known as a manufacturer of *garum* in Pompeii. It is true that elsewhere in the *Cena* local personalities are named, e.g. 44. 6 Safinius, 45. 10 Norbanus; but here Trimalchio seems to be describing a visitor who has come to the *Graeca urbs* from a distance and not merely moved from near-by Pompeii.

mavoluit : the forms *mavolo*, *mavolunt* are found in Plautus, Terence, and Naevius.

§ 6 assem habeas … : 'if you've only got a penny, you're only worth a penny; if you've got something, you'll be thought something.' Cf. Apul. *Apol.* 23 'tanti re vera estis quantum habetis', Lucilius 1120M 'tantum habeas, tantum ipse sies tantique habearis', Otto s.v. *habere* (1).

amicus vester : = 'I', 'yours truly', like 41. 3 *servus tuus.*
Trimalchio then goes on to refer to some tale of miraculous
transformation from rags to riches, like the story of the Frog-
prince. Petronius perhaps mocks him by making him turn to
a tale quite inappropriate to his own career: the Frog-prince
began as a prince, not as a frog.

Ch. 78

Mock funerals are occasionally mentioned elsewhere. Tacitus
(*Hist.* iv. 45) tells how the people of Sena insulted a senator by
holding a mock funeral for him in his presence. According to
Seneca (*Brev. Vit.* 20. 3), on being compulsorily retired, the
nonagenarian S. Turannius demonstrated by holding a mock
funeral for himself. Still closer to the account of Trimalchio's
bizarre behaviour is another passage in Seneca: 'Pacuvius, qui
Syriam usu suam fecit, cum vino et illis funebribus epulis sibi
parentaverat, sic in cubiculum ferebatur a cena ut inter plausus
exoletorum hoc ad symphoniam caneretur "βεβίωται βεβίωται";
nullo non se die extulit' (*Ep.* 12. 8). The resemblance has, however, not always been analysed with sufficient care. The eccentric outbursts of Pacuvius appear to have taken place long
before Seneca's letter was written, if he was a legate in Syria
in A.D. 19 (cf. Tac. *Ann.* ii. 79), but there is no reason to suppose
that they were quite ignored until Seneca recalled them—
indeed Seneca's use of *illis* implies that his readers could be
expected to remember. It is true that, although there is no
verbal similarity here between Seneca and Petronius, the
similarity in subject-matter has seemed significant to some
critics (e.g. Sullivan, p. 131, Walsh, p. 137); but Petronius
cannot be satirizing Seneca, who himself points out how absurd
Pacuvius was. Sullivan tries to deal with this difficulty by
claiming that the stories of Calvisius Sabinus (see 59. 4–5) and
Pacuvius are used for literary rather than parodic purposes;
but this in turn weakens the argument that elsewhere in the
Cena (e.g. at 71. 1 'et servi homines sunt') Petronius was
attempting to ridicule Seneca: it is inadvisable to satirize and
plagiarize from the same source.

§ 4 parentalia : in § 2 and in 77. 7 Trimalchio had been thinking
of his actual funeral, but now he is diverted to imagining the
parentalia, the annual commemoration of the dead. See Ov.
Fast. ii. 533–70.

§ 5 novum acroama, cornicines : cf. 53. 12.

dicite : 'play'. For this sense of *dicere*, cf. SHA, *Heliog.* 32. 8
'ipse cantavit, saltavit, ad tibias dixit, tuba cecinit, panduri-
zavit, organo modulatus est.' See Heraeus, p. 117.

§ 7 [qui ... regionem] : this phrase would hardly be needed by
a contemporary of Petronius, aware that the *vigiles* served as
a fire-brigade as well as performing police duties, but deletion
leaves the sentence incomplete. See Nisbet, p. 228: 'Perhaps
Müller goes too far when he implies that such an interpolation
cannot be ancient; it might have been made not to explain
who *vigiles* were, but to smooth over their abrupt introduction
in this context.'

§ 8 **verba dedimus** : 'gave him the slip'. Gellius (xvii. 2. 24)
expressly states that this phrase can be applied to a deception
not involving any speech.

fugimus : J. Révay (*CP* xvii (1922), 202 ff.) detects in this an
echo of the ending of the *Cena Nasidieni* of Horace (*Sat.* ii. 8. 93
'quem nos sic fugimus ulti . . .'). But Trimalchio's dinner surely
demands a sudden ending on artistic grounds. If Petronius
required to turn to literary sources for inspiration here, he is
more likely to have found it in the endings of mimes: cf. Cic.
Cael. 65 'mimi ergo iam exitus, non fabulae; in quo cum
clausula non invenitur, fugit aliquis e manibus, dein scabilla
concrepant, aulaeum tollitur.'

APPENDIX I

A. PETRONIUS AND TACITUS

Tacitus (*Ann.* xvi. 17 ff.; see Testimonia) describes a Petronius who, after serving competently as proconsul in Bithynia and as consul, showed himself such an expert in refined luxury that he was chosen by Nero as his *elegantiae arbiter*, a title which suggests supervision of court entertainments. Tigellinus' enmity towards him caused his downfall, and in A.D. 66 he was forced to commit suicide while in Campania. He is not said to have been the author of any work apart from a scurrilous document sent posthumously to Nero. Despite the *praenomen* C., given at *Ann.* xvi. 18, this Petronius may well be the same as the *T. Petronius consularis* mentioned by Pliny (*NH* xxxvii. 20), who on his death-bed broke a valuable vase in order to spite Nero, and the same as the T. Petronius of Plutarch (*Mor.* 60 e) who showed his obsequiousness towards Nero's extravagance by pretending to criticize his meanness.

Is the Tacitean Petronius to be identified with the author? Certainly the words *elegantiae arbiter* in Tacitus suggest a possible connection with the author, who is referred to as Arbiter or Petronius Arbiter in most manuscripts of the *Satyricon* and in some late writers (e.g. Terentianus Maurus and Fulgentius). In recent years this identification has come to be regarded as unchallengeable; on this view the author's position as *elegantiae arbiter* led to the use of Arbiter after his death as if it had been his *cognomen*. Tacitus' lengthy description of Petronius shows that he was in some unspecified way remarkable, but the failure to refer to him as an author has even been counted as an additional point in favour of the identification. The alternatives have not been properly examined in recent years. It is possible, for instance, that of the numerous Petronii, one, not necessarily of the highest rank but having the education, temperament, and ability required to write the *Satyricon*, was called Arbiter (the name is attested only three times: *CIL* x. 5490 (Aquinum),

vi. 12282 (Rome), *ILS* 2362 (Mainz); the first two of these refer
to slaves, the third to an ordinary soldier, but it is scarcely
credible that the name originated at so low a social level), while
by coincidence another, a man of consular rank of the same
generation or possibly rather later, possessing the temperament
described by Tacitus, was referred to either during his life or
afterwards as Nero's *elegantiae arbiter*. It should be pointed out
that Rose (pp. 44 f.) exaggerates the unlikeliness of such a
coincidence by assuming first the soundness of the identification with the Tacitean Petronius, and only then going on to
consider the possibility of Arbiter as a *cognomen*. Or again it is
possible that later writers, knowing only that the author was
named Petronius, wrongly assumed that he was the Tacitean
Petronius and hence either referred to him as Arbiter as if this
was his actual name or used it as a convenient means of identification.

B. PETRONIUS AND LUCAN

In ch. 118 the poet Eumolpus deplores meretricious standards
in epic, the reliance on glittering *sententiae* which have no real
connection with the subject; those who write about the civil
war (118. 6 'belli civilis ingens opus quisquis attigerit' suggests
that he has more than one poet in mind) must not dispense
with the divine machinery which was obligatory in earlier epic.
He himself will offer his own attempt, incomplete though it is,
to show what is needed. The poem which follows is usually
thought to be based in some way on Lucan's *De Bello Civili*,
left incomplete at his death in A.D. 65 but no doubt partially
available to some readers rather earlier than that. Now if there
are other grounds for supposing that Petronius was writing his
novel in 64–6, the inclusion of a poem which either parodies
Lucan or consciously seeks to surpass him would be decisive.
But the poem offered by Eumolpus does not parody Lucan—
and few readers would doubt Petronius' ability to write such
a parody if that had been his aim, nor again can it be taken as
a serious attempt to surpass Lucan. Thus more complicated
explanations of Eumolpus' poem have been felt to be necessary:
for example, Walsh (pp. 49 f.), although seeing it chiefly as
a derisive parody of the poetic style of Lucan, thinks that it

demonstrates how an incompetent poet like Eumolpus would write on the Civil War, and that Petronius is criticizing Lucan's innovations and the traditionalism of other writers. This analysis may be partly right, but the connection with Lucan deserves a closer scrutiny.

First, one or two general points should be considered. How much weight should be given to the fact that both Petronius and Lucan deal with the Civil War between Caesar and Pompey? This coincidence in subject-matter has perhaps impressed critics unduly; it might seem much less striking if we had a fuller knowledge of the themes chosen by poets who were at work in the first half of the first century A.D. (see H. Bardon, *La Littérature latine inconnue*, ii. 61 ff., 135 ff.). Likewise Eumolpus' criticism of those poets who dispense with divine machinery does not necessarily concern Lucan at all.

Long lists of echoes of Lucan found in Petronius' poem have been collected by Stubbe (*Philologus* Suppl. xxv (1933)), Rose, pp. 88 ff., Sullivan, pp. 170 ff., and others. Most of these echoes are unconvincing in themselves, and even more so when account is taken of parallels in Virgil and other earlier writers. Of Rose's 152 parallels the following have been given most weight by a number of writers:

(a) *BC* (=Petronius, *Sat.* 119 ff.) 1 ff.

> orbem iam totum victor Romanus habebat
> qua mare, qua terrae, qua sidus currit utrumque,
> nec satiatus erat

Lucan i. 109 ff.

> dividitur ferro regnum, populique potentis
> quae mare, quae terras, quae totum continet orbem
> non cepit fortuna duos.

If Petronius based his poem on Lucan, we should expect his opening lines to take up those of Lucan. The partial resemblance noted here with a later passage in Lucan is not an adequate substitute, especially since the main thought is not the same (Petronius: 'The Romans had now conquered the whole world, but were not content'; Lucan: 'Pompey and Caesar now ruled the whole world but they could not share it'). In view of this difference in sense, verbal parallels in other authors ought to be considered at least equally significant; cf.

> Virg. *Aen.* i. 236
>
>> qui mare, qui terras omnis dicione tenerent
>
> id. *Catal.* 9. 3 f.
>
>> victor adest magni magnum decus ecce triumphi
>> victor qua terrae, quaque patent maria
>
> id. *Aen.* vii. 100 f.
>
>> omnia sub pedibus, qua Sol utrumque recurrens
>> aspicit Oceanum, vertique regique videbunt

(*b*) *BC* 215 f.

>> incendia totaque bella
> ante oculos volitant
>
> Lucan vii. 179 f.
>
>> defunctosque patres et cunctas sanguinis umbras
>> ante oculos volitare suos

(cf. Cic. *Agr.* ii. 59 'volitat enim ante oculos istorum', Ennius ap. Cic. *Tusc.* i. 34 'volito vivos per ora virum')

(*c*) *BC* 117 ff.

>> vix navita Porthmeus
>> sufficiet simulacra virum traducere cumba:
>> classe opus est
>
> Lucan iii. 16 f.
>
>> praeparat innumeras puppes Acherontis adusti
>> portitor

(cf. Virg. *Aen.* vi. 413 'gemuit sub pondere cumba', *Consolatio ad Liviam*, 357 f. 'omnes expectat avarus / portitor, et turbae vix satis una ratis'

(*d*) *BC* 224 f.

>> debellatique Quirites
> rumoris sonitu maerentia tecta relinquunt
>
> Lucan v. 30 f.
>
>> maerentia tecta
> Caesar habet

Here the resemblance is closer (although cf., for example, Ov. *Fast.* iii. 641 'maestum tectum', *Consolatio ad Liviam*, 177 'consul init fractis maerentem fascibus urbem'), yet we are entitled to consider the possibility of a coincidence or of some lost source common to Petronius and Lucan.

Thus it would seem that in this question, as with the identification of the author with the Tacitean Petronius, a great deal of caution is required. If the weaker points in the comparison with Lucan are discarded, surprisingly little is left, and certainly not enough to forbid further discussion.

Lastly, a few words on the interrelationship between these two problems. If A.D. 65–6 was the date of composition of the *Bellum Civile*, and if it is in any sense a parody of Lucan, it follows that in order to dash off his parody while it was still topical Petronius must have written it almost immediately after Lucan's death, just as he is supposed to have made fun of Seneca just after *his* death. An earlier date of composition would leave him less unattractive as a person, even if it failed to give a precise explanation of his motives for writing.[1]

C. PETRONIUS AND SENECA

Various attempts have been made to date the composition of the *Satyricon* by means of parallels between it and Seneca's *Epistulae Morales*, which appear to have been written in the years between his retirement from court in 62 and his death in 65. Lists of possible echoes and borrowings are given by Rose (pp. 69 ff.) and Sullivan (pp. 129 ff., 193 ff.). Here there is space to take up only a few of these parallels and to indicate some counter-arguments.

(a) *Ep.* 12. 8, *Sat.* 78. (see note ad loc.) deal with mock-funeral scenes. But the mock funerals held by Pacuvius which are described in *Ep.* 12 date back to the reign of Tiberius (and in *Brev. Vit.* 20. 3 he refers to a mock funeral held by S. Turranius in the reign of Caligula). Hence it is implausible to imagine that such eccentricities remained unknown to Petronius until Seneca chose to mention them years later.

---

[1] I owe some of the material in this part of Appendix I to Mr. P. A. George, who kindly allowed me to see a draft of his article 'Petronius and Lucan *de Bello Civili*', *CQ* N.S. xxiv (1974), 119 ff.

(b) Trimalchio's poor memory for the details of mythology and poetry (see 48. 7, 50. 4–6, 52. 1–2) and his reliance on *Homeristae* to recite poetry for him (59. 2; see note ad loc.) are said to be based on the picture in *Ep.* 27. 5 of Calvisius Sabinus, a rich man who purchased slaves to recite the works of particular writers for him. The resemblance, is, however, not very striking. Calvisius is perhaps picked out by Seneca because, although not a freedman, he had the wealth and mentality usually associated with successful freedmen. The idea that Petronius must have had him in mind depends on the unsafe assumption that he was a freedman; but in any case information on his behaviour need not have come to Petronius through reading Seneca's letter.

(c) In *Ep.* 47 Seneca praises his friend Lucilius for treating his slaves considerately, and sees nothing shameful about sitting down at table with his own slaves. At *Sat.* 70. 11–71. 3, when Trimalchio, after allowing his slaves to invade the dining-room and to take part in the dinner, preaches a little sermon to his guests on the brotherhood of man, Petronius is assumed to be making fun of Seneca's letter. Yet it is hard to believe that this type of kindness towards slaves was peculiar to Seneca and Lucilius, and even the verbal similarity (*Ep.* 47. 1 ' "servi sunt." immo homines', *Sat.* 71. 1 'et servi homines sunt') should not be pressed too far; cf. Herodas 5. 14 f., where an angry mistress deplores the ingratitude of her slave lover ἐγὼ αἰτίη τούτων, / ἐγῶιμι, Γάστρων, ἤ σε θεῖσ᾽ ἐν ἀνθρώποις. Moreover Seneca himself goes on to suggest that generosity to slaves should not be practised to excess (§ 15 ' "quid ergo? omnes servos admovebo mensae meae?" non magis quam omnes liberos'), so that Trimalchio's words and behaviour would be inept if taken as a parody of Seneca's letter.

(d) *Sat.* 56. 7 'iam etiam philosophos de negotio deiciebat' (see note ad loc.) is said to be an echo of *Ep.* 88. 44 'Zenon Eleates omnia negotia de negotio deiecit.' But Seneca's words would be incomprehensible unless the expression *aliquem de negotio deicere* was in use, and it is unthinkable that Petronius should have been content to echo Seneca's abnormal expression by using the normal expression on which it was based.

Many of the echoes of Seneca detected in Petronius depend

on the assumption that Petronius had no other source of information available to him. In addition, diverse explanations have to be given of his use of Seneca (Sullivan himself notes this several times, e.g. p. 132)—occasional parodies of Seneca would surely be less effective if the readers who could appreciate them could also recognize frequent borrowings of material where no parody was intended. At the very least some of the collections of parallels should be drastically pruned, and even those who remain convinced that there are Senecan echoes should consider whether parallels with passages in the letters have perhaps been over-emphasized at the expense of parallels in his earlier works.

APPENDIX II

THE LANGUAGE OF THE FREEDMEN IN THE *CENA*

The language of the freedmen in the *Cena* (see Introduction IIC)
naturally contains features which would occur in the ordinary
speech of Romans of any social level, e.g. *constructio ad sensum*,
ellipse, proverbs, present tense in place of future. Parallels for
these features may be looked for in Cicero's letters and in the
plays of Plautus and Terence. But the freedmen's speech also
contains features which point more specifically to their lower-
class background. In this appendix some details of abnormalities of different types in the *Cena* will be given; but the reader
is advised to consult V. Väänänen, *Le Latin vulgaire des inscriptions pompéiennes* in order to appreciate the much wider range
of abnormalities from which Petronius has given a selection.
For a full study of the language of the *Satyricon* see D. C
Swanson, *A Formal Analysis of Petronius' Vocabulary*; his
work is, however, not as helpful as it might have been, since
he believes that no distinction is possible between the language
of the freedmen and that of Encolpius, and he therefore does not
usually classify separately the facts for each of these categories.

A. *Phonology*

au to *o*: 44. 12 *coda* (but 89 v. 38 *cauda*); 39. 12 *copones* (cf.
CIL iv. 3948, 6700), but 98. 1 *cauponi*; 40. 7 *lotam* (*totam H*);
45. 13 *plodo* (but 70. 10 *plaudebat*). Note also the story recounted
by Suetonius (*Vesp.* 22) 'Mestrium Florum consularem, admonitus ab eo *plaustra* potius quam *plostra* dicenda, postero
die Flaurum salutavit.' Cf. W. S. Allen, *Vox Latina*, 60 f.,
Väänänen, *Introduction*, 39 f.

Syncope: 44. 11 *bublum* (but 35. 3 *bubulae*). But 66. 3 *caldus*
(for *calidus*) should not be cited as a Vulgarism, since it occurs

also in narrative at 65. 7, and Augustus is said to have corrected C. Caesar for using *calidus*, the more affected form (cf. Quint. i. 6. 19).

Inserted consonants: 44. 18 *plovebat* for *pluebat*. But several examples sometimes cited of the insertion of *r* are doubtful. In Habinnas' speech *H* has *frustrum* at 66. 5, but *frusta* at 66. 7, as well as 35. 3 *frustrum*, 59. 7 *frustra* (both in narrative). In these cases the intrusive *r* looks like a scribal error; so also with 38. 5 *culcitras H* (Hermeros), cf. 98. 5 *culcitra L* (in narrative), and 38. 1 *credrae H*.

B. *Morphology*

(a) *Accidence*

NOUNS AND ADJECTIVES

Gender

In later Latin the neuter tended to disappear (see Väänänen, *Introduction*, 107 ff., Palmer, pp. 159 f.), a development illustrated in the *Cena*. Note these types of change of gender: masculine in place of neuter: 39. 4, 39. 6, 45. 3 *caelus*, 75. 10 *candelabrus*, 42. 5, 71. 1, 77. 3 *fatus*, 39. 4 *fericulus*, 47. 5 *lasanus*, 57. 8 *lorus*, 67. 6 *reticulus*, 57. 8 *vasus*, 41. 12 *vinus*; also 71. 1 *lactem* (for *lac*) (at 41. 11 *balneus* is conjectured by Gronovius for *baliscus H*); feminine in place of neuter: 76. 11 *intestina*, 66. 7 *rapa*, 44. 8 *schema*, 45. 9, 69. 1 *stigma*, 78. 1 *stragula* (narrative).

The reverse changes are also found, although less frequently: neuter in place of masculine: 50. 6, 66. 7 *catillum*, 46. 7 *librum*, 45. 11 *nervium*, 46. 8 *thesaurum* (see notes ad. locc. on the effective placing of the solecisms *libra* and *thesaurum*); neuter in place of feminine: 63. 3 *margaritum*, 75. 8 *quisquilia* (pl.), 76. 6 *seplasium*, 50. 6 *statuncula* (pl.).

Swanson, p. 253, points out that all 31 instances of change of gender in the *Satyricon* occur in the *Cena*. In fact almost all occur in the speech of the freedmen.

Declension

Apart from declension changes included above, note also: 39. 5 *cornum*, 44. 16 *diibus* (*aedilibus H*), 76. 5 *gustus -i*, 70. 2 *palumbus*, 46. 1 *pauperorum*, 68. 8 *strabonus*.

Back-formations

62. 13 *bovis* for *bos*, 45 4, 66. 3 *excellente*, 47. 4, 58. 2 *Iovis* for *Iuppiter*, 59. 1 *sanguen* for *sanguis*.

VERBS

Voice

There was a gradual disappearance of the deponent in Latin (see Väänänen, *Introduction*, 136, Palmer, p. 163), but in the *Cena*, as in early Latin, there are fluctuations between active and deponent forms.

Active in place of deponent: 63. 8 *amplexo*, 46. 1, 57. 8 *arguto*, 57. 2 *convivo*, 76. 10 *exhorto*, 46. 1 *loquo* (also 140. 8 *remunero*). Deponent in place of active: 45. 7, 64. 2 *delector*, 48. 4 *fastidior*, 47. 4 *pudeor*, 57. 3 *rideor*, 74. 14 *somnior*.

Note that fluctuations of voice in the *Satyricon* are almost entirely confined to the *Cena*.

Conjugation

69. 2 *defraudit* (for *-at*), 74. 14 *domatus* (for *domitus*), 50. 7 *olunt* (for *olent*), 53. 8 *vetuo*.

Miscellaneous

68. 6 *erudibam* (for *erudiebam*), 71. 10 *facia(n)tur* (for *fia(n)t*), 69. 6 (narrative) *farsus* (for *fartus*), 61. 8 *fefellitus* (for *falsus*), 77. 5 *mavoluit* (for *maluit*), 58. 5 *parsero* (for *pepercero*), 45. 10 *vinciturus* (for *victurus*).

(b) *Word-formation*

NOUNS AND ADJECTIVES

Some use is made of endings which suggest specifically vulgar speech:

-monium: 61. 3 *gaudimonium*, 63. 4 *tristimonium*.

-o, -onis (see Väänänen, *Introduction*, 92, Swanson pp. 78 ff.): 60. 8 *Cerdo, Felicio, Lucrio*, 46. 3, 71. 11 *cicaro*, 76. 10 *Graeculio*, 38. 8 *Incubo*, 39. 10 *lanio*, 58. 10 *Occupo*, 50. 5 *stelio* (*scelio H*), 63. 8 *vavato*.

-ax: 42. 5 *abstinax*, 52. 4 *nugax*, 43. 8 *salax*.

-osus: 57. 10 *dignitosus*, 57. 8 *lacticulosus*, 43. 4, 63. 1 *linguosus*, 38. 6 *sucosus*.

Diminutives are common in colloquial speech of any social level (cf. Fordyce on Catullus 3. 18). Swanson (pp. 7 ff., 84 ff.) lists many from the narrative sections of the *Satyricon*, but even so it is clear enough that diminutives are given rather more freely and effectively to the freedmen in the *Cena*: cf., for example, 58. 5 *comula*, 57. 6 *glebula, lamellula,* 58. 8 *sponsiuncula*; 63. 5 *audaculus,* 38. 3 *meliusculus.*

Popular compounds are likewise used more colourfully by the freedmen: e.g. 61. 6 *bacciballum,* 45. 11 *burdubasta,* 45. 5 *caldicerebrius,* 57. 3 *larifuga,* 45. 11 *loripes.*

VERBS

Some compounds are used in place of simple verbs (cf. 40. 7 etc. *comedo,* 69. 3 *debattuo*; one or two verbs have a double prefix (cf. 43. 4 *recorrigo*) as often in later Latin (cf. Väänänen, *Introduction,* 100). Frequentatives, desideratives, etc., are also used like simple verbs: e.g. 64. 2 *canturio,* 43. 6, 44. 16, 75. 3 *fruniscor,* 62. 14 *exopinisso.* This tendency is found in narrative as well, although to a more limited extent.

(c) Lexicon

Swanson (pp. xxvi f.) calculates that the Greek element in the entire lexicon of Petronius amounts to nearly 10 per cent; but the more vivid and uncommon Graecisms tend to occur in the speech of the freedmen: e.g. 62. 3, 67. 3 *apoculo,* 42. 2 *laecasin.* Note especially the Greek element in the language of Hermeros: 37. 4 *topanta,* 37. 6 *saplutus, lupatria* (a hybrid with a Greek suffix), 37. 9 *babae babae,* 37. 10 *babaecalus,* 57. 11 *athla,* 58. 7 *deuro de.*

C. Syntax

(a) Most of the abnormal uses of cases reflect the gradual move towards the establishment of the accusative form as an all-purpose oblique case (see Väänänen, *Introduction,* 118 f., Elcock, *The Romance Languages,* 60 ff., Palmer, pp. 160, 166): e.g. 46. 2 'te persuadeam', 58. 13 'maiorem maledicas', 44. 16 'meos fruniscar'; 30. 3 'foras cenat', 44. 14 'domi leones, foras vulpes', 47. 5 'omnia foras parata sunt' (cf. *CIL* iv. 3494 'foras rixsatis'). The accusative is also used irregularly with the preposition *prae*: cf. 39. 12 'prae mala sua', 46. 1 'prae litteras' (cf. Väänänen, *Introduction*, 119, Palmer, p. 166, *CIL* iv. 698 'cum discentes suos').

(b) Pronouns

 ille for reflexive: 38. 4, 38. 16.

 reflexive for *is*: 43. 1.

 ille for *is*: e.g. 46. 4 (see Väänänen, *Introduction*, 128 on the weakening of *is*).

(c) Negatives

For the pleonastic double negative cf. 42. 7, 58. 5, 76. 3, Väänänen, *Introduction*, 162 f. But although colloquial, this perhaps sounded less of a solecism to an educated Roman than one might assume (see note on 42. 7).

(d) Indirect speech introduced by quod *and* quia

The classical accusative with infinitive construction is several times replaced by an indicative clause introduced by *quod* or *quia*: 45. 10 'subolfacio quia', 46. 4 'dixi quia', 71. 9 'scis quod'. See Väänänen, *Introduction*, 173 f., Palmer 333 f., on the development of this construction in later Latin.

(e) Indicative in indirect speech

Once or twice the indicative is used in place of the subjunctive: 44. 1 'nemo curat quid annona mordet'. But note, as with the *quod* and *quia* clauses in (*d*), the restraint with which this abnormality is inserted.

INDEX NOMINUM

The names of Trimalchio and his guests are printed in capital letters

BERMEROS, 59. 1
Hermeros (gladiator), 52. 3
Hermogenes, 45. 9
Hipparchus, 40. 1
Homerus, 48. 7, 59. 4; Homeristae, 59. 2. 3. 6

Incubo, 38. 8
India, 38. 4; Indicus, 55. 6 v. 9
Iphigenia, 59. 5
IULIUS PROCULUS, 38. 16
Iuppiter, 44. 17, 51. 5, etc.

Laenas, 29. 9
Lares, 29. 8, 60. 8
Laserpiciarius, 35. 6
Liber, 41. 7
Lucrio, 60. 8

Maecenatianus (cognomen Trimalchionis), 71. 12
Mammea, 45. 10
Margarita, 64. 9
Mars, 34. 5, 55. 6 v. 1
Marsyas, 36. 3
Massa, 69. 5
Melissa, 61. 6, 62. 11
Menecrates, 73. 3
Menelaus (antescholanus), 27. 4 f.
Menophila, 70. 10
Mercurius, 29. 5, 67. 7, 77. 4
Minerva, 29. 3
Mithridates (servus Trimalchionis), 53. 3
Mopsus, 55. 4

Nasta, 53. 5
Neptunus, 76. 4
NICEROS, 61. 1. 3, 63. 1
Niobe, 52. 2
Norbanus, 45. 10, 46. 8

Occupo, 58. 11

Opimianus, 34. 6 f.
Orcus, 34. 10, 45. 9, 46. 7, 62. 2

Palamedes, 66. 7
Pansa, 47. 12
Pegasus, 36. 2
Petraites, 52. 3, 71. 6
Philargyrus, 70. 10, 71. 2
PHILEROS, 43. 1, 44. 1
Phileros (causidicus), 46. 8
PLOCAMUS, 64. 2
Pompeianus, 53. 5 f.
C. POMPEIUS DIOGENES, 38. 10
Pompeius (nomen Trimalchionis), 30. 2, 71. 12
Priapus, 60. 4
Primigenius, 46. 8
Publilius Syrus, 55. 5

Roma, 29. 3, 69. 9, 70. 3, 71. 12, 76. 3

Safinius, 44. 6
Saturnalia, 44. 3, 58. 2, 69. 9
Scaurus, 77. 5
SCINTILLA, 66. 5, 67. 6, etc.
Scissa, 65. 10
Scylax, 64. 7. 9
SELEUCUS, 42. 1
Serapa, 76. 10
Sibylla, 48. 8
Sicilia, 48. 3
Stichus, 77. 7, 78. 1 f.
Syrus, 52. 9

Tarentum, 38. 2; Tarentinus, 48. 2, 59. 4, 61. 6
Tarracinienses, 48. 2
Terentius, 61. 6
Titus, 45. 5
TRIMALCHIO, *passim*

Ulixes, 39. 3, 48. 7

Venus, 29. 8, 68. 8
Vergilius, 68. 5

INDEX VERBORUM

INDEX RERUM

66. 5; beet, 56. 9, 66. 2;
blood sauce, 66. 2; boar
served whole, 40. 3 (also *apri
gausapati*, 38. 15); dates, 40.
3; dormice, 31. 10; duck-
flesh, 56. 3; fig-eaters, 33. 8;
fish-sauce, 36. 3; hot water
with wine, 65. 7; *mulsum*,
34. 1; *oenococtus*, 47. 10;
Opimian wine, 34. 6; *ova
pilleata*, 65. 2; peacock's
eggs, 33. 4; *penthiacum*, 47.
10; pepper, 38. 1; *placenta*,
35. 4; *porcus Troianus*, 49. 9
f.; *scriblita*, 35. 4, 66. 3;
sow's udders, 36. 2
comic menus, 45. 4, 66 *init.*;
served hot, 31. 11, 35. 6;
surprises in, 33. 4 f.
funerals: burden on survivors,
54. 1; ceremony after nine
days of mourning, 65. 9; expense, 42. 6; mock-funerals,
78, cf. 26. 9; undertakers, 38.
14. *See also under* 'tombs'
future: periphrastic, 45. 4; for
imperative, 37. 3

games: ball-, 27. 3; *bucca, bucca
quot sunt hic?*, 64. 12; dice, 33.
2 f.; *micare in tenebris*, 44. 7;
wagers, 70. 13
genitive of quality, 49. 7
genius, 37. 3, 53. 4
gerund in ablative, replacing
nom. pres. participle, 75. 2
gladiators:
brutality, 45 *passim*; depicted
on commemorative cups, 52.
3, on gravestones, 71. 6, on
lamps, 45. 11; freedmen and
slaves as gladiators, 45. 4;
toy armour, 75. 4
types: *bestiarius*, 45. 11; *eques,*

45. 11; *essedaria*, 45. 7;
essedarius 36. 6; *Thraex*, 45
12.
glass, unbreakable, 51. 2 f.
Greek: studied early, 46. 5
words and phrases: *athla*, 57.
11; *babae babae*, 37. 9;
babaecali, 37. 10; *deuro de*,
58. 6; *eug' euge*, 58. 3;
gingiliphum, 73. 4; *laecasin*,
42. 2; *madeia perimadeia*,
52. 8; *malista*, 57. 10; *peri-
stasis*, 48. 4; *propin*, 28. 4;
Σίβυλλα τί θέλεις;, 48. 8;
sophos 40. 1; *topanta*, 31. 11

hair: used instead of towel, 27.
6; long-haired pages, 27. 1;
unguent on 65. 7
Homer, 29. 9, 48. 7, 59. 2
Horace, pp. xix f., 54. 1, 72 *init.*,
78. 8

imitations as entertainment during dinner, 41. 6
indicative: in indirect questions,
44. 1; present for imperative,
33. 1
indirect speech introduced by
quia and *quod*, 45. 10
infinitive, historic, 62. 5
inns: fraud, 39. 12, 62. 12; prostitution, 61. 6
interpolations, 26. 10, 29. 6, 30.
5, 36. 2, 44. 8, 58. 3, 60. 3, 63.
7, 73. 2, 3. 5

John of Salisbury, pp. xxvi f.,
51. 2 ff.
jokes, 35. 7, 36. 7, 41. 7 f., 48. 4,
50. 4, 68. 1 f.

locative for motion towards, 62. 1